THREE & Me

Three Actresses Made the Difference

My life's story and unlikely friendships with actresses Jill Ireland, Theresa Saldana, and Heather Menzies Urich.

How can I explain the incredible luck I had in befriending three remarkable women who would help me heal the scars of my childhood through their friendship, kindness, wisdom, and unconditional love.

Three & Me

ISBN-13: 979-8-9885107-3-4

Cover design by: Suzie Dotan
Cover Photo: Sandor Sigmond
Library of Congress Control Number: 2023910476
Printed in the United States of America
First Edition

THREE
& *Me*

Three Actresses Made the Difference

100 West High Street
Suite 604
Moorpark, CA 93020

Three & Me

AUTHORS NOTE: Some names have been changed in order to protect the privacy of a few of the individuals in this story. None of the name changes affect the main characters. The events described, as well as all conversations, are described as I remember them. All the events in this story are true to the best of my knowledge. When I was in doubt about certain facts, I researched them, and when they could not be verified, I chose not to include them in order to keep the integrity of the story honest. Also, there are a few F-Bombs dropped throughout the story. Some of my friends were very liberal with their usage, and it is reflected in the conversations. If you are sensitive to those words, I apologize in advance.

i

Sue Lika Dotan

ACKNOWLEDGMENTS

Before I begin thanking all the people who helped me along this way, I believe it is most important to thank Jill Ireland, Theresa Saldana, and Heather Menzies Urich for being my supporters on so many levels. Because of their love and friendship, I was able to trust women, and I am so glad I found that trust. I would be missing out on so much had they not taught me the inner beauty we all possess. They saw me for who I am, with no judgment, no prejudice. Without their love, their friendship, and their infinite wisdom, I know I would be less of a person than I am now. They are always with me, day in and day out. Not a day goes by when I don't think of them and all the wonderful parts of themselves that they shared with me.

I want to thank my father, Sandor, for showing me the right way to live my life. He was an imperfect father but a perfect human being. While I navigated his imperfections, he taught me patience because I learned that things can and do turn around. I love him more each day as I fall back on the education he instilled in me, or when I look at my son, or when I think of his love for the Almighty and his Angels. My dad's history never embittered him. He rose above all the evil in the world, and when he passed away, he taught me even more as he faced his death without fear or trepidation.

I want to thank my mother for all the laughter or humor I can find in many situations. Being Rita's daughter was definitely difficult, but I feel I am a stronger and more compassionate person because of those years dealing with the unknown person "behind the door." I inherited her love for animals which is such an important part of my life.

Thanks also go to my good friend James Camuso and his daughter Nicole, who both read my manuscript a bazillion times, shared their thoughts with me and gave me the encouragement to continue telling my story. Neither is part of the demographic I thought would enjoy the story, but they enlightened me to the fact that my perceived demographic is much broader than I thought!

I want to thank Paul McLaughlin, a friend and former employer from within the publishing industry, for taking the time to read my manuscript and offer so many words of encouragement. I was on the golf course in Palm Desert when he phoned to tell me that "memoirs are a difficult thing to write," but I hit it out of the park. I've been on Cloud Nine since that call.

To Beverly Werber, my editor, who called out areas that needed more explanation and helped me clarify my messaging. Thank you.

I want to thank Christine McCallum for reading my manuscript and letting me know that she felt closer to her mother-in-law, Jill Ireland, from reading it. A thank you to Sarah Boone, for reading the manuscript and offering suggestions that helped me sound a tad more intelligent.

I am also grateful to my partner Ron Friedman for being by my side and taking care of my every need. He has brought so much light and laughter into my life, as well as opened my eyes to the beautiful world we live in through travel to just about everywhere.

And lastly, I am so grateful for the people in my life who have made, either knowingly or unknowingly, my life so much happier. My friends are the best people on the planet, and just knowing they are there makes waking up that much more wonderful!

Three & Me

CONTENTS

Sue Lika Dotan

Me and Jerry. He was 4 and I was 5.

Three & Me

Me and my Aero. He was my best buddy for years.

PREFACE

It was almost as if I had walked through an invisible wall into another room I did not recognize. This room with the gray and wrinkled walls stared back with the acknowledgment that it had been expecting me for quite some time. Those wrinkled walls, mirroring those on my face, became a stark reality on my 70th birthday. I couldn't ignore my chronological age anymore by staying active, enjoying a well-lived life, or looking in the mirror with rose-colored glasses. My 20-year-old brain was forced to stare at the wall of a septuagenarian.

On the one hand, I was saddened—and maybe slightly bitter—at reaching an age I had always considered old. It came too fast for me to digest fully. Totally unprepared for this reality; I wasn't done being young and playful. I hadn't yet achieved every goal I had set out for myself. I wanted to transport myself back in time. To relive the great moments and to experience even more remarkable ones. I never climbed Mount Everest, for goodness' sake! (Yes, that was a dream I had.) I never became a spy for the CIA (yep, I wanted to do that too), learned all the languages I wanted to, hadn't yet reached my financial goals, nor had I felt I had given enough back to society. On the other hand, I felt lucky to have entered this room, filled with the subtle graying of the walls, the new wrinkles, and the wisdom of having lived so many years. So many of my friends and family (including my mother and brother) never got to enter their septuagenarian rooms, having left this earthly existence so many years too soon. And for all intents and purposes, it's a miracle that I am still here. Luckily, my journey is continuing, hopefully for a while longer, while so many others were cut short by disease, suicide, accidents, and war.

Three & Me

As I stared at the walls in this foreign but strangely comfortable place, images crystalized in my mind's eye—once a blur—but now sharp as a knife. The memories of my life began to surround me in my newly found room. My past had come to wrap itself around me like a warm blanket and lead me to the complete understanding that I would not be who I am today without all the good and bad experiences of my life. And that's when I decided it was time to tell my story of survival, filled with hope and inspiration.

My Nuclear Family.
My mom let her self "go" during
this period of time. She smoked a great
deal and played a lot of bridge.
Her sister only wore designer clothes.

ONE

My Nuclear Family

In a Midwest June of 1951, at 11:20 am, on a day I should not have been born, I opened my eyes for the first time. According to my mom, I was three weeks late, which I am sure frustrated her horribly with the discomfort of a pregnancy that would not end. Because I had no intention of leaving the warm and safe confines of her Uterus, the medical team decided I needed to be cut out of her belly. My mom was administered ether, a scalpel was used to slice open her belly and uterus, and I was successfully pulled from her body, leaving a huge ugly scar in the aftermath. She slept through the entire birth process—not uncommon in those days.

I was a low-birth-weight baby, born at just five pounds, two ounces. My mom was a three-pack-a-day smoker and not privy to that habit's scientifically proven side effects. (In the 1950s, the advertising industry promoted smoking as a "healthy, stylish" lifestyle. Its negative impact on pregnancy, lungs, and overall lifespan had not yet been acknowledged.) On the back of my skull was a divot with a birthmark known as a raspberry. When I was a small child, I was told that this birthmark represented royalty. I finally realized it doesn't because, after 70+ years of walking around with a raspberry on the back of my head, I have never heard of any royal, anywhere, with that same birthmark. I now consider it a way to "identify the body" should that need ever present itself.

The family I was born into was both a privilege and a curse. In the early 1950s, post-war America was beginning to recover. Men were home from war. They married pretty young, having been in the European or Japanese theaters, and quickly had 2.2 kids to ensure the continuation of the family name. Women were primarily homemakers. Men worked long, hard hours to provide for their families. Suburbs sprang up everywhere, giving rise to white picket fences, shirtmaker-styled dresses worn with aprons tied, and cigarettes in almost every mouth. Moms throughout the country aspired to be June Cleaver. My mom didn't.

Mom came from a family where the patriarch, David (aka Skeeze), was an entrepreneur. Outwardly, Skeeze looked like a box; such was his stocky build. Most photos show him with a cigar in either his mouth or his hand. He wasn't particularly handsome, but he seemed to have just enough personality to make him both a success and a failure. He made and lost more money in a single year than most people made in an entire lifetime. However, he somehow provided my mom and her two siblings with a luxurious lifestyle.

As a sign of her financial status (or to rub my mother's nose in it), my grandmother, Lottie, always wore a mink stole over a sleeveless cotton dress when they visited us in California. *(Who does that?)* My grandparents hated each other, and they hated my mother. But the person they hated the most was my father, a European immigrant. My mother had married beneath her station in their eyes, and it was more than my grandfather could take. He would exact his revenge and tear my mom's nuclear family apart long after his death, a private and secret delight he savored his entire life.

To hammer his disdain for my dad home, he secretly bestowed upon two of his children a gift of $30,000 each upon marriage, but not my mother. Unbeknownst to her, he put her money in a spendthrift trust that would prevent her from receiving any funds until she was well into old age. According to the terms of the trust, it would dissolve upon her 65th birthday or five years after the last surviving parent died, whichever came later. If that was not bad enough, Skeeze put my uncle in charge of the trust.

My mom never knew about the gifts to her siblings and certainly had no knowledge of that mean-spirited trust. Thirty thousand dollars was

My Nuclear Family

quite a considerable sum in the postwar 1940s. My Aunt Beatrice and her husband, Chester, used their money to invest in a business that became very successful, and they enjoyed a life of wealthy privilege. Aunt Bea wore only the most expensive designer clothes and shoes. She bought nothing off the rack. She'd drop designer names at every chance to my mom, who mainly wore muumuus purchased at the local discount stores. Beatrice had a beautiful body, having benefitted genetically from my grandmother's side of the family. Bea was built for designer clothing, and the designers loved having her as a loyal customer because everything she put on looked spectacular. My mom, however, was built like my grandfather, inheriting an unfortunate boxy body for a woman with such a beautiful face.

My Uncle Bob took after his father in that he was the entrepreneurial type, and he used his gifted money to invest in his businesses, which were also very successful. To his delight, he now had a cash reserve available to help float things when times became challenging or when cash was tight. He repeatedly dipped into my mother's trust during those tough times. Her money was his personal savings and loan without the payback.

To add to my grandfather's delight, Mom and Dad struggled financially after he decided to give up a relatively stable and lucrative position, selling insurance for Prudential. He had a lifelong dream and desired so much more out of his life. The selling was fine. Except he wanted to be a person who could heal other people, to be able to take away physical pain while simultaneously providing for his family. So, he put himself through chiropractic college, working several jobs to cover tuition, food, and the roof over our heads. Unbeknownst to my mother, he also supported his parents and sister. She would have had a fit had she ever found out.

As for Skeeze, even as a child, I could sense his dislike for us; he was that transparent. When my grandparents came to California from their home in Emmetsburg, Iowa, to visit us, they would always talk about and brag about their "real" grandchildren back home (my cousins). At a very young age, when I should have been happy with just about everyone and everything, I learned to distinguish between phony and genuine. I suppose I should be grateful to my grandparents for such a valuable life lesson. They taught me that family can be just a concept, at least in our family.

In my grandparents' unhappy marriage, the hatred between the two was always raging silently under the surface. From the moment he married my grandmother, Skeeze constantly accused Lottie of purposely getting pregnant so he would have to marry her. (Hard to believe they actually had sex of any kind, not to mention pre-marital sex.) Skeeze managed to shove this in my mom's face her entire life, repeatedly telling her she was never wanted and that it was her fault that his marriage was miserable. As if that weren't bad enough, he also told her the two kids who came after her were wanted. He never tired of reminding my mother that she ruined his life. Mom got the same tirade from her mom. Never wanted. Ruined her life, ad infinitum.

My grandparents on my mother's side were two toxic people who should have never met, let alone married, let alone had and raised kids. And as horrible as they were to my mom, they were equally nasty to my brother and me. Especially me. In a world and time where men were exalted and women were second-class citizens, boy children were held in much higher regard. I was the daughter of the daughter they never wanted. Until my grandmother's deathbed letter to me, where she apologized for how she treated me, I suffered her vitriol relentlessly.

# # #

My Nuclear Family

MOM

My mother, Rita Lee, was a small woman with a brilliant mind. She exuded a quiet beauty with her big brown eyes, demur smile, and bobby-pin-curled brown hair caressing her shoulders. The 1940s hairstyle she so favored was a look she wore her entire life, taking it to her final resting place. She never once changed it in all her years.

My mom was five feet tall and very bosomy, a feature the women from her side of the family proudly showed off. Unfortunately, she also got her fair share of her father's terrible genes. She was small in stature and had disproportionately huge bosoms and narrow hips. Because of the stomach scars from two C-sections and an appendectomy, her tummy protruded, adding to her box-like shape. By far, her best features were her legs, which were beautifully shaped, allowing her to show them off whenever possible with knee-length skirts or dresses. Her skin was porcelain white, never needing moisturizer, and when she passed at 69, she had no wrinkles. Her skin had never seen the sun. My mom preferred to be indoors her entire life, giving her the smooth, milky complexion of a teenager.

Skeeze used to tell my Aunt Bea that she was his beautiful daughter. He'd tell Mom that she was his intelligent daughter, thereby setting them up to despise each other. According to my aunt, how Skeeze categorized each of them used to bother her until she realized she was beautiful *and* intelligent. And that was true. My mother could only go with brilliant because she lacked that striking physical beauty her sister had, even though she was a shining beauty in her own right.

My mom's high intellect served her well during her school years, allowing her to skip many grades on her way up the academic ladder. She graduated from university while still a teenager, but not before she had at least one professor tearing his hair out. One day, my mom woke up feeling like she wanted to opt out of an extensive exam in one of her courses. She studied for it and knew she'd get an "A" if she took it because she always got "A's." But there was a point to be made, and she decided she would take it upon herself to make that point. So, she walked into the classroom before class began and asked the professor if she could speak with him. He agreed, and when he sat with her at his desk, he wasn't prepared for what my mother had to say. "With all due respect, Sir," she began, "It's silly for us to take this exam."

"And why is that?" her professor asked.

"Because," she said, "exams are meant only to discover what you don't know. And that makes no sense. You see, we could know much more about the subject matter than your exam will allow us to demonstrate. So, I will tell you everything I know about the material right now!" At this point, she began to discuss everything she had learned from that class, leaving nothing out while, at the same time, leaving an exasperated professor wishing he had never sat down with my mother to begin with.

My Nuclear Family

He had to interrupt her to begin the class. Students were already seated at their desks, staring at both of them. According to my mother, he dismissed her from the exam, and she got an "A."

However much I liked that piece of my mom's academic history and the creative spunk she showed, something happened to her as she aged. After she married my father, she basically spent her life hiding behind a deck of cards. As for my own academic achievements, well, they were never good enough for her. She would trot out all her old report cards and gloat. Of course, I could never match the straight "A's" she had. No matter how hard I worked or how smart I was, I could never, ever reach her academic success. It was something I dealt with all through my own academic career.

# # #

Eventually, the harsh winters of the upper Midwest, where we lived until I was three years old, became too much for my mother's fragile health. She was always sick with recurring bouts of pneumonia, one case right after the other in a long string of illnesses. No one thought to question her chain smoking. Instead, her ailments were always blamed on the cold, brutal winters. Her sick lungs were a massive problem in our household and quickly became more dangerous for my mom. Rita was never a healthy woman; her childhood was filled with diseases one rarely hears about, like scarlet fever, a burst appendix, and secondary infections from childhood diseases like mumps and measles. So, the decision was made to move the family out west to California. Dry heat, warmer temperatures, and the promise of better health were just what her doctor ordered.

A few months before the big move west, my parents decided to foster two young teen boys. They had become wards of the state and were placed into the custody of the Jewish Home. Needing the income that came with fostering and wanting to do something good (she was, after all, a trained social worker until she married), my parents decided to bring these two boys into the family. Instead of two young kids creating aggravation for my mom, she piled on two teenagers to cause even more.

We struck out on a road trip with a loaded car, four kids, and two adults, all of us on our way to a new life in California. My mom smoked the entire trip. I threw up into a towel the whole way.

My mom liked kids. In fact, I'd say she loved them. She just didn't like hanging out with her own. She used to say she loved seeing her friend's kids because she could ooh and ahh, and then hand them back when she was done. Mom should have been a working mother as far away from the house as she could get, staying away for as long as possible. She would have been so much happier as a professional, working in her chosen field as a social worker, helping society. Instead, because of the times, she was pigeonholed as a stay-at-home mom with two young children. My brother Jerry was born precisely one year, two months, and 20 days after me. Jerry and I would have benefitted from being in daycare, but daycare wasn't a thing back then. So, the three of us tried as hard as possible to make the situation work. Being a mom to young children, or being children to a parent, shouldn't have to be so difficult. But it was.

A social creature by nature with a quick wit and a bigger-than-life laugh, Mom was stuck with two rambunctious children she had no clue how to relate to, not to mention two teenage boys. She chain-smoked and played cards daily. She would invite her girlfriends over, set up the card table, and play bridge all afternoon. They *all* smoked. My brother and I were left to watch TV through the smoky haze as they played. When the game ended, always timed perfectly for my dad's arrival home, she'd make dinner, usually a variation of meat and potatoes. Afterward, she smoked some more.

It was apparent to everyone, including me, that Mom loved Jerry much more than she could ever love me. Jerry had big green eyes

My Nuclear Family

with lashes that went into tomorrow. He had an impish smile, was a bit of a scamp with freckles on his nose, and had a twinkle in his eyes that made my mom melt. Jerry could do no wrong. And if he did do wrong, somehow it was always my fault.

I'll never forget when he stole my mom's jewelry and handed it out to all the neighbors. He was seven years old, and I was eight at the time. I had no idea he did this. It was a cold fall day in the Westside of Los Angeles. The leaves falling from the large sycamore tree in front of our house were scattered all over the lawn and into the backyard. At the time, I was outside in the garage area playing with the dogs when the neighbors began calling, asking why Jerry was giving out expensive jewelry. When confronted, he was so afraid of my parents' rage that he looked them straight in the eyes and said, "Suzie told me to do it!" It was, of course, a huge lie, but one they swallowed hook, line, and sinker. That was all my mother needed to hear. She went ballistic. At this point, my dad was also furious, and he ran out into the backyard, literally lifting me off my feet (easy since I weighed maybe 35 pounds then) and carried me off to the living room, where he set me down harshly, at my mom's feet.

"Did you tell Jerry to steal my jewelry?" she demanded of me. I had no idea what she was talking about. In fact, I was utterly gobsmacked at the allegation. It would never occur to me to steal anything, let alone goad someone else, especially my brother, into doing such a thing.

I looked at them both and said, "No." It was the truth. Apparently, that answer didn't sit well with them because my dad immediately called me a liar. "No, I'm not!" I shook my head in an exaggerated protest. "I have no idea what you're talking about." And then I felt the sting of the slap across my face. My father was beyond furious and fully into a rage.

His voice grew louder when he asked me again if I told Jerry to steal the jewelry. Feeling the panic and dread well up in my throat, I said I didn't. Then he hoisted me up on his knee, and I felt the sharp pain on my rear end from being spanked. My dad's face was bright red, with spittle coming out of his mouth, when he told me it would only get worse until I told the truth. I was crying now, trying to make sense of being punished for something I had no part in while the real culprit, my brother, was just sent to his room with an admonition about not taking things that weren't his. Again, I stubbornly insisted I didn't know anything about it, let alone suggest Jerry do such a thing. Then the belt came off, and my behind got whipped again and again. As stubborn as I was, I wouldn't admit to something I didn't do. Finally, the spankings stopped, and I was sent to my room, the tears streaming down my face, burning into my memory the searing pain of the injustice of it all. To this day, I can still feel the pain of not being believed, a pain much worse than the beating I sustained.

That was the day I learned that you can't ever prove you *didn't* do something. There is no evidence of *not* doing it. I would go on to learn this lesson many times throughout my life. Years later, when we were both adults, my brother confessed about his great jewelry heist. My mother refused to believe it, telling me, "I know you were involved somehow. Jerry is just trying to be a gentleman right now."

Upon hearing Jerry's confession, my dad also disbelieved it; instead, he sided with my mom, as he mostly did. "Well, that spanking was then for the things you did that we never found out about," was all he could say. That was justice? Arbitrarily punish someone innocent because, at some point in their lives, they probably weren't! While shocked at the sheer ignorance of that remark, I again felt the sharp pain of being blamed for something I had no part in. It wasn't until many years later that my dad finally apologized to me for what had transpired. It was after my mom died; I guess it had eaten at him for years.

My Nuclear Family

It was no secret that when I was very young, my mom had a hard time with my appearance. For one, I didn't look like her at all. I was the spitting image of my father. For another, I was small for my age and could best be described as scrawny. The 1950s were all about *zoftig* and big buxom women endowed with Marilyn Monroe curves, big Jayne Mansfield chests, and the smoldering sexuality of Shirley MacLaine. Full figures were in. My mom and her sister and mother possessed what I lacked. My mom would harp on how skinny I was and how disgusted she was with how I looked.

Unfortunately, I always looked years younger than my actual age. I was in the 20-percentile if even that. On top of everything else, I would get nauseated by the constant haze of smoke wafting around the house, permeating everything it came in contact with. I couldn't eat. I would get yelled at about not eating and would try and force myself, but the smoke made me sick to my stomach. I found ways to pass the food under the table to a napkin which I would then throw away. I got good at chewing, pretending to swallow, and then chucking it into the napkin when no one was looking. When the dog was allowed in the dining room, I would pass it to her. The dog got fatter while I stayed skinny. I still can't eat anything if someone nearby is smoking.

Throughout my childhood, I never felt a close connection to my mother. I loved her like all children love their mother, but there was a palpable distance between us my entire life. To my recollection, she never hugged me, always keeping me an arms-length away. I think the damaged relationship she had with her own mother crippled her ability to relate to a daughter. But at the time, I didn't understand this. I was just confused about why my mom was lenient with Jerry and so hard on me. Years later, when confronted, my mom told me it was "because I was the older child." Happily, I never got resentful of Jerry. I loved him with all my heart.

# # #

Three & Me

My most vivid memory from early childhood with my mother is of her saving my life. I was just barely five years old. We lived across the street from Crescent Heights Elementary School at that time. I can tell you from firsthand experience that when people say pedophiles stalk the areas around elementary schools, they are right.

It was the summer before I was to begin kindergarten. I had some chalk, and I remember drawing pictures of dogs (which was all I could do then) on the sidewalk in front of our house. I was alone outside, which was common back in the 1950s. My mother was inside the house in the dining room, which faced the street, and was on the phone with one of her many girlfriends. I assumed she was watching me play but got distracted at the exact moment a young man approached me. I can still remember him vividly. I have a near-photographic memory, which is one of my talents. Recalling visuals has always been easier for me than recalling details through audio retention (although, for some reason, I can pick up foreign languages quite easily). I clearly remember that he was wearing a yellow Alpaca cardigan sweater over beige pleated pants. He had a collared shirt on underneath his sweater. He was slight in build and had sandy brown hair, the sides of which were slicked back with the front loosely falling onto his forehead in a Bobby Rydell style. At the time, I had no idea how old he was, just that he was a man. If asked today, I'd guess he was in his late 20s to early 30s.

"Hey, little girl," he began, "What are you drawing?"

I looked up at him. I remember he had a lovely smile. I smiled back at him. "Dogs," I said.

He stood there for a few seconds, not too long lest he be seen with me, and then asked, "Do you like candy?"

I looked up and answered an enthusiastic "Yes!" He motioned for me to come with him. I dutifully got up. "I have a lot of candy in my car.

See that car at the corner? That's my car. Do you want to come with me, and I'll give you some?" He began walking towards his car, five houses down, and I obediently followed him. I had to skip a few steps and trot a few others to keep up with his quick pace. As we got to his car, a brown 4-door sedan, he opened the back door. "The candy is in the car," he said. "You'll need to get in and reach under the front seat to get it. I'm too big for that."

As my kidnapping began to unfold, my mother glanced out the front window and saw that my chalk pieces were still on the sidewalk, only I wasn't around. She hung up the phone, opened the front door, and spotted me following a man she did not recognize. It took a quick minute for her to realize that I was in extreme danger. My mother, who did not possess one athletic gene in her small, bosomy body, suddenly became an Olympic sprinter! She began to run as fast as her legs would carry her, calling after me to stop. But I didn't hear her as I was already entering the back seat of the man's car.

I can still remember, to this very day, the horrible stench inside his vehicle. It smelled of something rotten and made me gag. As he closed the door, locking me in, I suddenly became acutely aware that I didn't like it back there. And then I saw her. My mom came flying in with the force of an E5 tornado and literally smashed her shoulder into the guy, pushing him to the ground. She quickly opened the back door and pulled me out with so much force that she actually pulled my shoulder out of its socket. I was in some pain but mostly embarrassed. I noticed the "nice" man on the ground and tried to make sense of everything happening around me. And then I started to scream. People came out of their doors, and my mom called out to them to call the police. The man got up, jumped in his car, and sped off. Then, I got the swats on my tush to end all swats. All the way to our house, the five-house walk of shame, Mom got her adrenaline-fueled fear and anger out on me with each smack on my behind.

Three & Me

Mom dragged me home, screaming at me the entire way that I was about to be murdered. I had no idea what murdered even meant until she screamed some more that within the next hour, I would be dead and my body discarded in some garbage dump somewhere. At this point, I went utterly hysterical. My parents had never talked to me about stranger danger, so until this exact moment, I trusted just about anyone and everyone. I knew what death looked like from a dead frog in my driveway, and I imagined I would have looked like that.

After what had to be a hysteria-laden conversation between my father and my mother, my dad drove home to pick me up and take me to Dr. Steindel's office. The doctor's office wasn't far away, and he needed to put my shoulder back in its socket. The police came while I was gone, and my mom gave them a report. To this day, I have no idea what happened to that man. Did he go on to kidnap and kill other kids? Was he caught? Or was it his first and last attempt because it went so badly? Had my mother not saved me that day, I would have ended up just another statistic, another headline, a piece on the local news, and missed out on my life. That's a heady reality, and I still shudder at the thought.

Through all the bad times with my mom—and there were plenty of those—I would ruminate about that summer's day. I still do. The fact is that my mother saved my life, so she had to have loved me. She could have let that man drive away with me in the back of the car had she not. No one would have been able to tie my imminent death to her. Instead, she found the inner strength and the adrenaline necessary to go after my would-be kidnapper. She snatched me from the jaws of death, who was dressed that day in a yellow Alpaca sweater and beige pleated pants.

# # #

My Nuclear Family

DAD

My father, Sandor, was born in 1920 in a small village outside of Budapest, Hungary. His good looks were striking: tall, swarthy, and lanky, possessed of emerald green eyes and chiseled features. His father, Louis, was a religious Jew, so my father was sent to yeshiva to study in an Orthodox environment. In the European religious community, children were expected to behave in a particular manner. As a youngster, my father found it difficult to conform to that behavior. He rebelled against the harsher elements of yeshiva life and was subsequently punished for his belligerent behavior. Many times, during his young life, he experienced the sting of punishment in his rear area. My grandfather, Louis, thought he was doing the right thing. "Spare the rod, spoil the child" aligned with his way of thinking and parenting. My dad took his licks, hoping he would grow up a good Jew. Corporal punishment was not yet considered child abuse. This practice continued throughout his childhood. It was something he brought with him into his own fatherhood.

Three & Me

By the time Sandor reached the age of 13—an age Jews consider a young boy to be a man—the world was beginning to change. Hitler and Nazism were quickly becoming a threat to most of Western Europe. In the pre-war era of Eastern Europe, the Hungarian government saw benefits in gaining Hitler's favor. With the rise of a passionate nationalism sweeping Europe, minorities became a target for the anger and rage simmering over the inequity of the economy and lack of shared wealth. There was the perception that Jewish businesses were thriving economically and a bias of belief that they, and they alone, were the main reason so many others were not. The Jewish population was targeted as the problem, and the solution to that problem was eradication. The Final Solution was about to be implemented a few short years later. Without real prompting from Germany, the Hungarian government voluntarily began rounding up Jews and putting them into pre-war concentration camps or prisons.

But before Jews were regularly rounded up, a small but significant event was about to occur in Hungary and within the Zsigmond household. It was Yom Kippur Eve in 1934, the holiest day in the Jewish calendar. My father, at 14, was on his way to the synagogue in the small village where his family lived. He was walking on the dusty and unpaved road he regularly took to see the rabbi when he was stopped and questioned by two young police officers. He recognized them both, knew who they were, and knew they knew him. Thus, he was surprised when they began to ask him questions. Because the village was small and everyone knew everyone and almost everything about everyone, he was perplexed as they peppered him with questions. "What's your name?" they asked him. He looked at them, puzzled. "I said, what's your name?" they queried again.

"Sandor," he replied obediently.

"And where are you going?" they asked of him.

"To the synagogue," he politely replied.

My Nuclear Family

Their demeanor scared my young dad as they demanded to know what he did for a living. "I'm a student," he answered. They then asked about his father, his father's place of birth, and what he did. My dad responded truthfully that his father was born in Romania, came to Hungary as a young man, fought in the World War for Hungary, was a decorated soldier, and had recently been a tavern owner. (World War II hadn't yet occurred, so it wasn't referred to as World War I back then.) My father searched the faces of the young policemen trying to get a read on the situation, as his discomfort level began to rise with each unfolding moment.

"You can go," they suddenly said to my dad when the questions were finished. As my dad wended his way towards the synagogue and Yom Kippur services, he had a feeling in the pit of his stomach that all was not well. He was right.

Not too long after the Yom Kippur encounter with the local police, my young father was home with his parents and younger sister when there was a banging on the door. My grandfather instructed my father to open it, and when he did, he was met with State Policemen armed with guns. "We have orders for Sandor Zsigmond. He is being transported to prison." Upon hearing this decree, his parents were nearly befallen by shock and immediately began to protest the order.

"He's just a boy!" they argued. But the police insisted he was "head of family," even though, just looking at him, anyone could discern it was an obvious mistake. With that, the entire family was instructed to take only what they could carry and meet gendarmes at the train station at a pre-designated time later that evening. They would travel to the prison on the outskirts of the village and were to be imprisoned with other political prisoners, criminals, and individuals considered enemies for other reasons.

As the police left the Zsigmond home, my dad's family scrambled to sell off some of their belongings, rationalizing that some money would help them should they need it. The people in the village heard about what was happening and went to the Zsigmond home to help them by purchasing items. The family was well-liked, and many in the town came to say their sad goodbyes.

My dad had a goat named Mukey, whom he had raised since birth. My father was always closely bonded with different animals, a trait I share with him. My dad's love for that goat took on the same intensity of emotion as it would for another human being. To my dad, life is meant to be cherished no matter what form life takes. Ultimately, for the goat's future well-being, he sold Mukey to a family he was sure would take good care of him. It was my dad's first real heartbreak.

In the middle of all the chaos, my dad realized he would have just enough time to go to the synagogue and tell the rabbi what was happening. With the speed of a young athlete, my father quickly made the run to the temple in ample time. The rabbi told my father to always believe in God and his angels. He instructed my father never to give up his faith and always ask God for guidance, even during dark times. My dad took these words to heart and, feeling like he could now face his destiny, bid the rabbi goodbye for the final time.

Along with taking that lesson with him to prison, my father took it with him daily until his last breath. He always kept his faith in God and the angels, even during the darkest times of his life—and of those, there were many. His love for the Almighty was his life's blood. Without it, he wouldn't be able to live. With that same love of God, he could readily face his death many years later as an old man.

As the sun began setting and the darkness began to envelop them, the Zsigmond family trudged along the cobbled pathways leading to the train station and an uncertain fate. My father resolved to survive and keep his family safe as much as possible. His young sister, Sari, quietly cried. She couldn't find the strength to be brave. The family headed to the train station just ahead of the designated time. The

gendarmes met them there. Escorted by the armed police, they boarded the waiting train, choosing wooden benches towards the back of the
car for their journey—each one lost in their thoughts and fears about
what was to be. As the train pulled out, my dad looked back at the
village behind him and sighed. He never saw his family home again.

The time they spent in prison for being Jewish was torturous. My dad
mercifully was housed together with his father. My grandmother was
housed together with her daughter in a separate part of the prison.
The days were harsh and filled with hard labor. The nights were short,
offering little respite from the day's hardships. There were no beds,
only wooden planks with a bit of straw. Both Dad and my Grandfather Louis worked long hours with little rest and even less food.
Thankfully, they were both strong and in good shape and could tolerate the beatings their bodies took.

Occasionally they would be allowed to visit with Aunt Sari and my
grandmother, trying to stay upbeat for their benefit. Throughout it all,
my dad faced each day with the same positive stoic attitude that got
him through most of life's miseries. He knew God was on his side.
While my dad was stoic, my grandmother was busy. She was reaching outside the prison for any help she could get at every chance.
Which wasn't a lot, but it would prove to be enough.

After many unsuccessful attempts to find anyone who could help
them—the Jewish community had effectively turned their backs on
them lest they, too, anger the Hungarian government—my grandmother discovered an organization for Hungarian veterans of the
World War. Through them, she found my grandfather's retired and
aging commanding officer, who remembered my grandfather well.
He intervened on their behalf, and they were eventually free to leave
the prison. But there were conditions. They couldn't go back to their
village. They had to relocate to Budapest and could not leave the city
without police permission. They had to check in with the police every month on the 1st and 15th. Any violation of any kind would send

Three & Me

them back to prison or get them deported. If deported, they would be destined to live in a netherworld at a border since no one in Europe wanted them. They were criminals in the eyes of the Hungarians and other European countries—just for being Jewish.

My father's family was one of the first Jewish families in Hungary to be imprisoned because of their faith. As history would eventually show, being Jewish in Hungary would become a huge liability. Not too long after my dad's imprisonment, Hungary began arresting their Jewish population around Budapest's countryside and putting them into camps. Then they sent these Jewish prisoners to the Auschwitz extermination camp in numbers far more significant than any other country in Europe, East or West. The Hungarian government was a prolific feeder to the Nazi extermination machine.

My grandmother's brother, Uncle Simon, lived in the United States. He had come to this country, settling in Wisconsin, way before any of the white nationalizations of Europe began. He found a foothold there and became a successful businessman. Larger than life, always with a cigar in his mouth and a huge, boisterous laugh, it was hard to believe that he and my diminutive and soft-spoken grandmother were from the same family. The few times I saw Uncle Simon, he always wore a white cowboy hat! That was his style, and it suited him well.

Once in Budapest, my grandmother sent him messages asking that he send the family tickets out of Europe. She described their dire situation and her recent ordeal as a prisoner. Budapest was quickly becoming ever more treacherous for the Jewish population. Anti-Semitism was everywhere, even permeating the Jewish community where they lived. Uncle Simon agreed, but he first had to go through the legal process of getting them through immigration because they had no papers.

Hungary did not recognize Jews as citizens; therefore, they would have no passports. He had to agree to sponsor them financially, and the U.S. government needed to believe that he could. So, while he waited for the United States to vet his financial affairs thoroughly, my dad and his family waited impatiently on the other side of the Atlantic.

Finally, the approval came and, with it, the tickets out of Europe. My dad and his family made their way to a ship named the SS Manhattan and headed to New York City via Genoa. He entered Ellis Island as *a man without a country,* as did his parents and sister. Uncle Simon Deutsch effectively saved their lives.

Once settled into his newly adopted country, my father studied engineering and took a job at one of Uncle Simon's businesses. But it wasn't to last too long because the United States was growing increasingly likely to enter World War II. Feeling restless and wanting to do something for his newly adopted country, he enlisted in the United States Army, attaining the rank of sergeant. (I found my dad's Army autograph book among his papers when he passed away. It is one of my most treasured possessions. His men called him "Sarge," and much love was expressed for him as a man and leader.)

While a soldier in the United States Armed Forces, he was recruited to Camp Ritchie, the Army's training base for army intelligence. Because of his language skills, high intelligence, and physically fit physique, my father was part of roughly 2,000 other Jewish immigrants who fled pre-war Europe and became a small cadre of war heroes known now as the Ritchie Boys. Basically, they were Jewish spies.

On December 12th, 1943, my father boarded the SS Queen Elizabeth en route to Glasgow, Scotland, officially entering World War II. He and other Ritchie Boys were back in the European theater as the United States and the Allies entered the war. His primary function during the war was to read aerial maps and root out enemy installations, using his training from Camp Ritchie. He was even at Omaha Beach and Utah Beach during D-Day. My father was proud of his service to this country. If he were alive today, he would be humbled to know that he is now part of American history, as his legacy is honored in the new Ritchie Boys Museum at the old Camp Ritchie in Maryland.

Because of his service in the Army, my father was granted United States citizenship in 1942. To him, his American citizenship was a badge of honor he was proud of until he died. He was as American as anyone born on this soil. I was lucky enough to find his discharge papers the year before he passed. They were in a box he handed me while cleaning out his closet. I used those discharge papers to secure him a military burial upon his death. As he lay dying on a rented hospital bed in his living room, I told him I could get him military honors. Tears rolled down his cheeks, and he whispered a soft but heartfelt "Thank you, Suzie. I'm proud of you." I was so grateful I could make a dying man, my dad, my hero, happy in his last hours.

# # #

Growing up from toddler to kid to teen, the friction between myself and my mother intensified. The more my mom distanced herself from me, or the more she verbally attacked me, the more my dad embraced me behind her back. He'd stand with her as she would punish me for what she perceived as misdeeds or backtalk. And then once she left the room, or I went into my bedroom's safe confines, he'd come in and apologize. If I went through a particularly bad experience with my mom, he'd go out and buy me jewelry. I still have some of the pieces he bought me. He knew something was wrong with my mom, but he loved her. He knew of her own sad and tumultuous history, so he never went against her in front of her face. But in private, he was my biggest fan, most of the time during my younger years.

My dad encouraged every inkling of talent I would exhibit. Monday nights were bridge nights for my mom and her cronies. That was the night my dad would educate me. Nearly every Monday night until I went away to school in Israel some 19 years later, we'd sit together, teacher to student. It started when I was just past a year old. He'd sit

My Nuclear Family

me down and teach me the alphabet painstakingly slowly so my infant brain could absorb what he'd say. He'd do this every chance he got when my mom wasn't looking. By 18 months, I could identify all the letters in the alphabet, and by two, I could link letters together, then words, and finally sentences.

When I was 18 months old, my eyes went wonky. I could go wall-eyed at will, scaring everyone I did that in front of. According to my dad, I enjoyed the looks of horror I would get when I'd walk over to someone and spread my eyes to the outer corners. Finally, my mom and dad took me to the pediatrician to try and correct my condition. While seated, I looked up and saw the eye chart. Suddenly, I began to blurt out the letters line by line to a stunned audience comprised of my mother, the doctor, and his nurse. Dad sat there proudly with a huge grin on his face. As my mom would relate the story, the doctor would point to a line and then ask me to read the letters. I dutifully complied.

Instead of being happy about it, my mom was irate! When we got home, she read my dad the riot act. How dare he go behind her back and not tell her what he was teaching me! Unfettered, my dad shrugged off the verbal dressing down and continued our lessons. But with a caveat. I wasn't allowed to tell her. I never did.

As a result of that early education, I read chapter books at a very young age and, in fact, had finished the entire *Nancy Drew Mystery Series* before I entered kindergarten, which did a couple of things. It set me apart from all the other kids, which wasn't so great at that age. And it got me in trouble because I was bored reading the primer *Fun with Dick and Jane* in class. I'd fidget, resulting in my constantly being sent to spend time in the cloakroom, staring at lunchboxes and coats, during most of my elementary school years. I learned more on Monday nights with my dad than I ever did in school. World religions, history, languages, science, the classics, art history, you name it, we covered it—all except math. My otherwise sponge-like mind would go dark when I saw numbers. It still does. I remember my dad trying to teach me binary numbers and creative ways to do math division, multiplication, etc. The look of frustration on his face made me sad, but I could not make sense of it. He eventually gave up on math, and we focused instead on the subjects I could absorb.

I loved learning about other religions and cultures. My dad taught me to understand the *Koran, the Bhagavad Gita, the New Testament,* and the Old in those lessons. We studied Hinduism and Buddhism and found links between all of the religions. I also loved exploring the Psalms. When I'm sad, I still take solace in them.

My Dad taught me about the human and holy *"spidits."* It was the common link in all religions. I was 20, in college, in a drawing class, when suddenly, I realized that his Hungarian accent turned the word "spirit" into "spidit!" All those years I thought we had, each of us, a spirit and a spidit! Without being overly silly, to this day, I try to embrace my own inner "spidit." Over the years, it has become a massive part of me and who I am!

Because of my father's Monday night sit-downs, I learned to embrace people of other cultures and countries. Learning the ins and outs of their respective religions and cultures helped me understand and respect them. I was never afraid of meeting new people. This served me well when I lived overseas. Through those lessons, I realized that peaceful relations come from an education and understanding of the other person in the room. The more you know and understand, the more you can have dialogue. When there is ignorance, fears crop up, and that fear creates hostility and separation. I see that too often in the world today, and it saddens me.

Probably the most valuable lesson my dad shared with me was the gift of seeing people for *who* they are and not what they are. Racism was a concept my father found utterly repugnant, having suffered through the racism rampant in Europe. So, on a warm California day, he put

My Nuclear Family

my brother and me in the car and drove to the Burbank stables. I remember him pointing to a horse and asking us what color that horse was. "Brown!" we called out. He then pointed to another horse, asking what color that horse was. "White!" we proudly exclaimed. I was proud of how easy this new game was! Jerry wasn't quite sure about what we were doing and felt that there had to be a catch because the answers were so easy.

Then my dad pointed to all the horses in the corral. "What do you see now?" he asked.

"HORSES!" I shouted out happily. I could tell my dad was pleased.

We then drove to a park nearby. People were there with dogs on leashes. He pointed to a dog and asked me what color that dog was. "Black!" I cheerfully answered. Then he pointed to another dog, asking the same question. "Yellow!" Jerry and I shouted in unison. He pointed to yet another dog without asking but expecting an answer. "Black and White!" we giggled. This was really easy. "And look at the park and tell me what you see?"

"DOGS!" we shouted.

"Excellent!" my dad exclaimed. He was clearly happy with how we were playing this game. "We're gonna get ice cream after our next stop," he said, making us giddy with joy!

My dad drove to Downtown Los Angeles. We got out of the car, and for the first time, I wasn't in a suburb of Los Angeles but in the heart of the city. We looked around, eyes wide open. There were people everywhere, actually walking on the street. Busses full of people were passing us by. The storefronts looked colorful, with merchandise displayed out in front. I hadn't seen anything like it. As I took it all in, my dad pointed to a woman across the street sitting on a bus bench. "What color is her skin?" he asked of us.

Three & Me

I studied her. Jerry didn't answer, but hesitatingly I asked, "Dark brown?" My dad smiled. Then he pointed to another person. He again asked about the color of the man's skin. This time I didn't hesitate. "Pink!" I said with a joyful giggle. My dad smiled again. Again and again, he would point out different people and ask me to define their skin color. Again and again, I made him smile. Jerry had stopped playing. He was bored, but he was still paying attention.

Then my dad motioned his hands to encompass our entire area. "And now, looking around you, tell me what you see?"

"PEOPLE!" And with that exclamation, my father picked me up and hugged me!

When we got back in the car, he explained that hating a person for their skin color, the religion they chose to follow, or the country they were born in is wrong. It was called racism. He told me that to be a good person in God's eyes was to accept everyone we saw as one of God's children. No one was better than anyone else. Every life mattered, no matter how rich or how poor. And how, as young children growing up, we had to carry this lesson with us our whole lives, teaching others along the way. And we did. As the last surviving member of my nuclear family, I still do. I raised my son this way. It's my dad's legacy and needs to be continued. My son will teach his future children that same lesson.

# # #

As time passed and I got wiser and more intelligent, my mom was beside herself. I found an ability to try to reason with her, and she realized that her power was slowly diminishing right before her eyes. Instead of retreating, my mom decided to fight fire with fire. Her attacks became even more vicious, her goal to break me, her words sharp weapons, honed through the years of abuse she suffered from her parents.

As much as my mom waged her personal war with me and against me, my dad encouraged me to grow and develop. He drove home the point that I should never ever depend on a man for anything I could do myself. His goal was to create an independent woman, which in the 1950s was almost unheard of. He would repeatedly tell me that I could grow up to do anything and everything I wanted and never to let the fact that I was a girl get in the way. I didn't.

# # #

Me, Jerry and Dad on a Yom Kippur day.
I was 9 years old.

Three & Me

JERRY

Mom would frequently tell the story of her bringing Jerry home from the hospital after being in an incubator for a long time. Apparently, I tried to bite his foot upon his arrival. Jerry was born a preemie. He spent the first month of his life in an incubator until he weighed enough to come home. He, too, was a C-section because back then, once your uterus was cut into, all subsequent births had to follow suit. That doesn't hold true today. Vaginal childbirth can follow if the woman has had up to two C-sections previously. But 1950s medicine was a whole other ball of wax than medicine today.

I don't remember ever feeling anything but love for my baby brother. I adored him. He was my best friend and my confidante. Most importantly, though, he was my full-time playmate.

We shared a bedroom until I was around six years old. When Louie, the older of the two foster brothers, left home and Jerry moved in with Davey, I had my own room. Back then, houses were your typical three-bedroom house, unlike the five-bedroom homes on the market today. My parents always got the main room. Davey and Louie shared a room, and Jerry and I had twin beds in ours. We'd talk until we'd fall asleep, or until my parents would come in after hearing us giggle and threaten us with the all-too-familiar, "One more peep out of either of you...." We knew that meant the wooden spoon or my dad's hand smacking us. We would instantly close our eyes and somehow fall asleep.

Jerry and I would often put ourselves in dangerous situations, either through our own naiveté or from watching cartoons and trying to emulate what we saw. Cartoon characters could get blown up, fall off a cliff, or be hit with hammers, cars, or baseball bats, and they'd be fine. Jerry and I thought we were as invincible as Elmer Fudd or Daffy Duck.

Pretending we were circus performers, we would use our beds as trampolines, trying to out-jump each other. Davey would sometimes "help" us by lifting us higher and then dropping us on the mattress to see what kind of bounce we could get. Once, Davey lifted me up, but instead of dropping me, he gave a little thrust and bam! I flew right into the wall! My tooth went through my upper lip, bringing about a trip to the emergency room for stitches.

I still have that scar on my left upper lip. I didn't cry, though. I really don't remember ever feeling any pain. Everyone thought that was strange, including the doctor. I remember putting my hand to my mouth, pulling it back with blood on my fingers, then calmly walking to my parent's room. Jerry followed me, crying. I tried comforting him, but he was inconsolable. My mom immediately cradled Jerry in her arms as my dad assessed my situation, eventually putting me in the car to get sewn up. Davey was in a state of shock and felt horrible. He tried wiping my little blood spot off the wall, but it just smeared. Later, as we grew older, he confessed that it was a hugely traumatic event in his life. As for the smear, I would look at it nightly until we moved out of that house.

One fine summer day, Jerry and I decided we'd make an elevator out of a large old boot box and some yarn we found lying around the house. My mom was a knitter back then, always knitting over-sized sweaters that itched. I found and took a knitting needle from my mom's knitting bag and punched holes in the four sides of the box. Then I threaded the yarn through each hole and attached a much longer piece of yarn at the top, where I had knotted off all four sides of it. The longer piece of yarn would be used to lower the elevator off the roof with my brother holding it and me sitting in the box. That was the plan, flawed as it was.

Once I finished creating the elevator, Jerry and I scampered off to the next-door neighbor's house. At that time, we were living on Crescent Heights Boulevard. The homes were built in the Spanish style, where they remain today—flat, Spanish-tiled roofs. Our house had a small structure on top that my father called an "angel house," which had a slant to it. We knew it would be too hard for us to climb up. But the house next door was absolutely perfect. It was flat on top! To make it an even better choice, there was a trellis on the side of the house, so we could climb up to the roof and easily haul our very light elevator up to the top. As little kids, we had no concept of boundaries, tres-passing, or any other legal technicality that should have prevented us from climbing on the neighbor's roof. It was simply there, and so it was ours to climb.

Jerry and I quickly made it up onto the neighbor's roof. We were look-ing down atop our driveway when we spotted a great area to lower the elevator with me in it. As we were getting ready for our big event, my mother happened to walk into the kitchen, which luckily faced the neighbor's house. She heard our voices and undoubtedly our laughter. Jerry made a speech about launching a rocket into space, and I was rolling around laughing at how silly he sounded. I had just about settled down after getting into the boot box when my mother ran out of the back door screaming at us. "YOU TWO GET DOWN HERE IMMEDIATELY!" she yelled towards the roof, struggling to see us from that angle. We didn't want to.

"No!" we shot back in unison. It was then that the neighbor heard the commotion and ran outside. She saw us on her roof and must have realized the potential peril we were in so dangerously high up. Two young kids on her roof were nothing to laugh about. She joined my mother in screaming at us to get down. We held fast. "Not until we lower the elevator!" we yelled back.

And then the neighbor yelled the magic words. "I'M CALLING THE POLICE AND HAVING YOU ARRESTED!" That did it. We scampered back to the trellis, leaving our elevator on the roof, and climbed down at record speed. We knew we would face the dreaded wooden spoon and steeled ourselves for very sore bottoms and backs, which ultimately came. We were sent to our rooms without dinner. I was okay with that since I hated dinner with all the smoke, but my brother cried. The next day the trellis was gone.

Jerry and I would go on to bigger and better adventures as the years passed. I was Davey Crockett to his Daniel Boone. When we finished that, we'd play a game called Flies Up, where we'd hit a red rubber handball into the air for the other one to catch. Tag was always fun, jumping hedges into thick ivy was heaven, and hide and seek always kept us entertained. When we were old enough to skateboard, we'd go over to the highly steep Kincardine hill and bomb straight down, bailing onto someone's lawn at the last minute as our skateboards careened across Castle Heights Boulevard causing some cars to swerve to avoid hitting them. Luckily, we never had a board get crushed. Often, we'd miss the lawn in our dive off the skateboard and go home with a severe and painful case of road rash. But we were back on Kincardine as soon as the scabs healed.

Three & Me

Jerry was my best friend. We'd ride bikes together, go to the gully together to look for pollywogs, and stay outside for as long as possible before we were called in to eat. Summers were our season. But as we got older, he gravitated more toward having guys as friends, and I was stuck by myself, painting portraits of dogs in the garage. Eventually, I had some friends that I could play with, but they were mostly boys. A little boy down the street, a year younger than me, was my buddy for a short while. His name was Donny. We were inseparable until his parents moved to Cheviot Hills, and I rarely saw him after that. It wasn't until 5th grade that I began to connect with other girls and actually had a best friend.

As kids grow up, so do kids' problems. Jerry was smaller than most other boys in his elementary school class. A couple of boys used to bully him, and he would often come home crying after a thumping. One kid named Robbie and another named Reggie delighted in making Jerry cry. They waited for every opportunity and struck him at will. He was their whipping boy.

When I was in 6th grade, and my brother was in the 5th grade, my dad, who would closely shave his head to match his bald spot, took Jerry in for the same haircut. It wasn't just a crew cut. Jerry's hair was buzzed entirely off, leaving a bald and crying 10-year-old boy. Jerry came home and ran into his room. I was horrified at what I saw. "Why did you do that to him?" I demanded. "He's going to get killed in school tomorrow!" My dad thought it looked great. (He obviously had no idea about the brutality of a schoolyard.) He thought the haircut brought out the brilliance of Jerry's big green eyes! "That's because his head looks green!" I shouted to no one as I walked away from my parents.

The very next day, as expected, all hell broke loose. In the morning, Jerry and I walked the usual route to school. I tried to keep the conversation light and funny. Jerry was morose and non-communicative. As soon as we stepped onto the school grounds, the shit show began.

My Nuclear Family

All of a sudden, kids from all grades began surrounding Jerry. They had never seen a bald kid before. They started putting their hands on his head to feel the baldness.

Jerry began to cry and lash out. But then, something very unexpected happened. A teacher who witnessed the chaos grabbed Jerry and put her arm around him, quickly ushering him toward the offices. I was, all of a sudden, the new focal point for the crowd of kids. "Why is he bald?" some kids shouted to me. "Is his hair going to grow back?" asked another. Children of all ages surrounded me. Some pushed me. "Your brother's bald!" others shouted. I began to panic. It was at this exact moment that I discovered I was claustrophobic. My heart beat quickly, my skin became clammy, and breathing was a chore. But, like my dad, I was as stoic as ever, never betraying my inner fear. I pushed the kids away from me and sought the sanctity of my class-room. Once inside, though, the same thing happened with the kids in my class demanding to know why Jerry was bald. Finally, the teacher broke it up and started class. I was in no mood to stay in school, angry at the world. When the 3 o'clock bell rang, I ran the whole way home.

Jerry was sent home earlier from the office, wearing a baseball cap a sympathetic staff member gave him. My dad came to pick him up, not fully understanding what all the fuss was about. Years and years would go by, and even into adulthood, the people I went to school with would always ask about the day Jerry's head was buzzed. It be-came one of those childhood experiences that refused to go away. As bad as that was, history was about to repeat itself 25 years later on a much more public scale.

Robbie and Reggie continued to beat my brother up after school ev-ery single day. Jerry always came home with a tear-stained face, and my mother went nuts. She finally got through to my dad that some-thing had to be done. I think she was thinking more about my dad calling up the parents and the school, but he had other plans.

Three & Me

He piled Jerry and me into the car and drove to a karate dojo on Venice Boulevard. We walked in, and I saw men in pajamas with different colored belts holding up their pants (or so I thought), making odd movements, and in the end, screaming, *"KiYaii!"* The sound of their voices reverberated off the walls, and I practically jumped through my skin. Jerry jumped behind my dad. My dad walked up to an extraordinarily tall and chiseled man with a crew cut and a deep voice. This man was wearing black pajamas, and his belt was black. He was barefoot, as were all the other men in the room. Jerry Packard, the dojo owner, the sensei, stepped forward with his hand outstretched to my dad's waiting hand.

After their handshake, my dad presented Jerry to Jerry Packard, who looked him over. "Take off your shoes, little man, and join the others on the mat. Try and do what we do." Jerry Packard's voice had a gentle but commanding tone as he nudged my brother toward the other group of men.

My dad gave Jerry a little shove, and he found a spot in the room among the men. He was the youngest one there. Kids karate dojos had yet to spring up across the country and were at least 30 years away from happening. Jerry was going to have to sink or swim in this new pond. He looked so lost, and I felt so bad for him. Men were kicking, pivoting, thrusting their arms in a combat position, pivoting again, then kicking, and Jerry could hardly keep up. I could see the sweat pouring down his little face. That lasted about 20 minutes until the session finally ended. My dad took out his wallet and paid Jerry Packard, who went into his office and came out with a white karate Gi (the pajamas) and a white belt, showing him how to wrap and tie off.

In a complete transformation, my brother immersed himself in Karate's sport, culture, and spirituality. He rode his bike to the dojo every day after school. On weekends, summer vacation, and any other school holiday, he would spend all day, every day, at Packard's dojo.

Soon the belts he wore began to change color. White turned to yellow. Yellow turned to orange, which turned to purple, then green, then brown, and finally, just before Jerry turned 15 years old, he achieved black. An achievement not to be minimized. He was the youngest black belt in the history of that dojo, going up against men to get it. He was breaking bricks with his hand or foot, splitting boards, and had the strength of three men. His achievement was huge, and word went out in school that he was never, ever to be messed with. That's not to say he didn't get into scrapes, but when someone tried to bully him, they lost. Jerry would first warn whoever wanted to take him on. If they didn't take heed, he'd usually lift them with one hand and give them a second warning. After the third warning, if someone still insisted on throwing a punch at him, he'd lay the guy out on the sidewalk and walk away.

In junior high school, Robbie and Reggie finally lost a fight with my brother while an entire group of kids watched. The fight was over in about one or two seconds. They never bothered my brother again.

*Jerry as a new recruit in the
Air Force.*

Jerry as a Black Belt on one of his Karate hikes.

## TWO

The Awkward Years: Junior High and High School

Both junior high and high school are probably the most brutal periods of most young people's lives. While navigating those years, so many variables come at you from all directions, not the least being: awkwardly changing bodies, reaching sexual maturity, zits, hormones, menstruation, etc. Throw in social hierarchies, and the humiliating experience is complete!

I accepted the fact that there were different cliques based on looks, family wealth, athleticism, and wardrobe. Believe it or not, colored socks were a status symbol when I attended school at Palms Junior High. The more colored socks you had, the higher your cred was. Popularity was the most crucial goal for most kids because, for the popular kids, the school was essentially theirs. The term we used, probably derived from the word "social," for the popular kids was "Sosha" or "Sosh" for short. Everyone else was relegated to the fringe, wondering why they weren't with the "in" group or trying to get in. Except me. I honestly didn't care about that because I had other problems. While I was always friendly, finding a real connection with most other kids was difficult. I didn't have the looks that fit the mold and definitely didn't come from wealth, as my dad had only recently graduated from Cleveland Chiropractic College and was starting his practice. I had no athletic inclinations (I was last picked for any team in PE) and definitely didn't have the clothes. (My mom shopped at Fedco, the Walmart of its time, instead of the trendy Beverly Hills shops the other girls' moms went to. And I wore white socks.)

During that period, my mom's paranoia and subsequent treatment of me progressively worsened. The year I entered junior high school, all hell began to break loose. The problem was that my mom would go

Me at 12

The Awkward Years: Junior High and High School

to her bridge club on Tuesday afternoons (on top of Monday nights), and during the bridge game, the other women would discuss the problems they were having with their own children. My mom would listen to their stories and somehow, in her mind, conflate their problem children with me. So, if a young teenage girl was a bit fast with the boys, I also had to be. Or if another young adolescent girl was shoplifting, I had to be doing that as well.

Let me be clear. I was not a sexually attractive 12-year-old. I would never have been able to finesse sexy. I looked like I was 8, and that's being generous. I had no figure. Indeed, I looked like a waif. Throw in the Oxford shoes my dad made me wear, a hand-me-down, and Fedco wardrobe; I know I looked about as sexy as a scarecrow!

So, you can understand how violated I felt the day I walked home from the bus stop after school and saw my mom waiting at the door for me with rage in her eyes. Before I could say "Hi, Mom," she slapped me hard across the face. "Slut!" she screamed at me. "You horrible SLUT!" I was too surprised to cry, although my face stung from her slaps. I didn't know the meaning of the word. I had never even heard it before. I was 12 years old and incredibly young for my age. "Just wait until your father gets home! Just *you* wait!"

Through flowing tears, I begged her to tell me what I did wrong. "You know what you did! You cheap slut! You know...."

"I don't!" I screamed back, holding my face. "Tell me what I did!" I could feel the red-hot pain in my cheeks as I shouted back.

"You're running around with boys! I heard about you... I heard everything! SLUT!"

I was stunned. *What boys?* There was nothing to hear. I woke up, took the bus to school until it was time to take it home from school, then came straight home. Then changed clothes and walked across

Three & Me

the street to Marty Root's house (he was three years younger than me) and played around-the-world with his basketball until we got tired, then played catch in the street out front. I had never been touched by a boy, let alone kissed by a boy or anything else my mom imagined in her increasingly sick mind. And once again, I was faced with proving something that never happened, *never happened*. It's impossible.

I went to my room and cried, wishing to be an adult so I could leave this craziness behind. Then my dad arrived home before he was supposed to come home. I could hear my mom screaming in the other room about me and her imaginary boys and the ladies at the bridge club and their daughters, and somehow through the insanity coming out of my mother's lips, he figured it out. "I'll go talk to her," I heard him say. "Just take care of dinner."

My dad knocked on my door and came in. He looked at me, not just as a dad but as a friend. He sat down on my bed, and I crawled into his protective arms and sobbed and sobbed. He didn't say anything; he just let me cry myself out. He put his hand on my head, caressed my cheek, and left. I didn't eat dinner that night, choosing instead to stay away from my mother in the safety of my bedroom. I was a huge Superman fan then, collecting all the weekly comics. I pulled some comic books from my collection and read them until I fell asleep. The following day, I woke up to a new bracelet from my dad.

# # #

I always tried to keep a brave face in school. Inside I was filled with insecurities about my appearance, our economic situation, and the unstable relationship with my mom. In grammar school, still at Castle Heights Elementary, I bonded with a girl named Lana. She had long light-brown hair worn with a pixie band over a cute flip. She had a pretty face, big beautiful eyes, and her sense of humor mirrored mine. She loved horses, and so did I, although I wasn't allowed to share that about myself. (It was a secret I had with my dad, who would take me out to the stables when finances would allow, so I could ride. Had my mother found out, that would have been the end of it.)

Lana and I became best friends. We were inseparable! We would have adventures together, like the time we snuck into the Nazareth House, a Catholic senior home near her house in Cheviot Hills. Somehow, we walked in unnoticed and entered the vast network of hallways. We were eating sunflower seeds and trying to be invisible in the marble hallways near the chapel. "Do you think we should get rid of the empty shells?" I asked. Lana shook her head in agreement. We found an "ashtray" just outside the chapel with a sponge-like object, so we dumped all our spent shells in the receptacle and walked into the chapel area. We were two young Jewish girls who had never been in a church. We were instantly mesmerized by the crucifixes on the wall, the paintings of Christ, and the carvings on the pews. We were silently taking in the surroundings when we heard a booming voice call out,

"WHO PUT THE SUNFLOWER SEEDS IN THE HOLY WATER?!" Lana and I froze, turning to look at each other before we both ran for the exit, as fast as our legs could carry us, straight back to her house. We didn't feel safe until we closed the door behind us, then we burst out laughing! I'm not sure what the divine punishment is for sunflower seeds in holy water, but I'd have to imagine that if Jesus Christ were watching, he'd have had a good laugh! (Jewish humor, maybe?)

I spent almost every weekend at Lana's home at sleepovers. Her mom, Melanie, was the mom I wished I had. She was normal. And she adored Lana. You could see Melanie's love for her daughter through the hugs, the desire to spend time with her, and how she spoke to her. There was no degradation, tension, disharmony, and, more importantly, no crazy accusations. Melanie respected Lana and cherished her.

Melanie called me "Sioux City Sue" in her thick New York accent. It was music to my ears because she used to say it out of genuine affection for me. Lana was so lucky. I loved my time there. Her mom made me feel like I mattered. I was able to exhale for a few days every time I visited.

Lana's stepfather owned an electronics store, so they were among the first to get color TV in the early 1960s. I still remember watching *Walt Disney's Wonderful World of Color* in their living room on Sunday nights. I also got to see the Beatles' first performance on the *Ed Sullivan Show* in Lana's living room. It was heaven.

Lana wore stretch-jean capris, which were all the rage back then. My mom refused to buy any for me, so when Lana outgrew hers, she handed them down to me. I remember those jeans being my pride and joy. I wore them until they literally tore apart. They were my first actual trendy articles of clothing. For my birthdays, I would ask my Grandmother Zsigmond, who shopped in Beverly Hills, for a new piece of clothing that was on trend and tried to slowly build a wardrobe that went with those jeans.

Being Lana's best friend was wonderful, but it would soon come to an unforeseen end. Lana's body changed during the summer between elementary school graduation and the first day of Palms Junior High. She developed a beautiful figure, and once she stepped foot on the school grounds that first day, she became the most sought-after girl in school. She was the celebrity of Palms Junior High and walked into the most popular clique on campus, owning it. Palms Junior High was her kingdom, and her popularity would last through high school graduation and beyond. She grew more and more popular as she became more beautiful each year.

On the other hand, I was relegated to the shadows of the fringe. Small, skinny, insignificant. I mourned the loss of my friend and the weekend sleepovers. Mostly, though, I mourned the loss of her mom.

# # #

The Awkward Years: Junior High and High School

Junior high school years for me represented a kind of hell that I imagine holds true for many kids. But my brother, because of karate, was becoming one of the most talked about kids on campus. His athleticism was being noticed. Not only was his body showing the effects of daily workouts, but his personality was also becoming quite large! He was busy setting records in PE, like most sit-ups or pull-ups. He developed a sense of humor, playing practical jokes on his teachers, like the time he told his entire PE class to go to the auditorium to see the movie *The Barefoot Surfer* (was there even a movie with that title?) and then running back to see the look on his teacher's face when no one showed up to class. He got busted when one kid went to find Mr. Kiino, the PE teacher, to find out why the movie was taking so long to start. My parents laughed when they got the call that Jerry was in the office because he stole a gym class and was being sent home as punishment.

While Jerry thrived, I suffered. I remember a slight crush on a new boy in school named Ken. I mistakenly confided my crush to a girlfriend who rode home on the same bus as I did. Ken was seated in the row in front of me, and, much to my horror, my friend got up, flopped down next to him, and told him of my crush. They both laughed at the revelation as I sat red-faced, wishing I could die right there, when he uttered, just loud enough for me to hear, "Wouldn't it be funny to see Sue Sigmond in a bathing suit?" Then they both laughed some more. It was more than I could take. My bus stop mercifully arrived, and I leaped off, sobbing with the embarrassment of it all for the entire three-block walk home. I already had a strong distrust for women, primarily because of my mom. That awful day on the bus made me realize that trusting girls as friends could also be treacherous.

High school started out like junior high school, the only difference being that I could walk to school instead of being stuck on a bus. I went to Alexander Hamilton High School in the Westside of Los Angeles. Full-figured women were still trending, but then something interesting happened. Twiggy hit the scene in England, and Thin was

Three & Me

IN! At least it was overseas, anyway. But in the microcosm of Hamilton High School, the old standards of beauty were still in play, along with who had the best wardrobe, best house, eventually best car, cutest boyfriend, etc., etc., etc.

In my first year at Hami, I quickly learned that football games were crucial. Even though we usually lost, it was essential to go and cheer on our team. (Our team consisted of mostly Jewish boys in shoulder pads and helmets.) One Friday night at a game, the unthinkable happened. I was standing and talking to a cute boy who was a year ahead of me. My hair had grown long and straight, an increasingly on-trend style because it was the look of the surf culture in Southern California. While not yet developed, my body was slowly becoming indented in the right places and protruding slowly in the other suitable places. This boy was clearly interested in me. His name was Gary Owen, and I swooned when he put his arm around my shoulder. We watched the rest of the football game together and walked to his car, still arm in arm, when the game ended. He drove a black Mustang, which I thought was incredibly awesome. Before he left, I got a sweet little kiss as he drove off, and just like that, I had a boyfriend!

How easy and innocent young love was back then. With one kiss, a romance was born. Compared to being older with the complications that result from age, wisdom, experience, and baggage, finding love at 15 is a gift to be cherished and remembered. I'll never forget that night in the bleachers.

Gary was in a boy's club on campus, and he gave me his club chain and pendant to wear around my neck. We were officially going steady, and I thought I had died and gone to heaven. Gary was all I could think of. I looked forward to his phone calls. I could hardly wait for weekends so we could go out on dates, and I loved kissing him. For the first time, I felt the happiness that being a part of a couple could bring.

My mother, God bless her, then felt the need to destroy it all as soon as she realized how happy I was. Was she jealous of me for being happy for the first time? Was she afraid? Or was it that because her childhood had been miserable, she was determined to make mine even more miserable? I had no clue then, and I have no clue now. But it didn't take long for my mom's harmful interference with my first-ever love to tear things apart. Gary and I lasted less than six months as a couple, and I'm surprised it lasted as long as it did.

He came from a good Jewish family. His father was a clothing manufacturer of junior clothing and drove a Lamborghini. Gary's car was his own. His sister also had her own Mustang. They lived in a big home on Motor Avenue in Cheviot Hills. His parents were so nice; his mom was clearly the kind of mother one would thrive under. There was nothing wrong with our going steady. It was young puppy love. But to my mother, it represented impending doom. For whom, I don't know.

She convinced my father that having a steady boyfriend in high school would lead to unwanted pregnancy (more bridge club gossip entering my upbringing), venereal diseases, drunkenness, drug use, and other teenage horrors. So, the machinations were set in place to end my relationship with Gary. I was told I could never have a boyfriend, and I had to break up with Gary. I was also told to date different boys each time I went out. I couldn't have two dates in a row with the same boy. I was told I had to be home by 10.00 pm sharp or I would be grounded. I was told I could not go to parties with a boy. My mother's paranoia played out in a big way. But she wasn't worried about me. She was concerned about what her bridge cronies would think of her if I decided to go down the dark path of heroin addiction and chain pregnancies. While I had no desire to do drugs or drink, or God forbid, smoke or have intercourse, my mother's imagination forced her down that fearful rabbit hole.

I was aghast at suddenly finding myself in a prison-like home life. Jerry, meanwhile, had an entirely different set of parameters. Because he was a boy, he enjoyed freedom. The old privileges I enjoyed as a kid evaporated into the dark abyss of my mother's imagination. All the kids my age went to dances, the movies, Picwood Bowl, or other places teens would hang out. Boys and girls were quickly finding each other. Car dates were standard. To my mother, cars represented portable bedrooms.

Because of my low self-esteem, I felt lucky that just ONE boy found me attractive enough to want me for his girlfriend, let alone attempt to find a new date every week, if at all. I was devastated. I reluctantly called him and told him of my new restrictions. I cried as I told him, and I could feel my heart shattering into a million pieces, then shattering into a million more. I was 15 years old and wanted a social life. Gary was upset at my new restrictions and what was happening. Somehow, we both arrived at a plan that should have never been on the table. We decided to sneak around behind my parents' backs. This was a hugely troubling moment for me. I was an honest person, and even at that young age, I had strong values. I didn't like not telling the truth. Telling the truth was the one thing I could rest my laurels on. My self-identity was based on that honesty. And now, I would enter into a phase of dishonesty, lying, sneaking around, and abject disobedience. I was going to defy what I considered unjust rules. And I would do it dishonestly. Now, not only was my heart shattered, but my self-worth also took a big hit.

We snuck around for a few months. I would take babysitting jobs across the street, and Gary would park around the corner and come and hang out with me. I would meet him at friends' houses. I hung out with him at school every day. We found a way to make it work until, one day; I got caught.

My brother, angry at me for something, ratted me out, and the next thing I knew, my dad was on his way to pick me up from Gary's house, where I was visiting on a Saturday afternoon. Jerry called to warn me that Dad was coming, so I went outside to wait for the inevitable tongue-lashing. I'll admit I was petrified. As he drove up, I remember feeling the knot in my throat tighten. As bad as I imagined it getting, I had no idea how bad it would get. The yelling started as soon as the door closed to his car. But that was nothing compared to what my mom threw at me once we got home.

Mom had decided to give me up. I was no longer wanted. She was finished pretending to love a child she couldn't. She had called the police and told them that she wanted to surrender custody of me to MacClaren Hall, an orphanage for kids or a holding place for kids waiting to be placed in foster care. It wasn't a good place to be. Mc-Claren Hall was eventually shut down because of short staffing. It housed innocent kids with kids who had committed crimes or had mental illness issues. Neglect and abuses were frequent at the facility. Clearly, my mother had done her research and found that suitable for the horrible daughter I was.

I was told to pack a bag, and then we drove to the Perdue police station in Westwood, where I would be surrendered. The entire drive to the police station was some of the worst moments of my life. I kept hoping that maybe it would be for the better. I would miss my dad and my brother but never my mom. And then the waves of sorrow hit me with the realization that my mom had made it abundantly clear how much she didn't want me as her child. I never cried that day. I wouldn't give her the satisfaction.

Once at the police station, my mom made it clear to the officers how much I wasn't wanted. Then a policewoman took me aside and spoke with me, trying to figure out the catalyst for this parental surrender. My father looked like one of the walking dead. He had gone from enraged to completely deflated, void of all feelings and emotion. I think, for the first time, he didn't know what to do. Go against his wife and protect his child, or stand with her and give up his flesh and blood. He was so obviously torn. The police picked up on my father's inner conflict and asked to interview him separately from my mother. Then,

Three & Me

he said he had no intention of letting me go. Things had gotten out of hand, and he couldn't stop the momentum of the hurricane that was my mother. He just wanted to scare me and teach me a lesson while, at the same time, letting his wife think she had gotten the upper hand. In the end, I was sent home with my parents. The police wouldn't take a surrender unless both parents were on board to sign me away. My mom was angry. My dad was relieved. I was scared and devastated. I went home with emotional scars that would take years to heal. Things had changed for me. I stopped trusting my dad. As for my mom? Well, the veil was lifted, the gauntlet thrown. My mom openly hated me now. That's a pretty tough pill to swallow for a teen. What I had done did not merit the extreme reaction and possible abandonment I faced. Any *normal* parent would have just grounded me.

My world was filled with the insanity my mother threw out. Every hurt she suffered as a child poured out of her ten times stronger when she directed it at me. She couldn't punish her parents, but me? I was fair game.

Gary broke up with me soon after. Talk about a double whammy! I felt my parents called his parents and made threats because it was in line with what my mother would do. I'd seen her do it with teachers regarding my brother. His parents probably said that being with me was not worth the trouble. Who could blame them? It wasn't. Even I could see that. While I mourned the loss of Gary, my mom reveled in my broken heart, reminding me constantly that I was pretty much worthless. Her favorite saying was, "Nothing is perfect, Suzie. And since you want a perfect life, you ARE nothing. Remember that!"

In June of that same year, I turned 16, which brought a certain amount of independence. I was gaining coping skills and tenuously learning to trust my dad again. Although initially strained, we slowly and carefully restarted our Monday nights together.

During the summer that year, a television show was being filmed daily at the beach at the old Station 8 in Santa Monica, near where the kids in my grade at school hung out. I was old enough to take a bus to the beach while Jerry spent all day, every day, at the dojo. My mom, with her new-found freedom from "watching" kids, played bridge daily, as my dad worked in his office from before dawn until evening. Summer meant freedom for me, and I took to it as a duck took to the water.

One summer beach day, I was lying on the sand, speaking with a friend, when a guy about my age approached me and knelt by my side. He grabbed my hand and asked me to come with him. I wasn't sure what this was about, but I got up and walked with him, trusting that I would be OK. He led me inside a circle of people surrounding the TV show's film set and placed me at the end of a long line of girls. I had no idea what was happening or why I was there, but a celebrity was nearby (one of the stars of *Peyton Place*, the hottest and most controversial television show at the time.) This celebrity announced through the mic to Michael Blodgett, the emcee, and host of the beach show, *Groovy*, that he chose the little girl at the end. So, I looked down the line of girls toward the other end of the line to see whom he was talking about.

Then I heard, "No, no. It's you! In the pink bikini." He laughed as he said it, and Michael Blodgett walked up to me and placed a massive firecracker in my arms. The date was July 3rd, and they were filming the July 4th show. I now had the official "Miss Firecracker" title and was awarded a few prizes. It was over quickly, and I thought that was the end of it.

After I filled out forms with my name, address, and phone number, I left the circle and the TV show and sat back down on my towel in the sand. Things were suddenly different. My 16-year-old body looked good in a bikini. I was no longer skinny but now "slim" (thanks to Twiggy). I had long dark hair down to my waist and a golden tan, and my facial features had somehow become more chiseled, showing off my high cheekbones. Who knew? All of a sudden, I was the center of attention. Guys who wouldn't give me the time of day or even look twice in my direction only recently were now vying to talk to me. I felt uncomfortable with this new and unexpected attention, especially after spending so much time in the shadowy fringes of high school society, so I packed my towel and hairbrush and took the bus home.

After the show aired the following evening on the Fourth of July, the phone rang off the hook. TV shows wanted me to come in and audition. Dance shows, particularly *Boss City*, wanted me on their show every chance they could. (I took a lot of friends with me each time.) My parents were fielding calls from producers, directors, and agents. I was excited. My parents, of course, said, "No way!" so Hollywood moved on without me. I wasn't surprised.

The phone also rang off the hook from guys who wanted to date me. Suddenly, I became a status symbol, a trophy, because of my new notoriety. But I soon discovered that most guys just wanted to have sex with me, and that was not on my agenda at 16. I got more careful with whom I chose to go out with. My mother, with her distorted logic, was thrilled because I had so many guys asking me out; it was easy not to have two dates in a row with the same guy. Little did she understand that trying to wrestle drunk and stoned guys off of me was much worse than my having a steady boyfriend, someone as nice and unassuming as Gary.

Just as I thought the hype about me was dying down, a photographer who knew I won the bikini contest took a picture of me eating ice cream at the beach, and it was published as a full page in the full-color tabloid-sized weekend edition of the *LA Times*. My mom was the one to find that photo. I was immediately grounded. She'd had enough of my body being plastered over print and TV media. Her bridge club ladies, no doubt, had a say in that too.

But there was one thing she couldn't control. People for years kept coming up to me saying they saw me on TV, either from the bikini contest on *Groovy* or *Boss City* or both. And they'd say they saw my picture in the *Times*. I had achieved a small slice of fame at 16 years old. And I'd be lying if I said I didn't enjoy it.

Another thing I noticed was that people treated me nicer because of that hype. It was a small lesson learned at a young age. I would watch this play out on a larger scale once I reached adulthood. In California, as superficial as this is—looks matter.

The day after Lana's16th birthday, she got her driver's license. I hadn't spoken to her in years. In fact, I had moved on from the friendship and was among the hundreds of students who admired Lana from a distance. She was the most prominent and brightest high school star at Hami. Her clique was comprised of all the gorgeous girls and guys. Even after I won the bikini contest, I still had no way out of the shadowy fringe at my school. At Hamilton, you are who you were. (It's still like that at class reunions some 50 years later.) So, I let them be who they were and continued to develop myself to be who I wanted to be. I had dreams I needed to make come true, and I didn't want to be caught up in the high school social hierarchy. Remember, I still wore white socks.

Lana was a July birthday girl. I had already won the bikini contest by the time of her birthday, and while male attention outside of school was something I wasn't lacking at the time, none was forthcoming from the guys in my school. The cool guys still ignored me, preferring the cool girls instead. But outside school, among the older guys who surfed, grew their hair longer, and became increasingly good-looking, they noticed me. And I was good with that. Lana's parents gave her a Sweet 16 party (something my parents didn't give me). I wasn't invited. Not a surprise since I wasn't in with the Sosh group. So, I was shocked when the very same day Lana got her driver's license, she drove her mom's late-model yellow Lincoln Continental over to

Three & Me

my house and picked me up. It was as if the years we hadn't spoken had never existed. We reconnected as friends, enjoying each other's company, and immediately reverted to being just two young girls who shared the same likes and dislikes. We drove around for hours, catching up. Out of all my memories with Lana, that ranks amongst the best.

I had become a fixture at the beach, enjoying the combined smells of the ocean salt water and the food carts. The cool brisk air, softly caressing my face, was my personal addiction. I couldn't get enough of it. I loved the feeling of the sunshine washing over my body and the sounds of the waves crashing on shore as I ran into the water, towing my rented raft behind me. Listening to the cries of the seagulls softly in the background completed the experience for me.

Going to the beach together became a thing. Regularly, we'd go down, if for nothing else, to meet guys and decide which ones to date. Lana had her white leather bikini, and I had my pink one. She filled out her bikini much better than I did mine, but for some reason, that didn't matter. Guys were attracted to us both, and we had our pick! That was one of my favorite summers. Every time I see the John Von Hamersveld poster for the movie *The Endless Summer,* feelings of nostalgia still wash over me. That summer was my Endless Summer.

This brings me to my "endless" date. Lana called me one evening. Some guy had misdialed a phone number, and instead of reaching his intended party, he got Lana. She liked the sound of his voice because, in her words, "He sounded cute." How can someone sound cute??? I didn't get it. To follow even more flawed logic, she had an absolutely HUGE favor to ask of me. This guy had a friend. They were both in the Navy, and she wanted me to go out with his friend, so I could try and figure out if the guy she was talking to was cute or not, even though I wouldn't be meeting her guy. (Good luck making sense of this one!) Didn't quite get that logic, but, hey, I was 16, and Lana was the dating expert between the two of us, so she was able to talk me into the date.

Well, the guy called me because Lana gave him my phone number. He asked me out for the weekend and asked me what I wanted to do. I told him I wanted to see the movie, *The Endless Summer,* but I wanted to see it in a theater in Hollywood, far away from where I lived, guaranteeing no one I knew would see me out with this guy if he turned out to be, dare I say it, a dud.

When he came to the door, I was horrified. I wanted to absolutely kill Lana for making me do this. Standing before me was a short man with the most enormous nose I'd ever seen, accentuated by his Navy crew cut. His eyes were too close together, and his teeth were an exercise in modern art. He was dressed nicely enough, and he seemed sweet, so I hoped the date would not be too awful and the time would pass quickly. The entire evening, though, he threw out all kinds of canned phrases. It didn't appear that he had an original thought in his head. I was glad we'd be watching a movie, so he couldn't talk much, but apparently, that didn't stop him. He chattered non-stop throughout the entire film. I nearly died when he looked me in the eyes and, with all sincerity, said, "Never love a sailor-man. They're always saying goodbye." I still giggle at that thought. As for forgiving Lana for that horrible "endless" date. Not on your life!

Once school started in September, Lana returned to being the superstar and hanging out with her clique. I rarely spoke to her during school hours, but we'd talk on the phone regularly, get together on weekends and cruise around in her mom's car. Even though we weren't social at school, kids knew we were friends. Guys would approach me, wanting to know what being friends with Lana was like. The guys in my grade were still not interested in me for me. But because of my ties to Lana, they fell all over themselves to speak to me. They somehow wanted to get "closer" to Lana, thinking I was a pipeline to her. There's a term for that today. It's called being the DUFF (Designated Ugly Fat Friend). Even though I was still skinny, I fit the bill in every other way. My experience being Lana's DUFF prepared me for what would come in my adult years. The curious

Three & Me

attention towards a friend of mine would only amplify as I got older. I learned quickly that if you pay attention to schoolyard behaviors, you will see those same behaviors play out in adults later on. They just occur on a larger playing field.

Lana always had the most popular boys as boyfriends. Her first real boyfriend in junior high school was a guy I had crushed on since I first laid eyes on him in 7th grade. He was in many of my classes, and I fell hard for him. John Keller had sandy blonde hair that fell across his forehead. His eyes had a cute squint, and he always looked handsome in a yellow button-down or plaid flannel shirt paired with beige Dockers or blue jeans. His smile was something I can still picture to this day because it was genuine, revealing the sweetness that lay beneath it. But mine was unrequited love, the silent crush that had to remain my secret. Because I knew, as nice as John Keller was, he was out of my league. He was out of my stratosphere, actually. Hoping to connect with a John Keller back then would be like me today, hoping that Brad Pitt would want to hang out. That is never gonna happen.

But it happened to Lana. They found each other, the two most beautiful kids in the school. They were the power couple on the junior high campus, and instead of being jealous, I was happy that at least Lana got the boy I admired.

She and the star quarterback became a couple in high school. Not only was he a jock, but he was also a straight-A student. He had the classic good looks of a Jewish athlete. Possessed of dark curly hair, a chiseled face, a ruddy complexion, intense eyes, and a body like a machine, he commanded attention in the hallways. He excelled at everything he touched. It was no wonder the two of them were attracted to each other because sometimes stars collide. And collide, they did. Their relationship was explosive, always full of ups and downs. He knew I was friends with Lana, so after each squabble or pothole they'd hit, he'd show up on my doorstep, asking me for advice on the how's, why's, and what-to-do's about the situation. Every time that dark blue VW Bug would park in front of my house, I knew I would be listening to the sad tales of a boy who loved a girl too much.

My friendship with Lana was on again, off again. Even now, we remain casual friends, occasionally getting together or speaking on the phone. Lana and I have a lifetime of scattered memories. Now Facebook keeps us up-to-date on each other's lives between visits. Once we speak or see each other, the connection returns, and we revert to being 12-year-old girls, putting sunflower seeds in the holy water again.

# # #

My home life was still a free-falling experience. While I was trying my hardest to stay out of my mother's way, my brother Jerry was enjoying his popularity in school way too much. He was a member of the Essex Club, a prestigious club for the cool guys. He got a job at Chuck's Steak House as a busboy and earned enough money in salary and tips to buy his own souped-up hot rod. His car was much fancier than the Plymouth Valiant my dad drove. Jerry had blossomed into a gorgeous teenage boy. His personality and smile were his tickets to many after-hours sex romps with an array of older women on the dining tables after the restaurant closed. (Imagine that the next time you go out to dinner somewhere!) Jerry walked into my bedroom one night and proudly showed me a photo of him atop a woman "doing it." She was bottle blonde, a lot older, and had enormous boobs that spilled out over the sides of his chest as he lay atop her. I learned later that my brother had a fetish for women on the heavier side.

Because of his loose sexual behavior, he caught gonorrhea and syphilis more than once. My dad would have to take him for antibiotics each time, but instead of getting in trouble with my mom, she laughed it off as "boy behavior." Let's remember, at 12, I was the slut in the family because a bridge lady's daughter kissed a boy. But my brother with venereal disease? No big thing.

Three & Me

One day my mom decided to clean Jerry's closet. She moved some items, and a shotgun went off, putting a bullet into the wall. That got her attention! For the first time ever, Jerry was in hot water. Completely freaked out, she immediately called my father, who ran out of the office, charging home to deal with my mom, who nearly got her head blown off. Once home, he dismantled the rifle and threw the pieces away. He read my brother the riot act, telling him he was damn lucky my mother wasn't killed. And Jerry was lucky! Accidental deaths from loaded firearms happen all too often. After listening to my dad's speech, nodding his head in agreement and feigning remorse, Jerry went out and bought another one, hid it better, and kept the ammo close by instead of leaving it loaded. My parents never knew.

After the gun episode faded, Jerry told me the disconcerting fact that he slept with a knife under his pillow. He'd hide it under the mattress every morning when he woke up. My mom never found it, so he hid it well. I wondered if Jerry wasn't showing early symptoms of my mom's paranoia and mental illness. (Yes, by that time in my life, I'd figured out my mom had a mental illness.) I didn't have much time to worry about it, though. As soon as he turned 18, Jerry joined the Air Force, and he was, for all intents and purposes, completely gone from my life. The baby brother I felt so protective over, who was at one time my best friend, had chosen a path I didn't understand. It would rip us apart for the rest of our lives.

The Awkward Years: Junior High and High School

THREE

Coming Into My Own

In Hebrew, each letter in the alphabet equals a number. The number 18 spells "chai," which translates to the word "life!" (Think *Fiddler on the Roof* and the lyrics to the song *L'chaim! To life to life, I'chaim!*) The eighth letter of the Hebrew alphabet is the first part of the word, while the tenth letter is the second—thus 18. In the summer of 1969, I had reached a birthday where legally, my parents couldn't control me. They tried, oh how they tried, but it was easier and easier to let the noise they made go in one ear and out the other. I was on my way to adulthood.

While I was in my junior year of high school—the year when SATs, college applications, and college visits were all a significant part of the high school experience—I got the news that I wouldn't be able to be a part of that excitement. While my dad's practice was growing and he was beginning to make some pretty good income, I was informed that upon graduation from high school, I had to attend a community college due to budget constraints. After that proclamation, I didn't bother sending out applications to colleges. There wasn't enough money for me to go to a four-year college, let alone dorm living. I was heartbroken because I would lose what I considered the right of passage from childhood to adulthood. It also meant I would be stuck at home, still in the crosshairs of my mom's fury.

Graduation Day came a few days after my 18th birthday. To no one's surprise, my mom started a massive fight with me on the morning of graduation over what, exactly, I don't remember. Then, after exhausting herself by yelling at me, she told me she was just too tired and upset with me, so she would not be attending my graduation. I was on my own. With that, she retired to her bedroom, still in the muumuu

Three & Me

Yaniv in our yard in Motza Illit, Israel

Coming Into My Own

she had put on when she got out of bed. *What parent wants to miss their own child's graduation?!* It's one of those life milestones that parents share with their kids. When my son graduated high school, my husband and I were proudly there. Nothing, barring nuclear war, could keep me away. But my mom? She didn't give it much importance. It was just another day in her life, and she'd spend it in bed.

When the time came, I walked to school, put on my cap and gown, and marched with my class to the cheers of other student's parents. I remember it being excruciatingly hot that June day, and I barely remember the ceremony. The other girls in the class wore pantyhose and fancy dresses under their caps and gowns, capped off with pretty shoes. I wore bright yellow knee socks and tennis shoes because I didn't own a pair of dressy shoes. I'm pretty sure everyone could see me as I was the only girl wearing socks (at least they weren't white).

I figured I'd wear something utterly wrong if I couldn't look like the other girls in my class. When the ceremony was over, I walked home alone while the other kids found their waiting families, received hearty congratulations, flowers, balloons, and loving kisses, and posed for pictures. I didn't bother looking for my dad or brother in the stands. Before I left for school, I heard my mom call him and demand that he not attend. He didn't. While others in my class probably have many photos from that huge day, I have none. There was no one to take them.

Throughout my senior year in high school and into college, I got a job working retail part-time at Judy's, a popular chain of clothing stores in their brand-new flagship store in Century City. Somehow my personality was conducive to selling to men. So, while all the other sales girls had to wear appropriate clothing like skirts and blouses, I got to wear bell-bottomed jeans because I had to climb a rolling ladder to reach pants. Up and down the ladder I would go hundreds of times a week. I only had to talk to men, and they would pile the clothing higher and higher, racking up huge sales. Whenever I told a guy I loved him in a particular shirt, it was sold. However, at $1.75 per hour with taxes withheld, I couldn't pay tuition, get an apartment, or even a car, so I resigned myself to being one of the kids who didn't get to leave home at 18. Lana had her own apartment in Brentwood by then. Her parents let her move out before her 18th birthday, and I'm pretty sure footed the bill.

I enrolled as an art major at Santa Monica City College and quickly learned to love that small college. The guys were gorgeous, the classes were a lot of fun, and I enjoyed the free periods between classes. Throw in the proximity to the beach, and it was not a bad way to knock out two years of school. I guess you could say I made lemonade out of the academic lemons.

I was also enjoying a busy social life. I'd befriended kids my age who had graduated from Culver City High School. A whole new world opened up for me then, and I dated many cute guys from that area. The only problems I began to have, were marijuana and sex. That was because I didn't want to do drugs, was completely afraid of getting caught and spending years behind bars, and the prospect of VD and pregnancy scared the living daylights out of me. Even though I began to be sexually active, intercourse was still off the table. Since everyone I knew was smoking weed, dropping acid, doing "shrooms" (mushrooms), and smoking hash, it got to be dicey for me since I was the only straight one in the room. I did get contact highs, though, and eventually, when I felt it was safe enough, I'd try taking hits of weed off of my friends' blunts. That didn't last long. I found out two things about myself. One, weed put me to sleep. Two, weed made me paranoid.

I was dating a guy in a rock band during that period. His name was Ron, and he was absolutely drop-dead gorgeous with long hair, big blue eyes, a perfect build, and a voice I could listen to over and over again. He smoked weed and hash and did opium. He tried to get me to do drugs with him, but I refused. It never dawned on me that the laws being what they were, if he were ever busted, I'd be busted with him since I would be in the same car with him and the drugs. He was such a cool guy that I overlooked the obvious until that one day. We had gone to the beach and were driving down Pacific Coast Highway when he asked me what I was doing Saturday evening. I told him it was the first night of Yom Kippur and couldn't go out.

"Yom Kippur?" he asked. "Does that mean you're Jewish?"

"Yeah. It does."

He looked at me briefly because he was still driving at about 60 mph, and I could tell he was lost in thought. After a minute or two, he responded. "That's OK. I don't mind."

Huh?! *How benevolent of him, not minding that I was Jewish!* Well, that ended that. I couldn't go out with him after he said what he said. Poor Ron couldn't figure out what he did wrong. His drug use didn't do him in for me, but his ignorance did.

When I was in college, Skeeze ran away from my grandmother. He drove cross country to live with us in our small three-bedroom house in Southern California. My parents were unprepared for his extended visit, unaware he was coming. Skeeze just appeared on the doorstep of the family he looked down upon at a house he used to consider beneath his station and moved into Jerry's old room. His visit distracted my mom from me because she had to focus on her father, which was a nice change. He wasn't in California long when he suffered a massive heart attack, so both my parents were very busy tending to him and his needs.

It turned out my dad saved my grandfather's life. Skeeze was feeling unwell on the morning of the day he was to have his heart attack. To everyone's surprise, my dad examined him and immediately called an ambulance. Skeeze was hooked up to lifesaving equipment in the

Three & Me

emergency ward of Brotman Memorial Hospital when the heart attack struck. He would have hit the floor dead if my dad hadn't taken quick action when he did.

I noticed my grandfather's behavior had shifted somewhat, becoming more palatable and slightly more likable. I'd visit him in the hospital, and he would tell me how beautiful I had become and how I was now his favorite among all the grandchildren. I knew it was bull, so I never fell for it. I have no desire now or then to hurt an old man, so I would smile and say, "Thank you." And then I'd forget about it. I hate to say it, but the damage was done, and I looked upon my grandfather as a man who was suddenly very old, ill, and somewhat pathetic.

I was largely left alone during this period, and I loved it. My social life became more enjoyable as my grandfather recovered at our house. It was the 1960's hippie era. I was attracted to guys with long hair. None of them were Jewish, though. It was mainly in part because the Jewish guys rarely asked me out. If they did ask me out, I wasn't interested in them either because they had crummy personalities, weren't my physical type, or were expecting me to spread my legs on the first date. I grew up in a neighborhood filled with Jewish American Princes who could do no wrong in their mother's eyes, which framed my view about dating them. Add the fact that they ignored me during my high school years, and I had no interest at all at that point.

On the one rare occasion when I went out with a Jewish guy, I had to fend off some very aggressive advances. At the end of a date, one guy named Dale stood on my porch, looked me square in the eye, and told me that I would grow up to be a loser simply because I hadn't slept with him. I had no idea how to react to such an audacious statement, so I ignored it and him.

My parents were panicking about my choice of guys to date, so they hatched a plan to send me to Israel for the summer in a program called "Summer in Kibbutz," where I would work on a kibbutz and be able to travel around Israel for an entire summer. (A kibbutz is a collective settlement based on socialism. Each member had a job within the community and, in return, got their food, clothing, home, education, medical and dental care covered by the kibbutz, and a yearly allowance for extras.) I wasn't that gung-ho about it, but at the end of the day, after I researched kibbutz life and found out it fell into lock-step with the hippie movement and commune philosophy during the late 1960s/early 1970s, I took them up on their offer. No money for college or dorms, but an overseas trip? No problem! I flew to the Holy Land in June of that year.

The first thing I did on arrival in Israel was fall in love with the kibbutznik in charge of our group. I first laid eyes on him in the middle of the night when he came to greet my group and show us to the shacks we'd be occupying. (Kibbutz life was pretty bare bones.) I couldn't keep my eyes off him. His piercing blue eyes, long curly hair, scruffy beard, and slim build struck me like a bolt of lightning. I made up my mind that he would be mine. His name was Yaniv Dotan. He had no idea what was coming. But as much as I wanted him as my forever man, some obstacles had to be overcome. When Yaniv first saw me, he couldn't believe someone would send a 12-year-old girl so far away from home to work on a kibbutz. That was a huge hurdle. Then to make matters worse, he had a girlfriend at the time and was not the least bit interested in me.

That would change.

Just about every single girl on the Summer in Kibbutz program who was sent to Ayelet Hashahar (the name of that kibbutz) with me crushed hard on Yaniv. He was almost the local celebrity within that small community. The members of his kibbutz all said he looked like Paul Newman in the movie Exodus and most of the single girls on the kibbutz had set their sights on Yaniv as well.

Three & Me

One day, a rumor circulated that Yaniv and his girlfriend had broken up. I wasn't sure it was true, but then I repeatedly heard that rumor. Friday night dinners were special evenings in the main dining hall. It was a beautiful room, not so much because of the décor—the tables and chairs were mainly utilitarian and largely uncomfortable—but the high vaulted ceiling, large windows, and beautiful artwork made the place stunning. Once inside, people sat with their families and/or friends. It was cafeteria-style serving, so everyone would pick up trays, stand in line, and self-serve their dinners. That would include grabbing cutlery, glasses, drinks, and Challah. On Friday nights, people would wear their best Shabbat clothing, ladies in skirts or nice slacks and men in white button-down shirts. People usually wore more casual shorts, t-shirts, sandals, or work boots on other nights.

I had previously spotted Yaniv in the dining hall with a beautiful girl with dark curly hair. In my mind, she epitomized female Israeli beauty. Now I saw him alone or with friends, without his girlfriend present. More importantly, they were not together at Shabbat dinner in the dining hall, so I surmised the rumors were true. We had a scheduled tour away from the kibbutz that Yaniv would chaperone coming up in the next few days, and I had made up my mind that Yaniv *would* notice me.

The Summer in Kibbutz program chartered a bus for our group, and our tour of Northern Galilee was about to commence. I was seated on the aisle when Yaniv walked past me and sat in the back seat. I wasn't about to let someone else grab the seat next to him, so I quickly got up and flounced down with a big smile on my face. He laughed out loud, but I could tell he was flattered. We talked and joked the whole way to Nazareth. I could see the other girls seething at my getting chummy with Yaniv, making the experience that much sweeter.

The entire five days of the tour were five days spent together, chatting and getting to know one another. While my mother possessed some demons, her sense of humor was her shining light. Thankfully, that was the one trait I got from her that I liked. I'm grateful daily for the ability to laugh, find humor and enjoy even the tiniest thing. Yaniv loved my sense of humor, and, as he told it, he fell in love almost immediately after I sat down on the bus next to him. Thankfully, he no longer saw me as a pre-teen.

Those beginnings of our courtship were so, so, so romantic. I was on cloud nine the entire time we got to know each other as we traveled around the country. I still remember walking the darkened alleys of the old city of Akko, situated on the Mediterranean Sea, hand-in-hand, listening to the Muslim calls to prayer from the mosques nearby, the waves crashing, and sounds of Middle Eastern music wafting from radios in the Old City courtyards. The cacophony was beautiful. Life was wonderful, and it would stay that way for some happy months. In the back of my mind, though, was the realization that I would return to Los Angeles to live at home with my parents again. That realization would bring me crashing back down to Earth. But for the time being, I would enjoy being madly in love with the most handsome, intelligent, and nicest man I had ever met. Yaniv was 22 years old and just out of his mandatory three-year stint in the Israeli Army, where he served as a paratrooper. He was trying to find his way in this new-to-him civilian life. At the end of the five-day tour, we were officially a couple. He was my boyfriend, and I was as happy as I'd ever been in my young life.

Yaniv and I agreed to have an international romance upon my return to the U.S. I would return to Israel the following summer to stay. I didn't dare tell my parents. I'd already experienced the pain of their interference with my first boyfriend, Gary Owen, and I wasn't about to let it happen to me a second time. But, like everything else at 3103 Oakhurst Avenue, my mother would eventually find her way to cast a pall on my happiness.

I was still working at Judy's, saving every cent for plane tickets. I wanted to visit Yaniv over the Christmas holidays, as there would be no

Three & Me

classes then. Before I left, I went to a gynecologist to see about birth control. The doctor I saw in Beverly Hills was named Dr. Hyman, of all names. (I wonder how many women came to him because of his name?) He fitted me with a diaphragm because I was too afraid of birth control pills. Too many of my friends packed on the pounds with the high estrogen levels, had sore breasts and experienced various side effects. I thought I would go a safer route and get the diaphragm. When I returned home, I tucked the device at the bottom of a drawer in a vanity I had in my room. I was sure it was safe there because I couldn't imagine anyone, including my mother, rifling through my drawers.

After I returned from Israel, Yaniv and I corresponded several times a week, sending love letters back and forth over oceans and continents. At that point, the mailman was my best friend, bringing me messages of love from far away. While my mother never said anything about these letters, I was sure she hoped time and distance would end the romance. I never imagined Yaniv's letters would prompt her to violate my privacy and rifle through my belongings. But she did. I was naïve to think she would afford me some privacy. She found the diaphragm. Like so many times before, she'd use this new excuse to make my life a living hell.

I wasn't home when she searched my room, which was probably not the first time she'd done so. She probably read Yaniv's rather steamy letters to me as well, as I kept them in a shoe box in my closet. So, on a beautiful Southern California early winter day, I drove home after school and parked my jalopy of a car at the curb in the same place I did every day. I was preoccupied with an upcoming zoology exam the following day, as I opened the door, thinking I would go straight to my room and study. My mom was there waiting with her wooden spoon in hand, whacking me hard across the face with it as soon as I entered the house. I was stunned. I was 18 years old! At some point, this needed to stop! She held up my diaphragm, shrieking that I was a whore, was a no-good, rotten daughter, and

Coming Into My Own

pretty much vomited up the exact hateful words she'd thrown at me my entire life.

This time though, I picked up the books I'd dropped and picked up my purse that had fallen to the floor, all while my mother was shrieking into my ear and swinging that wooden spoon at me, causing me to dodge repeatedly as I tried to gather my stuff. After a few blows to my back, I'd had what I needed and turned around to face my mother. "What is wrong with you?" I said sadly. "You're not going to break me. In fact, you can hit me until I'm dead, and you still won't be able to break me!" My mother's face was beet red, and I could tell her head was about to explode. She lunged for me again with the spoon raised, but I was too quick.

I opened and quickly shut the door behind me, jumped into my car, and sped away as fast as possible. She didn't chase after me, so I was sure she was calling my father to come home from the office to deal with this new crisis. Thankfully my mother didn't drive then—she was afraid to—which saved me from a possible chase. I pulled away, and while I was nursing the welts on my face from the spoon, tears now flowing freely, I drove to Santa Monica beach, where I had a friend named Pipeline, a man my parents were unaware of. Pipeline was about ten years older than me, and he had the perfect hippie apartment right on the boardwalk. I stayed with him, sleeping on the couch for three nights, never once talking to my parents.

Of course, my mother phoned the police. And, of course, the police said they could do nothing. I was of legal age. I had every right to stay away. Since I had committed no crime and was not the victim of one either, they would do nothing to find me. I spent the next three days attending class, coming home to Pipeline's place, sitting outside on his porch, and watching the waves crash on the shore. It was early December, and the air was brisk and healing. The soft breeze running across my face and into my hair made me feel better with each passing moment.

Three & Me

But I couldn't stay at Pipeline's forever. I had to eventually go back home if only to see if there was mail from Yaniv. When I walked in the door, I said nothing to my mom. My dad wasn't yet home. I went straight to my room and stayed there the entire night. A week later, the chill still permeated 3103 Oakhurst. But at that point, I didn't care anymore. Within days, I had a friend pick me up and take me to Los Angeles International Airport, where I would board a flight to London, then onto Tel Aviv and into the waiting arms of Yaniv for two blissful weeks of love. I was at peace. The chaos of my childhood ceased to exist once I was in Yaniv's arms and loving embrace. All was right with the world, and I became addicted to that feeling.

In June, I left my parent's home for the last time. Only they didn't know it then. They assumed it was just for summer and that I would enter UCLA that fall. I didn't dare tell either of them because I feared they would do something drastic. What exactly, I didn't know. But my imagination ran wild with the possibilities. I'd seen too much ugliness come out of my mother. Her hatred towards me grew exponentially with every passing month of my life. My mom was a beast behind closed doors. I knew deep in my heart that she couldn't stand the idea of me living happily ever after, somewhere she couldn't reach me. All that ugliness in her had to have a target. Ugliness, which was created and nurtured by her own parents, the two people she was supposed to trust most in the world.

< **FOUR** >

Finding A Home Far Away

As soon as I stepped off the plane, I knew this was where I could heal, grow, and expand my horizons. In the early 1970s, Israel was behind the modern civilizations of the United States and Western Europe. Israel had a European influence in its street signage, metric system, storefronts, curb rails, and products. But with the Army budget taking so much out of people's income in the form of taxes, there wasn't much left for luxuries. Additionally, purchasing any item had so much duty attached to it that even something as simple as makeup was almost cost prohibitive. Cars? When I arrived in Israel, VW Bugs were selling for around $2,500 in the United States, but in Israel, with all the import fees and the duties, that same car was selling for $16,000. About $100,000 today! Highly sought-after Levi's jeans were selling for more than the equivalent of $80—almost $600 today! The cost of a telephone was astronomical, costing thousands of dollars for each line because there was very little infrastructure at the time. Few private households had a phone. It took years after signing up for a phone to install one. Product availability in Israel was limited to primarily Israeli-manufactured goods, which were also expensive and scarce.

I didn't care about the inconveniences of living in 1970s Israel. The Six-Day War was three years prior, and Israel was in the process of rebuilding. It was an exciting time to be there. No phone meant my parents couldn't reach me except by mail, and not having a car was no big deal since there was an excellent public transportation system in place. I loved it!

Yaniv was in the Army Reserves when I touched down. He was supposed to have been released the day before I arrived, but he left his

We had our wedding on a cold day in January. My parents boycotted.

*Yaniv as he looked
when I met him.*

Finding A Home Far Away

gun on a train, and another soldier saw it, took it, and reported him. Yaniv was sentenced to Army jail for two weeks because forgetting or losing your gun is a military crime. It wasn't the first time Yaniv lost his rifle, so they doubled up on the sentence.

Once he got out, we spent my first month in Israel on his kibbutz but made plans to leave. He got a paying position as an outside contractor at another kibbutz in the middle of Israel, in the countryside close to the town of Ashkelon. Kibbutz Ruhama was a considerable hike from the bus stop on the main road, but it was worth it. The weather was always moderate because the kibbutz was so near the ocean. The surrounding scenery was rural farmland, and the kibbutz itself, while not as rich as Ayelet Hashahar, was still pleasant. The landscape was dotted with tiny homes that belonged to the members and beautiful lush gardens that emitted an atmosphere of idyllic peace.

We lived in a single room that made studio apartments in the United States seem like mansions. We ate all our meals at the dining hall, so, small as it was, the size of the room was just fine for us. Typical of most dwellings at that time in Israel, except for new construction, there was no central heat or air conditioning—just a window. On scorching days, the stone walls would radiate heat back at us, especially at night, making sleeping with any covering other than a single sheet impossible. Our bed was comprised of two very narrow twins that we pushed together to create what would be considered a full-size or double by today's standards. Mattresses were three inches of foam rubber with a zippered cotton cover placed on a metal spring frame. Getting sheets to stay tucked was a nightly challenge.

While Yaniv worked in a paying position, I was a volunteer, picking apples. I quickly made friends with everyone and somehow found myself in the esteemed position of head of the apple-picking crew! Instead of the hard farm labor of picking apples, I sat in the shade and instructed the pickers on which bin to place the full buckets. It was a relatively easy and pleasant job. We'd start the day at 4.00 am and

73

be done by noon, with the rest of the day to hang out by the pool or hitchhike to the beach nearby. I made friends with an Irish Red Setter, who would run after me every morning as I sat on the tractor bed with the other volunteers. He would spend the day hanging out with me in the apple orchard, then follow the tractor back to his home when we wrapped up. His owner was delighted at his dog's new-found friendship with me, and I was equally happy with it! I have had dogs my entire life, but this was the first time I found myself without one, so this dog's offer of friendship was a much-needed and appreciated gift.

Before I left Kibbutz Ruhama, I wrote to my parents at the end of the summer. I told them I had decided to stay in Israel and apply to the Bezalel Academy of Art and Design in Jerusalem. I found out there were scholarships available, and so I set to the task of working on a portfolio for the following year's admission. And I'm sure you know by now that news flew over like a lead balloon. My mother was furious but could only be angry in a letter instead of face-to-face, which must have intensified that fury.

I knew that because the letter I got back was full of vitriol and included an ultimatum. I was either back in Los Angeles on October 1st, or I would be dead to her. I don't know if she shared what she wrote with my dad because when the deadline passed and I never showed up, he wrote to me as if nothing had happened. I had witnessed how my mom cut off contact with many people during her life, so I wasn't too surprised to read the threat in the letter. I knew she'd make good on it. But I really didn't care at that point. I didn't show up and had no desire to. I figured that whatever happened between my mother and me would be what it would be. The important thing was that she was thousands of miles away, and her anger had no bearing on my life anymore. Or so I thought.

Yaniv was accepted into the biology department at the newly established University in Be'er Sheva, an under-developed frontier town, for that current academic year. Be'er Sheva had a very rudimentary infrastructure with few paved roads. Donkeys and other beasts of burden were more apt to be seen lumbering down the streets than cars or trucks. There were busses, though, plenty of them. Be'er Sheva, at least, had that.

The town center of Be'er Sheva was paved, but the outlying areas were all dirt. There was no landscaping, no grass, and no flowers. When I first arrived, I saw primarily old and unkempt buildings shaped like boxes sticking out on top of dirt. Even our tiny house on Oakhurst was beautifully landscaped, in sharp contrast to this barren landscape. I walked downtown and bought some art supplies because I wanted to draw what I saw to remember my first overseas apartment. If that same building had been in the United States, it would have been condemned as uninhabitable, written up with violations of every code in existence. But to me, it was heaven.

I did have one sadness, though. Looking out our apartment windows, I'd see the starkness of the buildings against the light brown dirt. I longed for greenery. I longed to see black soil instead of light, sand-colored dirt. I never realized how much I would miss grass. I had gotten used to the kibbutzim (plural for kibbutz), which had substantial park-like areas of grass, trees, and flowers. But Be'er Sheva was a different kind of place. It was like I'd landed on the moon. Most of the citizens of Be'er Sheva were of Middle Eastern or North African descent, coming from areas like Morocco, Algeria, and Yemen. Culturally they were completely different from Israel's Jewish citizens of Western European origin. Two slang and derogatory words were used to describe the two different cultures. "Vooz-Vooz" was a descendant of Western heritage, while "Chak-Chak" was the term for people of Northern African and Middle Eastern descent. I was a Vooz-Vooz and an oddity in Be'er Sheva at that time. I was picking up Hebrew, my brain quickly processing the new language. I knew what people were saying when I walked into town. I was called a Vooz-Vooz more than once.

Three & Me

I witnessed many heated clashes of the cultures among the population right there in the middle of town. In Be'er Sheva, people walked around with a short fuse. It would take little for a verbal confrontation to start. Taxi drivers yelled at other taxi drivers. Women yelled at shopkeepers. Bus drivers yelled at customers. It seemed that verbal conflicts between the inhabitants of Be'er Sheva were constant events. I noticed this on a slightly lesser scale in the rest of Israel. Israelis definitely walked around with short fuses and could erupt at the slightest provocation. Yelling was a very dominant part of communication back then.

The new university brought a whole host of new problems to Be'er Sheva, not the least of which was student housing. University students were not welcome, even though they would contribute to the local economy. The long-time town residents weren't happy with a much younger and more Western demographic, so they behaved with particular hostility. Break-ins and thefts were a big problem. Teenagers hurled rocks at strangers—something I'd witnessed and been a victim of too many times to count.

Violence towards strangers was also common. I remember riding my bicycle to work. (I worked at the computer lab at the university.) As I cut my way across a big dirt lot, I found myself surrounded by teenage boys who were also on bikes. One rode up next to me and asked me in Hebrew if I was afraid. I didn't know why he'd ask such a dumb question, so I told him I wasn't. He said, "Just watch," peeled off to the right, circled, and came at me directly from the side, slamming his bike into mine. That impact threw us both off our bikes in a massive crash, creating a cloud of rising dust and dirt. When I picked myself up, I saw I was OK with just a few minor scratches. And my bike was fine. I was surprised to see him still in the dirt when I looked at him. I realized he was a bloody mess from his face and mouth, and he'd bent his front wheel. I offered to help him, but he swore at me, so I left. That was pretty much a typical day in Be'er Sheva in 1971.

Another time I was on the bus when a young man with an intellectual disability boarded the bus. He was traveling alone and innocently made his way to the back of the bus, where a group of teenage boys sat. They immediately pounced on him, tormenting him, spitting at him, and burning his arms with their cigarettes. As the guy cried out in pain, I got up out of my seat and told the gang of hooligans to leave him be. They were so surprised that a girl would stand up to a group of guys that they forgot about the guy and focused their hate on me. I was able to diffuse the situation by telling them I could take them all on and would if they didn't shut up. Not sure what to think; they swore at me in Hebrew but otherwise backed off. That's when I learned there was much power in words and attitude. I showed no fear. Only confidence. It worked.

Being from California, I wasn't prepared for demonstrations of rage and anger between strangers. In California, there is a vast zone of personal space, and in Be'er Sheva, there was none. It was odd to me for the longest time, until my first trip to New York City in 1973, when I realized that it wasn't so much the Israelis who were hot-headed, loud, and abrasive; it was the same with many New Yorkers. Apparently, being in crowded streets, suffering hot, humid weather, and paying dearly for most things puts people on edge.

Despite all its oddities, I enjoyed our time there. I found it romantic. Two kids setting up our own space and working towards our futures together. Yaniv studied at the university, and I worked in the computer department. He applied and was accepted to the Hebrew University of Jerusalem as a biology major. I applied to the Bezalel Academy of Art and Design and was accepted with a full scholarship. I didn't need my parents' money. We were self-sufficient, and it felt great.

I also found a dog! Longing for books to read, I went to the local library. That little doggie was roaming around the library with no owner in sight. She ran up to me, wagged her tail, and smiled; it was love at first sight. I picked her up and took her home. I would have a dog

Three & Me

in my life again, and I couldn't have been happier. She would stay in my life for 17 more years until she crossed the Rainbow Bridge.

In the summer of 1972, my parents planned a trip to Europe. My dad had brokered peace between my mother and me by then, and he, unbeknownst to her, was sending me $100 per month, which I put into a savings account. My dad suggested I meet them in Italy. Flying to Greece was $30 at that time. He bought and sent me a Eurail Pass, which was good for unlimited first-class train travel in Europe. I took the money he'd sent me and planned to backpack through Europe after seeing my parents. I planned to go all the way north to Sweden, where I would visit and stay with friends. With the book Europe on $5 a Day in hand and a backpack, I set out to meet my parents. After visiting Greece and spending three days on the famed Orient Express, I was on my way to my first parental reunion—filled with mixed emotions.

I was pleasantly surprised to see my mom in a different light as well as a different setting. She was ebullient, fun, hilarious, and, most of all, nice. She was a different person, whether it was because she was in a foreign country, her new status as a successful man's wife, or just time away from me. I loved the time we spent together in Rome. My parents stayed in an upscale hotel, but I preferred a hostel. I figured distance seemed to be working, so why ruin it?! However, it didn't take long for them to bring up a conversation regarding my return home. They broached the subject once or twice, but I was adamant about staying in Israel with Yaniv. At this point, they were empty nesters, my brother was in the Air Force, and I think they wanted a kid at home. My mother, for whom taking care of kids was a 19-year nightmare, actually missed us. The time I spent with my parents in Italy was among the best moments I remember. I don't know if it was because we were always together with the people from their tour or if my mother possibly accepted that I was an adult. There wasn't one nasty jab, no recriminations, and no disharmony. It was shocking and fabulous at the same time.

Finding A Home Far Away

Upon my return to Israel after my European travels, Yaniv proposed marriage. I remember it like it was yesterday. We were staying with his aunt and uncle in their Tel Aviv home, lying in bed after making love, when he asked me. I said, "Yes" quickly, lest he changes his mind!

When we took the bus back to the kibbutz the next day to inform his parents, I could also use the kibbutz phone to call my parents with the good news. I was happier than I'd ever been. Yaniv and I were utterly compatible, had similar goals, and I couldn't imagine spending my life with anyone else. We were two youngsters in crazy mad love. Yaniv's parents set about planning a kibbutz wedding, and there would be nothing for my parents to do except come and celebrate. Because of the frugality which defined most of my childhood, I thought that at least there was one piece of good news—the wedding wouldn't cost my parents a dime. The kibbutz would pay for everything since Yaniv was the son of kibbutz members and a former member himself. I was gushing with excitement when I made the call.

All the goodwill of the European vacation and our time in Italy evaporated with that one call. A new frost was ushered in; cold silence was on the other end of the line. After what seemed an eternity, the first words out of my dad's mouth were, "I immigrated to the United States to build a good life for my future family—for you! And now you are running away from this country to marry a man who isn't a citizen of this country! He's poor! He's marrying you to get United States citizenship; why can't you see this?" I was stunned. Here was my father, formerly a poor immigrant to the United States, who married an American Citizen, adopting the same prejudices my grandfather had levied against him! Those same prejudices he despised were now being hurled back onto me. I never saw THAT coming!

I could hear my mother screaming in the background, "Put me on the phone with her!" My father passed the receiver to my already irate and screaming mother. "Listen, Missy! If you think you're going to get married to an Israeli and have us schlep halfway around the

Three & Me

world to watch you throw your life away, you are sadly mistaken! We won't be coming!" With that, she hung up. I stared emotionless at the receiver as the dial tone sounded, signaling the end of what should have been a conversation filled with love and shared happiness, but instead turned into the ugly I was so accustomed to.

Yaniv watched my once-happy face, bigger-than-life smile, twinkling eyes, and excitement deflate right before his eyes. He shook his head and hugged me tightly. "It's OK. Don't worry. They'll come around." I know he felt his chest slowly moisten with the tears flowing from my eyes. First, my graduation. Then my marriage. I was all alone in the most significant moments of my life. I morosely thought that if I died while they were still alive, they would also find or fabricate some reason to boycott my funeral.

Yaniv and I did get married on January 16th, 1973. But that morning, we woke up to a huge dump of snow in Jerusalem, effectively shutting the city down. Pretty to look at, but the realization that we had to get from Jerusalem to Northern Galilee for our wedding that night was one of sheer panic. We looked at each other in complete disbelief over that huge obstacle of snow and realized we had only two choices. Try and make it, or cancel. We found out the trains were still going, so we decided to trudge the three or so miles through blinding snow to get to the train station. We miraculously made the last train, and we sat relieved in our seats, grateful that we would be able to attend our wedding. It was beautiful. The snow was white beneath our feet, and we said our vows those many years ago. Two young kids madly in love.

The evening was beautiful, and I felt like the star in my own fairy tale. The kibbutz did a beautiful job of decorating the banquet room for the event. My friend, Maple, made my dress. And the kibbutz pampered me with a spa treatment and professional hair, nails, and makeup for the ceremony. I got the complete bridal treatment. True to their words, my parents never showed. But my mom's cousins, the

Scharfs, were living in Israel then, and they came, so my family was represented. The once-dreaded snow actually provided a beautiful backdrop for our special day. While I was dressed in white, so was the earth below my feet.

After Yaniv and I returned from our very short honeymoon in Natanya, I started to get strange letters from my mom. I think my mom's friends were horrified that she didn't attend her only daughter's wedding because suddenly, my mother did an about-face. She told people they didn't attend because my father passed a kidney stone, and travel was out of the question. She omitted that she refused to attend, didn't buy plane tickets, or made travel arrangements that she had to "cancel" at the last minute because of a "kidney stone." It was a lie. This was probably the one time her bridge club cronies disapproved of her behavior.

As my mom tried to save face with a growing cadre of detractors regarding the wedding, we were suddenly invited to Los Angeles, where she would throw us a huge party with all her friends in attendance. I had no say in the guest list and honestly didn't care. It was her party. We would just attend. I was leery at first and a little afraid of going to my childhood home with my new husband. If there was one predictable thing in my life, it was my mother's unpredictability. However, I thought it through. We could always leave if it got unbearable. I would ensure we would have enough money on hand should that be necessary. Those were the days when airlines didn't charge penalties for flight changes. We had our return tickets, and changing the date would be as easy as making a phone call.

Upon our arrival, my mom caught me by surprise when she immediately and absolutely fell in love with Yaniv. With his handsome face, genuine kindness, and high intelligence, it was hard for my mother to resist. She paraded him around like a brand-new trophy she had won in a bridge tournament. She was smitten. My dad liked Yaniv too. He saw a lot of himself in Yaniv.

Three & Me

My parents were on their best behavior during that summer visit. It was definitely above and beyond what I had expected it to be. After six weeks of calm, we left in September to take a road trip across the country before returning to Jerusalem. I left reasonably happy that some old wounds appeared to be healing. Once we reached Boston in October of 1973, all hell broke loose, but this time it had nothing to do with my parents.

We were scheduled on a flight from Boston to Tel Aviv on the evening of October 6th. October 6th was Yom Kippur, and we celebrated it with my mom's cousin, Mitzi, and her family in Lexington, Massachusetts. Yom Kippur would have ended at sundown, well before our flight back to Israel. However, Israel was attacked on two fronts on that Yom Kippur Day, the holiest day of the year for Jews. In Israel, most soldiers were home, and the government was shut down, leaving only skeleton crews to keep the country running when troops from Syria invaded Israel in the wee hours of the morning.

The Syrian forces advanced far inside Israel, expecting resistance where there was none. Confused, they just stopped where they were, waiting for new orders on what to do next, as they never expected to get as far as they did. Thankfully, the Syrian confusion and subsequent pause gave Israel time to mobilize and answer the Syrian invasion. The realization was lost on no one that had the Syrians not stopped when they did; they could have gotten so much further inside of Israel, causing much death and destruction. Egypt attacked simultaneously on the southern border, also catching Israel with its pants down. Soldiers were quickly mobilized. In Israel, even after men finish their mandatory tour of duty, they are permanently considered reserve soldiers until they age out at 60. They can be mobilized at a moment's notice, and that's precisely what happened with lightning speed. Because it was the holiday, most able men were home or in the synagogue and were easily located, quickly rounded up, and sent to the two fronts.

Back in Boston, Yaniv was beside himself with anxiety. He was a paratrooper and wanted to join his unit, but the Israeli airport was closed—no flights in and no flights out. I, on the other hand, was afraid for his life. He already had a massive chunk of thigh missing from shrapnel hurled at him during the Six-Day War. We stayed in Lexington for two stressful days until we got the call that EL Al Airlines would fly us back that day, effectively returning Yaniv to his unit.

When the El Al jet landed on the runway of the darkened airport due to the blackout, only our plane was taxiing on the minimally lit runway. I got chills as I peered out of the window onto the tarmac. It was eerie. Ben Gurion Airport was typically a hub of activity with planes taking off and landing. We were alone in the sea of blackness; even the cabin lights were low. There were no other planes around, no tourists, only men returning to fight, accompanied by their saddened but supportive families. My heart was in my throat as we deplaned and walked towards the terminal. I walked painfully towards that terminal with tears in my eyes. I knew I'd have to say goodbye to Yaniv within the next minute or two, not knowing whether or not he'd return home safely to me. Right before we entered the terminal's open doors, I impulsively kissed him and told him to stay safe. As I feared, he was ushered away by the soldiers waiting for him, as well as the other men on our flight, just one minute later. I was now alone with my thoughts in a country at war and took a taxi with headlights blacked out for the ride home to Jerusalem.

Upon arrival at the little guest house we rented in Motza Illit, a suburb of Jerusalem, I could see everything was wrong from the minute I opened the door. Because of the rules of a blackout, no lights were allowed. I didn't need light to know I came home to a mess. I found dirty dishes and sticky counters with trash strewn about everywhere, and somehow through the darkened and smelly mess, I found a note from our house sitter, Simon. At the onset of the war, he left for a kibbutz and took our dog, Shemesh, with him so as not to leave her alone.

Three & Me

I was crushed. I didn't even have my dog for comfort or company. It was fall, and Israel was in the midst of a heat wave. The apartment felt stale from the closed windows, stifling heat, and rotting food. I quickly opened the windows to air the place out and for some much-needed ventilation. I then set to the task of making the home habitable. Tired from the transatlantic flight, the toll of three days of anxiety, the unexpected but necessary clean-up, and saddened at finding myself in a war zone with no Yaniv and no dog, I fell asleep only to be woken up by the sound of thunder crashing overhead. At first, I thought it was bombs blasting, but I soon felt the rain coming in through the open window and realized it was a storm. My first night back in Israel was a long one. The actual war was over within weeks. However, Yaniv's cousin was killed an hour after the cease-fire on the Egyptian front. That hit me hard. We attended his wedding before we left for the States. Yaki and his bride were a striking couple, and it saddened me to realize his new bride was now a widow. Yaki's death struck so close to home that I had difficulty reconciling his passing. I cried for his loss, and even today, 50-plus years later, I still think about him even though I barely knew him. A beautiful life cut short by an enemy's bullet.

Eventually, Yaniv was allowed home, and we tried to live as normally as possible after the war. It wasn't even a week when, on a Saturday, there was a knock at the door. We opened it to see a soldier from Yaniv's unit. They came to pick him up under a "Tzav Shmonah" (Section 8), an Emergency Mobilization. Syria had begun a war of attrition, and Yaniv's unit would be stationed in Israeli-occupied Syria. Yaniv quickly changed into his fatigues, signature red boots, and red beret, looking ever like the paratrooper he was. Grabbing his backpack and his M-16 rifle, he kissed me goodbye, and the next thing I knew, he was gone again, just like that. At least I had my dog with me this time.

While he was away, Yaniv sent me love letters, the kind that kept me going during our year apart and would continue to keep me going

Finding A Home Far Away

during that period. He would include pictures of himself sitting on the veranda of an abandoned building in Mazarat Bet Jeaan, a small village in Syria while doing guard duty. He adopted a horse that was roaming the town and would send me pictures of him running and playing with the horse when he had time off from his shift.

Mercifully, Yaniv would be released for a weekend off every three to four weeks and would thumb rides home for a much-needed visit. In Israel, if one sees a soldier with his or her thumb out, picking them up is considered a good deed so they can get home quicker. Yaniv's visits home would make for some very passionate and loving time. Nothing like a good old-fashioned war to really spice up the bedroom!

The war of attrition lasted six months, and there were casualties daily due to skirmishes. Whenever I heard the news, I would pray Yaniv was safe from mortars or gunfire. Thankfully, my prayers were answered, while sadly, others weren't. Finally, after over half a year, a cease-fire took hold, and Yaniv was discharged from his reserve duty.

During those six months when Yaniv was gone, I befriended a girl on the bus into Jerusalem. Her name was Sara Greenblatt. Sara had a fresh face, needing no makeup, and long curly hippie hair. Her smile lit her up, and I instantly liked her. On the bus ride, she told me about her boyfriend, who was an explosives expert. He somehow shot himself in the foot with his army issue gun and was released from duty. Sara was relieved he was home and out of danger. One day on the bus and entirely out of the blue, Sara invited me to have dinner with her family. I was ecstatic. I hated being alone every single night of the week, pining for Yaniv. I still had my dog, whom I talked to all the time, but I thought it would be nice to actually have a human conversation.

That evening, Sara brought me home to her parents, who lived in a huge house on the street below our guest house. They were American ex-pats who had immigrated to Israel many years before. Sara's dad, Chuck, was a research physician at Hadassah Hospital, while her mom, Joannie, was busy running an alternative high school on the outskirts of Jerusalem. When Sara brought me home with her, they opened up their hearth and their hearts and became my Israeli family. To this very day, I consider Chuck and Joannie my Israeli parents, and Sara and her sisters, my sisters. I spent almost every night with them watching Israeli television while Yaniv was in Syria. (We didn't own a TV.) When Yaniv came home, we continued the tradition, including Friday night Shabbat dinners. Chuck would take care of me when I was sick, Joannie taught me how to cook (my mom never did), and I enjoyed family life for the very first time. I don't think Chuck, Joannie, or Sara knew how essential they were in building me up as a person. From their friendship, I left the little girl behind and became officially an adult.

One summer, my parents announced they were coming to visit Israel on a tour. My mother went shopping in preparation for their visit. She bought Yaniv and me a whole closet of new clothes. Of course, she shopped the jobbers in downtown Los Angeles, getting great prices. But the haul she brought with her when they came was pretty impressive. My parents also stopped in England, purchased a television for us, and shipped it to Israel. I was absolutely giddy with joy when it arrived. Israel, at that time, had one television station only. However, my antenna was able to receive the Jordanian television airwaves, so I watched plenty of Jordanian soap operas. The end result was that I picked up spoken Arabic in the Jordanian dialect. *Kif Halek!* (Translation: "How are you?").

My parents' presence in Israel meant they would finally meet Yaniv's parents. Ruth and Arieh Dotan initially had a bad taste in their mouths because of the wedding boycott, the same wedding they were so proud of. That all changed when the two families finally met on the kibbutz. My mother was charming, warm, and absolutely delightful. Of course, it didn't hurt that Yaniv came from a very prominent Israeli family. There was status to be had in the pairing of Yaniv and

Finding A Home Far Away

me. Yaniv's uncle, Yisrael Geffen, was one of the original Hapalmach fighters during the fight for liberation from British rule. Yisrael married Moshe Dayan's sister, Aviva, and they had three daughters and one son. Moshe Dayan was the most famous general in Israel and globally. During the Six-Day War in 1967, troops commanded by Dayan captured Jerusalem. His iconic eyepatch was recognized the world over.

Yisrael's son, Yonathan, became a famous Israeli poet, scriptwriter, and author. Yonathan's son, Aviv, became the biggest rock star in Israel in the 1990s. He was standing on the stage next to Prime Minister Yitzhak Rabin when a religious fanatic assassinated Rabin. To be linked to that family, even as loosely as the links were, was pretty prestigious. Moshe Dayan had passed away by the time I married Yaniv. His widow, Ruth Dayan, came to watch us wed on that snowy January day. Once my mom learned this, I could tell she was kicking herself for not coming. There were other notable people in attendance that January night in 1973, including but not limited to members of parliament. My mom was just then beginning to learn what her pettiness cost her.

If that linkage to Moshe Dayan and the Geffens weren't enough, Yaniv's mother, Ruth Geffen Dotan, was very well connected politically in her own right. She was friends with many Knesset members (MKs) and prime ministers. The Knesset is the governing body in Israel, much like Congress, although based on a parliamentary system. She could easily reach out to prime ministers, MKs, and other power brokers in Israel. (She once sent an MK running out of the Knesset to meet me at the gate with an antenna in hand for my new TV. That would be like Kevin McCarthy or Adam Schiff running out of the Capitol to do the same thing.)

Additionally, Ruth was good friends with Arieh Ben-Gurion, nephew of the first prime minister of Israel, David Ben-Gurion. My mother and father quickly befriended him and remained friends until he died. Thus began my mother's need to clothe every notable individual in

Three & Me

Israel. Arieh Ben-Gurion, as well as others, ended up receiving many shipments of new clothes from my mother.

My mother was in heaven! Her daughter had hand-delivered prestige of the highest level within her Jewish bridge club community! She had status now. Her bridge ladies were very impressed with my mom hobnobbing with the Israeli elite. I saw right through her, and I'll admit I was annoyed at the way she decided to roll in on Ruth's tailcoat. I couldn't stop her, though, so I accepted that the new bonds of family were a reality, and I figured it was better than what I had faced before. My mom celebrated her new-found in-laws with many trips to Israel and, of course, many shipments of new clothes to Ruth. I believe that after the glamour and social climbing wore off, they ended up forging real friendships.

To my way of thinking, my mom went "Israeli overboard." Every Israeli visiting or living in Los Angeles was somehow "adopted" by her. They got new clothes as well as regular dinner invitations. They would never face a holiday alone if my mom had something to say about it. By this time, my parents had bought and moved into a beautiful home in Bel Air, a chic and expensive neighborhood in the foothills north of Sunset Boulevard. My mother threw dinner parties regularly—any excuse to have one. After Yaniv and I returned to live in the United States, it became common to find my mom's dining room table filled with many newly arrived Israelis waiting to eat. When Yaniv's brother, Amnon, moved to Los Angeles, he too became a regular fixture at my parent's home. My mom was expanding her family, one Israeli after another. It was actually kind of nice.

## FIVE

Celebri-Tease

As I stated before, animals were and are a huge part of my life. I get so much spiritual strength from them. The traits that animals have, like patience, expressing honest emotions, bonding, and never killing for sport, are traits that I wish the human species would have more of.

Horses were a huge part of my dad's life growing up in Hungary, and he transferred that equine love onto me. He made sure I learned to ride western saddle when I was growing up. In Israel, I rode sporadically, and that was only on trails. One crazy day, me and Yaniv, along with the stable manager for Yaniv's kibbutz, went for a ride into the Golan Heights. We rode for three hours before we realized we had accidentally crossed into Syria. We just turned around and went back the way we came in. I would say luck was on our side that day.

After I completed my degree at Bezalel, we moved back to the United States in 1977, and the first thing I did was find a barn to train in. I couldn't afford a horse then, but I wanted to ride regularly nonetheless. Our apartment was in Brentwood, and I found a barn in Old Topanga Canyon called Mill Creek, owned by Cory Walkey. She held a large string of school horses that would be perfect for taking lessons. Mill Creek was nestled in a wooded area of the Santa Monica Mountains within Topanga Canyon. Driving to Mill Creek always put me in a good mood because I would go along Pacific Coast Highway, hugging the coast before turning up into the canyon.

The muted sounds and smells of a horse stable are among my favorite in the world. I love the quiet chewing sounds of horses as they eat their hay, the sweet smell of fresh shavings in their stalls, and even

Me and Aero sharing grief together. My heart was broken that day.

Celebri-Tease

the scent of fresh horse manure. Listening to a horse whinny or nicker gets my heart pumping every time. And if the whinny or nicker is directed at me, that would make me smile the whole day.

At Mill Creek, I trained under the tutelage of Lynn Whitley. She had the patience of Jove, coupled with a beautiful sense of humor, and I looked forward to every lesson. I would ride as much as my wallet let me, never once thinking that the sport had an element of danger. In my mid-twenties, fit as a fiddle, weighing under a buck, I didn't care if I fell off. I'd dust myself off and get back on. Bouncing came easy for me back then.

It was Lynn who suffered a catastrophic horse accident, though. A horse had reared backward and fallen over onto her, crushing her pelvis and breaking her leg. It was an injury that would waylay her for many, many months. Eventually, Cory hired a trainer, Donna, to take over Lynn's lesson schedule. Donna is the daughter of a golden-screen actress with a larger-than-life personality and a smile that could melt ice. She wanted her own business as a trainer, so she convinced another girl and me to move to a new stable she planned to lease. Being young, naive, and trusting, I followed her to a small backyard stable in the San Fernando Valley, less than seven minutes from my house. (We had purchased a home in the Valley by then.) Mill Creek was a fancy private stable. Apart from the sheer beauty of its surroundings, it was so clean you could literally eat off of the floors. Mill Creek also boasted big stalls, giant riding rings, and competent staff who would care for the horses. The stable primarily catered to Three-Day Event participants (dressage, cross country, and stadium jumping), and the horse owners mostly showed at away horse shows.

While close to my home, Donna's new place was a funky backyard barn. It was literally in someone's backyard. It had little to no staff, a tiny ring, and weird stalls. However, this was a whole new experience for me. It was a hunter/jumper barn, not an event barn—so I was excited to be part of what I thought was a grass-roots beginning

Three & Me

of something big. Donna told me I needed to buy a horse, which I obediently did. (So young, so trusting!) I was making good money in my design/ad business, and buying a horse seemed the next logical step. Donna said she found a good one, so we went to the seller's home, and I bought a mare named Spring, just on sight. If any of my equestrian friends read this, this is the point where they cringe and smack their foreheads over my naiveté and stupidity. I had no idea at the time that I was supposed to try the horse first, maybe even bring the horse back to the barn on a small feed lease for a week or two (or three) to figure out if we were a compatible fit. Donna, the trainer, should have told me to bring my saddle and get on the horse. She didn't. It would be the first of many costly omissions from a person I put complete trust in.

Once we brought the mare back to our backyard stable, I hopped on her and quickly discovered something I should have known before buying her. *Spring was nuts!* She only knew two speeds. Fast and faster. Jumping her was absolutely crazy. She went out of control on the approach to and after every fence. Finally, after nearly getting killed and watching my hair turn grey, I told Donna that this was not the horse for me. This was after we went to a horse show, and I couldn't get around the course without looking like an idiot and scaring myself witless. We returned to where we bought Spring, and I had to cough up more money to trade her in for a beautiful bay gelding that I named Buster. Buster supposedly had a "hitch in his git-along," whatever that meant.

Again, I wasn't advised to get on and ride Buster. We just took him home. I lucked out this time. He was a real gentleman. Another thing Donna didn't educate me about was getting a horse vetted for soundness. It's called a pre-purchase exam. I was told his "hitch in his git-along" would be a non-issue, and I believed it. (Again, so young, again, so trusting!)

Through Donna's mom's connection to the film industry, two of her other main customers were also from that industry. My now lifelong

Celebri-Tease

92

and dear friend Tracie Hotchner trained with Donna and brought with her to the barn her Godmother, Joan Rivers, and Joan's then 10-year-old daughter, Missy (aka Melissa Rivers). Both Joan and Missy were charming around the barn and at the local horse shows. Edgar Rosenberg, Joan's husband, would come to the shows and quietly cheer his daughter on. It appeared that Donna's efforts to build a show barn were showing signs of success. Usually, the established, well-known, or "A" barns attracted big celebrities, but right out of the gate, Donna snagged one of the biggest!

This period in time was my barn honeymoon. I was in love with my horse and in love with being part of a small but growing barn—exciting times for me. I had no idea the world of showing was so much bigger than our little patch of ground, and I would soon find out just how big that world was.

Donna recommended that the Rosenbergs purchase a small bay mare for Missy. Again, a quick sale. Sadly, the horse was not a good match for her. At the time, Donna had us showing at the one-day local shows but convinced us that we were part of the big leagues. So, when our horses didn't do well, we all felt terrible. Missy would exit the ring frustrated and sad over her and the horse's poor performance. I felt awful for Missy; she was such a sweet kid. I never liked to see kids become sad in any competition, especially her. So, I'd let her hop on Buster at the shows, and they did well together.

After one such horse show, Joan was very grateful for my gesture of lending Buster to Missy, so she extended an invitation to watch her set that evening at the Comedy Club on Ventura Boulevard, located conveniently near my house. I quickly accepted. She gave me the time she'd be on and said she'd leave our names at the door for free entry. She told me she'd leave four tickets for us. I was excited about seeing the show and invited two friends to join us. When we got to the club at the designated time, we were told at the door that Joan had not given our names, and it was already sold out. Edgar was standing near

Three & Me

the door, and he heard the conversation. He nicely walked over and apologized, saying Joan was incredibly busy that day, and her promise to us probably slipped her mind. Ultimately, I blew it off; Edgar had apologized, and his explanation seemed plausible.

But I was wrong. That scene would play out again, and I wasn't so willing to be understanding then. While at a horse show, I brought my 35mm Pentax camera with a 200mm lens to shoot photos of the show. Missy had just won her first-ever blue ribbon on her new horse, Toby. (The other was thankfully sold.) I thought it would make a nice photo, so we attached the blue ribbon that Missy had just won to the side of Toby's bridle, and I shot a photo of a smiling little girl with her winning ribbon. I owned a downtown design studio and sent all my films to Newell Color, a substantial professional color lab with professional-grade prints. I had a beautiful 18"x24" color print made, mounted on foam core, to bring with me the next time I went to the barn. That photo embodied the love between a child and her horse. Simply beautiful. Missy was incredibly photogenic, and Toby had very kind eyes, which came through in the image. When I handed the photo to Joan, she absolutely loved it. She was demonstrably grateful and, in a moment of generosity, invited me to have dinner with them the following night. She gave me her address and told me to arrive at 6.30 pm. It never dawned on me to call and confirm the dinner before I left the office, especially in light of the Comedy Club mix-up.

Joan's home wasn't far from my parents' home, about a mile away as the crow flies, and I quickly found it. I parked my car in the cul-de-sac, walked to the gate, and buzzed. A male voice on the other end answered through the intercom built into the gate post. I figured it was her personal assistant. I gave him my name and said I was expected for dinner.

Silence. "Hmmmmm," I thought, "this isn't good...."

The male voice on the other end of the intercom cleared his throat. "I'm sorry. Joan is having a business dinner tonight, so I'm afraid you won't be able to attend."

"Are you kidding me!" I was trying very hard to keep my cool. I had driven an hour in traffic and rain to get there, freaked that I might be late, and now I find out THAT invitation was fake too! "Are you sure?" I asked him, hoping he was making a mistake and getting the dates mixed up.

"I'm quite sure," came the reply. "I'm sorry," and with that, he disconnected the intercom, leaving me standing there in utter disbelief, feeling thoroughly humiliated for believing that Joan Rivers would want me to come to her house for dinner. Still facing the long and torturous drive from the Westside of Los Angeles to the San Fernando Valley, I resigned myself to the stupor that takes over in traffic. Everyone knows the 405 freeway is the worst in the country, especially at rush hour in the rain. And so was my mood. Lesson learned.

The next time I went to the barn, I behaved as if nothing had happened. And that was largely because nothing HAD happened. I still liked Joan. She was a sweetheart. And I was nuts about Missy. But I was beginning to understand the difference between huge celebrity and bigger anonymity and reconciled that I needed to understand my place in the Los Angeles hierarchy. It felt like the social structure of high school all over again. At least I had a point of reference to help me realize what my societal station was supposed to be.

At some point, Donna moved us from the backyard barn to a legitimate boarding facility, which was run by a cowboy who was a bit odd. Finding that place uncomfortable after a few months, we moved again to a better boarding stable in the same Chatsworth neighborhood. We were now at White Oak Stables, and I loved it there.

The night of the non-dinner, I was feeling stupid and wanted to forget the "unvitation," I figured that getting on my horse would be an excellent way to brighten my mood, so I tacked up and got on Buster. I walked into the ring, and suddenly, I felt from his few steps that he was "off" behind. He wasn't moving right. And that was just at the walk. I thought maybe he was stiff from being in the stall all day, so I walked him around a few more times to try and loosen him up. I could feel his hindquarters gimping along, and I wasn't quite sure what to do. So, I asked him for the trot. The back legs felt worse. He was definitely lame, so I got off and put him in his stall. Right then, I understood what a hitch in his git-along meant. He was crippled.

Every day, I'd take him out to see if he was better, and he was the same every day. He wasn't healing. I called the vet, who, upon examining him, told me I needed to send him to Dr. Baker's surgical clinic in Chino for further examination. I did as I was told and sent him. Late the next night, I got a phone call from Dr. Baker, who was considered the Equine Vet God. "I'll get right to the point, Suzie. Your horse will never be able to jump. Actually, I don't think he'll really ever be usable except for maybe a walk-trot horse. He's got osteochondritis dissecans in his stifle [knee area]. He's bone on bone. I'm sorry."

That phone call blew my head apart. I couldn't believe that the horse I was emotionally invested in, not to mention financially invested in, was basically unusable. I was heartbroken as well as devastated. Now what?! It wasn't only money I was losing. It was an animal that I had grown to love. I was torn. I couldn't afford two horses. I didn't want to put him down, either. He was too beautiful a soul. Finally, Sam Perlow, who owned White Oak Stables, told me I could donate Buster to the Kidney Foundation. He would be donated to a facility that used horses as therapy for children with disabilities. Walk-trot was all they needed in a horse. I could take a write-off, and Buster could be useful and help children. So that's what I did, although saying goodbye to Buster was painfully difficult. It broke my heart to ship him off, and I still regret not finding him a nice field somewhere where he could be a horse. But no one, especially Donna, told me there were options like that.

Once again, I found myself without a horse. Donna said she'd find me a good one, but this time she said I had to spend some really big bucks. (You'd think by this time I'd know better... but rose-colored glasses cloud one's perception...) Having learned from Buster, I specifically told her I wanted the new horse vet checked before paying for it. Donna agreed. I still didn't get to try any horses, not realizing that trying a horse out was standard practice in the sport. A few days later, Donna said she found a great horse at Tommy Lowe Stables. A chestnut gelding named Bolero. He was expensive. Donna said the vet was coming out the next day, and she would call me with the results. Again, I had no idea that the purchaser of a horse should be the one getting the vet results. At that point, I was too trusting and new to the hunter/jumper world. When a trainer finds you a horse for purchase that you actually then buy, they get a commission of 10%. The seller pays 10% to their trainer, who markets the horse for sale. After Donna called me the next day with the "great news" that Bolero passed the vet check, I wrote her a check for the horse plus the 10% commission.

It was late summer when I bought Bolero, and he seemed to be perfect. I was thrilled. I finally had a horse I thought was clean in the legs and a known show horse who knew his job. Unfortunately, as soon as the weather cooled with the onset of fall, things started to go south. Bolero began stopping at the fence instead of jumping. Donna blamed me for riding him poorly. No matter what I did, Bolero would stop, and he'd stop dirty, lowering his head, which meant I would fly off his front end. I would take many trips up "Mane Street" during that period.

An annual Thanksgiving Week horse show at the Earl Warren Showgrounds in Santa Barbara is fondly known as the Turkey Show. Donna informed us that we all had to go to that show. It would not only be our first big away show, but it was a show that everyone went to simply because it was so much fun. She wanted to establish a "presence" within the showing community.

I was excited about going. I had beautiful equitation on a horse and had won plenty of blue ribbons in that division. My thin build, long legs, and perfect leg and arm positions helped me win almost every time I entered an equitation class. Sadly, my high hopes and excitement came crashing down as the days unfolded. No matter how hard I tried, I couldn't get Bolero around a course of jumps. He stopped at the very first fence. After three refusals, you are asked to leave the ring. After one refusal, the judges stop watching you because you will not place, so why bother? My face was flushed with shame every time I exited the show ring. I didn't have one happy moment.

Donna blamed me and my lack of riding skills for turning a famous show horse into a stopper. After that miserable week at the Turkey Show, I'd reached the end of my rope with Donna. Because, I reasoned somewhat logically, if the horse did so well in training with Tommy Lowe, then I should move him back to Tommy and finally get myself into an "A" barn instead of Donna's small potato operation. I called Tommy and asked him if I could move into his barn and become a customer. The answer was a "yes." Donna was angry that I left her barn, but, in hindsight, she must have been afraid of what I would find out once I got to Tommy's. And she would have had good reason!

The next day I called a hauler and had Bolero moved to the Paddock Riding Club, a lovely facility near Griffith Park. I met with Tommy in his office, expecting an entirely different conversation than the one we had. "We need to put you on a different horse," he said. "I've got a little chestnut gelding named Nocky who jumps really cute. He's the right size for you, and you'll have nothing but fun on him." (My brain hiccupped at this point.) "Then, we need to get rid of Bolero, and I have someone I know who can sell him. He's a man's horse, to begin with. And he's dead lame. He's got Navicular. You knew that, right?

That can be treated in any number of ways, but he's also got the dirty stop in him that a big man can overcome. Not someone your size. He's all wrong for you."

My head spun as I tried to make sense of all of this. My brain wasn't really computing what Tommy was saying because it went against everything Donna had told me about the horse. Tommy looked at the look on my face and, for a second, paused, then continued. "I was surprised you bought him. I mean, I was astonished. He failed the vet check. Then when Donna called and said you still wanted him, I was completely speechless!" (This is the point in the conversation where my heart rate doubled, and I felt like passing out.) Tommy thought for a moment. "Was it the cheap price that made you go for him?" he asked.

CHEAP PRICE?!!!!! I paid a premium for that horse I now knew went into Donna's pocket. I was shocked into silence. I wasn't expecting any of this, but here was the down low on the horse, straight from the horse's mouth, so to speak. Finding out the horse was lame and a dirty stopper was terrible enough. But finding out I paid five times the actual price of the horse plus a 10% commission on the inflated price, well, I had no words to describe my stupidity. At that point, I learned one of the biggest lessons of my life: to be involved in anything that requires money and substantial purchases. Trust no one on a horse sale unless I can have possession of a horse on a lease for at least a week to a month. I resolved to make the vet my very best friend on a purchase. For the rest of my time in the horse world, I have lived these rules and have had the benefits of many wonderful horses and experiences. Yes, there have been occasional hiccups, but never on the scale of the Donna disasters. (In the end, I sued Donna and won a judgment that was never paid.) The last I heard, she moved out of state.

Three & Me

Me and Jill in her remission years. She was gorgeous!

The Empress And The Queen Meet

## SIX

The Empress And The Queen Meet

After our talk, I left Tommy's office in a massive state of shock, trying to figure out how I could have been so gullible. As I made a right turn out of his office to walk down the barn aisle that led to the parking lot, I looked up in surprise. Right before me was an entire barn aisle filled with horses owned by the same family. Every stall had a plate with each horse's name and owner. On this particular barn aisle, each horse was named after a fancy car, "Stutz Bearcat," "Phaeton," "Bentley," "Rolls," "Limo," and so on. Charles Bronson and Jill Ireland owned all of those horses. "Oh great," I thought. "More Celebrities..."

At the time, Charlie was one of the hottest male actors in the world, especially overseas. Of *The Great Escape* and *Dirty Dozen* fame and his new *Death Wish* franchise, Charlie represented the epitome of Hollywood's image of the man's man. Jill Ireland had her own claim to fame beyond being married to Charles Bronson. She was a contract singer and dancer in her birthplace, England, and had married David McCallum of *The Man from U.N.C.L.E.* television series. David has been blessed with longevity in a fickle industry and is currently playing Ducky, a medical examiner, on the long-running *NCIS* television series. (An interesting side note: At this writing, he is the only living actor from the movie, *The Great Escape*.) Jill also starred as Spock's only ever love interest on *Star Trek,* the original TV series, and went on to star in *Shane*. (I still have the hat she wore in *Shane*.) And she played opposite Charlie in 15 of his films. After they were married, he didn't want her playing the love interest of another man, so he cast her in his movies.

From my earlier barn experiences with Joan Rivers, I learned my lesson about celebrities. They are meant to be admired from afar. I would avoid the Bronsons at all costs. I figured that they could live in their celebrity world, and I could live in my regular-person world, and all would be right with the Universe.

On weekdays, Tommy would give either private or semi-private lessons. Mornings were usually taken up by the amateur riders (people like me competing in the amateur divisions as opposed to the professional divisions), which was anyone over the age of 18 — basically adults. The afternoons were primarily taken up by kids who were in school earlier in the day. Because I had a business to run in downtown Los Angeles, a good 30 minutes away, I could only ride with Tommy during the week if it was very early in the morning or later in the afternoon. So, it was one weekday afternoon, soon after my move into the barn, that I drove out for a lesson on Nocky.

Before I got on, I needed to go to the ladies' room. I walked over to the structure housing the restrooms and opened the door. As I entered, my eyes lit upon a slim woman in a sleeveless top, britches and boots, long legs, long arms, a long neck, and blond curly hair to her chin. I suddenly realized it was Jill Ireland combing, brushing, and styling her hair. She had just gotten off a horse, and I assumed she didn't want to go home with helmet hair. My first impression of her was that she was absolutely stunning. But I said nothing as I passed by and took care of business. When I finished, I quickly washed my hands in the sink beside her and noticed she was busy applying lipstick. I hurried out.

While on my way to the barn aisle where Nocky was stabled and where all my tack was stored, a little girl about eight years old ran past me with the speed of light. Thinking nothing of it, young girls were always running around barns; I continued walking when I heard a man's voice call out, "Zuleika, get back here right now!" THAT caught my attention! Everyone calls me Suzie, but my

The Empress And The Queen Meet

real name is Sue Lika, which is a name my father gave me after Potiphar's wife, Zuleika, in Jewish and Muslim traditions. Instead of spelling it Zuleika, he Americanized the name by breaking it into two. He softened it with an "S" rather than a "Z." (My father's last name of Zsigmond in Hungary was Americanized to be Sigmond in the United States.) It never dawned on me that someone else had my name. (On a 2023 trip to Morocco, in a Jewish Synagogue, I found a memorial for a woman named Suelika, which was also amazing to me.)

I looked around and saw no one looking at me like they wanted me to "Get back here right now." But I did notice that little girl who had run past me go over to a Latino man wearing a white shirt with dark trousers. Without connecting the dots, I continued over to Nocky's stall, wondering who and how someone knew my real birth name. I would find out soon enough.

That first weekend I was in Tommy's barn, I participated in the 9.00 a.m. group lesson. Jill was in the same lesson as were others. She gave me a friendly smile, something she did for everyone in the lesson, and I politely smiled back. Tommy put us through our paces, drilling us, correcting everything from leg position to posture, to hand position, to eye position, as we rode around the ring in circles. Every lesson began with a flat session, which means walk, trot, and canter only. No jumping yet. This warmed up the horses before they were asked to jump a course of fences, but it also warmed up the riders to make sure their position on the horse was as correct as possible. Tommy was a stickler for proper equitation, and there was to be no sloppiness by any rider in his lessons. He put the fear of God into us. But we all loved his lessons. At that time, he was a legend in the horse show circuit as a trainer and as a judge.

After every lesson, I'd exit the ring and hot-walk Nocky around the property before I put him away. Jill would ride up and ask if she could join me, but I always had an excuse for why not. I was quickly running out of reasons. Finally, after one lesson, as I was leaving to hot-

Three & Me

walk Nocky, I heard Tommy's booming voice call out, "DOH--TAWN...
HALT!" I pulled up Nocky, stopping on a dime, with a sick feeling in
my stomach, wondering what, if anything, I had done wrong. I sat on
my horse, facing straight ahead of me (perfect position on the horse),
all the while waiting for an explanation as to why I was commanded to
stop. I got my answer. He screamed out, "WAIT FOR BRAWN-SON!"

Wait for Bronson? Huh? That wasn't something I expected to hear. But
I was afraid to move lest I anger Tommy. I waited for Jill to trot over to
me. She greeted me with a huge smile, and I smiled back, confused
about what was happening. "Hi, Suzie," she said. "Have I done something to offend you?"

Trying not to fall off my horse at this point, I quickly said, "Oh my
gosh, NO! You've done nothing wrong!"

"So then, why won't you talk to me? I mean, it's as if you're avoiding
me."

I cleared my throat to give myself time to form the correct answer, but
what the hell? I decided to tell her the truth. "Well, I am avoiding you."

Jill looked stunned and a little amused at the same time. "And why is
that?" she asked.

"It's nothing personal... It's just that you're a celebrity. And I don't
want to know celebrities." There! I said it.

Jill looked over at me and burst out laughing. With a little twinkle in
her eye, she quickly shot back, "I rather like that! What are you doing
for lunch?"

Lunch was going to be at her place in Bel Air (oh gosh, not another
Hollywood invitation), but instead of giving me her address, she told
me to follow her home from the barn (big sigh of relief). She drove a

The Empress And The Queen Meet

blue Rolls Royce with the license plate JIB. No matter how bad traffic was between the barn and her house, I could easily find her car on the freeway—the only old-style Rolls in a sea of Japanese vehicles. We pulled up to a mansion near UCLA on a street with three houses in total. I parked in the expansive circle driveway near Jill's Rolls. As we climbed the seemingly endless stairs from the driveway up to the entrance to the Spanish/Italian villa-style mansion, I was taken aback by the immensity of the property. I lived in a small three-bedroom Encino home at the time. Her garage was probably bigger than my house and backyard combined!

As we entered the house, the first thing Jill did was walk me over to Charlie, who was reading a newspaper in his study. She wanted to introduce me. "Charlie," Jill began, "remember I told you about the lady in the barn who was always avoiding me?"

Charlie looked up at Jill, then at me. "Is this her?"

"Yes! This is her! And do you want to know why she avoided me?" Jill asked Charlie, all the while grinning. She didn't wait for Charlie to answer. "It's because I'm a celebrity! She doesn't want to know any celebrities!"

Charlie started laughing. He was thrilled. Usually, people were trying to get to know them *because* of their Celebrity, and they both hated the phoniness! Standing before them was someone of the opposite persuasion, and it was a breath of fresh air. Charlie got up off his chair, extended his hand, and said, "It is very nice to meet you....?"

"Suzie," I answered.

"Well, it's certainly nice to meet you, Suzie!" And just like that, they were no longer celebrities but incredibly lovely people whom I would grow to love like family.

Three & Me

Our friendship started out like most friendships. Commonalities, hanging out, phone calls, lunches, parties, and the like. We both found the same things funny, were horrified by the same things, and absolutely loved animals. It was a nice getting-to-know-you period with Jill. At the time, because Charlie was such a huge star, I tried to minimize my contact with him. But that didn't last long. Charlie was a warm presence, and he enjoyed Jill and me having a good time. He welcomed me with both arms wide open.

There was one other thing that made the connection stronger between us. It was, of all things, my name. Remember the little girl running past me that day in the barn? Well, that was Zuleika Bronson, their daughter! We shared the same name, albeit hers was spelled with a Z. Jill told me she named her daughter after Zuleika Dobson, a character in a book whose name had the exact name Genesis as mine. Charlie loved introducing me to new people saying, "This is our good friend Sue Lika, and there's my daughter, Zuleika!" He loved the reactions from people on hearing the two strange-sounding names. He'd always let loose with a little chuckle after the introductions.

Besides their daughter, both Jill and Charlie blended families from previous marriages. Charlie brought Suzanne and Tony. Jill brought Paul, Valentine (Val), and Jason McCallum. Jason was adopted at birth but, funny enough, grew up to look a lot like Jill.

Jill and I had been friends for about a year when Yaniv decided he wanted to go to Israel to visit family and friends over the Christmas holidays. His job as an engineer gave him ample vacation time so he could have an extended vacation back "home" with his family. He left a week before I did.

The following week it was my turn to head over to Israel. I was lucky enough to be seated next to the emergency door, which gave me more legroom, and for a 12-hour flight out of New York, more room was a good thing. Or so I thought. It didn't take long after we were airborne for me to realize something was wrong. Cold air seemed to be coming in from somewhere, and no matter how hard they tried, the cabin crew couldn't figure it out or remedy the situation. It was a full flight so no seat change would happen. They brought me more blankets, but it kept getting colder. No matter what I did, I couldn't get warm. Before advancements in air filtration, planes were basically viral bombs. Because I was so cold, I'm sure my immune system was a bit disabled, and I managed to catch something horrible.

Upon landing in Tel Aviv, I was already feeling quite punk. Yaniv met me at the airport, and during the three-and-a-half-hour drive to the kibbutz, I began to feel worse and worse. The following day, I woke up sick as a dog. High fever, chills, sore throat to end all sore throats, and absolutely no voice. Not even a squeak. I was miserable. But we were in Israel, and I had to be social; I didn't have the luxury of staying in bed. So, I gobbled fever reducers and cold remedies and put on a brave face. I had a virus, and it was a big one. The virus invited some of its best friends over to party in my body and even invited that nasty bug, bronchitis, to the soiree. I ended up coughing my way around Israel. I still couldn't talk, so I smiled a lot. When I got to Jerusalem and the Greenblatts' house, Chuck pulled out some brandy and made me drink it. It stopped the coughing briefly, giving me a much-needed respite.

Yaniv would stay in Israel a week longer than me because I had a job in New York for one of the Big Eight accounting firms. It was January in New York City, and it was a particularly cold month. My virus was quite happy with the situation, throwing all kinds of surprises for me. This virus had too many friends. One of those friends decided to go down into my kidneys and multiply.

When I finished my job, I flew home to Los Angeles. Yaniv arrived on a separate flight the same day, almost when I did. We drove home from the airport together, and as happy as I was to see Yaniv, I felt like dishwater that had been let down the drain. I fell asleep early that night, but in the back of my mind, before I fell asleep, I remember wondering why my back hurt. I have a serious bodily problem. My problem is that I don't feel physical pain like most people do. I have a very high tolerance. Consequently, when I realize something is wrong, I am in terrible shape.

# # #

When I was 16, I caught a virus at the beach after a rainstorm. This was years before warnings came out about avoiding the water for a full two weeks after a rainstorm due to viruses and bacteria. Two days later, I got a headache. I'd never had a headache before, so I had no idea what intensity to expect. This one was a doozy. But, as I said, I don't feel pain like others do. So, I toughed it out for another two days, each day my head worsening. Finally, I started vomiting. My dad came into my room, having heard me retch in the bathroom, and put his hand on my forehead. I was on fire. He broke out the thermometer, and I registered 105° F. He immediately called Dr. Steindel to come over. (Doctors still made house calls then.) Long story short, Dr. Steindel sent me to County General Hospital in Downtown Los Angeles because they were the only hospital with a communicable disease ward at that time. When we arrived at the hospital, an attendant came out with a gurney, hoisted me from my prone position in the back seat, and gently placed me on the gurney.

I was quickly ushered in for a spinal tap (not much fun). Then they threw me in a ward that resembled a cage. I was glassed in. Nurses wore all kinds of protective gear, making me feel like I was in space somewhere. No one could visit me in person. They could only talk to me through the glass from a telephone on the other side, like being in jail. I needn't have worried, though. The only visitor I had was my dad. My mom stayed away. My diagnosis? Viral spinal meningitis. And I thought I just had a headache.

The Empress And The Queen Meet

During one summer in the early '80s, things changed at Tommy Lowe Stables. There was a new and well-known trainer at the barn. Her name was Shari Rose, and she and Tommy somehow got together at a horse show. They became not only life partners but business partners as well.

I was in heaven over the new change! Shari Rose, without a doubt, was one of the best trainers I've ever had. She watched how I rode, sat, and held my hands and then found me the perfect horse. When I tried him, he did everything he could to convince me to be his owner. The horse chose me. It worked. I had him vetted, and probably because of his young age —he was a three-year-old—he vetted clean, so I bought him. His name was Aero, and he became my partner for his entire career, spanning 15 years.

I missed Aero for the two weeks I spent in Israel and New York. The following morning after I arrived from New York, I scampered out to the barn to get on him. As I rode Aero around the ring, I noticed my lower back was beginning to really bother me. It was a dull ache, but it was becoming more noticeable. But me being me, since I wasn't in a great deal of discomfort, I tossed it off as being just one of those aches. Until the vomiting began. Vomiting always seemed to get my attention, so I called my doctor. When I handed him the urine sample, even I was impressed with the brown color in the vial. The virus had gone deep into my kidneys, and I was in trouble. I was immediately thrown into the hospital and administered massive antibiotics. I was to stay there for over a week.

Jill called me at the hospital to cheer me up. She made plans to visit the next day after she was done riding. But Jill never showed up, and she never called. This wasn't like her. I called the house, and no one answered. I knew something had to be wrong, so I got worried. She finally called me later that night. Apparently, while she was jumping her horse, Stutz, he forgot to put his feet down after the fence. He tucked to jump but then failed to untuck his landing gear, crashing with a considerable thud to the ground. Jill flew off and fractured her leg. It was a bad break rendering her nearly helpless. Her leg was placed in a large cast, and she was not only hobbled for the foreseeable future, but she was also miserable. We chatted about us both being out of commission, me trying to cheer her up, and she trying to cheer me up. I still remember the sadness in her voice. It would be the same sadness I would hear years later when her cancer was discovered.

When I left the hospital, I was instructed not to ride or do anything to jiggle my kidneys. They still needed to heal from the trauma I had put them through. Jill couldn't ride either, so I would go over to her house, and we'd just hang out together, chatting about everything but nothing in particular. Jill had her own dressing room in the mansion. It was a bedroom overlooking a golf course and had a veranda. We'd sit on the veranda, the breeze flowing through our hair, softly caressing our faces, while the California sun, even in winter, warmed our bodies. Those were idyllic times for us. The world seemed right. Our lives seemed right. And for the most part, it was. Thinking back, though, I wonder if the cancer in Jill's body had begun to grow at that time. Was a renegade cell desiring something bigger out of life, figuring that turning cancerous was a way to the limelight—the old "go big or go home" kind of thing. I have no idea how long cancer takes to develop or when the immune system decides to turn a blind eye, but looking back, I'm pretty sure that Jill was a ticking time bomb around that time.

Eventually, Jill's leg and my kidneys healed. Every year the Bronsons would spend all summer at their farm in Vermont, aptly named Zuleika Farm. They owned an old purple brick house with three stories, on acres and acres of beautiful pastures, with horse corrals, riding rings, lakes, and forests as far as the eye could see.

They left for Vermont in June that summer, and I would follow in July. Yaniv was busy and wouldn't really miss me. Besides his Bachelor's degree in Biology, a Master's degree in Neurophysiology from Hadassah Hospital, and another Bachelor's degree in Electronic Engineering from USC, he was working on another Master's degree, this time in Engineering. Yaniv collected degrees like most people collect stamps, and my being gone would be one less distraction to get in the way of his studies.

Jill and I had a wonderful time for the two weeks I was there. I had the only bedroom on the third floor across from the attic. It got pretty hot up there, but I would open the window and let the breeze softly put me to sleep. We rode horses every day, hung out by the lake sunning ourselves, our entire selves (yep, totally in the buff), enjoyed lunches and dinners in the quaint town of Woodstock, and shopped the cute country stores. Vermont was more humid than Los Angeles, but I quickly adjusted and loved the softness of the air on my skin—definitely country living. My favorite icon from those Vermont days was the "Soup Can," one of the earliest SUV's that I can remember. The Bronson Soup Can had a faded orange chassis with a black top that made it look like Campbell's Soup packaging. We'd take the Soup Can out every time we went into town. It was pretty beaten up, but I loved its jalopy vibe.

One day Jill had a great idea. We would go for a long trail ride through the forest surrounding the property. Off we walked toward the tack room. Jill would ride a beautiful grey horse named Robby because her leg was still healing, and he was the safest ride for her. I would get on a large bay Connemara pony named Turtle, whom I adored. The skies were blue, and there was nary a cloud. The sun was warm, and a slight breeze rustled the trees. We were in the middle of joking about our breasts being sunburned as well as our bums when Charlie rode up on his motocross dirt bike. "Jill," he began, "maybe you shouldn't go on a trail ride right now. I heard thunder."

Jill walked out of the tack room and waited and listened. Nothing. No clouds. No thunder. Only bright blue sky. "Charlie, I think you're hearing things," she said with a small chuckle. So, we continued to tack up, mount, and start our adventure. Charlie rode away on his bike, convinced he heard thunder.

The trail ride was breathtaking. Unlike California, Vermont is full of lush vegetation; bushes, forests full of trees, green meadows, and many babbling brooks. We chatted aimlessly about every kind of subject imaginable. Jill and I never lacked for conversation. We could discuss the pros and cons of a particular paint color for hours, such was our ability to communicate. Mostly, though, I remember talking a lot about Tommy Lowe and his new arrangement with Shari Rose. We loved the new trainers that came with the merge. Shari came with a whole cadre of assistant trainers who were absolutely lovely to work with, and they brought a whole new perspective to riding and showing. We did agree that we both missed the Tommy Lowe group lessons, as they became a thing of the past.

As we were chatting away, I heard the sound of rushing water nearby. We were in a really thick forest at that point. We couldn't see the sky. We couldn't really see much in front of us except the immediate trail we were on, and we certainly couldn't see very far on either side of us. "Jill, is there a creek nearby?" I asked.

"Why yes, yes there is!" Jill responded.

"It sounds like it's pretty big!" I exclaimed. Jill agreed, and we continued on. The sound of rushing water was getting louder and louder, and I wondered if we would find ourselves blocked by a raging river. Before long, we were out of the forest and into a clearing, a large grassy meadow behind the Bronson's home. It was pouring rain. (So that's what I heard!) The skies were angry and throwing lightning bolts in every direction. The roar of thunder was huge. Both Jill and I were immediately soaked by the torrential rain. Something caught my eye

The Empress And The Queen Meet

at the other end of the meadow. Squinting my eyes, I could make out Charlie standing outside with his arms crossed. "Jill, why is Charlie standing outside in the rain? It's weird that's he getting soaked when he doesn't need to."

Jill looked over toward Charlie. Her face grew grave, almost pensive. "I know what he's thinking."

"What could he possibly be thinking right now?" I asked, slightly amused. Without missing a beat, Jill gave me my answer.

"He's thinking we're going to be struck by lightning. He knows the horses wear metal shoes, and we're now the tallest objects out here." Jill said it so calmly that I didn't know if she was serious or kidding. But it struck me as making good sense, so I looked over at Jill and told her I was pretty much out of there!

"Good idea!" she laughed, and we high-tailed it out of the storm at a pretty good gallop back to the safety of the stable area.

Once we put the horses away and returned to the house to shower and change into dry clothes, we sat by the fireplace and sipped hot tea. Charlie was still angry with us for going out, but he eventually softened up, knowing we were back home and safe.

When I was with Jill, I would admire her many wonderful attributes, and I aspired to be the kind of person she represented. There were no mean thoughts anywhere in that wonderfully sharp brain of hers. In fact, I was always amazed by Jill's humanity towards others. Her kindness was genuine and bottomless. One needn't be a member of the Hollywood elite for her to show—even to strangers—compassion, support, or utmost respect.

Her generosity was legend. Jill loved to shower her friends and family with gifts. She shopped for Christmas gifts all year round. For her

Los Angeles people, she had a special hiding place under a window bench in the Bel Air House. For the Vermont Christmases, she'd leave the gifts she found in Woodstock upstairs in the attic until it was time to put them under the tree. It never failed that when we would be out somewhere, she'd find something and say, "This would look perfect on Katrina," or "Antonio needs a new coat," or some other good reason to buy that gift. When Christmas came, everyone in Jill's circle had multiple gifts showered on them. To this day, I have all the gifts she gave me as keepsakes and reminders about what a wonderful person I had as my best friend.

When the Bronsons returned from Vermont at the end of that first summer of our friendship, Jill began to get ready for the party season. She and Charlie would go to many black-tie affairs during the fall. One day she looked at me as if sizing me up. She had that Jill Ireland Bronson scrunched brow, letting me know she was definitely thinking of something. "Darling, do you have any ballgowns?" She asked. I just about fell over backward. I grew up pretty poor, lived in still-developing Israel, and moved back to a small home in Encino. How the hell would I have ballgowns for one—and two— *Why would I have ballgowns?!*

I laughed pretty hard as I said, "No... but I do have a fancy pair of bejeweled jeans in my closet."

"Well, we better find you a ballgown pretty quickly," she laughed. "Because we are going to go to a very fancy ball in two weeks. Charlie just bought a table at the gala for the *Princess Grace Foundation,* and you're coming with us!"

I was gobsmacked. Never would I have believed I would be one of those people to step out of a limo. To start off at the Princess Grace Foundation was mind-boggling! Of course, I found a dress, and the perfect shoes, had my hair done, bought a nice tux for Yaniv, and we were ready. There was no way I would miss out on an opportunity like that!

The Empress And The Queen Meet

The morning of the day of the gala, my mom asked me to stop by her house to fix something for her. She knew I was going to go to the ball with the Bronsons. I'd just had my hair done in Beverly Hills, and her house was on the way home, so I stopped by. I had a key and could let myself in, usually through the back door. When I spoke with her earlier in the day, she was chatty and friendly. The woman that greeted me as I entered was in a rage. She immediately attacked me, screaming at me for being so pretentious as to go to a ball, having my hair done, pretending I was beautiful, acting like I was better than anyone, and on and on. The weird thing was that she kept calling me Beatrice, her sister's name. I was defenseless. I kept telling her I wasn't her sister but to no avail. No one was home but us. She unleashed such a tirade of hate that I walked out in tears, shaking, unsure if I could compose myself enough to go to the gala. I was so distraught that I wasn't even sure I could drive home safely. I pulled my car over when I was a few blocks from my mom's and sat there in shock, vacillating between crying and shaking.

To make matters worse, a photographer I worked with on many jobs offered to come and take photos of Yaniv and me when we were dressed to the nines. I still had to get home, shower, put on makeup, and get dressed. Puffy red eyes wouldn't do, so I forced myself to calm down, think good thoughts, and regulate my breathing. After a while, my efforts were working. I could regain control of my emotions and focus on the rest of the day. I put my car into gear and pulled away from the curb where I left my mom's tirade behind.

Once I got back home, everything fell into place. Mark, the photographer, came and took pictures of a beaming couple. We did clean up nicely. Especially Yaniv. His deep blue eyes against the black and white of the tux shone like two beacons. I chose sparkle for my debut on the party circuit. My dress could best be described as something close to the coat in *Joseph and the Amazing Technicolor Dreamcoat*. It was a shimmering rainbow of colored sequins set off nicely by my dark complexion. Dare I say it; we were glamorous! Jill taught me

Three & Me

that the fancier the dress, the more understated the jewelry, so I chose a simple strand of coral to go around my neck.

We rode with Jill and Charlie in the limo to the event. If I remember correctly, it was held in the main ballroom at the Beverly Hills Hilton Hotel. On the way, Charlie looked at Yaniv and remarked, "Yaniv is very handsome, and I bet the paparazzi are going to go nuts trying to figure out who he is once we step out." I agreed with him. Then he also remarked, "And the same goes for you. We are going to drive them crazy!" He got a huge chuckle out of this. As it happened, Charlie called it. Jill stepped out first, then Charlie, me, and Yaniv. The flashes of the cameras popped all around us. I heard a few photographers say, "Who are those two?" It was fun pretending to be "somebody," if only for a magical night.

That evening was one of the best evenings of my life. I danced with Prince Ranier and his son Albert that evening—absolute magic. Jill was full of pride watching me dance with the two princes. As I write this, I can still feel the excitement I felt. I imagined I was on top of the world, and I believe I really was for some brief moments. Jill and I would reminisce for a long time about my dancing with two princes in one evening. A once in a lifetime event.

The very next morning, I got a phone call from my dad. He was very agitated, but through the conversation, I understood my mom's fits of rage the day before. My dad explained that my mom's brother had been diagnosed with pancreatic cancer. It finally came to light that my grandfather, long since dead (he passed away when I was in Israel), had created that $30,000 trust for my mother. Upon hearing the news of Uncle Bob's diagnosis, Lottie, my mom's mother, called him and inquired about the trust. Uncle Bob told her the truth. The money was gone. He'd spent it on his business endeavors and never returned any funds to the trust. Since my mom never knew about the trust, he figured no harm, no foul. Lottie was taken aback. Not so much because my mom was out the money—that didn't matter to her.

It was more along the lines of her son dying a dishonest man. *That,* she couldn't allow. He was her golden boy. And she wanted him to go to Heaven as such.

Instead of leaving well enough alone, Lottie called my mother and told her the whole story with the last words, "You can't let your brother die a dishonest man. You have to do something about it."

My mom was astounded that a trust had even existed from as far back as it did, the news taking her entirely by surprise. According to my dad, all the hurt and pain of her childhood came flooding back. How could her parents do that to her? How could her brother do that to her? Again, she was reminded about how little she mattered to the family. It was too much for her. If that weren't bad enough, she then found out about the ugly conditions of the trust, practically guaranteeing that she would only receive the money as an old woman. (I did the math. Had my mom lived long enough, she would have seen the money at the ripe old age of 75 years old!) Then there was the financial part of it all. There should have been hundreds of thousands of dollars in that trust when my mom cashed out. Now there was none.

A lawsuit would rip the family apart, but my parents sat down and carefully thought things through. My mom had never been treated as one of the family. She was always disliked, the child conceived out of wedlock, causing two hideous people to join in unholy matrimony. And she was the black sheep who married an immigrant without two dimes to rub together. She lived on the West Coast with two scrawny kids, unlike their other daughter's healthy, strapping children. To say she was looked down upon would be an absolute understatement. So, the decision was made to sue my uncle for the actual worth of the trust in 1987 dollars.

The lawsuit did tear the family into so many different factions that it was hard to keep up with who hated whom more. In the end, the bad guy was my mother. How could she sue a dying man?

Everyone seemed to forget the fact that she was the wronged party. She wouldn't have sued a dying man if my grandfather hadn't created the hideous trust, to begin with, or if my Uncle Bob hadn't used it as his personal savings and loan. But that wasn't considered. My mom was now public enemy number one for immediate family members and beyond. I was incensed at what relatives were saying about and to my mother.

Yaniv was the shining light in my mom's life during this dark period. He would spend many evenings with my parents when he would stop by on his way home from work. He was utterly disgusted with the backstabbing family I hailed from.

I couldn't get it out of my head, either. I would spend many hours filling Jill in on the twists and turns of my family saga. She was equally horrified. What got her the most was when she heard about the deposition. Lottie, when deposed, admitted that the trust was set in place because of my grandfather's hatred toward my father. The original trust documents actually spelled that out in my grandfather's own words! While the money he gave his other children helped them succeed financially, he delighted in watching my dad struggle through challenging years.

I like to imagine that Skeeze is up in Heaven, twisting and turning with the knowledge that my dad, who achieved financial success on his own sweat, is also lauded as an American Hero. His bio with his legacy is part of a museum. (There are books and movies about the Ritchie Boys, calling each one of them heroes.) I take great satisfaction in imagining that he's probably died a thousand deaths over this. (I can dream, can't I?)

The lawsuit was finally settled after my uncle succumbed to his cancer. His widow, my Aunt Esther, a woman I loved madly, made good and repaid the trust money that my uncle had used, settling on a dollar amount acceptable to the courts and my parents. Nothing, however, could change the terms of the trust, so my mom still had to wait. My Aunt Beatrice was named trustee and paid herself a fairly hefty salary for her troubles. That resulted in more court. More bad feelings. More hatred. Finally, the court ordered the trust to be placed with a banking institution as trustee until it dissolved. My mom never got her money. She died before my grandmother did; as the only survivor, the trust became mine. My grandmother passed away at the age of 94. In her letter apologizing to me for her behavior, she said she hoped the money I would receive five years after her imminent passing would help put salve on the wounds she created. I did receive the money, but there was little left in it after all the salaries, fees, and whatnot were taken out.

# # #

Jill and Charlie took Yaniv and me to many black-tie events that fall. It was fun glamming it up, finding fabulous ball gowns, and pretending to belong in the room with all those wealthy and famous bigwigs. Jill would lend me one of her furs for each season, so I'd fit in. (It was part of the gala culture to walk in with furs back then, nothing I would ever do now.) I met many stars from that era, Elizabeth Taylor among them. (Those eyes!) There were others as well, Roddy McDowell, Charlton Heston, Tab Hunter, and Shelly Winters, to name a few.

Once the gala season was over, Jill went in for her annual checkup. She had always had cystic breasts. When she had her mammogram, a small lump was detected. Because of her cystic history, she was told to re-examine six months later. Thinking nothing of it, she went home to live her life.

Six months later, right before leaving for Vermont for the summer, Jill went in for her follow-up mammogram, thinking everything would be just fine. The doctors had given her the impression not to worry, so she hadn't. But that's when the hammer usually hits. You think you're cruising, but suddenly you hit a massive brick wall called Life. After this new mammo, they told her there was a good chance she had cancer, but they needed a biopsy to be sure. Jill was stunned by the news, as was Charlie. When she told me the news, I was heartbroken.

The day of the biopsy arrived. When she was about to go under, she signed a form saying that if they found cancer, she agreed to undergo a radical mastectomy. In the end, that's what happened. To make matters worse for Jill, during surgery, they found cancer had also spread to seven nodes. As Jill once told me, "That's like being told you're going to die for sure." Anything over five nodes was a certain death sentence at that time. That little lump had grown over the six months to become a raging cancer storm within her breast and now threatened her very life. Jill was only 48 years old at the time of diagnosis, with still so much life left to live. Instead of giving up, Jill resolved to live as much of that life as she could. She transformed into a warrior—even Wonder Woman would pale in comparison. Jill wouldn't give up without a fight, and fight she did.

I felt helpless when I was faced with her diagnosis. What could I do? How could I even begin to help my friend? I didn't want to lose Jill to evil cells hiding in her body that wanted to kill her. I wanted the cancer gone, and I decided to be the best friend Jill could ever have. I would help her through it all! I just wasn't quite sure how yet.

Jill's team of doctors had settled on a course of treatment involving eight rounds of chemo to be administered once every three weeks for six months. In light of this new reality, Jill looked around at her surroundings and decided that owning a mansion with all the furniture and trappings accompanying it would only drag her down on her road to recovery. She wanted to purge herself of the burden of carrying all that weight. She wanted out, and she wanted out now! Charlie agreed they would rent a house on the beach on Pacific Coast Highway in Malibu while she was undergoing chemo. They also found a newly built home in Cross Creek in Malibu. It was a one-story home, about a third of the size of their Bel Air home, and they purchased

The Empress And The Queen Meet

that as well. It would take a long time to complete the renovations Jill wanted, but it would be her forever home when it was done. It would also be where she would take her last breath.

While they were renting in Malibu, I would drive to the beach house to hang out with Jill. She had placed eight stones on the coffee table from the sand below. After each chemo session, she would walk down to the water and throw one stone in, watching the tide carry it away. She got strength from throwing in each stone, one more step towards wellness, something tangible she could see. I was with her several times when she threw the rock out to the ocean. I understood how she got strength from each stone carried away by the tide. I felt that sensation of hope also.

While Jill underwent chemo, Charlie watched a great deal of television to kill time. He was into the TV series, *Murder She Wrote* with Angela Lansbury. It was something we could all do together. Charlie also liked *The Golden Girls,* and we'd wind up laughing together at the situations those ladies would get themselves into. Especially Betty White! While those were hard days, we silently hoped for the best possible outcome. We were living as normally as possible, and it helped. Silly TV shows helped. Angela Lansbury and Betty White helped!

While recovering at the beach in Malibu, Jill picked up a microphone to a tape recorder and began to tell her story. She "wrote" ferociously, telling her tale about her journey through cancer. She'd send the tapes out to be transcribed and have typed pages delivered. Then she could send out for multiple copies. While still in its infancy, personal computing had not yet entered the mainstream. One day when I walked into the beach house, she thrust a bunch of pages into my hands and said, "Do me a favor. Go into the corner and read what I wrote." Obediently, I sat down and read what would be the beginnings of *"Life Wish,"* her first book. Because I had spent so much time with her during her journey, it read almost like a diary to me. I loved it immediately. Jill would always go back and re-work what she'd written, so each time I came

Three & Me

over, I would get the same 100 pages again. I was dying to get to page 101, but it took a long while for that to happen! I was able to recite almost perfectly those first 100 pages. It would become a running joke between us. I still have her original typed manuscript before the book was published. Every so often, I go back and read those yellowing 100 pages just for old times' sake.

# # #

During this period, several things were happening in the background of my life. The first involved my brother. Jerry was a chiropractor specializing in personal injury, unlike my father, who had a family practice. Jerry championed breaking up a peer review committee that operated under a pay-to-play scheme. Bluntly put, it was extortion on a sophisticated level, using insurance companies as leverage.

If a chiropractor paid dues to the group, their patients' insurance claims would pass peer review. If they didn't join, well... Who could say, right? Long story short, my brother refused to join, got peer-reviewed, his patients' claims denied, then got even. He sued in the courts and won. Happy ending, right? Wrong. After the peer review racket was broken up in the courts, the involved chiropractors lost their cash cow and weren't too happy about it. Some of them were high-ranking officials in a state association. My brother said they began harassing him in ways he hadn't imagined would happen. They went after his license, and they won, robbing him of his livelihood. But my brother played into their hands. Emboldened from winning the dissolution of peer review, he went after them under the Racketeer Influenced and Corrupt Organizations Act, the federal statute used to break up the Mafia and other organized crime. RICO is tricky to prove, and my brother's lawyers were ill-prepared for that fight. My brother became obsessed with this battle. It was all he could talk about. The more obsessed he became, the more insane he seemed. I hate to say this, but I was loathe to be around him. All I would hear about were his court battles. There was a question in my mind about his emerging paranoia and schizophrenia, coupled with an undiagnosed bipolar condition which made being around him much more challenging. But I wasn't paying attention to the loud warning signs going off all around me, and I would dearly regret it in the coming years. I wasn't a very good sister at all.

As if things weren't going askew enough with my sibling, my grandmother happened. She lived in an assisted living facility in downtown Rochester, Minnesota, near my Aunt Bea, the "good daughter." It gets oppressively cold in Minneapolis during the winter, so during the winter of 1984/85, my grandmother decided to visit her other daughter, my mother, in Bel Air, California, where temperatures were primarily mild all year. Now that my mom had a beautiful home in the prestigious neighborhood of Bel Air, Lottie found it appealing to visit for the winter. My parents' Bel Air home was now acceptable to Lottie's standard of living. I couldn't believe my parents welcomed her, but I guess they figured the damage caused by the trust was done, so why not?

It was a late afternoon in January when I was in the neighborhood and wanted to stop by and say "Hi" to my mom and dad. I let myself in with my key and walked through the house looking for them when I ran into my grandmother standing in a darkened dining room off the kitchen. It was almost surreal because she just stood there, motionless in the shadows behind the table. "Hi, Granny," I said, about to ask where Mom and Dad were, but I didn't get the chance.

"You are a rotten person," she screeched right out of the blue. "You were a rotten child then, and you're a rotten person now! Don't think I don't know that about you!"

Well, I wasn't expecting that kind of welcome. But OK. I've heard worse. The thing that struck me, though, was the vocabulary she used. Those were the exact words my mom would use on me. "Rotten kid" was thrown at me in most of my mom's tirades. Now here was Lottie using those exact words. And then it hit me. My mind connected the dots as Lottie was busy trying to break me down. My mother was only repeating what she'd heard from Lottie throughout her life. She knew of no other way to relate to me. Her mother had destroyed her so entirely that she became her mother. And just like that, I found so much compassion and love for my mother. Nothing about her feelings and actions toward me was her fault. The vicious monster on the other side of the table was the responsible party. Finally, I understood my mom, and I immediately forgave her.

It was then and there that I looked at Lottie and gave it right back to her. "Stop!" I said, "You are a hideous mother, grandmother, and human being. You seem to think that putting my mother down and putting me down somehow makes you superior. It doesn't! It just makes you pathetic!"

She stared at me, aghast at what I had said. But, true to form, the ugly inside her had to win. She started shrieking at me about how I had just proved how terrible and rotten I was. And then it happened. I began to laugh at how ridiculous this old sick-minded, cold-hearted woman really was. Much to her chagrin, I still laughed as I walked out of the house. I could still hear her screaming at me as I pulled my car out of the driveway. It would be the last time I saw Lottie or spoke with her. I don't hate her, but I have no love for either of my mom's parents. I sometimes wonder about that deathbed note asking forgiveness. Was she channeling that day in my parents' dining room when she wrote it?

#

Jill finally finished her eight rounds of chemo. She looked beautiful. Jill was never too sick from the drugs, except for the first few days after each treatment. Her hair never entirely fell out; instead, it fell out in small patches, leaving bald spots sporadically around her scalp, but it now grew in thick and curly. Within months she would look like she'd never had chemo.

The Empress And The Queen Meet

Because of her radical mastectomy, Jill had to wear an uncomfortable and hot prosthetic breast. She would complain about it regularly. She was also very tender around the scar and newly insecure about her looks. She felt maimed and deformed. Plastic surgery was not an option her doctors recommended.

Because of the type of cancer she had, and the number of nodes where it was found, they felt that any implant might mask a small tumor until it was discovered too late. If anyone should have had reconstructive surgery, it was Jill. It would have gone a long way toward her rehabilitation and self-identity. Today, reconstruction is routinely done at the same time as radical Mastectomies. The oncology surgeon does his job then the plastics docs step in and do theirs, thus eliminating the need for two surgeries.

As Jill got stronger, she moved back into the Bel Air house while the new Malibu house was undergoing renovations. She had to relinquish the rented beach house to the owners, but it had served its purpose well. I was going to miss that house. There's something so life-giving about listening to the sounds of the crashing waves. I can understand why people want to live on the beach. It's energizing. Jill felt the same life-giving energy from the ocean as I did, and she resolved to buy a beach house when one became available.

Later that year, during the summer, when we were in Vermont together, Jill was especially feeling sorry for herself. She was an actress, after all, and her looks were her paycheck. Looking down at herself, she could only see one lump instead of two. I decided we needed to do something about her mood. So, I came up with the idea to take topless photos of ourselves. We would call it the three-tit photos. So, with the Polaroid camera in hand, we had another friend point the camera and shoot our three tits. They came out great. My two, and Jill's one, and oh, how we loved those photos! It was to be our legacy as friends. Unfortunately, Jill told Charlie about the photos. He was scared to death that they'd end up in the *National Enquirer* or some other tabloid. (There were no negatives, but OK.) He ended up confiscating the Polaroids. Charlie now had photos of my two tits and Jill's one. Oh well.

We also decided to form a club called the "BSC" (Blue Snatch Club), where we would dye our pubic hairs blue. We never got around to that since Brazilians were taking hold, but we held true to the "Ladies of the BSC" right up until the end.

Jill had a make-up person and a good friend named Alan Marshall. He used to call her "The Empress," which was funny because my mom used to call me "Queenie" or "The Queen" when she wasn't angry with me. I swear, it sounded like she was calling for a dog every time I heard, "Queenie, time for dinner!" In fact, if any of my friends heard it for the first time, they'd be looking for a dog until I told them that Queenie was me. After I heard Alan call Jill "The Empress," I told her about me being the Queen. We both got a kick out of it. I told her that being an Empress was far more prestigious, which she enjoyed.

This being the mid-1980s and Alan being gay, it wasn't a surprise when he became one of the first of the walking shadows. He was diagnosed with Pneumocystis AIDS, which scared the living daylights out of Jill. Because I had done pro bono work for AIDS Project LA, I was educated enough about AIDS not to fear someone who had it as long as I didn't engage in unprotected sex or was exposed to blood. But Jill didn't have the benefit of my knowledge, and no matter how hard I tried to explain AIDS to her, she was still deathly afraid of Alan. Her heart was broken because his diagnosis at that time meant certain death, but she still wanted to distance herself from him.

One day when we were sunning ourselves topless on the back deck of the Bel Air house, she brought the subject of Alan up. "Darling, would you do me an absolutely huge favor?" she asked.

The Empress And The Queen Meet

"Sure," I said without thinking twice. "What's up?"

"I want you to take care of Alan. You need to replace me as his center of attention."

"What?!" I asked, completely stunned. I wasn't even sure Alan knew I was in the same room when we were all together; he was so mesmerized by Jill.

"Alan needs you. Yes, I know he has Jimmy, but he also needs to obsess about a woman... Let him obsess over you. I know you're not afraid of AIDS, and even though my fears have proven unfounded, I am still healing from cancer and don't want to take any chances. Chemo kills your immune system, you know..."

I stopped Jill right there. "I'll do it," I said. "If it makes you feel better, I'll care for Alan."

Jill was thrilled. She immediately picked up the phone to call Alan and let him know that because her immune system was compromised, she could only be a phone friend for the time being but that I would be his little buddy in her stead. For some unexplainable reason, Alan seemed pleased with the new arrangement. I was confused but willing to help Jill and, in turn, help a dying man. I was learning about humanity from my friend, and it was beginning to show.

I was literally thrown into the then-controversial world of AIDS. It was a whole different set of parameters from my pro bono work doing graphics for AIDS Project Los Angeles. In my work for APLA, I dealt with the hard facts of the number of cases, symptoms, preventions, etc. There were no faces yet attached to AIDS in my life. But Alan put a face to the crisis, bringing a whole new set of emotions, understanding, and sympathy.

Three & Me

Alan was a feisty son of a gun. He would say the most outrageous things to see how hard and how far he could push me or challenge me. Physically, he was a diminutive man with a sharp tongue and a sharper sense of humor. The frailty of his thinning body aged his appearance far beyond his years. He was in his 50's, much older than me. I was in my early 30's at the time. As frail as he was, he was very much in command. He had recently undergone a face and neck lift. His already tight face stretched even more tightly as he lost massive amounts of weight due to the disease.

Alan obsessed over beautiful women despite being gay. He was a movie and television makeup artist, aware of every flaw in a woman's face and how to fix it. Boy, did he have a field day with mine! Right off the bat, he commented on my nose (it's crooked). My high cheekbones were something he drooled over. He always had a comment every time he saw me. "Girl, do something about those eyebrows!" he'd often say. "Oh my, Dearie, did you put on a pound or two? I can see it in your face!" There would be no hiding physical flaws from Alan.

Alan lived with his partner, not too far from me, in a condo in Woodland Hills. At the time, I was still in my little Encino house, not too far away. I'd pick him up and take him places he wanted to go. He loved horses, so I'd take him to the barn, and he'd sit in the bleachers as I rode. Then we'd go to lunch somewhere where it would become a test of wills between Alan and me. He would buy a drink, then offer it to me, "Do you want a sip?" he'd tease. Ugh. I knew HIV wasn't detectable in saliva, so I'd reluctantly take a sip, to Alan's great delight as well as my own chagrin. I've never been one to want to swap straws with people, and I have to admit, AIDS or no AIDS, I was grossed out!

Alan glommed onto me like flypaper. It drove Yaniv crazy at times. Like when we'd all go to a movie together, Alan would flounce on the seat next to me, leaving Yaniv and Jimmy to fend for themselves. Yaniv ended up sitting either next to Jimmy or next to Alan. Alan always took the seat closest to me if we went out to eat together. I was his, and he wasn't letting anyone, even my husband, get in the way of that. Thankfully, Yaniv was a kind-hearted soul who recognized Alan's situation and allowed him his little eccentricities. He'd occasionally grouse about it, but he knew at the end of dinner or at the end of a movie, I was going home with him.

The polaroid before the 3-Tit polaroid.
Fearing it would fall into the wrong hands, Charlie
took the boobie shot and locked it up.

Three & Me

Theresa Saldana and me. We could have been cast as cops in a TV show! We fit that blonde and brunette typecasting!

Sue Lika Dotan

## SEVEN

A Victim No More

Charlie filmed the movie *The Evil That Men Do* in Mexico, and the actress, Theresa Saldana, was cast as his female lead. Alan provided makeup for her during filming, and they struck up a lovely friendship that continued after filming wrapped. As good an actress as Theresa was, she became more famous for being a stabbing victim. *Evil* was filmed shortly after that hideous event on March 15, 1982.

It's a well-known story—it was all over the news at the time and was later a TV movie, *Victims for Victims: The Theresa Saldana Story.* Theresa also penned a book, *"Beyond Survival,"* which detailed her life before, during, and after the attack. Sadly, too few young people know what occurred that day in 1982, let alone remember Theresa, so here is the *"Reader's Digest"* version.

A man, Arthur Jackson, was obsessed with a movie actress while he lived in Scotland and England. He wrote her letters and tried to get to see her, to no avail. She died, not at the hand of Jackson but from something else. Instead of this being the end of his obsession, he transferred it to Theresa after seeing her in the movies *Defiance* and *Raging Bull.* Jackson was considered a drifter. No one knows how he got the money to hire a private investigator, but he was able to secure the phone number for Theresa's mother, who lived in New York. Using the ruse that he worked for famed director Martin Scorcese and needed to reach Theresa to cast her in another movie, he cajoled her into giving him Theresa's home address in California. Ever the supportive mother, she only wanted to help her daughter out. She had no idea that production companies don't contact talent directly. It is ALWAYS

131

through an agent. She never, for one second, thought she was putting her daughter in harm's way.

Jackson made his way to Theresa's rented house in the San Fernando Valley and waited for her outside her home. I believe the legal term is "lying in wait," which he did patiently. He was in the street when she walked out her front door. As soon as he saw her, he approached her and said, "Miss Saldana?" When she innocently replied in the affirmative, he pulled out a knife and began stabbing and hacking away at her. He had a crazed mission that day. His mission was to kill Theresa and then be executed by the people of California, so their souls could be married in heaven forever. Let that sink in for a minute!

Theresa screamed as loud as she could from sheer panic and pain. A Sparklettes delivery man named Jeff Fenn heard her screams, saw the attack unfolding, and quickly came to her aid. He wrestled Jackson off Theresa and held him until the police and the paramedics arrived. He saved her life that day. Jeff was an amazing and brave hero when he stopped the attack from progressing further. That few moments in time would alter the trajectory of his life. He moved on from being a water delivery man to a long and successful career in law enforcement.

I met Theresa one day when we were doing an Alan handoff. Like me, Theresa became a support network for Alan once he was diagnosed with AIDS. Alan had to have been thrilled. He had me part-time, and he had Theresa part-time. Theresa and I hit it off instantly. She had a dry sense of humor, just like mine, and whenever we did an Alan handoff, we'd all hang out together at a restaurant or a park, or wherever, and talk.

It didn't take me long (basically two minutes) to notice the mangled fingers on her hands, which were defense wounds from the knife attack. Theresa always wore high-collared pink blouses to hide the scars on her chest. The fashion trends during that period of the 80s

A Victim No More

were big curly hair, Guess Jeans, and outfits with giant shoulder pads. Jill wore them constantly. So did Theresa. She wore oversized wide jackets over her pink blouses with big bows. She did everything she could to hide the stabbing, but the emotional and physical scars were always there, front and center.

Two years after the attack, Jackson was sentenced to the maximum sentence at the time, which was 12 years (the two years awaiting trial were credited as time served), but he could be released after only seven years. There's that little thing called overcrowded prisons so that sentences could be slashed for good behavior.

When I asked Theresa why Jackson didn't get more time behind bars, she chillingly said, "It's because I didn't die." Hearing those words from someone I knew and liked sent chills up my spine. I had no idea that in just a few years, I would listen to something more chilling, something that, to this day, I can't ever forget. And I would hear it from Jackson himself.

133

Theresa drove a cute little Miata sports car with the top usually down. I always wondered about that because she still had severe PTSD and was afraid to go anywhere alone, especially at night. Eventually, Theresa and I would meet for lunch in various restaurants around North Hollywood/Studio City without Alan. She felt safe in the places she regularly frequented because the proprietors knew her and were protective of her.

While Theresa and I played the trade game with Alan, his disease progressed rapidly. He was treated with the standard protocols of the time using the drug, Pentamidine, which made him very sick. He would complain about all this treatment's side effects while bemoaning that it didn't appear to be helping. Reflecting on those early days of the AIDS pandemic, I realize just how little the world cared. Unfortunately, I could spot anyone who had it based on their gauntness and the haunted look in the person's eyes. Alan had that haunted look.

I was literally watching someone die a painfully slow and horrible death and felt helpless in the face of it.

I don't know if this sounds callous, and I am sure there will be people who disagree with me, but if it were legal, I would have helped Alan end his life back then. He practically begged me to do just that on more than one occasion, but I would talk him out of it, telling him that science was hopefully working on a cure. After watching Alan waste away to his last hours, I am so grateful that California is now a right-to-die state. No one should be made to suffer the way Alan did. I believe in the cocktail. I believe in euthanasia which is starting to become legal in a few countries.

Eventually, Alan ended up in Saint John's Hospital in Santa Monica. Theresa and I would visit him nearly every day, which got tricky with work and my other obligations. Every day was worse than the day before. I could smell death on his breath, the rot wafting up from his dying insides. He reeked like a living cadaver. But he wouldn't die. The next day, I thought, would be his last. Nope. And it went on like that for literally weeks. I asked the nurse how it was possible that he could still be alive. She told me that AIDS patients were usually young men with healthy hearts that kept them alive long after they should have died. While everything else appeared to be shutting down, their hearts kept ticking. This was the case with Alan. Other than having AIDS, he was a specimen of good health.

One day I was at the hospital, sitting in his room, wondering just how long his body could stand the ravages of the disease when he woke up from his coma and asked me to come over to him.

"Darling, come here. Please come close. I want to ask you something." At that exact moment between life and death, I thought something profound would be said regarding him standing on the precipice. So, I walked over, getting closer but not that close where I could smell the death emanating from his mouth.

A Victim No More

Softly, I replied, "I'm here, Alan. Can you see me?"

"Darling, please be honest with me. I want your absolute honest opinion." He paused slightly, and I wondered what deeply profound thought was going through his head with only precious hours left to live.

"Yeah, Alan. I'll always tell you the truth."

He was silent for a bit, his face contorted. Then his hands rose slowly, pointing towards the end of his bed. "Tell me, Suzie! What do you think of that horse's legs? Do you think he's sound?"

I stopped in my tracks. What do you say in a situation like that? I had heard that the dying sometimes wake from comas hours before they die in what is commonly called a surge. But I wasn't expecting it to happen. After my initial shock and unsure what to say or do, I did what I felt was right and told Alan that the horse was as sound as a horse could get. Pleased, Alan closed his eyes. He passed during the night.

When I called Jill with the news that Alan had passed, she was heart-broken. Alan was a loving and loyal friend to her over the years. His passing not only made her grieve for her friend but also mirrored her fears about her mortality and her own illness. AIDS was a quick death relative to her situation, but she was hoping for life as an option, and any mention of death would throw her into a depression.

Alan wanted to be cremated, so Theresa, Jimmy, and I got his ashes and spread them in a garden of roses. I'm pretty sure how we did it was illegal, but we could hear Alan directing us to the red ones, so we bid our friend goodbye at the cemetery in an unconventional way. Hopefully, Alan's spirit is alive in that rose bed. I can almost hear him telling a flower, "Darling, you really need a bit more rouge. This shade is absolutely perfect for you. ... Here, let's try some on."

Three & Me

Jill continued to heal, and she continued to write her book. I enjoyed reading the first 100 pages a zillion times until, finally, I was allowed to read more. It was an easy read, especially since I was so involved in the journey she was taking.

Reading what she wrote brought me even closer to her inner thoughts and feelings about battling such a disease. I was happily surprised to find out I was part of the story. But I was saddened at the same time that the story even needed to be written. I would close my eyes and try and wish her cancer away permanently so I'd have my friend with me forever.

One night, Jill and Charlie were out at a restaurant in Malibu when Michael Viner and Deborah Raffin approached them. Michael introduced himself as a talent manager, boasting a large and famous clientele, including Jacklyn Smith of *Charlie's Angels*. Deborah was a well-known movie-of-the-week actress and as sweet as one could be. According to Jill, Michael had a reputation for being a bit of a hustler, but he managed to talk her into representation for her book. His hook to reel her in was that he understood cancer since he was also recovering. (We'd find out later; however, that wasn't entirely true (although he did die from cancer many years later).

That night was the beginning of a business relationship between Jill and Michael. Deborah was added delight. From that day on, we would go out with them regularly. I remember driving in the back seat of Michael's car with Jill and Charlie when I heard a phone ring. We were going up Coldwater Canyon, and I couldn't figure out where a ringing phone could possibly be coming from. Michael picked up a receiver built into the console between the two front seats and began conversing. Jill, Charlie, and I were floored. Michael was probably the first person I ever knew with a car phone! After that, we all got them.

Charlie was preparing to film *Death Wish 3*, and Deborah was cast as his female lead. I'm pretty sure that Michael had a hand in that. Some scenes needed to be shot in New York City, so off we went. Michael and Deborah were always with us socially as we did New York together. Michael was incredibly friendly to me. He considered me part of the whole Jill and Charlie deal. I thought his sentiments were genuine, and I believed, for a very long time, that they were. He was all about Hollywood; his friends were only industry people; he had no use for regular Joes. In fact, Michael spent mornings, every single day, with Larry King at Nate and Al's in Beverly Hills. So, to be accepted by Michael Viner seemed like a huge deal.

Jill was turning 50 in April and decided to have a huge bash. She rented out one of the ballrooms at the Los Angeles Equestrian Center, which boasted a high-end reputation back then. I did the invitations for the party with a photo of Jill jumping over a five-foot fence (no helmet, though) and the tagline "Jill is Jumping into a New Decade." I was super excited about the party, and so was Jill. Of course, we went shopping, and I bought a beautiful outfit and could hardly wait to wear it. I also picked out a nice sport coat and pair of slacks for Yaniv. We were ready to party!

In the second week of April, Charlie flew to New York City to be on the *Today* Show to promote *Death Wish 3*. Jill called me the first day Charlie was gone and asked if I wanted to go paint the town red with her. Who could turn that down?! Not me! Yaniv was going to be in a class that night, leaving me with nothing better to do, so I happily accepted the offer! Off we went. We went to different clubs, always the trendiest, danced like crazy, ate as if we'd never seen food, and shared a few glasses of wine. (I just sipped a little.) We laughed at how silly we probably looked, like two teenagers carrying on. But it was a blast. We didn't get home until the wee hours.

When I woke up later that morning, the room turned upside down and spun like a dreidel. I had a horrible case of chills from a high

Three & Me

fever, and every bone in my body ached. Only a hoarse grunt came out when I tried talking to my dog. Wow. What had hit me?! Yaniv had already left for work when I woke up, leaving me feeling slightly abandoned in my hour of need.

Then my phone rang, and when I picked it up and tried to say something, only a croak, and some strange sounds came out. I heard a weird kind of noise in response. It was Jill. She was as sick as I was. We both tried laughing, but it was too hard. I tried whispering, which worked better. "Are you sick too?" I whispered, barely audible.

Jill could hear me, and in a faint whisper back, I heard, "Darling, this is a nasty bug we've caught!" Then she gave a little chuckle, accompanied by a prolonged, wet cough.

At the same time, we both realized that her party was exactly one week away! "Oh my gosh, Jill," I whined, "Your party!" At this point, we both regretted the night before. We figured we'd picked up influenza from one of the many people at the different clubs. It was a seriously contagious bug!

When I hung up with Jill, I called my dad and whispered that I was sick. He drove over and gave me an adjustment to my back and my neck. About an hour later, my fever broke without the use of fever reducers. My headache also went away, and I could stand without feeling dizzy. My dad would come and repeat the adjustments daily, and I soon felt better and better. My body could heal itself much faster with the aid of my dad's adjustments.

When Charlie got back the following day, he was furious. He wasn't angry about us going out and having fun; he was freaked by the germs that came with Jill's flu. Charlie was a huge germaphobe. If he so much as heard you sneeze over the phone, he was afraid he'd catch whatever you were sneezing. Charlie was also angry that we'd both gotten so sick right before the party. As I write this book, we are in the fourth year of the Covid-19 pandemic. I used to make fun of Charlie for being such a germaphobe, but occasionally, as I wear my mask, social distance, and take other precautions, I look upwards and utter, "I'm so sorry, Charlie. I'm so sorry I made fun of you. It turns out you were onto something way back then."

That flu knocked out any appetite I might have had. Already slim, I lost a massive amount of weight during that week. When I tried on the outfit I'd bought weeks before, it literally just hung on my body. I looked terrible.

Jill, too, was slowly getting better. Our voices gradually came back, and we'd chat on the phone. I was getting better quicker than she was, even though she was taking prescription medications to help her along. A couple of nights before the party, my phone rang. There was no caller ID back then, few answering machines, and no cell phones either. I was surprised to hear the voice on the other end when I answered it. It was Charlie. He was concerned about me making it to the party. "Charlie," I told him, "I'll make it. No matter what. But I probably won't look too good."

Charlie's response? "Oh, don't worry about that, Suzie. Lots of ugly people have been invited, and they'll probably all be there!" *THAT was supposed to make me feel better?!*

We had a really good laugh when I told Jill about Charlie's response. Of course, Charlie was trying to cheer me up, but in his own Charlie way, he muddled the entire thing! It wouldn't be the last time, either. Years later, we were driving on a highway in Vermont. The car in front of us didn't look like it had a driver. "See that?" I said to Charlie. "That's my destiny! One day, I'm going to be the little old lady behind the wheel that no one sees!"

There was no bigger tease than Charlie Bronson. In his way of thinking, it was OK when he teased, but he hated it if someone else picked

Three & Me

on me, or worse yet, if I picked on myself with self-deprecating humor. "That's not true, Suzie," he said. "You can still grow. In fact, I'm still growing. Whenever I go shopping, I need to buy a bigger size!" OK. That one knocked me to the floor. I tried hard not to laugh, but it took all I had not to.

Jill and I somehow pulled it together enough to make it to the party. Jill looked radiant in a spectacular outfit. And me, well, I had to scramble to put something together that fit, but I pulled it off. Yaniv, of course, was as handsome as ever. No one knew he wasn't some famous actor, and people would ask him repeatedly, "What were you in?" or "Do I know your work" or something equally outlandish.

After the party, some weeks later, when I was at the Bel Air house, Jill and I were in her dressing room, just passing time. I had finished reading more pages from her book. While I was practically memorizing every page word-for-word, something in the book bothered me. I had kept it to myself for all these many months. But sitting in that room and chatting with Jill about anything and everything, I decided I'd ask her about that one sticking point.

"Jill, in your book, you write that you lost a lot of friends when you got your cancer," I began, "but I haven't noticed much difference, really." I paused. "So, who left?"

Jill suddenly grew very serious. "I had quite a few people in my life who may not have been close friends, more social than not," she said. "And I have never heard from any of them. It's almost as if people are afraid of catching cancer. Or they don't know what to say to me. So, they just leave quietly." She paused, clearly thinking about what she had just said. "Good riddance, right?" She looked around the room. "Less weight to carry with me. Just like this house. I can hardly wait to get into my new home. Get rid of all this heavy weight off my shoulders—the burden of things. I want fewer things in my life. I only want quality in my life right now, Suzie. And that goes for people as well as possessions."

A Victim No More

Listening to her speak about how important it was to carry less weight, I realized she was right. So many people get caught up in needing bigger and better. Collecting people as well as things. Maybe those people brought status socially, but they also could be a considerable burden of toxic personalities or other negative attributes. I was quick to accept Jill's concept as a mantra for my own future. Less is always better (well, except for clothes). Carrying less human baggage was something I would make a priority. I learned so much from Jill during our time together, but this one lesson is one of the best. I'm now not afraid to eliminate toxic people from my life, thanks to Jill!

Jill was entering into a proactive wellness stage. Forced marches around the UCLA campus became a big part of our routine. Jill would open her stride, and it was all I could do to keep up. Pretty soon, I found myself going to Phidippides, a running store in Encino, to buy the perfect shoes for how I moved. It was owned by Kathy Kusner's boyfriend. Kathy was a famous Grand Prix rider on the horse show circuit who competed on the world stage. She brought home the team silver at the Pan-Am games in 1967, and in 1968, she was part of the United States Olympic Team. She was also a good friend of Jill's for many years. Kathy was in the store when I went in to buy the shoes and enjoyed hearing about why I needed to buy them. Her boyfriend fitted me correctly, and thankfully, with those shoes on my feet, I was quickly able to keep up with Jill.

Diet became extremely important to Jill. She researched cancer-preventing food sources and decided on a macrobiotic diet. Well, that meant I also ate seaweed and rice every time we were together. Thankfully, this phase didn't last that long. What did last, though, was the anti-sugar diet. I got off sugar, and so did Jill. To this very day, I don't ingest more than 40 grams per day, including the sugars found in food naturally and all processed sugars.

Holistic medicine, as well as conventional, was something she experimented with. Unfortunately, she landed in the examination rooms of a couple of sketchy people who sold her a bill of goods. My dad was a chiropractor and guided me to a combined holistic and conventional path many years prior, so my spider senses tingled every time Jill met with a charlatan. Thankfully I was able to give her my two cents worth and steer her away.

Finally, it happened. Jill's book, "Life Wish," was published. She began a robust public relations and marketing push, going on talk shows, giving interviews to different magazines like People and Us, and, to my delight, throwing book parties. I got to go with her when some of the TV tapings were local. I was delighted with the initial success of her book, having been a part of it for so long. She hired a young and talented publicist by the name of Lori Jonas, who has gone on to become one of the top publicists in the country today. (She discovered Seinfeld, among many other successes). I honestly believe Lori was critical in the book's success.

I attended the book party at the Bistro Garden in Beverly Hills. Jill had given me a beautiful outfit that didn't quite suit her anymore because it had a sheer bodice. I think the fact that she had to wear a prosthetic breast in her bra cup was the reason behind the gift. It was absolutely a beautiful outfit. My hair was now long and blonde, having been slowly lightened over the last two years. "Darling," Jill once said to me, "You know you won't be able to have dark hair forever, right?" I wasn't expecting to hear that, that's for sure. I asked her why not, and the response was immediate. "Because the older you get, the lighter your hair color should be. Otherwise, you look older than you should. Why do you think hair grays?"

"Because the roots run out of color, and we're living longer than we were originally designed to?" I responded.

"No, darling. It's because the skin ages and lighter tones suit that aged skin better."

Mind you; I was in my mid-30s when I heard this. I didn't think of myself as aging. But I thought about it and concluded that maybe she was right. After that comment, anyone older than 50 with dark hair stood out to me. So, I began adding subtle streaks to my hair until I was officially blonde two years later. And I've stayed that way, only now I'm adding darker low-lights to the blonde.

Another thing Jill alerted me to was the length of my hair. "Darling, you know at some point you will have to cut your hair much shorter than you wear it now." I was perplexed and asked her why. "Well, it's mostly because you have a young body. You're slim and petite, and someone will look at you from behind and think, 'My, she's a cute girl,' except when you turn around to face them, they'll think you're a hag!" Upon hearing that, I went inwardly psycho. She made me acutely aware of age with that one comment. And the funny thing is, now that I'm 70+, I actually worry about people seeing me from behind and thinking I'm young. Then, when I turn around, they'll look at my face with the word "hag" going off in their heads! If all of that weren't enough, Charlie informed me a long time ago that the older one gets, the more their lips disappear. No wonder I'm a head case about age!

I learned a few things from Jill about parties, especially with high-powered people attending. Some people walk into that situation and literally work the room, going from individual to individual. Then there are people who walk into a room, grab a drink and find a spot to settle into, letting people come to them. The latter of the two options suited me. So, at the book party at the Bistro, I went to the bar, ordered sparkling water, and stood at the corner of the bar sipping my drink. Men flocked to speak with me. Jill had gone into a private room to be interviewed by "People Magazine," and when she emerged, she couldn't help but notice the group of men surrounding me.

One of the men was Jerry Rubin from the Chicago 7; only I didn't know that then. He was an anti-Vietnam War protestor who was prosecuted with conspiracy charges. He was also charged with crossing state lines with the intention of causing riots. He was convicted at trial, but the Circuit Court of Appeals then voided the incitement conviction based on judicial misconduct. It also voided the contempt citation on the grounds that it required a jury trial.

As we spoke, I had no idea who he was, just that his name was Jerry. I did think, though, that he was pretty good-looking. He was not tall but well-dressed in his suit and tie. His dark hair and winning smile completed the picture. Surprisingly, he asked me out after we had chatted for a while. I had to tell him thank you, but no thank you. I was married. He handed me his business card anyway, just in case my situation changed. Not looking at or knowing what to do with the card, I slipped it into my purse and forgot about it.

Some time passed after the book party, and I forgot about the guy named Jerry. Then news reports surfaced about Jerry Rubin, one of the Chicago 7, being killed while jaywalking in Beverly Hills. When I saw his photo on TV, I gasped. I ran to get that purse. Tucked away in a pocket was his card. When I pulled it out, it said: Jerry Rubin, Chicago 7. I was literally chatting with history and had no idea. It wouldn't be the last time this happened.

After the book party ended, Jill and I quietly talked about the event upon returning to her house. "Well, you certainly know how to draw attention to yourself rather quietly," she said. "Well done! I liked that people came to you rather than you flitting around. Very classy, I must say." I was pleased to hear that. The last thing I ever wanted to do was embarrass Jill. My old insecurities sometimes crept up on me, throwing me back to my awkward junior high and high school self. I was happy that Jill was happy.

Jill would leave for Vermont in less than a month, and I already missed her even though she hadn't yet left. I had plans and a plane ticket to follow a month later. When I finally arrived in Lebanon, New

Hampshire, my luggage didn't. I flew from Boston to Lebanon on one of those super small commuter planes. It was a 12-seater. I never imagined such a small plane would lose my luggage. When the plane landed, the pilot got out and handed people their bags.

Mine was nowhere to be seen. I went into the parking lot to meet Chuck, the caretaker for the Bronsons' Vermont property. "Where's your luggage?" he asked. I told him it was missing. Once we got back to the house, Charlie asked me the same question. When I told him it was MIA, Charlie called the airline. Travel wasn't as computerized as it is now. Today it's almost impossible to lose a bag with Apple Tags, bar codes, and new systems in place. But back in the 1980s, not so much. Charlie reached an agent on the phone, and when he identified himself as Charles Bronson, the airline staff began falling over themselves to help. My bag arrived within hours of his phone call. They found the bag in Boston and flew it up as quickly as they could for Charlie. I wondered what would have happened if I had made the call. I would have seen my luggage at some point, but probably not a few hours later.

Jill and I had made plans to do a movie-thon. We wanted to rent and watch old movies for 24 hours non-stop. We bought a bunch of popcorn, hot dogs, and some candy. All we needed were the movies. We all piled into the Soup Can and headed to the Powerhouse to rent videos in Lebanon. Once there, we saw that all the rental movies we wanted were in the new VHS format. Jill and Charlie had a Betamax. We looked at Charlie, batted our eyelashes, and begged him to buy a new VCR. At the time, they were selling for about $1,600.00. A bit expensive, so Charlie hemmed and hawed. He hated change. He looked at his watch. It was already 7.00 pm. "Why should we buy it now? *Who will* assemble this thing in time for you to watch your movies? Why can't you two pick movies that are made for Betamax?"

"I'll put it together, Charlie," I said. Charlie looked aghast. He didn't think anyone but specialists could do anything with electronics, let alone a woman.

"You're going to put it together?" he asked incredulously. "You can't do that! How can you do that?"

I laughed. "Charlie," I said. "I assembled ours at home and my parents' VCRs and some of my friends." At this point, Charlie had no choice. He bought the VCR while Jill and I went crazy picking movies to rent. Jill couldn't stop laughing at Charlie caving so quickly.

As promised, I hooked up the VCR and set the clock and the timer. It took just a few minutes. To say Charlie was dumbfounded would be an understatement. As I was cleaning up the plastic, the wire ties, and the box pieces, Charlie got up and went into the garage. He was wearing his robe and slippers when he left. We could hear him banging around in the garage from inside the breezeway. Charlie eventually emerged with a beautiful wooden box in his hands. I was still on my knees on the floor when he presented it to me, almost like a Samurai presented his sword. Confused, I took the box. When I opened it, I saw the most pristine tool set I had ever laid eyes on. The tools practically sparkled. It was apparent these were no ordinary tools but a costly collection instead. Clearly, this had been a gift to him from someone, a gift that he had found no use for; until now.

I looked up at Charlie, baffled as to why he presented me with this toolbox. "Can you fix the antenna?" he asked. Jill about fell over. I nodded yes, and, indeed, fixed it. From that point on, Charlie had a whole new respect for me. I could tell him something, and he'd do it. If anyone else heard me tell Charlie how to do something or what to do in a situation, they'd cringe, waiting for what they thought was the inevitable explosive reaction. Instead of exploding, Charlie listened to me and took my suggestions. Jill used to laugh, telling anybody who would listen that I was the only person on the planet who could tell Charlie what to do.

A Victim No More

Toward the end of my stay, Jill and I told Charlie that we wanted to go to Doobies in Woodstock. Restaurant by day, dance club by night, it was one of the big hangouts for locals. A great band was playing, and Jill wanted to go out on the floor to dance. I did too. The musical beat was making it impossible to sit still. We had been dancing for a bit, enjoying the freedom of cutting loose, when a couple of the local guys decided to turn the dance floor into a mosh pit and slam dance. Slam dancing was just taking root in clubs across the country, but it hadn't yet hit Woodstock, Vermont, until that night. One of the guys made a beeline straight for Jill, and another made one toward me. Almost simultaneously, we were slammed. I flew into the railing while Jill was knocked in her chest, right at her scar. She let out a loud scream from the pain.

Within a second, Charlie jumped over the rail to the dance floor, quickly nabbed both guys and lifted them off their feet by the collars of their shirts. He was as angry as I'd ever seen him. Charlie had them against the rails, one hand on each guy, and from a distance, I could see absolute fear in their eyes. With a stern warning that if he ever saw them touch either one of us again, he would do some severe damage, he let them go. The guys wisely left. Jill and I looked at each other in wonderment. Then we both started laughing. We'd never seen two guys exit so fast in our lives. I guess it helped that Charlie was a famous "vigilante" from his *Death Wish* franchise.

The Vermont House.
The Soup Can is to the left.

Three & Me

Jill, the day she got her star. (Joan Rivers is in the background.)

The Other Shoe Always Drops

## EIGHT

The Other Shoe Always Drops

Later that same year, Jill and Charlie went to Vermont for the Christmas Holidays. I flew in to join them. We were all sitting around the living room when Jill suddenly vomited. Rushing to clean up, Charlie and I both had a look of dread on our faces. What did this mean? Then she started moaning in excruciating pain. Her back was killing her. Charlie quickly called a local doctor, who rushed over. We sat in the other room as Jill was examined behind a closed door. We were both silent, trying to hear what the doctor was telling Jill.

When the examination was over, the doctor called us in. Jill was suffering from a bad case of Shingles; the rash was slowly beginning to appear. Joyful at the news, Charlie and I hugged each other and breathed sighs of relief. The doctor couldn't explain the vomiting but said extreme pain can cause nausea. As Charlie and I silently did the happy dance, the doctor wrote a prescription for us to fill that would help alleviate her discomfort. Jill, meanwhile, looked at us like we'd both lost our minds. "Why are you both so happy I have Shingles?" she demanded. We both just stood there, feeling a tad sheepish. Shingles is not something you want anyone to have.

Charlie was the first to speak, "Jill, we aren't happy you *have* Shingles. We're just so happy that it is *just* Shingles and nothing else."

I nodded in agreement and could only come up with a feeble "Yeah."

Jill gave us both a scornful look, smiled suddenly, and said, "OK, I forgive you both. Now get me my medication. Quickly, mind you. I'm in serious pain!"

Three & Me

Grateful we'd dodged a bullet, Charlie and I rushed into Brownsville to fill the prescription. Life felt so good as we drove and cracked jokes along the way. Jill didn't have cancer. I was young and having the time of my life. In my carefree moments, I didn't see 1988 coming at me like a freight train. I would have some happy-go-lucky months ahead before March barreled down on me, changing my life forever. Theresa, who was stabbed on March 15th, would always say, "Beware the Ides of March." She was right.

# # #

Years earlier, when I lived in Israel, constantly under the threat of a terrorist attack, I needed to learn how to shoot automatic rifles. I was not too happy about that because, personally, I never liked guns. It didn't matter whether other people had guns; I just personally never wanted one. The Israeli army issued an M-16 rifle to Yaniv to keep at home during his civilian time off. We kept it near the coat rack, behind a wall, close to the front door. I kept the magazine on the shelf above the coat rack. Every morning I would have to look at that damn rifle, and I hated it.

At that time, we lived in a beautiful guest house owned by the Flanter family at the junction where three roads met and funneled into the main highway. Before that, we had a smaller place down the street where I spent the Yom Kippur War. Dana Flanter, at ten years old, was a very precocious little girl. I gave her English lessons then, even though she didn't need them. She told me that there was a beautiful apartment that had never been used at the bottom of their house. Dana being Dana, marched me over to her mother's kitchen and clearly stated that she wanted me and Yaniv to live below them in the apartment. Her mother, Shifra, was amused by Dana's forthright command. After Shifra spoke to her husband, Gideon, about it, it was a done deal. We were moving in. I loved my time there.

The Other Shoe Always Drops

Terrorist activity had ramped up in Israel during that period. A few months prior, on July 4th, 1976, while the United States was celebrating its Bicentennial, terrorists had fireworks of their own to set off. I was actually moments away from being blown to bits by a bomb set off at Zion Square. I stood on that corner twice that day, patronizing a camera store/photo lab named Photo Prisma. I was halfway up the street on my way back to school when a refrigerator rigged with a bomb blew, killing 75+ people. So, when I was told that our neighborhood was assigned guard duty to rotating households, Yaniv took me out into an open area near the mountain and taught me how to shoot both an M-16 and an Uzi.

It took me a while to get used to holding a rifle correctly without getting the painful kick onto my shoulder, but I eventually figured it out. My automatic weapon of choice, however, was the Uzi. It had a strap, and I could hold it at my hip and spray. That was fun, as long as I was shooting at the dirt or a hill. I could never imagine aiming at any living thing—the opposite intent of learning to use the rifle.

151

A few years later, when we were back in the United States, my brother took great pleasure in driving Yaniv and me out to the firing range in the hills above Hansen Dam. Yaniv was a good ex-soldier. He delighted in shooting at targets. Me, not so much. But I had to be a good sport and fire away since Yaniv loved it so much. Because I already knew the ins and outs of an M-16, I asked Jerry if I could shoot his. His rifle was semi-automatic, not fully automatic, like in Israel. The United States gun laws (thankfully) prohibited fully automatic weapons.

Unfortunately, or fortunately, depending on how you look at it, I have excellent hand-eye coordination. This allowed me to shred the bull's eye easily. I was a better shot than Jerry, who practiced relentlessly. My brother was astonished at my accuracy, as was Yaniv. Jerry had multiple friends who were in the LAPD. He kept telling me I should become a cop and then a sniper. Yeah, right! No, thank you. I was only playing Annie Oakley occasionally to make them both happy. I had no intention of shooting guns ever.

# # #

One evening Jill phoned me up. "Darling, I'm sending our van to Shari and Tommy's to pick up our horses, and we're going to pick up Aero also. I leased out Sycamore Stables down the street, and I think you'll like it much better." I told her to go ahead. Driving over the hill to Malibu would be better than driving from Encino to the barn near Griffith Park.

Jill had finally moved into her Malibu home, downsizing to 15,000 square feet from the mansion in Bel Air. The Malibu house still seemed incredibly large to me, but it was laid out nicely with a great open concept, high ceilings, and beautiful high-end appointments, and it had a nice flow to it. One of the rooms Jill had built during the remodel was a meditation room right off of her expansive walk-in closet. The meditation room became our substitute for her Bel Air dressing room, and we'd hang out in there. Charlie also purchased a beach house for Jill on Old Malibu Road. We'd go to the beach house often to enjoy the incredible energy of the ocean, where I often spent the night.

On a day when I was happily enjoying the Malibu sunshine, the light breeze against my skin, and the sound of my horse's hooves as he cantered around the ring, my brother was beginning his march toward his end. All the pieces of his life's puzzle were being assembled, troubled piece by troubled piece. Just a few remained to complete the puzzle that I would try and solve for the rest of my life. He was working on those pieces at a fevered pitch.

A few years prior, Jerry bought a ranch-style home in Northridge, put in a pool, and hosted many swim parties with his friends. Inside my brother, a perfect storm was brewing that would lead him down a deadly path. For one, he blew a lot of cocaine, which can cause paranoia. He also had the genetic predisposition from my mother to become paranoid schizophrenic. He was presenting signs to the trained eye, but no one caught on. Except I could tell, something was very wrong. He was either hopped-up or down-down. But did I say anything to anyone? NO. Did I try to talk to my brother about these odd behaviors and his drug use? NO. So, what exactly did I do? NOTHING. I pulled away. I could help a friend recover from cancer. I could help another deal with her post-stabbing PTSD. And I could help an AIDS patient die. But did I do ANYTHING to help my brother? NO. I'm still haunted by my inaction when my brother needed me most. I will be haunted by it until the day I am wrapped in my life's tapestry as I am laid to rest.

While I was riding my horse on that beautiful Malibu day, my brother put on a crash helmet, got into his souped-up Buick, and took off like a bat out of hell. It didn't take police long to witness him speeding dangerously down the streets of Los Angeles. When he raced onto the freeway, cops' lights blazing behind him, he added the California Highway Patrol to the parade of black and whites following his car. Jerry was now the object of a high-speed chase. Eventually, tired of racing around the city, he pulled up in front of his house. (WTF?) When he got out of his car, the cops and the CHP officers pounced on him, beating him to a bloody pulp during his arrest, and hauled him off to jail. This is what happens when you engage in a high-speed chase. Adrenaline pumps ferociously through the pursuing officers' veins. It becomes a visceral chase, and once they nab their perp, usually all hell breaks loose. It's not something I condone because once someone is handcuffed, they are rendered defenseless, so physical punishment isn't necessary. But try explaining that to a group of alpha males chasing someone. I believe such behavior harkens back to primal hunting behavior. There is no chance for a peaceful end to a high-speed chase.

Jerry was horrified at the beating he got. For some inexplicable reason, he wasn't expecting it. He was a black belt, after all. Black belts don't get beat! My parents also were aghast. Me? I had no idea that Jerry even did this. No one told me. I only heard about it from the radio, a small news snippet about a high-speed chase ending safely with no one hurt. That was it. I had no idea it was my brother they were talking about. My parents eventually bailed Jerry out of jail, and he returned home bruised and battered.

As for the reason for the chase? Jerry alleged that chiropractors from that now-defunct peer review were trying to assassinate him. (Chiropractors? Really?) He would point to bullet holes in his house where they allegedly fired at it. He claimed his dog was kidnapped and then mysteriously returned. He had a whole host of odd allegations. I heard some from him on the last day I saw him alive: Thanksgiving dinner at my parents' home. I could hardly wait to get out of there; the insanity was just too much for me. The stories were incredible. My mom and dad, as well as Yaniv, believed his tales. I can't blame them for their gullibility. Parents always want to believe their children. There was some credibility to some of what he said. He did successfully eliminate a giant cash cow for some corrupt individuals. But all of this? Bullets? Dognapping? It was too much for me to swallow.

Being me, I pushed the insanity of Thanksgiving quickly out of my mind. I figured at some point Jerry would tire of all his battles, or at least age out of them, and find some peace somewhere. I still had no idea he was waiting to be tried for his high-speed chase because I didn't even know he had had the high-speed chase. Such was the lack of transparency in my immediate family.

# # #

In early December of that year, Theresa called me to let me know she was admitted to a hospital in Beverly Hills for pain management. She lost the feeling in her legs and feet and couldn't walk. Of course, I went and visited her. Theresa looked very happy when I entered the room, but I had nothing to do with her happiness. It had to do with her feeling safe inside the confines of the hospital walls. Security was tight getting into and out of that hospital. I attributed the heightened security level to the high percentage of narcotics used for pain that were stored on the property. For Theresa, that security was her saving grace. No one in except those she wanted in. She loved the set up in the hospital, and she participated in all the group therapies.

I thought she'd be out fairly quickly, so I went and visited her every day for the first two weeks. By about the end of the second week, I realized she wouldn't be released any time soon. She still couldn't feel her feet. I wondered if this wasn't part of her PTSD, this need to be hospitalized. I'm not a doctor, psychologist, or counselor, so I'm only guessing that some of her symptoms may have resulted from having been stabbed by a lunatic. Since I'd known Theresa, she was always in and out of hospitals. It worried me that perhaps she wanted to be hospitalized just for the safety factor. She was a single woman living alone, and Arthur Jackson had begun sending her messages from jail, threatening that he planned to kill her with a gun the next time he tried. He wanted her dead. If I were in that situation, I might react the same way as Theresa. So, I never judged her. I just went along with everything, being as good a friend as possible.

While still in the hospital, she met another patient, a tall, ruggedly handsome man named Phil Peters, who was also an actor. He was well known in the soap opera *As the World Turns* and had roles in The *Commish* and other productions. Theresa fell for him, elated to have a strong man beside her. The feeling was mutual. Phil adored Theresa. So much so that they eventually married. She sounded like a schoolgirl when she called me after their first meeting. She was smitten, and I was so happy for her.

# # #

I've always had truly vivid dreams when I sleep. The funny thing about my dreams is that I actually remember them. One night in February

1988, I dreamt I heard a knock at my front door. When I opened it, my brother, Jerry, stood on my doorstep, holding the same M-16 I used on the shooting range.

"Jerry, what are you doing here? And why are you holding that gun?" I asked.

"I'm sorry, Suzie," he said. "This is something I have to do. I have no choice." His voice sounded sad in my dream.

I woke up in a sweat and in a panic. What the hell did THAT mean? Yaniv was sound asleep beside me, but I was wide awake. It seemed so real. Was Jerry coming to shoot me? Was he coming to tell me he was going to shoot somebody else? AND WHY THE HELL DID I BELIEVE IT WAS A WARNING?! Was I becoming as paranoid as my family?

It was just a little after 4 a.m. My dad would be in his office at that time of day, preparing to treat the actors, producers, directors, and film and TV crew members that had to be at work early in the morning. So, I dialed his number. His receptionist wouldn't be in until 8.00 a.m. He would be responsible for treating his patients and answering his phone for the first four hours of his long workday (not that too many people called at those hours). The answering service picked up my call. I didn't want to leave a message so early in the morning, afraid I would worry my dad. I hung up.

Debating whether or not it was a good idea to call my mother or a really terrible one, I finally gave in. I had been through the trenches with her, and I reasoned that getting an earful for waking her up wouldn't be the worst thing that had happened to me. So, I called her. She picked up, and I heard a groggy, "Hello?"

"Mom!" I began, "I just had the scariest dream..."

The Other Shoe Always Drops

She cut me off. "You woke me up in the middle of the night to tell me you had a nightmare?" She did not attempt to hide her contempt for being disrupted from a sound sleep.

"No... Mom... Listen!" I had such urgency to my voice that she stopped protesting and actually listened. I told her about my dream. The reaction I got was *not* the reaction I was expecting. She burst out laughing. OK. So that threw me for a loop. "Mom, what's so funny?"

"You are! You're the funny one!" She continued to laugh. "*You just dreamt you had sex with your brother! The gun is a phallic symbol.*" She laughed some more, then told me she was going back to sleep and ended the call.

SEX WITH MY BROTHER?!!! Well, she could have said anything to me but that! I definitely was *not* dreaming about sex with my brother. That idea was so gross; I literally wanted to take a shower after hearing it! After that, I walked in circles around the living room, went into my backyard and stared at the stars above, and hung out with my now awake dogs. I did anything to stay awake, afraid that if I fell asleep, something terrible would happen. By the time Yaniv woke up to leave for work, I was already showered and dressed, looking slightly like the mad woman from Borneo.

"What's up with you?" he asked me. "I woke up earlier, and you weren't in bed. Now you're dressed, and you look terrible!" I told Yaniv I had a nightmare, but I didn't tell him what the nightmare was about lest he, too, tell me the gun was phallic. He shrugged, kissed me, and got ready for work. Sometimes it seemed like Yaniv was blissfully unaware of the storms swirling around in my head. He was so even-keel, and I was in a range of emotions from 1-100 on a daily basis.

As I look back on the dream that night, I wonder, was my subconscious throwing all the red flags my brother was exhibiting together

157

and signaling that danger was coming? I believe it was. Brains absorb snippets from life and then assemble everything in the background of the subconscious, sending it back in many ways. In this case, I believe that is what provoked my dream. The trick is to recognize what your brain is telling you and to listen to it. Again, I feel I should have acted on my quickly emerging fear that a horrible event was about to occur because when it did, it was the most significant punch life could throw at me.

California evokes strong reactions from people, but whether or not they like the politics, hate the taxes or the cost of living, or are afraid of earthquakes, floods, or fires, there is one thing that almost everyone can agree on. The weather is fantastic for 12 out of 12 months. If you have rain at the beginning of the week, it can quickly turn warm and then hot. In Southern California, you can drive to a ski slope in the morning and be surfing in the afternoon at the beach. California has it all. Mountains, lakes, rivers, beaches, year-round golf courses, deserts, and forests, and it is home to just about every outdoor recreation imaginable.

Two weeks after my dream, on March 9th, 1988, I woke to a typically blue and cloudless Southern California sky. Temperatures were forecast to be in the mid-70s. Perfect weather for just about anything. In general, I wake up with my tail wagging. I am immediately happy, talkative, and energetic, ready to face the new day's challenges. I am the kind of person you'd like to swat while you're trying to wake up. Yaniv had a hard time that morning with me chattering in his head as he tried to have a little peace before he began his day. He was grumpy as he left the house. On the other hand, I happily talked to the dogs as I got ready for work.

I had a photo shoot scheduled at a North Hollywood giftware company. I was art directing the photography for products that would be in the next year's catalog. After that, I had plans to drive out to the barn for a photo shoot there. Jill wanted photos of Zuleika jumping her horses and various barn shots for an ad showcasing Zuleika Farm in one of the equestrian magazines.

John Oliver, the photographer, and I were in the warehouse at the gift-ware company. We had created a photo studio in one of the corners, erecting a seamless background, setting the lighting, and arranging the products for the shoot. I had a scheme sheet telling me which products would be in what category and which products would be on which page. There were hundreds and hundreds of items to be shot. The catalog usually was over 100 pages long. It was a colossal undertaking keeping every detail straight. This was being done in the era before digital cameras. We had to painstakingly light each shot and then shoot Polaroids. After that, we corrected the flares or shadows, then shoot another Polaroid. We would repeat this process until the many items in the shot were perfectly lit. It could take hours to get one shot. Then we'd have to shoot a test and send the transparency to a lab to ensure the exposure and color were correct. If it was, we committed to film. Then we moved on to the next shot. It took many weeks to shoot a catalog of this magnitude.

159

The radio droned on in the background as white noise while we worked. Shot after shot, we slogged through the many products. We had a mandatory break at lunchtime because the warehouse staff took theirs. I left the darkness of the studio area to go into the beautiful, bright sunlight of that March day. It was cold in the warehouse, and I relished the sun's warmth on my body. I wanted to go grab a sub sandwich close by. I got in my car, closed the door, turned on the ignition, put my car into reverse (I drove a stick shift), and backed up as the radio kicked on with the noon news. I was in a zone, not really listening to the news, when I thought I heard my brother's name mentioned. Puzzled, I stopped the car, now acutely aware of what was being said. When you hear something you're unprepared to hear, your mind does funny things. In this case, my mind would not connect the dots with the information coming to me over the radio waves. According to the news, my brother was dead from gunfire on the floor of the

Van Nuys Courthouse. For a second, my mind just blanked it all out, then suddenly kicked in with the realization that I really did hear that. WHAT THE HELL HAPPENED?

It took a minute to absorb, but I still wasn't sure it was Jerry. I parked my car, ran back into the offices, and asked if I could use the phone. (Not sure why I did that because there was a phone in my car.) I dialed my parents' number, and my dad answered. MY DAD ANSWERED AT NOON! That was enough to let me know this was bad. He was never home at that hour. He worked from 4 a.m. to 6 p.m. every single day except Thursday. This was a WEDNESDAY!

"Daddy?" That was the only thing I could say. Then silence.

I heard him softly say, "Yes, Suzie. It's Jerry."

My head exploded. Grief grabbed me by the throat, and I felt suddenly suffocated. I couldn't breathe. I was staring at the walls of an office, wondering if this was a dream or reality. My baby brother, my partner in crime, Daniel Boone, to my Davey Crockett, was full of bullet holes on a cold tile floor, his life's blood oozing out, his brains spattered randomly on the courtroom gallery. I couldn't wrap my mind around it. Feeling numb, like I was free-falling into a dark abyss, I walked out of the offices and told the receptionist I wouldn't be back that day. As I walked towards my car, I looked up at the sky. It was the most beautiful blue I'd ever seen in my life. I couldn't grasp how the sky could be so blue, how the birds could still chirp as they flew by me, and how the sun could feel this good when my world just literally imploded. I got in my car and left, to where I had no idea.

Waves of grief came at me from all directions. If I could visualize that sensation, I would suggest that it felt like white cannon balls from multiple cannons fired at me again and again and again. The waves and the cannon balls kept coming. I was sobbing, not sure what freeway I was on or why I was even on a freeway, to begin with. I called

The Other Shoe Always Drops

a longtime school friend and successful psychologist, Bradley Salter, from my car phone. He was able to talk me down enough so I could orient myself and my location.

I thought of going to my parent's house in Bel Air, but the thought of facing them made me cringe. I couldn't. I partially blamed them. But mostly, I blamed myself for what had happened. Going there would be too painful. I didn't know what I'd say to them. I also knew that Yaniv would go there immediately once he found out. I tried calling Yaniv at work, but I couldn't find him. I knew I'd talk to him before the day was over. I decided to drive to Jill and Charlie's house in Malibu.

Over the past few years, I confessed my feelings and fears about my brother to Jill. I told her about my dream after I spoke with my mom. While my mother decided I was dreaming of sex with my brother, Jill saw the dream as a warning. When the news came over their radio about a gunman dead in the Van Nuys Courthouse, Jill knew immediately who it was.

161

It was Charlie who opened the door when I rang the bell. His face was ashen. He threw his arms around me in a protective embrace. I sobbed into his arms, the kind of gut-wrenching sobs that only the most profound grief could manufacture. Jill ran over and put her arms around me, leading me into the meditation room, where I sat in a stupor. Sometimes there are no words for a situation. Sometimes shared silence can be just what someone needs. Jill knew that instinctively. She sat with me, sometimes hugging me as I cried, never once leaving my side.

Charlie was in his own state of shock. He paced around, trying to figure out how to make me feel better. He decided apple juice would be just the thing. "Here, drink this," he said as he gently offered the glass to me. "It might make you feel a little better."

I dutifully complied, drinking every drop. I handed the glass back to Charlie with a weak smile. He took off and refilled the glass with more apple juice. I swallowed that glass too, and, you guessed it, he ran and filled yet another glass and another. I don't remember how many glasses of apple juice I drank, but suddenly, my stomach churned and flipped upside down. The day's events and all the juice caused my stomach to protest violently. I ran to the bathroom and upchucked it all right into the toilet.

Taking shelter in Malibu was just what I needed. I could compose myself in front of people I didn't need to apologize to. I was able to garner strength through their gifts of love and understanding. After about six hours, I could drive over to my parents' house to face what I really didn't want to—the truth.

Yaniv greeted me at the front door when I arrived. He gave me a huge hug, the kind where I could feel he wished away the day's events but knew he couldn't. The first thing my mom did was show me Jerry's wallet. He'd dropped by the night before to give it to them. They told me he had given his car to Yolanda, his girlfriend, the night before. At this point, I'm wondering why they didn't call somebody. Why didn't they call the police? These were the classic behaviors of someone intent on committing suicide.

(I snuck around with a boy when I was 15 and was taken to the police! But the lunacy of my brother's behaviors brought no such reaction.) Had they called, Jerry would have been locked up for his own protection on a 5150. I have no idea what went through their minds on March 8th. Jerry could have been saved. My heart deflated, and my anger rose, but I knew this wasn't the time for recriminations. I could see and feel their hurt. Expressing my feelings would only hurt them more, and it wouldn't bring Jerry back. Nothing would.

Jerry committed suicide by cop. The week before, he had gone on trial for the high-speed chase that no one had told me about. He was convicted of speeding in a trial, but no one told me about either. Unfortunately, my brother had conflated the speeding trial with all

The Other Shoe Always Drops

of the litigation he had going on with the state over his license, with the chiropractors he'd neutralized, and with his RICO trial. In his now delusional mind, he saw the speeding trial as an all-or-nothing, make-it-or-break-it deal. Because he had lost that trial the week before, he walked into the courthouse, took a judge and a prosecutor hostage, and demanded a new trial. He didn't understand that he was only convicted of *speeding*. A traffic violation! A misdemeanor!

His mind wasn't his own. He had wallowed in self-pity at home, obviously festering over this "huge" loss. He then made his plans. On March 9th, he woke up and immediately snorted a lot of cocaine and prepared to die. He'd written several suicide notes, which he mailed right before entering that courtroom. (They all hit on March 10th.) He knew he wasn't walking out alive. A bailiff shot and killed him after Jerry fired at him first. Thankfully, the bailiff, who was shot in the stomach, survived after surgery, and no one besides my brother was hurt. Still today, I am grateful there were no deaths other than my brother's. And as far as the fear that Judge Harwin and then-prosecutor Jessica Silver felt that horrible morning, I am still so very sorry they had to experience that.

The irony of what happened that day hit me hard. While I was shooting photos, my brother was shooting bullets. To this day, it's hard for me to use the terms "photo shoot" or "shoot" when talking about photos.

Until then, no one had entered a courthouse with a gun and triggered a gunfight. At least not at the Van Nuys Courthouse. Those metal detectors you see in courthouses today? Courtesy of my brother. He became the biggest news story the country over. People in little towns heard about my brother's last stand. And it was a story that wouldn't die. It was everywhere I went, allowing me no chance to grieve privately. Photos appeared in the paper and on the news of my brother's older Springer Spaniel, Boo Boo, labeling her a vicious guard dog. I ended up taking Boo Boo home with me, and I can tell you she was

Three & Me

no guard dog. At that point in her life, she was blind and deaf, not to mention the fact that Springer Spaniels are bred for their sweet dispositions.

I don't know how many people have had to open the morning paper and see a full-size photo of a close relative, in this case, my brother, lying dead in a pool of blood. I'm still scarred from the headlines, the photos, the news footage, and the sensationalized media reporting exaggerated facts. At least I can manage it now. At first, I was ashamed and embarrassed. Then I became angry with myself for not doing enough to stop him. And now? Well, every time I hear of a shooting, my heart shatters. I wish there were a way to tell every potential gunman out there that not only are they hurting their targets and those families, but they are killing their own families at the same time, sentencing them to a lifetime of shame and grief. My dad died with tears of sorrow over my brother's last stand staining his cheeks. My mother died from a broken heart, having lost the will to live. Me? I go on. But I know, and now you know, I am the sister of a gunman. It's nothing I can change. History is cast in stone. It is always there, never to be altered in any way. Sadly, I lived this history.

Harkening back to the sixth grade when Jerry had his hair completely buzzed off, the curious children demanded answers. As adults, they still demanded answers from me. I felt thrown back to that time, fending off the curious "rubber-neckers." In the aftermath, I got calls from all over the country from people I either hardly knew or people I didn't know at all, demanding answers. An extended family member, who was utterly agitated many months after Jerry's death, called me, demanding I explain to him everything that happened. The pain inside me would not subside. Whenever some idiot thought I owed him or her an explanation, they cut away at my heart. For the record, I don't owe anyone any explanation. Life is what it was. I can't change it.

The night after my brother's shooting, I went to Jill and Charlie's for dinner. Yaniv wanted to go to my parent's house. Being left alone with

The Other Shoe Always Drops

my thoughts was more than I could handle. Additionally, my parents were planning Jerry's funeral for the next day, and I couldn't take that. I was still too angry with them for standing idly by when he divested himself of his worldly possessions.

A film shoot was taking place in the house across the street from Jill and Charlie. At the time, Wink Martindale owned the house and had leased it out as a location to a production company. After dinner, Jill and I wanted to see what was going on. Once Charlie caught wind of our idea, he put his foot down. "You are not going into that house!" he commanded of both of us. "You're going to be recognized!" We both looked Charlie straight in the eyes and said we wouldn't go.

Charlie went into his study to drink his Campari, something he did every night until he found out a couple of years later, that boiled bugs gave it a rich red color, at which point he stopped cold turkey. (Charlie was too creeped out about drinking boiled bugs to ever pour another glass again.) As soon as Charlie was tucked away in his study, Jill and I snuck out the back door and went across the street to the movie set. We couldn't tell what kind of film or television project was being shot, so we found our way to the craft services table and helped ourselves to some fruit. As we were standing around trying to blend in with the production, one of the crew looked over and recognized Jill. He nicely came over and told us it was a closed set, and we had to leave.

So, with our tails between our legs, we headed out of the film set towards Jill and Charlie's house. But there was one problem. The back gate had been locked. We couldn't enter through the front door because we'd run into Charlie. Looking straight at me, Jill uttered the words I didn't want to hear. "You're going to have to climb the wall and unlock the gate," she said.

I had no idea how I was going to scale that eight-foot wall. After what seemed an eternity trying to figure things out, I looked at Jill and told her I needed to somehow get on her shoulders. The two of us looked ridiculous trying to pull that off, but somehow, I managed to get onto Jill's shoulders and pull myself up to a standing position. We were so wobbly that we could have crashed easily and fallen. I grabbed the top of the wall, hoisted myself over the top, and then froze with fear as I realized I had to jump eight feet down to the cement pathway.

"Jill, that's a huge drop! How the hell am I going to make it down?"

"Very carefully, Suzie. Charlie will kill us both if you injure yourself!" *Well, those were comforting words!*

I decided to consider it a dismount from a very large horse. It took a while, but I managed to maneuver myself around to hang from my fingers and let myself drop with a thud to the ground below. It hurt like a son of a gun, so it took me a while to get back up and unlatch the gate.

166

Sheepishly, we let ourselves in the back door where Charlie was waiting with his arms folded. "I was wondering how you planned on getting in," he said, very much annoyed with the both of us.

"Charlie, how did you know we went over there?" Jill asked.

"I looked out the window and saw you both walk across the street after I told you not to go. They busted you, didn't they?!"

Jill and I sheepishly admitted we shouldn't have gone. Then we went into her meditation room and laughed at how funny the entire thing was. For a brief moment, I felt normal after my brother's actions. For that, I was so incredibly grateful.

Life wasn't easy in the aftermath of Jerry's death. He was a gunman. In the press, he was labeled a *lunatic gunman*, words that cut right through me for so many reasons. I remembered the little boy, the sweet freckled nose and long eyelashes. I mentally recalled all the good and couldn't reconcile his last years on earth with my memories of him as the beautiful child I grew up with. How could that gunman be my baby brother? How could he even be dead? He was a ball of happiness and energy until he got consumed by those awful lawsuits. It was a reality I struggled with for many, many years. I needed an out. And I needed it badly.

With gratitude, I headed to Vermont to visit Jill and Charlie on their fall trip. After six months of media coverage, it would get me away from Los Angeles and the constant articles about my brother in the *"Los Angeles Times."* I was so grateful to finally get a break.

It's cold in Vermont in the fall. In fact, there was a 90-degree differential between the San Fernando Valley of Los Angeles, where I lived, and Vermont. So, there really isn't much to do besides hang out around the fireplace, go to the Woodstock Inn for lunch or dinner, or bundle up and walk. And there was always television.

The World Series was on, and Charlie and I were glued to the TV set. Jill was not into baseball at all, but I was and still am. She sat in the sitting room and read while Charlie and I cheered on the Dodgers. They were up against Oakland, and the teams were well-matched.

Unfortunately for me, I wasn't going to ride out the entire world series in Vermont. My flight home was right in the middle of one of the critical games. I was going nuts. If the Dodgers lost, they'd be out. Charlie drove me to the small airport in Lebanon, New Hampshire, and we listened to the game on the radio. Once we got to the airport, Charlie came in with me to check in and asked the gate agent if we could hang out in the parking lot instead of at the gate. This was way before 9/11, so the gate agent agreed, saying someone would come to get me right before takeoff. The airport is teeny tiny, so there's minimal action. As Charlie and I listened to the radio, the game appeared to be heading in the right direction for the Dodgers. A bit later, I saw a plane land. A few people disembarked, and after a few minutes, we both saw the pilot running on the tarmac, headed directly toward the parking lot. He approached the car on Charlie's side and told him I needed to board. I hugged Charlie goodbye, and the pilot and I walked to the plane together. The Dodgers won that game.

When I was back home, Charlie and I continued to follow the Series together over the telephone. To our mutual delight, the Dodgers won the Series. A hobbled Kirk Gibson had ended the Series with a beautiful walk-off home run in the bottom of the ninth. We cheered like maniacs watching Kirk Gibson make his painful way around the horn. Jill was convinced both of us had completely taken leave of our senses, but we didn't care. We were both too happy with the win!

Once I was back in Los Angeles, it was the same old, same old. Months and months would go by, and still, the story would not die. Whenever I thought I could watch the news again or pick up a newspaper, there would be another story in the front section referring to my brother shooting up the Van Nuys Courthouse. I got to the point where I wanted off the crazy ride I was on.

I was an instructor at the Art Center College of Design back then, and they opened up a Swiss campus in the town of Vevey, right next to Nestle's headquarters. Instructors were encouraged to spend a term on the Swiss campus, bringing an American slant on design to Europe. Europe, from a design standpoint, was always the trendsetter. Art Center was more of an American institution, especially in automotive design, and American instructors were much in demand.

I threw my name into the hat to go to Switzerland, and, luckily for me, I was accepted into the program. I had an excellent reputation as a tough-as-nails instructor. My classes were much anticipated by students. When I arrived in Switzerland, my reputation had preceded me, and an enthusiastic group of students awaited my arrival.

Yaniv hated the idea of me leaving for those months, but he under-stood I needed an out. He had watched me under the pressure cooker that was now my new normal and agreed that changing scenery in a foreign country was an excellent way to heal. Additionally, he was working on yet another degree, and my time away would give him the peace he needed to concentrate on his thesis, so he became whole with my decision to live abroad for a few months. While happy for me, Jill and Charlie were sad to see me go, but they, too, understood.

The day before I was to fly to Switzerland through London, a Pan Am flight leaving London for New York blew up 40 minutes after takeoff over Lockerbie, Scotland. I hated hearing about aviation disasters, especially since I was nearly in one myself. In 1976, I was on TWA Flight 1 out of JFK headed to LA when we had one of the closest near misses in aviation history for that time. The pilot banked hard right, putting the plane's wings nearly perpendicular to the ground to avoid a collision. It all happened in what seemed like slow motion, so it was difficult to tell how close to death we actually came that day. It registered only when I read the news reports about that near miss in "Time Magazine."

When I arrived in a still-shocked London, the plane was met with armed military. They escorted us all off the plane. Those whose final destination was London went one way, and those who were connect-ing were ushered into an amphitheater of sorts. It was a large room with concrete steps that we were supposed to sit on while we waited for our connections. Our luggage was taken off our arriving flights and searched and scanned. We then had to ID our bags before they were loaded onto our connecting flights.

We were not allowed to talk. We could read quietly. There were no backs to the stair seats, so sitting still quickly became highly uncom-fortable. If we moved around too much, a guard came over and told us to sit still. If we had to go to the toilet, we had to raise our hand, and an armed person would escort us to and from the restroom. My itinerary had a five-hour layover, which meant I was stuck in that room, on those steps, under guard for that duration. I prayed my flight would leave on time. Every minute in that horrible room was excruciating. No food or water was available, adding to the discomfort. I saw one person completely lose it, arguing with one of the guards. Apparently, he moved around too much. He was taken away. To where I had no idea. Just that he never returned. It felt like I was in prison.

Finally, my flight was called for boarding. Everyone on my flight was ordered to stand up. We would be collected individually and placed in a straight line which we were not allowed to breach under any circumstances. Armed guards then escorted us as we marched single file to our flight. The airport was eerie as we walked to our awaiting plane. There were no crowds. No passengers in seats near the gates. No airline personnel were anywhere except the one lone steward who would check our boarding passes. The lights were dimmed, and the fading sunlight added to the macabre appearance of London Heathrow Airport. The only time I had ever seen an airport that empty was when I landed in Israel during the war.

After that arduous journey, I landed in Switzerland and spent the first night at my friend Paul Hauge's house. He had a colossal chateau that he shared with another friend of mine, Hal Frazier. Paul and Hal were the co-chairs of my graphic design department, and it was wonderful seeing them. After staying up late and chatting endlessly, I finally got to sleep in a most comfortable bed and nodded off into a deep and untroubled sleep for the first time in months.

I quickly found a great apartment, which I loved, near the Chateau Chillon, an 11th-century castle with a torture chamber. My apartment was the Grand Hotel, where it was said Mussolini once stayed when it was still a hotel.

I unpacked my suitcase and settled in. The next day, I took the train to Marseilles, which put me there on New Year's Eve. Huge mistake.

Marseilles is a horrible city filled with drunken sailors and many crooks. Especially at New Year's! However, I was on my way to a town called Grasse to meet a friend of my friend, Cartie Donohoe, who kindly offered me the use of a car for the time I would be in Europe. I toughed it out in Marseille for the night, woke up the next day, and caught the train to Grasse. After being hosted for a few days by Cartie's girlfriend—now his wife and her family—it was time to drive back to Switzerland.

The drive was magical. Europe is a most beautiful place, even in winter. The skies were a dark gray and never seemed to let the sunshine in, but the vast green of the meadows, huge mountains, quaint towns —it was all so breathtaking. I'm a Tour de France junkie. I never miss it. And I imagined that I was driving on the same roads and doing the same climbs that the Peloton travels during the month of July.

The time I spent in Switzerland was healing. No one knew who I was, and no one cared to know. Anonymity suited me: no imposing questions, no stares, no pity. I could be me for the very first time in nine long months. I could let my guard down, hop on a train, go up to the ski slopes, or watch the hot air balloons in Chateau d'Oex, and no one gave a rats patootie who my brother was. It was liberating!

I missed Yaniv horribly. I missed my dogs. And I missed our new kitty, Abba. However, being outside the United States was the best decision I made. My parents, initially, weren't happy about it, but Yaniv visited them regularly. It turned out that Monday nights were now a Yaniv and my dad thing. Every Monday night, they would have a session when my dad taught, and Yaniv learned. They mainly studied Kabbalah, a subject my father was an expert in. My mother cooked dinners for Yaniv, showered him with baked goods, and basically spoiled him. While I was gone, they had Yaniv to help them through their grieving process. He was more of a son to them than a son-in-law.

Three & Me

In the late 1980s, there were no smartphones. There were no apps. There was no WhatsApp. In 1989 the Internet was a fledgling industry based on dial-up phones. And there was no email, except for the few enthusiasts who were into Compuserve. Overseas calls were still costly. I had a telephone in my apartment, which was only suitable for local calls. To call overseas, I had to go to the post office and pay an exorbitant amount of money for a short call of a few minutes.

One night I had a dream that something was wrong with Jill. I woke up with a sick feeling in my stomach, so I resolved to phone her later that day when the timing would be amenable to a transatlantic phone call. I was eight hours ahead of Los Angeles and didn't want to wake her. I waited until much later to arrive at the post office.

I called Jill with some trepidation, but she sounded fine when she answered the phone. At least her voice did. She felt slightly down before I called but was very happy to hear my voice. Then I heard just the faintest of coughs. Nothing terrible, but it was there. She coughed a few times during our short call, and it worried me. I didn't say anything, though. I just asked her how she was doing. She told me her neck hurt and that she went to the doctor to find out why. She told me what the doctor had said. "Jill, stop being an actress and imagining that every ache and pain you experience is cancer!"

Hearing that, I was floored. I couldn't imagine any doctor saying that to a recovering cancer patient. Jill told me that her celebrity would always get in the way of good medical care. Doctors were human and were subject to the same prejudices or adulations about celebrities as the general public, especially those in their care. She would tell me how diagnoses were often missed or mixed up during her lifetime in the limelight.

Jill asked me when I was coming home. I told her I would be back in a month. Before we hung up, I heard the words I'll never forget, "Come home, Suzie. I need you here."

The Other Shoe Always Drops

I returned home to Los Angeles on a weekend when Jill was at a celebrity gala in Palm Springs. I was pretty bummed that she wouldn't be the first of my friends I saw. Yaniv was thrilled to have me back home, although that meant he had to put up with all the clatter and chatter I would make. Studious Yaniv was still working on his thesis and craved alone time so he could study. My dogs were pissed I was gone and tried giving me the cold shoulder, but that lasted about five minutes. Even Boo Boo was thrilled I was back. Abba, the cat, gave me the cold shoulder for about two days and left a strategically placed poop on my pillow before she forgave my dereliction of duty to her.

I was beginning to blend seamlessly into the rhythms of our house and was happy to be home. The hoopla surrounding my brother had thankfully died down during my absence. I finally felt comfortable again. Upon my arrival home, it felt like we were on a "second honeymoon" of sorts. It felt good to lie in bed and explore our bodies again like we did when Yaniv returned from his stints in the army those years ago.

173

The Sunday evening before Jill was to return from the desert, she called me from her hotel room. She was crying, angry and scared. "Jill, you have to speak slower. I can't understand what you're saying." All I heard were snippets between sobs, and it had to do with the tabloid press "What is going on?"

"You won't believe this," she began haltingly. "But a reporter from a huge tabloid came up to me at the party...." She sobbed louder and couldn't get the words out. I sat there listening to her sobs and heard that slight cough again. My heart sank.

"What about the reporter?" I asked. I heard Jill take a long slow breath before she answered. I waited. I knew this would be pretty bad, and I was steeling myself for the inevitable bad news, waiting for the other shoe to drop. And then it did. "He asked me how I felt about getting a terminal diagnosis. How I felt about cancer returning aggressively..."

"Wait! WHAT?!" Did I hear that right? Did a reporter from one of the big tabloids receive Jill's medical report before she did? Holy crap! I was speechless and momentarily at a loss for words. I could hear Jill crying on the other end. "How did that happen?" I asked her. "I mean, did you go in for tests? Did you have any symptoms? Who the Hell was the Pipe?" (A Pipe is someone who feeds stories to the tabloids. It can be a limo driver, a disloyal friend, a hotel worker, a hospital worker, etc. Tabloids usually pay their Pipes excellent fees to keep the stories coming.)

Jill responded sadly, sniffling through it all. "I wasn't feeling well. I have this little cough that won't go away. So, I went to the doctor, and they ran some tests. I'm supposed to go in Monday afternoon for the results when I get back to LA, and now this jerk reporter basically tells me that I might be dying!" She waited a moment before she continued. "One of the office staff must have leaked my records. Those sneaky reporters follow me around, waiting for news, and then they pounce. I wonder how much they paid whoever gave them my records. And I hope whoever leaked it knows how badly he or she hurt me. The worst thing is that I can't even reach my doctor on the phone to talk to him. To find out if this is even true! How am I supposed to sleep tonight knowing I might be dying right now?!" She started crying again, and my heart broke for her. The most wonderful woman on the planet, the best friend I've ever had, the most compassionate, caring individual alive, did not deserve to hear her prognosis through, of all places, a reporter from a tabloid!

We spoke for a while longer. Jill had been so strong and supportive of me in my darkest moment, and I needed to be there for her. We bandied around some other explanations for that jerk reporter's crass comments to her. Maybe he was fishing for a story, or perhaps he wanted to see a reaction to some horrible news that he was just making up—things like that. But it always came down to Jill having pain in her neck and a nagging cough. We couldn't explain those things away. The more we spoke, the more reality set in, and we both began

The Other Shoe Always Drops

to realize that a new journey was about to start. Where would it end? We had no idea.

Monday morning, Jill entered her Jaguar and drove from Palm Springs straight to her doctor's office. After she told him what the reporter had said to her, he sat silently for a moment before telling Jill he was so sorry that her records were leaked. He would make it his mission to find out who did it. When she heard this, Jill realized the reporter had the facts about her. She WAS experiencing a recurrence. And worst of all, she COULD DIE! The doctor told her that she had inoperable tumors in her neck and that the cancer had metastasized into her lungs as well. He would work with her to assemble a team to treat this new onset of illness.

After speaking with Charlie and telling him the news, she called me. She was resolute. She would fight this battle with every weapon available, but this time she would find a new team of doctors. She'd lost faith in the ones she had before. "Suzie, they never gave me a high enough dose of chemo the first time around!" she said. "I knew it when my hair didn't fall out. Only small patches, remember?"

"Can you enroll in some clinical trials?" I asked her. "I've read books where people's lives have literally been saved by being in clinical trial after clinical trial. They get medications and treatments not yet approved by the FDA, so being in one puts the patient on the cutting edge."

Jill thought about that for a moment. "That's an excellent idea!" She seemed to perk up at the thought. From that moment on, Operation Save Jill was in full swing.

Not knowing what I could do to help her at that exact moment, I got on my bike and decided to beat myself up in the hills. The Santa Monica Mountains have an endless supply of steep climbs that average around two to four miles in length. I grabbed my water bottle, threw it in my cage, and pedaled towards Stunt Road off Mulholland Drive. Stunt has some pretty steep and grinding grades, at least an eight percent going to 10 percent with some gnarly turns. With each pedal stroke, I imagined I was killing cancer cells. With each small advancement of my wheels up the hill, I pictured medication eradicating Jill's illness. My imagination ran wild on my bike rides. I wanted to nuke those cancer cells, and if the sheer power of my mind could do it, then I would go all out, pedal stroke by pedal stroke.

# # #

After the success of her book *"Life Wish,"* Jill began writing a new book aptly titled *"Life Lines,"* which told the story of her son Jason's struggles with drug addiction. Jason's birth mother was addicted to heroin, and when little Jason scooted out of her body, he was addicted too. His first few months were torture as he went through withdrawal. None of this knowledge was available to Jill and David McCallum when they adopted him. It was a closed adoption, the norm at the time. They just figured he was a fussy baby with colic. Years later, Jill would eventually learn the truth about poor Jason's rough start in the world.

Unknowingly, Jason grew up with a propensity for addiction. He was an extremely handsome young man, especially when he hit his teenage years. Thick, jet-black hair, strong features, a dimpled chin, big bushy eyelashes, and a winning smile opened doors for Jason wherever he went. He was slim, and his body was shaped into the perfect inverted triangle. Clothing of any kind looked incredible on him. When Jason was only 15, he caught the eye of a woman twice his age, the wife of a rock star. Her husband was always on the road with his band, so she had time for extracurricular activities. She set her sights on Jason, and he, being a healthy 15-year-old boy near the peak of his sexuality, was quickly drawn in by the beautiful and seductive woman. She introduced him to cocaine and sex, a combo he couldn't resist. It took practically no time for Jason to become hooked on her and the cocaine.

His body needed drugs to survive, on the same level as people required air. He was born an addict, so it took no time at all for his body to crave the artificial stimulation that drugs brought him. Sadly, he would battle drug demons his whole life, and Jill, ever the doting mother, would fight tooth and nail to get sobriety for her son. While her book on cancer spoke of her journey back to health and held positivity behind the pages, this new book effort took an emotional toll on Jill. It was hard to write.

Jill hired an editor to help her with this second book, having learned that a book editor is a valuable tool when writing. Michael Viner suggested Vernon Scott. Vernon was then the entertainment editor for UPI (United Press International). They met, and their creative chemistry was instant. Vernon loved Jill's writing style, and Jill enjoyed working with a man who was so positive and upbeat about her talents. He gave her some badly needed confidence, and the partnership seemed to work.

Soon that work partnership spilled over into a friendly and comforting friendship. It didn't take long for Vernon to become one of the people in Jill's inner circle. At times, Vernon would "bark" at me if he thought I was in his way, or he'd cut some snide remark aimed at me, maybe out of jealousy. Eventually, he accepted me as Jill's friend, and we cautiously developed a friendship based on our mutual respect and admiration for Jill.

Vernon was a man who was surrounded by stars everywhere he went. He was much sought-after because what he wrote about someone would go over the wires and be picked up by news outlets worldwide. He was a powerful man in Hollywood who could make someone's career take off. At some point, I felt he had a bit of a man crush on Charlie. While Vernon could boss me around (which he did quite often) or chum with Jill's other friends, I saw his insecurity fully displayed when he was around Charlie.

One day, we all decided to go to lunch. Charlie was driving, and he couldn't find a parking space. He kept circling and circling the parking lot. I couldn't take it any longer. "Charlie!" I said, "Follow that woman. She's going to her car. Then you can take the spot when she pulls out." Of course, Charlie hemmed and hawed, at which point I said, "Charlie, do you want to keep going around in circles, or do you want to park?"

Vernon was in the back seat with me. He looked aghast at what I'd just said. He hand-signaled that he thought I was nuts. But Charlie followed the woman to her car, waited for the space, and parked. When we got out, Charlie high-fived me. Vernon almost had apoplexy. Jill just laughed. After that, Vernon was nicer to me. And we began to have a relationship where we could rib each other well.

178

Months before I left for my stint in Switzerland, Jill was sent a script from a small production company. She was to play the mother of a drug addict. It was a minimal role but one she wanted as she was feverishly writing about that very subject. She accepted the part for scale pay. It was a quick production turnaround, with a private screening held at a theater on the lot at Universal Studios. Jill didn't tell us much about who wrote the script, who financed the movie, or any other facts. But she wanted us to come to the private screening. Charlie, who had read the script, begged off. I should have taken that as a red flag.

It was just Jill, me, and Vernon who went. We arrived pretty late. The speeches about the movie had already begun. We took seats in the very back row. Soon, the theater darkened, and the film started. It took me exactly two minutes to realize I was about to watch a profoundly Evangelical Christian movie. It wasn't the most fantastic script, and the film plodded along quite slowly. I moved uneasily in my seat as the boring storyline progressed. Jill had a few scenes right at the beginning. It was nice to see her up there on the big screen, looking healthy and happy, but after that, I didn't know what to think about the rest of the movie. Boredom does strange things to me. First, I fidget. Then I fidget some more. Then I look to see if anyone is as miserable as me. I found that shared boredom with Vernon. Initially, we sat quietly, throwing glances at each other during some of the slower scenes. But we made it through the movie. After the theater lights went on, a very tall man in the front row stood up with his back to us. He raised his hands as if he were in church and was going to lead us in prayer. And then he turned around and did exactly that. It was Billy Graham. His church had bankrolled the movie, and he asked the audience (or, in this case, the "congregation") to rise in prayer for the success of the film.

I was stunned. I wasn't expecting a church service, nor was I expecting Billy Graham to lead it. Vernon elbowed me in my side, which caused me to let out a small gasp. Jill sat on the other side of Vernon, and she had no idea he elbowed me. As small of a gasp as it was, Billy Graham heard me. I surmised he must have had the acute hearing of a wolf. He shot a dirty look in my direction all the way to the back of the theater. That dirty look didn't escape Vernon, so he began to tickle me. I tried to quietly fight him off to no avail. Again, Billy Graham stopped talking and looked directly at me, firing off his visual bullets. That gave Vernon more ammo. He then tickled me with both hands, and I couldn't keep the laughter in anymore. I was laughing and biting into my arms, trying to be as quiet as possible, but God help me, I couldn't keep quiet enough! Suddenly, Billy Graham's face reddened with anger, and he began running up the aisle toward me. I didn't need to wait to see what would happen, so I jumped out of my seat and high-tailed it out of the theater, hoping Billy Graham would see I left and go back down to the front and continue his sermon — no such luck. I learned something new that night. Billy Graham had the legs of a sprinter! Not only did he follow me out of the theater, but he caught up with me outside in about five strides! The reach that his

179

legs had was astounding! As he caught up to me, he grabbed the back of my collar, effectively curtailing my escape.

I turned and sheepishly looked at him. He was angry; oh boy, was he mad! Not knowing what to do and afraid of what might be coming next, I thoroughly apologized to him up one side and down the other. I told him my friend was tickling me. I told him my friend was trying to get me in trouble. I told him I was so, so sorry for the disruption. I apologized profusely. Billy Graham was still angry, but I could tell he was softening up a bit. I kept talking and pleading while my mind was racing. I was desperately trying to get one of the biggest Evangelists in the world to calm down. And then it hit me. Compliment him! Suck up to him! Appeal to his ego!

"I'm Jewish! And I've never heard a voice as powerful as yours, ever! Your command of the audience was remarkable!" I blurted out. It was beginning to work. I could see a softening in his eyes. His grip on me loosened. "Seriously," I continued. "You really are amazing!"

Billy Graham dropped his hand to his side. "Do you promise to behave?" he asked.

"Oh, absolutely!" I said that with a considerable amount of earnest intent and enthusiasm. We then walked back to the theater together. Jill and Vernon's eyes were wide with surprise. Especially when Billy Graham said goodbye to me as he returned to the front of the theater. In fact, just about everyone in that theater had wide eyes. I quietly sat down and didn't say another word. I was afraid lightning would strike me if I did.

# # #

When Jill had her first bout with cancer, she used to tell me that people from all over the world would send her articles about miracle cures or suggest different doctors or hospitals, exercises, or diets. And

The Other Shoe Always Drops

she used to complain about it because she said she had no way of knowing if any of those suggestions were good or not. She became resolute in following her own path, trusting her own instincts and judgment. Jill would politely decline if anyone would suggest a new doctor or regimen. So it was, upon confirmation that the cancer had aggressively returned, that she chose her own path.

She found a cancer center in Texas. She put all her faith in them, as they appeared to be on the cutting edge of therapies. Jill was a warrior. Nothing would stand in her way of accumulating more time to watch her daughters grow, to watch her sons succeed, and to be there for Jason. If she had to crawl through fire, she would. And she did.

She and Charlie, as well as their personal assistant, flew to Texas to begin therapy. I would be coming later in the week. Jill had a port surgically inserted around her heart to draw blood and administer drugs. After that, she began chemotherapy. This time it was different from the last time. Before, in her first bout, chemo was administered via infusion every three weeks. This time it was one week on, 24/7, and two weeks off. They would combine chemo with radiation for the inoperable tumors in her neck. Sounded like a solid plan.

I arrived later in the week. Everyone was staying in the Hilton. My friend Shari, whose father was Barron Hilton, had her dad's office contact the hotel to secure a suite upgrade for me. I threw my stuff into my suite and went to find Jill in hers. I was pretty unprepared for what I would see.

Jill was lying in bed, and it appeared like she had knitting needles sticking out both sides of her neck. These "knitting needles" were conductors of sorts for an experimental therapy that she was trying. She was in obvious pain and couldn't move her head in any direction. I chatted with her briefly that night and deduced that she was feeling optimistic. Her optimism made me feel optimistic. Again, I was hopeful. We all were.

Three & Me

One day, when we were all back in California, I got a call from Jill's assistant. She asked if I could fly to Texas with Jill and Charlie the following week. Jill was having some problems with massive swelling in one of her legs. I, of course, said yes. The limo picked me up and took me to the airport to meet them. We flew into Dallas, and a limo met us there. During the flight, Jill began to feel worse and worse. By the time we got into the car on the way to the Cancer Center, Jill was doing her best just to function.

I don't remember if it was an MRI or a CT that was ordered, but Jill was having difficulty breathing and could not lie down. She was afraid of drowning. She needed the imaging for diagnostic purposes to determine why so much fluid was accumulating in her legs and her chest. The imaging would be done in a tubular enclosure on a table that moves back and forth.

Jill had a massive anxiety attack as they tried to get her to lie on the table. She absolutely couldn't. She was crying and begging the technicians not to make her lie down. She was also screaming in pain as they tried to move her legs. I was allowed to accompany her, partly to help ease her anxiety and partly because Jill insisted. I was trying to assess the situation, which was going downhill pretty quickly. I studied the expanse of the tube they wanted Jill to lie in. I'm really good with spatial analysis, and I concluded that I could crawl into the machine from the opposite end and keep Jill's back high enough for her to breathe. Upon hearing this, Jill relaxed immediately, knowing I would be in the machine with her and would not let her drown in her own fluids. I laid down on my stomach with arms outstretched to support her back. It was excruciating being in that position for what seemed like an eternity, but I supported Jill with just enough lift in her back for her to be able to breathe.

Once the images were done, Jill was admitted to the hospital nearby. There was an underground tunnel between the Cancer Center and the hospital. Charlie was silent, lost in his own thoughts, the worry apparent in his facial expression. I pushed Jill in a wheelchair through the tunnel. There were mirrors along the way, lining the wall, which I found to be strange. Most people traveling through the tunnel would be oncology patients who probably didn't need reminders of how they appeared. All of a sudden, Jill yelled, "STOP!" Charlie and I quickly snapped out of our thoughts and focused on Jill. Was she OK? Was this a critical situation? Do we need to call for help? We were definitely on edge.

Jill looked back at me. "Look in the mirror!"

"What?" I asked, at this point completely confused.

"Look in the mirror!" she demanded. "Tell me what you see!"

If there's anything I hate, it's not understanding what's being asked of me. But this was Jill, and she was in serious physical distress, which made me very nervous. I didn't want to upset her; I felt she was trying to tell me something. At that moment, I wasn't very good at picking up on exactly what that was. So, I answered truthfully. "I see us."

"Exactly!" Jill said. She was pleased with my answer. Now I was utterly befuddled. But if it made her happy, then I was happy. "Do you see it?" she then asked.

Just when I thought I'd skated through the first question, the next one was a doozy. I wasn't sure what "it" was, but I would try again. "Ummmm. ... No!" I couldn't lie. I had no idea what she was talking about.

I'm not sure how she did this, but she reached up from the wheelchair, grabbed my chin, turned my face towards the mirror, and blurted out, "WE HAVE THE SAME FACE! You and me! We have the same exact Roman nose. We have the same cheekbones. We have the same chin. Our lips are very similar. WE HAVE THE SAME ROMAN-LOOKING FACE!"

Three & Me

The thought that I looked like Jill never entered my mind. But once she lost all the weight (which wasn't much), she was right. We looked a great deal alike! It was almost eerie. Many years later, upon the death of Charlie Bronson, Jill's son Paul went to Vermont for his burial. (His new wife wouldn't allow me to come.) While at the Vermont house, Paul had entered the attic to go through some of Jill's old paintings. Among her many talents, Jill was also an artist, as was Charlie. But Jill stopped painting in the early 1960s. Back then, I was still a kid turning into a pre-teenager. Jill had done a self-portrait during that time. As Paul went through the paintings, he found that painting, a portrait of how I look now. He brought it back to LA to give me as a most beautiful gift.

When he phoned me, he told me to drop whatever I was doing and get over to his house as quickly as possible. He made me close my eyes before I could see what he'd brought back with him. I couldn't believe I was staring at a portrait of me, painted when I had no idea who Jill and Charlie were and was too young to even look like that. It was Jill in that painting, and it's me in that painting. It's the both of us. Like Jill said, we have the same face.

On top of everything surrounding Jill's recurrence, I was juggling my business, teaching at Art Center, was concerned about my marriage, and needed to take care of my horse, all while trying to be the only surviving child for my parents. That wasn't enough. I became obsessive about cycling to relieve the stress. I began riding over 200 miles per week. I kept a log, a cycling diary of sorts. Calories in. Calories out. Miles ridden. I was obsessed with the weight of my bicycle, each gram had to be relevant, or I'd find something lighter. By the time I was finished with my bike, it weighed 15.2 lbs. Definitely scary light!

I had a regular weekday ride that was 22 miles, and I rode it five days a week. Then on weekends, I would ride centuries (100 miles) through sponsored rides for charity events or my own routes. I got Yaniv into cycling as well, and it was one activity we loved sharing

The Other Shoe Always Drops

together for most of our marriage. Already slim, cycling slimmed me down even more. Charlie used to call me "the slab," contending that if I turned sideways, I'd disappear. My light weight, my light bike weight, and my muscle-to-mass ratio gave me an edge in climbing. I could climb any mountain faster than most men (except the pro-riders). I could drop them on rides. I preferred out-of-the-saddle climbs, leaving men behind with mouths gaping. I rode every chance I got. On some days, I'd ride down to the barn, put chaps on over my bike shorts, ride my horse, take off my chaps, then ride my bike the 20 or so miles back home.

# # #

Meanwhile, during this time, things started to really begin to go well for Theresa. She had a darling baby girl named Tianna, was married to Phil Peters, and was a huge victim's advocate. She founded the organization "Victims for Victims" and gave wholly of herself to help other victims of violent crime. I met some of her cohorts within the organization, all sweet women with horrible tales of rape, beatings, attempted murder, torture, physical abuse, and other such horrors. One day I had the brilliant idea to get my design class at Art Center to design a poster that the organization could sell to help it fundraise.

Theresa came to my class and met with my students. Her dynamic personality made a big impression on everyone. She showed the defensive wounds on her hands, and the students in my class were transfixed by her every word. When she wrapped up, the entire class erupted in applause. I was so proud of her. The students enthusiastically took that project on, and it was a huge success. Additionally, I was lucky enough to get the printing of the poster donated, so every dime "Victims for Victims" made on the sale of the poster was theirs.

Outwardly, things looked great for Theresa, but Arthur Jackson was simmering in his jail cell. His release date was looming, just a year away. He began to relish his upcoming freedom and started a huge campaign of terrorism directed toward and against Theresa. He vowed that he would finish his job and complete his divine mission. He sent a barrage of notes echoing those threats. Sufficiently scared, Theresa went to the police. According to her, they initially blew it off as rantings by a madman who was locked up. Lovely.

Theresa tried unsuccessfully to live her life as normally as possible. She stopped driving. She was too afraid. She had no idea whether or not Jackson hired anyone to kill or stalk her, as his letters threatened. Even though her building in Los Angeles was New York in style with a doorman, which provided a layer of protection, she was still uneasy. To get anywhere, Theresa had to hire a driver to take her. When I wanted to see her, or she wanted to see me, I'd drive to Hollywood and visit in the safe confines of her condo.

One day she called me up and asked me to come over. When I arrived, a pleasant-looking man wearing an expensive suit sat with her and went over her personal security planning. His name was Gavin de Becker, a major provider of protection to the stars. He took the threats from Jackson seriously. He mapped out plans for Theresa while trying to get police and prosecutors interested in preventing disaster. He felt the threats were absolutely credible. I believe he was instrumental in what would ultimately lead to new charges filed against Jackson. I loved the way Gavin was proactive and energetic. He seemed to have all the answers and instilled badly needed confidence in Theresa.

Then Theresa found Model Mugging. It was a game-changer for her. The founder, Matt Thomas, himself a black belt in karate, told his classes about an experience of a good female friend of his. She was also a black belt. However, she was still raped. He was deeply troubled by this. He realized that karate is a standing form of combat. Men fight men mostly vertically. They attack women horizontally. He decided he'd find a way to teach women how to defend themselves against attacks by men. He interviewed convicted rapists and murderers and concluded that men fight women differently by throwing

The Other Shoe Always Drops

them down on beds or on the ground. He also realized that most self-defense classes are basically theoretical. Moves may be demonstrated but not practiced on another person.

Additionally, while little boys scuffle with each other as youngsters, girls don't. Women have little idea of how to really fight. Or how it feels to kick a guy in the nut sack or to fight their way out of a jam. So, they flail or resist, giving the assailant the upper hand. Using his own martial arts skills, Matt crafted a program based on the information he garnered through his research. He would use "real" assailants dressed in protective gear to physically "attack" the women who took his classes. His students would learn firsthand, and probably for the first time ever, just how much energy it took and how quickly they had to think while under attack. The point was that his female students would learn that they could fight back intelligently. During the class, the "muggers" would sneak up on their "victim," mainly attacking from behind or the side and sometimes from the front. The mugger would then throw the victim down on the mat, call her derogatory names (research showed that men deride women during attacks), pull her hair, and render her helpless. The muggers would basically do all the things an actual attacker would do.

Theresa loved this course. And, of course, she begged me to take it with her. Down I went to the studio, and after listening to Matt Thomas speak, I was hooked. I took that course a bunch of times and ended up being double-mugged and triple-mugged. The instructor demonstrated the skills and the moves necessary to defend oneself and then set up the muggings. It was great. It was also a great way to get rid of stress!

I did break my thumb a couple of times and walked out of the studio with plenty of sprains. But I walked out with a great skill set. Even today, if I get a funky vibe from a guy, I'm already assessing him, looking for the areas where he's weakest while preparing to defend myself.

Three & Me

Jill and Charlie didn't go to Vermont that summer because of Jill's treatments in Texas. But they had a bit of a break and flew to Vermont in October 1989. I had plans to see the Rolling Stones in LA at the end of October and was really looking forward to it. I'd seen the Stones in San Francisco when I was still in college, and it was one of the best concerts I'd ever attended.

Then the phone call came. Jill was in a panic. "Darling, I need you to come to Vermont tomorrow," she said with an immediacy to her tone.

"I've got tickets to the Stones. Can I come after?" I asked, hoping.

"I've got to have you here with me. My hair is beginning to fall out from the chemo, in huge clumps, really. Donald Trump's office just phoned me. Apparently, Donald Trump is dedicating a piece of land in Central Park as 'The Jill Ireland Garden of Hope.' He's sending his private jet to pick us up. I can't do this without you. I just can't. Please come."

How do I say no? I couldn't. I told her that, of course, I would come. She had already arranged for their regular limo driver to come to get me, had already bought the plane tickets, and by the following morning, I was on a flight headed to Boston, connecting to Lebanon, New Hampshire. But not before I called a good friend of mine, Ron Osborn, and gave him my tickets. He drove over immediately and picked them up. I think Yaniv was secretly relieved he didn't have to go to the concert. He was much more of a classical music kind of guy. (Ron told me I missed the show of a lifetime. He said the Stones were amazing. Sigh.)

When I reached the Vermont house, the first thing that struck me was the enormous weight loss Jill had undergone in the few weeks I hadn't seen her. Throughout all the years of our friendship, she'd always wanted to be thinner, bemoaning middle-aged weight gain. She'd go on the Atkins diet, the macrobiotic diet, or any other fad diet that was trending at the time to lose a few pounds. However, to find solace in carrying just a few extra pounds, she would invoke one of her favorite sayings, "Face or Fanny." In other words, a bit more weight to the tush to keep your face from taking on a gaunt appearance.

Jill and Charlie were both happy to see me. Jill was pleased for the support I'd bring and Charlie for the company. He was a huge tease, but it was hard to tease someone who was as sick as Jill was, so I was fair game! The first thing Jill said to me after we'd all said hello and hugged was, "Darling, come into the bathroom. We need to pull out all my hair! My scalp is very itchy, and I can't stand it." Dutifully I followed her into the downstairs bathroom, where she sat down, and we both began to pull out clumps of her hair. Her wigs were waiting in her bedroom, so she wasn't worried about having a bald pate.

Once we finished pulling out her hair, we went into her bedroom closet to find something appropriate to wear. We both knew it was already cold in New York City, so we had to find something warm. And we had to find something that would fit her nearly skeletal frame. We knew that whatever outfit she chose was one she could cover up with her long, camel-colored coat.

The following day, we drove to the small airport in nearby Lebanon. As scheduled, Donald Trump's private Learjet touched down on the runway. Jill got on first; then I did, and then Charlie. Our luggage was loaded into the small hold below, and we took off for New York City. It was my first time on a private jet, and I was awestruck at how easy it was to get somewhere. The ride was smooth, and we soon landed at La Guardia Airport. A limo was waiting to whisk us into Manhattan. Donald Trump was then married to Ivana Trump, and they owned the Plaza Hotel, one of New York City's most prestigious hotels. We were to be their guests.

Three & Me

We were immediately greeted at the hotel by welcoming staff and escorted up the elevator to the Penthouse Suite overlooking Central Park. The elevator stopped inside the suite, not in a hallway, which impressed the hell out of me! There were bedrooms and bathrooms and more bedrooms and more bathrooms. All were little mini-suites within this huge penthouse area. There was a living room with a giant television, a formal dining area with a massive dining room table that could seat about 18 people, a chef's kitchen, a huge outdoor rooftop area with an outdoor kitchen, and enough room to throw a huge party had we wanted to.

Ivana Trump apparently liked the perfume Chanel No. 5 because there were little bottles of it in all the bathrooms. Jill and I quickly ran into the many bathrooms, collected all the perfume bottles, and divvied them up between us. To this day, I still have some of those contraband bottles in my possession. Memories.

After we were settled and raided all the bathrooms, we decided to order room service because Jill was tired from the stress of the journey. She begged off to nap, and Charlie and I were left to try and find something fun to watch on TV. As we looked at the menu, we were blown away by the prices. A hamburger was $36! A hamburger! Remember, this was in 1989 when a good burger cost around $6.00 tops.

The next morning, Jill was going to be interviewed by Joan Rivers. Joan was no longer filling in as a guest host for Johnny Carson but had her own show, aptly titled *The Joan Rivers Show*. The dedication of the Garden of Hope was a big deal, as Jill's illness was big news, even in little towns and around the world. It was surprising how many people knew of her battle. This was before social media, although the *"National Enquirer"* and *"Star Magazine"* were widely read. Both were prolific in producing articles about Jill, with horrible photos of her and morose photos of Charlie on too many covers to count!

Joan rented a large and luxurious suite a few floors below us. Both Jill and I walked in for Jill's Interview the following day. Joan was delightful, surprised, but happy to see me. We chatted for a bit before the interview commenced, and cameras rolled. I must say, Jill was absolutely radiant. Ever the actor, once the lights came on and the camera started rolling, she gave a brilliant performance of health and happiness. Her sense of humor came out in a big way, and the two women appeared to have forged a friendship during the course of that interview. I loved watching them both. By the time the interview ended, Joan had stopped being Joan Rivers, the comedian and talk show host. Instead, she stood before us as Joan Rivers, a wonderfully warm and caring person. I have to say; it was really lovely to be part of that. Inwardly, I had to laugh, though, because of the irony of it all. Joan Rivers was the main reason I never wanted to befriend Jill, to begin with. As it turned out, she was the exact reason we *did* become friends. Life. Right?!

Later that morning, the ceremony for the dedication was to take place. Jill and I went upstairs, and she refreshed her makeup (lights can make it run or melt) from the morning interview, re-arranged her wig, put on a cute bowler-type hat, her camel-colored coat, white turtleneck sweater, and slacks. She was ready. Jill, Charlie, and I went to the lobby to catch the limo to the dedication site.

It was a beautiful, brisk fall day in Central Park. I looked out the car's window on the extremely short ride over and saw people enjoying their afternoon in the park. New Yorkers are used to crazy weather, the kind of weather people from Los Angeles don't understand. What are seasons in Los Angeles? We rarely need to listen to a weather report because it is always the same weather. But in New York City, there are actual seasons. All four of them! And fall is absolutely beautiful. I noticed the trees changing colors, some having already shed their leaves. A slight breeze blew a few dried leaves across the grass as dogs played and families walked.

As we pulled up, I saw paparazzi everywhere. Jill was headline news for the tabloids. Even mainstream news outlets were interested in Jill's journey. There were other photographers besides the paparazzi waiting for Jill's arrival. News crews from the local stations were there; they would later syndicate the footage to the rest of the country. As Jill stepped out, some photographers stepped in right behind her, cutting Charlie and me off from Jill. One photographer pushed a branch out of his way, which ricocheted back and smacked me in the face. Unknown to me, another news crew filmed Jill's approach to the Garden of Hope and captured me getting smacked in the face. Of course, that was the clip broadcast around the world!

When we watched the news back in the living room of the penthouse, Charlie was the one who spotted the branch hitting me square in the face. He let out a huge laugh and, pointing his finger, looked over at me and said, "Did you see that, Suzie? You're on the news!" Charlie couldn't get enough of that snippet of film. It kept playing on the news at different hours and on various news stations. Each time I got smacked, Charlie laughed. Actually, so did Jill. Eventually, I got over it and began to laugh as well. I was still annoyed at the photographer, though.

The ceremony for Jill made her feel fabulous. She was on Cloud 9 the entire day and managed to have enough energy to really enjoy the festivities. Donald Trump wasn't there, at least to my knowledge. If he was, I never saw him. But it was gracious of him to create that little Garden of Hope for Jill in Central Park, to send his jet and put us up in a luxurious penthouse. Seems like a lifetime ago. Years later, I went into the park to find the garden and couldn't. I've scoured the park many times since, asking people if they know where it is, and no one does. I really hope it's not gone but just well hidden.

We flew back to Vermont the next day, still excited that Jill had a little piece of Central Park in her honor. I enjoyed being on the Learjet, telling Charlie that this was something I could get used to. He laughed

The Other Shoe Always Drops

and said he thought the same thing. It wouldn't be the last time Charlie and I flew on a private jet as we continued Jill's journey together.

Media coverage about Jill's illness was reaching a fevered pitch. Everyone who knew me closely knew about it. Everyone else who knew me peripherally, now thanks to my getting smacked by a branch on national television, knew I knew Jill. And so, it began. The curious outsiders, as well as the people who truly cared about Jill, all wanted to know how she was doing. I was careful with what I would say, usually something beige like, "She's doing much better," or "She's a warrior." I didn't want to reveal private details about my friend, so I kept everything about Jill close to my chest. Charlie and I had significant discussions about the paparazzi. He gave me clues about spotting them and how sneaky they can be when trying to get a story.

I already knew how they would get "pipes" to feed them info, paying handsomely for big stories. Jill learning about her recurrence from a reporter is one example. The other example was a simple limo ride we took to an alternative medicine doctor in Las Vegas. The driver was a pipe. The next issue of a major tabloid ran an article about Jill visiting "Quack doctors in a desperate attempt to save her life." I was becoming well-versed in pipes and in the tactics of the tabloid press by this time.

# # #

One cloudy day, I was out at the barn riding Aero. One of the things I love most about riding horses is the camaraderie and partnership you form with your mount. Aero and I had an excellent partnership as well as a great relationship. He always knew when I needed to get on and do mostly nothing. No jumping, no real workout, no nothing. I liked the sound of his hooves padding the sand footing in the ring, the quiet among the noise. I enjoyed watching his ears twitch and change positions as he tried to either hear something or focus on what he heard. On that cloudy day, I was into the nothingness about

Three & Me

riding when a woman with a huge smile on her face rode up into the ring and began walking next to me.

"Hi," she said, with an absolutely colossal smile in her voice. I noticed her eyes sparkled, and I instantly liked her. "I'm new to the barn," she continued, "and Rob and Cyndi thought I should meet you. (Rob and Cyndi were my horse trainers at the time.) "My name's Heather!"

I was drawn to her openness and her friendly disposition. "Hi back! I'm Suzie. This is Aero," I said, pointing to my horse. "And who's that?" I asked, pointing to her beautiful bay gelding. She introduced her horse to me quite happily. She said his barn name was Doobie because he was a "Doo-Bee" (a throwback to the *Romper Room* TV show from the 1950s), but his show name was Baron von Trapp. People give their horses show names based on a multitude of reasons, like a character in a movie, a book, a comic book, or maybe a band name, or a cute phrase of sorts. Aero's show name was Clark Kent from "*Superman*" comics which I devoured my entire childhood. Upon hearing Heather's horse's name, I figured her favorite movie was *The Sound of Music*. I never gave it a second thought.

Heather and I chatted a bit as we walked around the ring. I was surprisingly happy to have the company. Usually, when I'm lost in thought, as I was before Heather rode up, I prefer to be alone. But Heather was great company. She filled me in on her recent life, telling me she and her family just moved back from Boston after her husband finished working there. She was trying to sell a huge house, which she called "The B-Word," but the real estate market was soft, and she was afraid they would lose money on the sale. IF it even sold.

Soon and quite easily, Heather and I became barn friends. We'd ride and then hang out, especially at the horse shows. One day, Heather invited me to her house for lunch. I knew her last name was Urich, but I never connected any of the dots from the information she shared. To me, she was Heather, a charming woman who was just a year and a half older than myself, who, wonderfully enough, was easy to talk to, laugh, and have fun with.

She gave me her address in Encino, which was close to where I was living, only she lived south of the Boulevard while I still lived north of the Boulevard. If you've ever lived in the San Fernando Valley, you'd know that the houses south of Ventura Boulevard were far more expensive, much larger, and had larger lots than homes north of Ventura.

I drove up to a lovely ranch-style home up a hill from the road. Heather met me at the front door and gave me a tour of her house and huge yard. She was doing some renovations, so some areas were torn up. As I discovered, Heather was always building, renovating, or changing residences throughout her life. Five years in the same home was almost unheard of.

Heather and I were in the front living room when a cute kid with dark hair falling into his face came screeching through like a blaze of lightning. He disappeared into the kitchen, then ran back out again, spotting me! Without knowing who I was, this little boy— Heather's son, Ryan—at ten years old, gave me a blow-by-blow account of the spawning habits of Alaskan salmon. Little Ryan stole my heart that day. Ryan and his dad had just returned from a fishing trip in Alaska, and Ryan was still excited by the adventure he got to share with his dad.

About a minute later, Robert Urich (*Vegas, Spencer for Hire,* etc.) walked through the living room. Heather introduced me. I pretended not to be shocked. I wasn't expecting Bob, having failed to connect the Boston house with *Spencer for Hire* or Baron von Trapp, with Heather being one of the children in the movie. All of it went right over my head. For example, if Heather and I were talking about something, and I'd say, "So...?"

She'd respond in song with "...a needle pulling thread..." and I would shake my head, wondering why she was so obsessed with that song! It didn't occur to me that she was in *that* movie!

Just like the Bronsons, Heather and Bob were two regular people with all feet firmly planted on the ground and whose values matched mine. There was no Hollywood veneer, no pretense, no believing their own hype. They were wonderfully regular people.

In time, Heather would become my go-to when things started going south with Jill. I could trust her not to talk to the tabloids because I knew she hated them as much as the Bronsons did. I could share with her my feelings, fears, and disappointments up to a certain point. I've never really, until the writing of this book, shared all that I knew or felt. It's taken me 33 years since Jill's passing to finally open up about my experience.

# # #

At the beginning of November 1989, Jill got the phone call no mother ever wants to get. Her beautiful son, Jason, died suddenly. His poor body couldn't take any more drugs. Not even legitimately prescribed drugs. According to Jill, Jason was on physician-prescribed medication. He was in his bathroom when he swallowed the pill and died. His heart just stopped.

I adored Jason and secretly cheered him on in his quest for sobriety. Jason was such a lovely young man. He was funny, personable, and treated everyone with such kindness. He lived a tortured life that ended way too soon. Born an addict through no fault of his own, he died a recovering addict. Jill was absolutely heartbroken. When Jill told me about Jason's death, I worried about how that would impact her health. Parents should never have to bury their children. It's out of the natural order. I watched my parents bury their son. And now I would watch Jill bury hers. That other shoe didn't stop dropping.

The Other Shoe Always Drops

At the end of 1989, late in December, Jill was feeling pretty terrible. The chemo was taking its toll on her, but worse yet, she kept filling up with fluid in her chest and legs. Michael Viner arranged for us to get the Warner jet, a luxurious 727 airplane, to fly Jill, Charlie, and me to Texas. The limo picked us up and drove us out onto the tarmac at Van Nuys Airport, where we boarded the plane. Donald Trump's Learjet paled in comparison to the Warner jet in size and luxury. The interior of that airplane blew us away. The entire back end of the plane was a luxurious restroom. The toilet was basically a throne! It had armrests and a padded back you could lean into. On either side of the plane were couches that could be used alternatively as beds. The kitchen was in front of the aircraft, complete with a restaurant-style dining booth.

Jill wanted to lie down during the flight, so she chose one of the couches. Charlie and I sat in the booth in the kitchen, pulled out a deck of cards, and began to play Gin Rummy. I quickly learned Charlie was absolutely terrible at that game. He kept giving me the cards I needed and never entirely picked up the cards that he needed. I would end up winning, and I hated that. It's OK to win at a game, but it's another to keep winning when your opponent feels bad about losing. So, I tried as hard as possible to lose but couldn't seem to succeed. I knew the cards Charlie needed by what he was picking up from the pile, so I'd try to give him the cards I had where I knew he could get Gin. Nope. He wouldn't pick them up. I wanted to hit him over the head and say, "Charlie, pick up the damn card!" Instead, I kept throwing my cards away, trying to avoid Gin at all costs. Finally, Charlie won! I was thrilled but pretended to be disappointed. That made Charlie's victory over me that much sweeter for him. Phew!

Above the oven was a TV screen showing the GPS flight path, our exact location, how many miles traveled, and how many miles left. Basically, the same screen so common on aircraft today but wasn't readily available in 1989. Charlie and I were transfixed. The technology blew us away. Now you can look at a smartphone with GPS and

197

pinpoint precisely where you are, where you want to be, and where you've been.

When we arrived at the private airstrip outside of Dallas, Jill announced that she felt well enough to eat. The driver dropped Jill and me off at the shopping mall across from the hospital, then took Charlie to the Four Seasons Hotel, where we would all be staying.

Jill and I went into TGIF Fridays for lunch before her appointment. She was scheduled to have a great deal of imaging before her doctor's appointment. We were a bit early, so we grabbed a table, ordered a couple of burgers, and chatted for quite a while as if nothing in the world was wrong. The normalcy of the moment didn't escape my notice, and I was grateful for it. We laughed like we always did when talking about men, which we always seemed to do. In the middle of that lighthearted moment, Jill suddenly turned pale. She put her hand up to her mouth, got up out of the chair, grabbed my hand, and we ran into the bathroom. Jill vomited all the lunch she had eaten and felt lightheaded and dizzy. Then she vomited some more until nothing was coming out. I helped clean her up before we went back to our seats. Leave it to Jill to make light of it. "I wonder if I should still pay the bill," she cracked.

While Jill and I were at lunch, Charlie rented a car. We needed transportation between the hotel and the hospital. Jill and I walked from the restaurant to the hospital and met Charlie there. She checked in for her tests while Charlie and I hung out together in the waiting area. Her doctor's appointment wasn't scheduled until the next day so that the images would have time to be reviewed by the radiologists and reports written.

On the way back to the hotel, while stopped at a red light, we felt a rear-end impact that was so strong Jill's wig flew right off her head. I was in the back seat and took the brunt of the accident in my lower back. Charlie got out of the car to assess the damage.

The Other Shoe Always Drops

We were crunched, as was the car that hit us. The driver, a very young man, was very apologetic about the accident. He pulled out his license and asked Charlie for his. Charlie didn't want to give him his license and instead told the guy not to worry. He didn't need to pay for anything. It was a rental car that was fully insured, so that the rental car company would take care of it. The young man was pleased by the news. Suddenly, he looked at Charlie and said, "You know, you look a lot like that actor, Charles Bronson."

Charlie nodded his head and confessed to the young man that people say that to him all the time. "Only Charles Bronson is a lot taller than I am, and he's much better looking."

After studying Charlie for about a minute, the young man looked him right in the eye and said, "I guess you're right. Charles Bronson is pretty good-looking."

I heard it through the window, as did Jill, who was still trying to pull herself together from that rear-end bump. It had deeply unsettled her already fragile state. When Charlie got in the car, I began kidding him, saying, "Yeah, that Charles Bronson is a pretty good-looking man, isn't he?" At this point, we all began to laugh.

The next day we all woke feeling relieved that Jill would see the doctor. Her leg had swollen to nearly twice its normal size, and she could hardly walk. When we arrived at the Cancer Center, Jill was placed in a wheelchair, and I rolled her into one of the examination rooms. When her vitals were all taken and charted, we were escorted into a darkened and cold room. Just the lights from lightboxes and computers eerily illuminated the area. There was a small office inside this larger space. Jill went in to speak with her oncologist. Charlie and I stayed on the outside, leaning against a wall, when we both heard what we never ever wanted to hear.

Three & Me

"Well, Jill," her doctor began with a bit of an edge to his tone. "I'm going to suggest you inquire immediately about arranging a hospice situation for yourself." I had to catch myself as I heard this. This doctor was blunt and to the point. "I'm afraid there isn't much more I can do for you. Your tumors are growing aggressively. They've stopped responding to treatment. You need to get your affairs in order."

Charlie practically collapsed on me. I suddenly had to support him, which wasn't easy, while trying to keep my own legs from buckling. Then I heard Jill, sounding suddenly like a child, begging her daddy for one more trip on the merry-go-round. "Hospice? What do you mean? I don't understand! How much time? I'm not ready yet."

The doctor told her that she had a few more months left if she chose highly aggressive therapy; otherwise, her time was imminent, days, weeks, a month, maybe. Jill chose time over imminent death. She chose a hard path. When he said aggressive treatment, no one could even imagine the hell Jill would go through to eke out more days, weeks, and months. As I said, Jill was a warrior.

Charlie was shocked into silence. I was the one Jill and Charlie both leaned on in hearing this news. I tried comforting Jill as best as I could. Charlie had mentally gone somewhere else. He had finally met the enemy who would beat him. This wasn't a film script. This was a disease that was all too real. And even though we had seen Jill slowly decline, the idea of her dying was something we hadn't yet wrapped our minds around.

As I pushed Jill in her wheelchair through the underground tunnel toward the hospital, she was a broken spirit. The air was heavy with our sadness. Our complete despair was evident in our hunched-over postures. But I had to give her hope and strength. I'm too optimistic a person not to do otherwise. I began to tell her that it was her choice to outlive expectations and that she could put her mind to accomplishing the impossible. Soon Charlie came out of his funk and began to

The Other Shoe Always Drops

cheer her up also. "Jill," I said. "No one knows your expiration date, not even the doctors. They guess. That's all. You're a warrior; you've walked through fire and led the way for so many followers. You're amazing. Don't let this guy get you down.

A few months back, Jill was undergoing a procedure at the Cancer Center. No one but the medical staff was allowed in the room with her. I walked into the waiting area to hang out while the medical team worked with her. It didn't take me long to realize that I was the only person there who had my own hair. Everyone else was wearing a baseball cap, a wig, a scarf, a knit hat, or other head covering. I quickly realized that I was the only cancer-free person in the room and that I was a curiosity to the others. One woman asked me, very politely, where I was from. I told her I was from California. She told me she lived in Oklahoma. I asked her how she had come upon this Cancer Center, hoping she'd tell me what a great place it was, its high cure rate, etc. "Oh, I came here because that actress Jill Ireland comes here," she said matter-of-factly.

Stunned, I asked why? "Well, she's the wife of Charles Bronson, you know." I nodded, not wanting to give away that Jill was the reason I was there. The woman continued, "So, I reasoned, if this is good enough for Charles Bronson's wife, then it's good enough for me."

As I recalled that conversation I had those many months ago, I now told Jill about it. "Whether intentionally or not, they are getting patients BECAUSE you are here! Maybe his bluntness is masking his disappointment in your prognosis."

Upon hearing my speech, Jill perked up. "You're right!" she said. We finally reached the admitting area, and Jill was immediately admitted to the hospital. Not too much later, she had a minor procedure to insert drains into her chest and leg and was given Lasix (a diuretic) to drain the fluid from her body. Charlie and I returned to the Four Seasons, had a small dinner together, each of us lost in thought, then said goodnight. Maybe the next day would bring better news.

It was December 31st, 1989. A new decade was being ushered in at midnight. I phoned Yaniv and told him about the the death speech. Yaniv couldn't believe it. That doctor either knowingly or unknowingly, took away her hope and nearly took away her fight. After I hung up with Yaniv, I sat in bed, watched TV, waited for midnight, and fell into a fitful and unsatisfying sleep.

At some point in the middle of the night, I woke up with the sheets feeling wet and sticky. With a lot of dread, I felt the blood pouring from between my legs. Cupping myself, I ran into the bathroom and sat on the toilet, where blood flowed out of my body endlessly. This was no ordinary period. This was a bloodbath! I was sure it was a result of the rear-end collision from earlier in the day. I sat in complete despair on that toilet for over an hour when finally, the flood began to ebb, and I could use a Tampax that would stay in place for more than 2 minutes. Weak and a bit dizzy, I returned to the bed and began tearing the sheets off. It looked like a murder had taken place, and I was absolutely mortified. I threw all the sheets in the bathtub and ran cold water over all the blood, trying to dilute it. Then I poured the shampoo out of the little bottle hotels give you, hoping to remove some of that stain at least so it wouldn't set. It seemed futile. Finally, I caved and called housekeeping to explain what had happened. They sent up a sweet woman who gathered the now wet and bloody sheets from the tub, placed them in a giant plastic bag, and then set to task making my bed with fresh new sheets. The cramps were coming on fierce and sharp in nauseating waves, and the Aleve I took didn't make a dent in the pain. Welcome to 1990. If the last 24 hours were any indication, this year would be a rough go.

Miraculously, I managed to get a few more hours of sleep, albeit fraught with the events from the day before and filled with the sharp

The Other Shoe Always Drops

pain in my pelvic area. By the time I had pulled myself out of bed, Charlie had already left for the hospital. I took a cab and found Jill and Charlie in her room. She was hooked up to IV and was being administered more chemo. They both took one look at me and, in unison, said, "WHAT HAPPENED TO YOU?!" Ugh. The last thing I wanted to do was tell them, but Jill managed to pull it out of me. I was that pale!

Charlie insisted I go down to the ER, which I absolutely refused to do. Since I hadn't eaten anything, they suggested I get some nourishment in me and go grab lunch. So, I went to the TGIF Fridays across the way. When I walked in, the hostess was very sweet and asked me how my mom and dad were doing. Huh? Was this a Southern hospitality type of greeting? I responded that my parents were both doing great, and the hostess seemed pleased by the news.

As I was seated, a few customers in the restaurant came up to ask me how my mom was doing. I was perplexed but told them my mom was okay and thanked them for asking. I wondered if I was rude in not asking them how their parents were doing and vowed to ask the next person who approached me. No one told me that in Texas, people cared greatly about one's parents!

The waitress finally approached my table, and I placed my order. She also asked me how my mom and dad were doing. I told her they were both fine and asked her about her parents. She smiled but was clearly confused as to why I asked about her parents. I realized that I was having trouble with this Texas custom.

After a few more people asked me about my parents, I decided that Texas had to be one of the friendliest states in the country. As I walked back to the hospital, musing about the southern hospitality these Texans were showing me, two more strangers stopped me to ask about my parents. Wow! Texas certainly was friendly!

Three & Me

I made it back to Jill's room and told them about all the friendly people in Texas. They both just looked at me like I'd just arrived from Mars. Then they burst out laughing. Charlie was the first to speak. "Suzie, they think you're our daughter!" *(OH MY GOD!)* My cheeks began to flush with embarrassment! "They were inquiring about us!" Yep! Now it all made sense. What must that waitress have thought when I asked about her parents? She must have thought I'd gone completely mad!

I felt like a complete idiot as I settled into a chair and pulled out one of Gary Larson's *"The Far Side"* books I had brought. I have a very sick and twisted sense of humor, and Gary Larson's books were right on target. Besides, I've always loved the comics ever since I was a little kid, hailing back to my Superman days as well as the Los Angeles Times funnies! I was far too upset over the events of the last 24 hours to actually read an actual book, so this was perfect.

Jill had closed her eyes for a short nap. Charlie was engrossed in his own Daniel Patterson book. We sat like that for a few hours until Jill woke up needing to vomit. Charlie handed her the dish, and when she was done, she looked up at me as I sat directly across from her bed. "What dribble are you reading?" she demanded.

I lifted the book and showed her. Clearly disgusted with me, she let me know it. "Suzie, how are you ever going to go to a dinner party and have an intelligent discussion with someone?!" she demanded. "People expect intelligent discourse, not something from a comic book!"

I sheepishly put the book down in my lap. "I'm sorry. I needed something light to distract..." Oops. I caught myself.

"Distract you from *what?*" Jill had a fire in her eyes.

I had to think fast. "Distract me from my cramps. I didn't want to obsess about them." Jill's gaze softened, and she attempted a weak smile.

The Other Shoe Always Drops

"OK. That's fine," she said softly. "I just didn't want you to forget any of the Fine English Lady Training I put you through. You can read your book if it helps you."

As she closed her eyes, the chemo and other drugs entering her veins, I sat back in my chair and recalled all the Fine English Lady Training she had given me over the years. I was Jill's *Pygmalion*, her *Fair Lady*. The most important thing to remember, she would tell me, is dinner party decorum. How to dress, how to converse, how to eat, how to sit, when to sit, who to speak with, when to get up, when to speak, and so on. There were a million moving parts to a dinner party, as she explained it to me. That was the first big lesson. The second big lesson was how to enter a room. How to effect poise and elegance with just a single stride. Then once in the room, where to sit, how to sit, where to stand, how to stand, and how to start a conversation with someone. The third lesson was speech.

Jill hated the way Americans sounded, so she would constantly pick words and make me say them "correctly," as in "bawth" as opposed to "baaath" or any other "A" sounding words. And yes, she did make me walk with a book on my head. Crazy as the entire thing sounds, I loved her Fine English Lady tutoring. Crazier still, I will fall back on those lessons learned quite often. Jill's Fine English Lady Training was spot on in so many ways. Where it really came into play was in business meetings. I could walk into a crowded boardroom, where most attendees were men, and hold my own. She would have been proud.

After her chemo was administered, Jill got a chance to rest. But then she went into radiology and was zapped and zapped some more and then some more. The inoperable tumors did stop progressing from all that radiation exposure. But Jill suffered horrible radiation burns on the outside that had to be tended to, which was nothing in the face of what I considered a bigger tragedy. She lost her melodious voice. Her vocal cords were burnt to a crisp. Radiation doesn't just burn you on the exterior; it burns you equally on the interior. To Jill's horror, she was now constantly bringing up bits of phlegm. She would find it necessary to spit into a tissue constantly. Her voice was reduced to nothing more than a hoarse whisper. Her biggest fear was an insufficient supply of tissue boxes and a readily available wastebasket. Cancer was not very pretty, and the treatment sometimes can be far worse.

On our last day in Texas, Charlie and I checked out of our respective rooms. We had to return the car later that day and needed gas. Charlie drove around the area, looking for a full-service gas station. I wondered why we passed by perfectly good gas stations, so I asked him.

"I need full-serve, Suzie. These are all self-serve stations."

"Oh My God, Charlie!" I uttered in complete exasperation. "Pull into the next station! We'll be in Oklahoma before you find a full-serve!" Charlie's eyes went wide. He confessed he didn't know how to pump gas. "It's OK, Charlie. I do."

We pulled into the next station, and I exited the car. I also told Charlie to get out of the car, as I would teach him how to pump gas so he'd never have to be in this position again. I showed him how to find the gas cap release in the car, then I taught him how to use the credit card, pick the correct gas, lift the handle, insert the handle, and pump. Well, Charlie just loved it. He was thrilled that he was now able to pump his own gas! I gave him a big pat on the back for a job well done!

Once we got Jill home to California, she was in a total state of panic, fear, resolve, and utterly dependent on others. A private nurse was hired to come to change her dressings; those burns on her chest were something else! She also had to take blood, administer medications, check her chemo pump, and do a whole host of other medical duties. I remember this nurse as being such a lovely woman with a kind hand and a gentle way about her. But she wasn't full-time, so Charlie became Jill's caregiver. Which if you knew Charlie, this was not exactly the role he was going to be very good at playing.

The Other Shoe Always Drops

On my end, the new year started off slow from a business standpoint. I decided to go on hiatus from work for a few months to help Jill and Charlie. I kept my teaching position at the Art Center College of Design because I needed some income. Art Center was only two days a week, allowing me lots of freedom.

I rode my bike over the canyons into Malibu to Jill-sit while Charlie went to play golf or get out of the house for some fresh air. I'd help change her dressings and do whatever else Jill needed. If she needed to barf, I'd hold the bowl. If she needed more tissue boxes, I ensured she had a few boxes within reach. If she needed to sit quietly, we sat quietly. And all the while, I was happy to help my friend, never once feeling sorry about what I was giving up or missing to do so.

Sometimes Vernon would come over, and we would all sit around when Jill was up to it. We'd crack some terrible jokes, or Vernon would regale us with stories of his flings with famous actresses from back in the day. (Wink, wink, if those stories were true, which I'm sure they were, Vernon lived quite the life!) We enjoyed Vernon; he was full of personality and never at a loss for words. He kept us both entertained.

Jill's burns slowly healed, but her voice never did. It never came back. Gone was the cute and soothing voice she had. It was as if she were "debarked." Instead of a full-throated bark, the only thing coming out was a faint raspy sound. It was tough for me to say goodbye to her voice. It must have been torture for both Jill and Charlie. Her voice was so much a part of who she was. Her kindness came out in her voice. Her brilliance came out in her voice. Her love came out in her voice. And now, in its place, only a raspy whisper came out.

To this day, I'll watch one of her old movies to hear her voice again. My favorite movie is *From Noon Until Three*. That movie almost mirrored her everyday life, and I love it. It was also Jill's favorite movie. I still watch it when I'm feeling down. It is all Jill.

Three & Me

One day in early March, I rode my bike over the canyons to Jill-sit. I took a longer route this time, up over a grinding climb that was Kanan Road. Once over the canyon, I headed south to Jill's Serra Retreat home, which wasn't too far from Pepperdine University. Before I reached Pepperdine, along Pacific Coast Highway, there were a series of roller-coaster hills. In other words, undulating climbs. Not too many, but they have a healthy grade to them.

I was climbing one of the hills when I heard something inconsistent with regular traffic coming from behind me. I heard a car approaching closer than it should, so I looked over my left shoulder. And then I saw it. An SUV driven by a young guy with his buddy leaning out the passenger side window, arm raised and taking aim. It looked as if he was going to throw something. And then I felt it, the pain scorching through my back as I crashed my bike on the asphalt below. The car with the two guys sped off. I was left on the road, trying to clip out of my pedals while at the same time trying to recover from the sharp pain in my kidney area. They had thrown a rock at me while going 50 miles per hour. So that rock hit me with a 50-mph velocity. It not only knocked me over but bruised my back and my kidney. I had blood from road rash on my elbows and knees and could hardly stand without pain. Somehow, I managed to get back on my bike and finish the last hill before it was all downhill to the Bronsons house. (Later I would discover blood in my urine.)

When I got to Jill and Charlie's, Charlie took one look at me and was absolutely aghast. Reluctantly, I told him what had happened. "Get in the car! We're going to find those guys!" Charlie said. He was angry. The only other time I'd seen that anger flash in his eyes was the time at Doobies in Vermont when the slam dancers slammed us.

"Charlie, they're long gone," I said. It made no difference. Charlie and I piled into his car and cruised Pacific Coast Highway, looking for a needle in a haystack. We never found them, and I'm glad we didn't. God knows what Charlie would have done if he'd found them.

The Other Shoe Always Drops

When we arrived back at the house, I cleaned up and hung out with Jill for the rest of the day while Charlie left to play golf. My knee had stiffened badly when it was time for me to go. I called Yaniv and asked him to come and pick me up. Before I loaded my bike onto Yaniv's truck, Charlie, who was back from his golf game, came out, again expressing his regret at not finding the guys who nailed me. "Don't worry, Charlie," I told him. "Karma has a way of making pretty good payback. They'll get theirs one day." Charlie nodded his head in agreement, and I could tell he felt better. But I wonder. Did Karma bite them in their respective butts? Probably not.

On the days when I would take care of Jill, it appeared on one level as if Jill was doing better; on a whole other level, she really wasn't. Sometimes her white blood cell counts would get low due to the chemo, so it was dangerous for anyone to be around her. I'd have to stay away, and Charlie was left with just the nurse to help him—something he usually dreaded.

Two significant events were looming on the horizon. One was Jill's 54th birthday on April 24th. The other was her son Paul's wedding scheduled for the beginning of May. There was also talk about Jill receiving a star on the Hollywood Walk of Fame. According to Jill, you had to be nominated and then accepted by the Hollywood Chamber of Commerce to get one. Jill was nominated and accepted, which was truly exciting. Usually, someone else, other than the recipient, pays for it. When Jill got her star, I know $14,000 was raised towards it.

On April 24th, 1990, Jill's birthday, Hollywood held a celebration in honor of Jill Ireland Day. Her star at 6751 Hollywood Boulevard was right in front of the Crown Books store. I thought this was magical because of her new-found career as an author. Unfortunately, like many other brick-and-mortar stores, Crown Books has gone out of business. The last time I was at the site, there was an empty building in its place.

Jill wore a beautiful outfit, an off-white, almost light pink pleated skirt with a matching top and jacket. I couldn't help but notice how frail she was. But her smile went from ear to ear. Her hair, while short, was her own. Joan Rivers was one of the attendees at the event. I was happy to see her, as was Jill.

There is a celebratory custom where invited guests come to a luncheon in the recipient's honor. The luncheon was fabulous—good food, good company, and lots of good cheer. The entire day was beautiful. The weather cooperated with warm sunshine. There was so much positive energy and love flowing; it was infectious. Jill looked radiant though frail. Her voice wasn't hers, but the emotion behind it was the same, as was her sharp wit and sly sense of humor. I was grateful to Vernon Scott because I believed he had a big hand in getting Jill her star.

Jill sharply declined after the star ceremony, and I feared that this journey would be over before any of us were ready. She already had to be rushed to emergency once, and I was walking on eggshells because of what could come next. I hoped she would hang on for her son, Paul, and future daughter-in-law, Christine's wedding at the Four Seasons at the beginning of May. Jill had the constitution of a Pitbull—nothing would deter her from what she set her mind to. And I could see that she had set her sights on the wedding.

Paul is Jill's oldest child. He was engaged to a beautiful French-Canadian model named Christine. Not only is Christine beautiful outside, but she is also lovely inside. She is sweet and caring and everything Jill would want for her son. I remain friends, to this day, with Paul and Christine and feel privileged to have their friendship. Their daughter is the granddaughter I know would make Jill proud. She benefits from Christine's good looks and Paul's handsomeness. She has Paul's spirit for adventure, her mom's poise, and Jill's twinkle in her eyes. Deep in my heart, I know that Jill is whispering softly into Paul's ear at night, "Well done, son. Well done."

The Other Shoe Always Drops

Miracles do happen. We were five months post death speech, and Jill was still very much involved in life. She hung in there with a purpose that defied medical odds. It was she who would determine her departure date. Not any one of her doctors.

Jill made it to the wedding. She witnessed her firstborn wed the woman he loves, although she had to lean heavily on Charlie for support. But the ceremony was beautiful, and I could see the happiness on her face. I could also see the fear in Charlie's expression. Years later, I still recognize that fear in some of the photos from the wedding. His eyes tell it all. Jill was slipping away.

After the wedding, Jill went straight home. She was weak. The cancer was growing, and breathing became increasingly a chore. We would speak on the phone multiple times daily until she couldn't. My heart was tearing apart. My best friend in the entire world, a friend who always had my back, loved me unconditionally, and supported me in so many ways, was slowly disappearing in front of my eyes.

I couldn't visit her anymore. She wanted to preserve what little energy she had left. Except, I couldn't accept that. So, on Mother's Day, I drove out to visit Jill for just a few minutes. That probably wasn't the best idea, but I couldn't stand the thought of her leaving without me seeing her one more time. Uninvited, I went anyway. She was in the living room, and I could tell she felt terrible. I only stayed a minute or two. When I was leaving, I turned away from her and called out a "Bye Jill!" like I always did.

"Stop Right There!" she commanded, anger flooding her raspy voice. "TURN AROUND AND SAY GOODBYE TO MY FACE! DON'T YOU EVER SAY GOODBYE TO ME WITH YOUR BACK EVER AGAIN!" Her eyes flashed lightning.

And that's when I knew. I would never see Jill alive ever again. Tears filled my eyes, and I whispered, "Goodbye, Jill." We looked each other in the eyes for the last time. She knew it, and I knew it. The lump in my throat was growing. I felt at that moment that all that was good in my world was sitting on that couch, her body failing her, her soul wanting to exit. How could I say goodbye? I still can't. I turned and slowly left. Jill crashed about an hour after I left and was taken to St. John's Hospital by ambulance. She died at home five days later on Friday, May 18th. But not before she cracked one last joke.

A goose some months prior had taken up residence in their large backyard. Jill loved the goose, as did everyone who got to know her. On her deathbed, Jill looked up at Charlie and said, "Charlie, please don't cook the goose." And then she slipped away.

Jill and Charlie at one of their parties.

The Other Shoe Always Drops

## NINE

Life Goes On

J ust as I did the day after Jerry died in a hail of gunfire, I picked myself up and threw on riding clothes. I needed to be at the barn. I needed the validation of life that riding provided me with. There is something in the power of a horse, the rhythm and un-spoken communication that makes me feel whole again. It's prac-tically a spiritual experience for me when I'm feeling down. Being outside, feeling the sun and the wind, is almost an aphrodisiac for life itself.

My heart was hurting, but my mind was trying to tell me that Jill was OK now. No more pain. No more suffering. Sadly, though, no more life, the one thing she desired most. I knew, even then, that I would feel the loss many times over throughout my life, and I have.

Loss is inevitable. Knowing that and experiencing it is basically an oxymoron. On the one hand, all living things must die at some point. I know that. We all know that. On the other hand, the sense of loss and the ensuing heartbreak resulting from that loss brings me to the point where the loss is almost too hard to comprehend. So, then I begin to rationalize the pain away, or, as in my brother's case, a hard-fought refusal to acknowledge it even happened.

I learned through Jill's passing that the pain I felt, the same pain I felt when Jerry died, was actually the love I felt for each of them. Once I realized that, I began to accept the pain as a reaffirmation of my love. I've learned through loss that life is filled with both pain and love. The pain helps me remember the love, and the love allows me to forgive the pain. It's a symbiotic coupling of emotions.

213

214

The day Jill passed, Theresa and I visited her star. I placed a rose.

Life Goes On

Being on a horse is how I process grief, so I could hardly wait to get to the barn. As I was just about to leave the house, the news of Jill's passing hit the airwaves. My phone rang, throwing me into a conundrum. Answer or not answer? Let the machine get it? Screen it? I was torn. In the end, I answered it. Theresa Saldana was on the other end. She had a sadness in her voice. "I just heard," she said. "Why don't you come over, and we'll walk to her star on the Boulevard. We can place some flowers there."

I began to cry quietly. Theresa heard my sniffles. "Listen. You don't have to talk. But I have something very important to tell you about death."

Huh? I wasn't expecting to hear that. Talking about death, especially on that day, really wasn't what I wanted to do. But it was Theresa on the other end of the line. So, I decided to give it a go. "What about death?" I asked her.

"I'll tell you when you get here. What time are you coming?"

I told Theresa I needed to ride Aero first. Absolutely had to. It was a fairly short hop from the Equestrian Center over Cahuenga to Theresa's Hollywood Boulevard apartment. "I figure I'll get there around 2-2:30ish." She was good with that.

Of all the drives in Los Angeles, the 405 included, the drive I hate the most is the drive into Hollywood. Even with the proximity of the Equestrian Center, traffic was always something to be concerned about. In Los Angeles, it can sometimes take hours to go two miles, depending upon the time of day, weather conditions, and whether or not there was a fender bender or a serious car accident. Driving in LA is an ever-changing experience. Hollywood, though is not only a freeway gamble. It's a street gamble as well. Cahuenga Boulevard (the most direct route) passes by the Hollywood Bowl on its way to merge with Highland Avenue. Highland has its own set of problems,

Three & Me

not the least of which is the poor synchronization of traffic signals as well as the proximity to the Church of Scientology Celebrity Center on Franklin Avenue. It's possible to end up waiting at the intersection of Highland and Franklin for an endless amount of time as cars, maybe two or three at a time, make it through the green before it yellows and then turns that awful shade of red. As it happened, on that day in May 1990, traffic was light, and I made it to Theresa's building in good time.

I pulled into the underground parking lot, handed the attendant my keys, and entered the lobby, where they announced my arrival to Theresa. Theresa came down the elevator with her toddler, Tianna, in a stroller. I was blown away by how Theresa was dressed. She was in a wide-shouldered royal blue blazer paired with blue jeans. I think it was the only time I'd seen her dressed that casually, wearing clothes with a tighter fit than usual. She usually wore pink tops, flowing pants or long skirts, loose blouses, and finished off with a wide-shouldered jacket. And there was usually a very big pink bow in her hair.

She came over and immediately hugged me. Because her building was on Hollywood Boulevard (near Highland), we could walk to Jill's Star. On the way, I purchased a single pink rosebud. I would place it on Jill's star for as long as it would last on the heavily foot-trafficked sidewalk. The three of us arrived at the star quite quickly. Earlier in the day, the Hollywood Chamber of Commerce had placed a huge wreath on an easel at the site. That made me smile for two reasons. One, because she deserved that recognition. And two, because it would provide a temporary block over her star so my rose could spend some quality time with Jill before being kicked away by an unaware pedestrian.

I looked down at her star and slowly put my hand over her name, remembering back to less than a month prior when she was there, when we all were there, as she received the recognition and adulation she so deserved. To most people, especially the young and

Life Goes On

healthy, a month is a drop in the bucket of seemingly endless time. At this moment, it was the difference between a life lived beautifully and a life ended. Twenty-four days had passed since we'd all gathered at that exact spot, cheering her on. Twenty-four days in which her body methodically, purposefully, and relentlessly completely shut down.

I reflected on Jill's battle. It was as if she were trying to plug a leaking dike. She would plug up one cancer hole, and two holes sprung up. She tried to stick her finger in those two holes, and another three to four holes sprung up. She tried as hard as she could to plug up all the holes, but the cancer kept throwing more and more at her. It seemed that her soul needed to leave her body and was determined to do so. Watching Jill through the process, I concluded that once your soul finds the determination to go, it finds a way despite medical intervention. Life can be prolonged through medical science, which is a wonderful thing, but once your soul is recalled for the final time, it's the end.

I looked up from the star and took in the surroundings. Gone were the crowds. Gone was the double-decker bus filled with adoring fans. Gone were the attending celebrities. And now my best friend was also gone. This star on Hollywood Boulevard was the only tangible thing remaining to commemorate her all-too-short life.

I got up off my knees and walked back with Theresa and her baby to her place. I marveled at the wonderful and crazy energy the Boulevard seemed to have. It was urban. It was gritty. The atmosphere was as close to Times Square as any area in Los Angeles. As I walked down Hollywood Boulevard with my friend, I realized that Theresa had carved out a quasi-New York existence in her little corner of Hollywood by living in a high-rise with a doorman. I gave her credit for her effort to turn an Orange into an Apple.

As we walked, I remembered that I hadn't yet asked her what she meant when she said she wanted to tell me something important about death. It had been in the back of my mind the entire day. As if she read my thoughts, at that exact moment, Theresa opened the door to the discussion.

"Do you remember when I told you I had something important to tell you about death?" she asked. I nodded. "I must tell you it is the most wonderful feeling you'll ever experience. Dying is incredible! So, don't feel bad for Jill. She just went through the most beautiful experience she could ever have."

Well, I wasn't expecting that, as I thought morosely to myself that maybe it's the most beautiful, but it's also the final experience. "I don't get it. Isn't dying filled with gasping for air, feeling your heart stop, panic, all that stuff?" I asked, utterly bewildered.

Theresa shook her head. "Do you remember when I was stabbed?" she said. "Well, I was at the Hospital, and I was hemorrhaging blood from all the stab wounds. I coded. I basically died right there on the table. All of a sudden, I felt myself going towards a very big and bright light, and I had the most wonderfully euphoric feeling wrapping itself around me. I looked down and saw my body on the operating table. I could see myself. I felt like I was getting farther and farther away and lost myself in the wonderful experience of death."

"Holy Shit, Theresa!" I was literally stunned. I've read about near-death experiences. I even read the book *"On Death and Dying"* by Elisabeth Kübler-Ross. The common theme always seemed to be the bright light. The euphoric feeling Theresa was describing wasn't something I'd come across before.

Theresa then continued. "The doctor was afraid he was losing me. All the monitors and machines I was hooked up to started to beep, so he reached into my chest and began to massage my heart while the others were able to stem the bleeding. IV bags full of blood were literally being poured into my body. My heart began to beat again, and the next thing I knew, I was back in my body. I couldn't help but feel disappointed because I loved the feeling of dying more than I was afraid of dying. But that was before I was a mom. Now I'm back to being afraid of dying, but only because I'd be leaving Tianna — not because I'm afraid of death."

It was then that I found complete comfort in Theresa's words. Those words continue to comfort me, especially in the face of impending loss. I recall our conversation that day when someone I love passes. Her description of her experience brings me back to a sense of well-being. I had to believe her. Who would know better than someone who was clinically dead and then brought back? I surmised no one would, and I took Theresa at her word. I was grateful we had that talk, and for the first time in the days leading up to and after Jill's passing, I felt myself begin to smile from within.

Charlie had Jill cremated, and her ashes were returned to him in a large urn. He'd had a beautiful mirrored box made to keep Jill's ashes safe until he could get to Vermont and keep her at the place she loved so much. One night when I was visiting him, soon after he got Jill, he motioned for me to come to the other side of his massive desk. "Here, Suzie, pick this up."

"What is it?" I asked him. "It's really heavy!" I put the box back down. Charlie shot me a wry smile, and his eyes twinkled with just the right amount of mischief.

"It's Jill," he said proudly. "I had her cremated." I just sat down in the chair and shook my head. No words. None.

Charlie chose the Four Seasons Hotel to hold her memorial. It was the same hotel where Paul and Christine exchanged their vows just a short time prior to Jill's passing. The irony struck me hard. The two events couldn't have been more different. One was a celebration of two people uniting in love; the other was a celebration of someone's

Three & Me

life gone too soon. Two different celebrations just weeks apart. I chose to wear the same outfit Jill had given me for the *"Life Wish"* book party. I wanted to wear something that embodied and symbolized my friendship with Jill. I also donned a special necklace she gave me one Christmas years before. When I entered the room, I held my head high and made my back as erect as it would go in my bid to be the Fine English Lady I was trained to be. Charlie was already seated with the rest of the family in the front row. I gave him a hug and found a seat off to the side. As I sat down quietly, I looked around the room. I recognized a great many faces, many of them from Jill's various parties, others more closely tied to the family. As I looked to one side, I felt someone sit beside me on the other side. When I turned, I looked into the eyes and sweet smile of former First Lady, Nancy Reagan. Back in 1988, Jill testified before Congress about the medical costs of cancer. She was awarded the American Cancer Society's Courage Award by President Reagan, an award she was very proud to have received.

During that period of time, Nancy Reagan, herself a breast cancer survivor, and Jill struck up a friendship. Jill would tell me all about their phone calls, brainstorming about breast cancer awareness. Soon after she took her seat next to mine, Mrs. Reagan held out her hand to me and introduced herself simply as "Nancy Reagan." There was none of the "don't you know who I am?!" baloney. She was warm and friendly. I liked her and saw why Jill liked her also because it was hard to resist the smile that radiated from her genuine warmth.

To my other side, a young actress named Tracy Nelson sat down. It was apparent that she was distraught; the tears were already flowing from her eyes. I immediately realized who she was. Jill was very fond of the young actress involved in her own fight against disease. She once told me that she was mentoring Tracy Nelson, the daughter of Ricky Nelson. According to Jill, Tracy was battling Non-Hodgkins Lymphoma at the same time Jill was going through her journey with breast cancer. Sometimes Tracy would call when I was at the house, and I would hear Jill's side of the conversation. Jill absolutely adored her and told me how happy she felt that she could help answer Tracy's questions, allay her fears, and be a cheerleader in Tracy's recovery. I'm pleased to report that Tracy is herself a warrior and is still very much alive today after successfully battling cancer too many times. I know Jill would be so happy about her survival.

During the celebration of Jill's life, friends and family got up to speak, voicing little snippets of memories from their relationships with Jill. It soon became my turn to get up on the dais and speak. There was no way I could capture the entire friendship, all the fun, all the laughter, all the shared experiences, as well as my part in her journey in a short speech. I opted to keep my eulogy light the way I think Jill would have wanted it. I spoke about what I was wearing, that the outfit was a gift from Jill. I spoke about my Fine English Lady Training, and I made sure to pronounce all those annoying "A" sounding words with "AH" sounds as if I was genuinely British.

Charlie was chuckling in his seat in the front row. It was the first time he laughed during the entire celebration of her life. He knew what I was talking about. He got it. And that's all that mattered to me. I honestly felt Jill was sitting by my side as I spoke. I had a smile on my face and in my heart as I felt Jill so very close to me. When I finished, Charlie gave me a nod of approval. I smiled back at him and walked back to my seat with as much poise as I could muster. As I was about to sit down, Nancy Reagan grabbed both my hands and told me how much she loved my speech. She had a tear in her eye but a smile on her face.

Also in attendance was a very well-known and highly respected book author and editor at the *"Hollywood Reporter,"* who was very close to Jill. Her name was Marcia Borie. She was a large woman with a bigger personality. Everyone loved Marcia, including me. Marcia would be the last speaker of the day. She took her spot in front of the mic and shared a dream she had about a little bird. In her dream, the bird approached her in the backyard of her home shortly after Jill passed. Marcia felt that the little bird was Jill. It was a cute story, but it never quite ended. Marcia rambled on and on and on. Soon people were shifting in their seats, uncomfortable with the incoherence and the long-winded tale. Finally, Marcia concluded her story, then went home, and, for some unknown reason, she died. She was just 60 years old at the time.

Charlie called me the following morning to let me know Marcia had passed away during the night. I was shocked awake. Marcia? Dead? I couldn't believe she had died. I felt terrible, especially since I was one of the people who really wanted Marcia's speech to wrap. Talk about feeling guilty! Because Marcia was Jewish, she would be buried the next day. Charlie said he'd come to pick me up before the funeral, and we'd go together.

When we got to the Hollywood Cemetery on Santa Monica Boulevard, we ran into Dr. Ray Weston, who at one time was Charlie's doctor as well as my own. Ray decided to hang out with us during the formalities. When it came time for burial, we were ushered into a mausoleum where her coffin was placed on a crane. She was to be placed in the nose-bleed section way up top. Marcia was, as I stated before, a very big woman. Consequently, she had to be placed in a very big coffin. From all appearances, it was an expensive one, with beautiful wood-grained finishes and a slick sheen that reflected the surrounding ambient lighting.

The crane was raised until Marcia's coffin stopped before the prepared opening, where she would slide very carefully into a wall for the rest of eternity. The employees began the chore of pushing the coffin into the slot. Initially, the coffin started to go in, but suddenly, with a huge screech from wood against marble, it stopped partway through. The casket was stuck. The employees tried pulling the coffin out. Nope. Marcia wasn't going to budge. Then, much to our horror, the employees began to bang on Marcia's casket, trying to somehow dislodge it and push it into the opening. The noise from the banging was deafening, bouncing and echoing off the marble walls of the mausoleum. In absolute abject horror, Charlie and I had our gaping mouths covered with our hands when Ray turned around and said, "Good God! They're going to wake up Marcia." Charlie and I looked at each other, not quite knowing what to do. Normally we would have laughed at such a well-timed joke, but laughing at something as morose as this...? Thankfully, we both were able to stifle the impulse.

After many futile attempts to dislodge Marcia, a funeral director entered the mausoleum and told us all to leave. I took one last look at Marcia Borie, hanging up high, halfway in and halfway out of her final resting place. It was almost as if she decided that maybe she didn't really want to be there after all.

# # #

One morning I was taking a shower, and as I was lathering up, I noticed a gray pubic hair! What The Hell! I completely freaked and immediately began to swear like a sailor. I wasn't ready for that terrible discovery. I was still in my 30's—far too young, or so I thought, for gray pubes. I pulled that sucker right out of my girl area faster than you could say, Jack! Then I quickly washed off, threw my towel around my body, and ran to the phone to call Jill to tell her about the sudden and huge new transformation my body was making! I was halfway through dialing when I realized she wasn't there. I burst out sobbing uncontrollably. It was at that exact moment that the finality of the loss finally hit me. I hated the emptiness of the dial tone, as well as the emptiness in my heart.

A few months after Jill's passing, I met with a client in Westlake Village for lunch. At the time, I was driving a white BMW 318is. During that period, there was a rash of carjackings involving white BMWs with women drivers. After my lunch in Westlake, I had another meeting scheduled in Valencia with Answer Products, manufacturers of

Motocross and Supercross accessories. My Westlake client told me the quickest way to Simi Valley would be to get on the 101 Northbound to the 23, exit at Olsen Road, and follow it up to the 118. (The connector between the two freeways was still years away from being built.)

While I was driving on the 23 freeway, a souped-up car pulled up next to me in the other lane. The driver appeared to be a 20-something Latino male with long jet-black hair, a narrow face, a square jaw, and some scraggly facial hair. What stood out most about this guy was that his arms were light brown and completely hairless. He had an open sunroof, and his arm was sticking out of it, signaling me to pull over. Well, this is Los Angeles. If a guy is signaling for you to pull over, he probably plans on killing you, raping you, robbing you, or all three. I had no intention of pulling over, so I shook my head "No." He stayed right next to me in the other lane, never once leaving my side. My exit was coming up, so without signaling and traveling just beyond the actual exit, I suddenly turned right, crossing over the little triangular section that separates the offramp from the freeway. I figured he'd never be able to pull that off from where he was. Except he did. I was in the right-hand turn lane when I noticed him pulling up next to me again in the left-hand turn lane. I had a bad feeling about this guy.

Back in the early 1980s, I was a witness for the government in a huge Ponzi scheme case. My testimony put six defendants behind bars. One of the Federal agents I worked closely with, a man named Kent, once gave me this great advice; "Suzie, if you think you're being followed, make three right turns. If that car is still with you after that, you're being followed."

Remembering that sage advice, I made a right turn. He made a right turn. I made another right turn. He made another right turn. I made the third right turn, and yep, t---*here he was. So, I gunned it. I took off like a bat out of hell because I was on a fairly deserted stretch of road. Well, it turns out his car was as fast, if not faster than mine. He was right on my tail. I saw a signal ahead of me, and I was praying I could make it. When the light turned red, I slammed on the brakes, quite literally screeching to a halt. It was then that I looked out my rearview and saw him stand up in his car, emerging from out of his sunroof, completely enraged. His car was actually shaking with his anger! He screamed that I would never get away from him, there was no escape, I was going to be his, etc. Talk about a crazy man! But instead of being afraid, I realized he didn't have a gun because he would have already used it if he did. So, I thought, "Let him scream." Because I was stuck at a light, I wasn't driving. I used the pause to hit 911 on my car phone, reaching the Simi Valley Police Department.

I explained my situation, and the officer took down my number in case of disconnect and gave me directions to follow. He asked me to describe everything that was happening. The guy was still yelling at me, pumping his fist in the air through the sunroof. When the light changed, I followed the officer's directions to some unknown destination. Finally, I was instructed to make a right turn down an obscure street, and there, at the end of the road, were a bunch of black and whites waiting for me.

The guy behind me took one look at the police cars, threw his car into reverse, and took off with officers in pursuit. The officers interviewed me to make sure I was OK; then they provided me with a motorcycle officer to escort me safely out of Simi Valley. That motorcycle officer stayed on my tail not only out of Simi but well into the San Fernando Valley. Funny thing about having a police escort right behind your car. No other car wants to pass. It didn't take long for the freeway in front of me to become totally void of cars. I literally had a parade behind me. Just before the 118 meets the 405, the motorcycle officer flashed his lights and waved goodbye. I returned a wave of gratitude feeling lucky the experience was behind me. I could hardly wait to tell Jill!

Three & Me

Again, that horrible feeling hit my stomach with the realization that I couldn't. So, I called Theresa and told her. She was convinced this guy intended to murder me. Of course, she would think that. To her, most men of ill intent have murder on their minds. I was less fazed than I should have been. I easily blew the whole thing off, telling her I never really felt like I was in grave danger. I was more excited by the really cool police escort! I was battle-tested from living in Israel, and it would take a lot more than that lunatic to scare me. Except Theresa was right. He probably did intend to murder me. I just didn't realize it yet.

A few years later, on the same freeway, a young co-ed from Moorpark College was murdered. I looked at her photos, and there was a slight resemblance to me. Hmmmm. I wondered if it was the same guy who had chased me. There was just something eerily familiar about that murder, and I kept ruminating about it. I'd thought of calling the Simi Valley Police and having them look up the details of my chase, but I figured it was such a long shot that they wouldn't connect the dots. Battling with myself over this decision, I made the call anyway. They took notes but, being police, never called me back. They had bigger fish to fry and were probably already closing in on the actual murderer anyway.

Not too long after, the murderer was indeed caught, and his picture was plastered all over the news. I found myself staring at the guy who had chased me years earlier. Turns out he was the Simi Valley rapist who had, at some point, graduated from rape to murder. His name was Vincent Sanchez. As I looked at his photo, his features stood out to me. He possessed that same jet-black hair, square jaw, and light brown, hairless arms. It was only then that I got chills up my spine! He absolutely was, without a doubt, up to harming me at the time of the chase. My mind went crazy, imagining all the horrible things this man probably thought as he chased me down. The mental "What If" game can be a dangerous game to play, and I played it well.

Life Goes On

And then I recalled that summer's day back when I was a little kid, re-living the experience, smelling the stench in the back seat of the would-be kidnapper's car. Was that death I smelled back then? What if it was?

CECIL YATES/DAILY NEWS

Sport getting harder to enjoy
Designer Susie Dotan exercises her horse at the Los Angeles Equestrian Center where boarding fees for the mounts will be increased by 6.3 percent in June. Dotan is disappointed with the increase and says her horsemanship hobby is "becoming the

Riding my horses always got me through
the really tough times. On the day Jill
passed, I went out and rode Aero.
A photographer from
the Daily News *shot my photo.*
This showed up in the paper three
days later.

Three & Me

One of my favorite outfits.
Jill Ireland gave me this beautiful knit ensemble.
I wore this to her book party
and I proudly wore it to her memorial.
(Also, that was the 80s, so I ended up
with big hair when I glammed up.)

TEN

Learning To Read The Room

After Jill died, I spent a lot of time with Charlie. We both needed each other's company during that transition period. Charlie would look at me and say, "Every time I look at you, I see Jill." Each time he said it, I would feel conflicted. On the one hand, I liked having physical likenesses with Jill. She was a gorgeous woman. I also strived to be more like her, and how she treated others. Many times, even now, I quietly think, "What would Jill do in this situation?" Then I follow what I believe would have been her path forward. On the other hand, when Charlie would tell me that, I'd feel terrible, wondering if my resemblance to Jill brought him pain.

I know Vernon Scott was hurt by my appearance. He ran into me at a typesetter's office in Chatsworth a couple of years after Jill's passing. I smiled when I saw him because he was so much a part of Jill's last chapter, only I didn't get the response I was expecting. His face went sheet white upon seeing me. "I can't look at you," he said in a voice betraying a huge panic. "You look too much like her! You remind me too much of Jill!" And with that, he bolted, leaving his work behind. I never saw him again after that.

In the immediate aftermath of Jill's death, I fell into a regular schedule. I'd work during the day and head to Charlie's for dinner. Yaniv attended classes almost every night during the week, so he was happy I could have some company while he was gone.

During that period, I was designing snowboard graphics for Kemper Snowboards, as well as creating catalogs and advertising/marketing materials for them. I was deeply immersed in the snowboarding culture as well as the sport itself. The top manufacturer at the time was

Burton Snowboards. (It still is number 1). I knew that Burton Snowboards was founded by Jake Burton Carpenter. David McCallum, Jill's ex-husband, and father to Paul, Val, and Jason, married Jake's sister, Katherine Carpenter. I loved that. There were just a few degrees of separation between us. I thought this connection was amazing. (Unfortunately, Jake Burton Carpenter also succumbed to the ravages of cancer just a few years ago.)

Charlie knew I loved snowboarding, so he'd go out and buy snowboard videos that we would watch after dinner. Then we'd play pool. Charlie taught me how to play, and I got pretty good at it. It's because of Charlie that I have a pool table at home. Every time I rack up, I can still hear him lamenting, "You left me no good shots, Suzie! None!"

On every night that I ate dinner with him in Malibu, Charlie would walk me to my car and give me a huge bear hug as we said goodbye. I know the entire world thinks of Charlie as the "tough guy," and to a large extent, he probably was. But Charlie gave the best hugs I'd ever experienced. It was where he was able to convey his genuine affection for me through those strong arms of his.

One night as I was saying goodbye, Charlie asked me if I could consider leaving Yaniv for him. That caught me completely off guard, but I wasn't thinking as a widowed man thinks. I was thinking about how I think, which was in a different direction altogether. I didn't know what to say or how to say it, so I stumbled. First, I told him I was flattered. Then I told him that Jill was still so present that I would feel like I was cheating on her. And then there was Yaniv. Our marriage was becoming less of a marriage and more of a partnership. Yaniv was always busy with school and work, and I hardly saw him. And when I did, he was always studying. It was only on Sunday that we would get together and have fun. But I wasn't ready to leave him. I still loved him.

Learning To Read The Room

Charlie told me how he and I would be a good fit. He told me that I reminded him of Jill. I had a lot of her same qualities. And we were already great friends. (Not only did we watch baseball games together on the phone, but I got him into watching the Tour de France. Charlie went as nuts as I did when Greg LeMond beat Laurent Fignon on the famous time trial back in '89!) Not knowing what else to say, I told Charlie I'd give it some thought.

I used to drive a BMW that had about 125,000 miles on it, which is really nothing for a BMW, but one day I heard a strange noise and saw smoke coming out of my car through my rearview mirror. I discovered that I had a cracked manifold that would cost $10,000 to fix. I thought repairing it was tantamount to throwing money away. Time for a new car! I drove over to a BMW dealer and bought one. That same night I drove the new car over to Charlie's. The evening was the same as it always was. We ate chicken curry, Charlie's favorite dish, then watched snowboard videos and played some pool.

That night when he walked me to my car, he noticed it was new. "You didn't tell me you got a new car, Suzie. I am so relieved you did. I worried when you drove the old car through the canyon at night until you called to say you're home safe."

What most people didn't realize about Charlie was that he was a huge worrywart over the people he loved. When Jill and Charlie lived in their Bel Air house, Charlie could hear the accidents on Sunset Boulevard. He'd cringe and hope it wasn't someone from the family. When someone left the house, he was worried until they came safely back. That was Charlie. So, when he said he was relieved I got the new car, I knew he meant it.

I gave him a ride around Serra Retreat in it, and he liked my new car. I drove a stick shift (and still do), and Charlie thought that was pretty cool. I pulled up in his driveway, he gave me a hug before he got out, then I drove home.

Three & Me

The very next night, I drove to Charlie's after work. We ate dinner. Watched videos. Played pool. Then he walked me to my car. When we got to my car, Charlie looked at it and said, "New Car? You didn't tell me you got a new car!" At first, I thought he was kidding me, especially because he was always such a tease. But then he launched into the same speech about being worried every time I drove the canyon at night in the old one. It was almost word for word, the same exact speech I'd gotten the night before.

I thought about it the whole way home. Was Charlie yanking my chain? At first, I thought so. But as he continued to speak, I realized that he was seeing my new car for the very first time. Again! So, I called his son and told him what had happened. He told me that, in all likelihood, Charlie was teasing me. He assured me that I didn't need to worry. I kept protesting, but he was convinced Charlie, being the big teaser and kidder that he was, oversold it that night. I wasn't convinced but decided not to make a big deal of it. If his own son wasn't worried, then I should just mind my own business.

Eventually, I had to tell Charlie that I had a great deal of love for him but that I couldn't leave Yaniv at that time. It just didn't feel right. Had this been another time, I could see Charlie and me together because I really did love him. But the timing was so very wrong. So, Charlie moved on.

At that time, I didn't realize that men who have been happily married for many years and suddenly find themselves widowed have a strong need to find someone to be with. Divorced men are quite the opposite. They are soured on relationships and especially soured on marriage. Looking back on it, I realize that I was the natural choice for Charlie's post-Jill relationship search. I was already in his life. I knew his wife and his family. And I basically knew Charlie. But at the time, I was completely oblivious to the needs of a man suddenly finding himself alone. I had stayed in the same role as a family friend and never realized that being in that role would put me in the line of succession.

Learning To Read The Room

At dinner one night, Charlie announced that he was quietly dating a woman who wanted to get her claws into him. Paul and I were at the dinner table that night. We both kidded him about whomever she was. He was lamenting that his new lady already wanted him to meet her parents. According to Charlie, he could feel the vise tightening around his neck. But knowing Charlie, the way I knew Charlie, I think there was a bit of a brag behind the complaint. His new lady was younger and very attractive. I hadn't yet met her, but Charlie told me she worked for Michael Viner producing audiobooks. She met Charlie when she produced Jill's audiobook, *"Life Lines."*

I still visited Charlie while he was seeing his new lady, until she began staying over at the house. One night, I went to dinner at the house with Jill's son, Paul. Without warning or provocation, Charlie's new lady let me know through her behavior that I wasn't really a welcome guest. The nicest women can suddenly turn territorial if they feel any kind of threat from another female. I guessed that Charlie told her that he asked me to have a relationship with him and that I declined. Or maybe it was because I was Jill's best friend. Whatever the reason, the hostility was thick.

When I left that night, I knew I wouldn't be able to see Charlie as long as they were together, and I respected that. I was officially persona non grata with the new lady. Charlie and Jill were in my life for many years, and his new woman's appearance in Charlie's life meant that they were now both gone from it.

Kim stepped into Charlie's life seamlessly. She even began riding the horses at the barn. Kim's time at the barn left an opening, which I gladly took advantage of. I'd call Charlie during the mornings when Kim was off riding at the stable down the street, and we'd have nice chats. He told me he bought Kim a house in Calabasas because he wasn't quite sure about her at that time and wanted to make sure she'd have somewhere to go to if things didn't work out. We'd talk about Jill and reminisce about the good times, but those conversations would eventually come to a sad end.

Three & Me

Charlie's memory began to decline. I never found out if he had dementia, Alzheimer's, or some other condition, but something was
clearly wrong with his cognitive functioning. I'd seen the preview
of his decline that night with my new BMW. His son and I stayed in
touch, and we spoke one night after Charlie had gotten in his car to
drive into town from Malibu. As he explained it, Charlie suddenly got
disoriented. He had no idea where he was going, had no idea where
he had been, and had no idea how to get back home. Thankfully, he
had a phone in his car and was able to reach someone. According
to his son, Charlie was sufficiently scared from that experience, so
much so, that he began to withdraw into his own cocoon, effectively
creating a smaller world for himself.

Months later, I got a Christmas card in the mail. It was from Charles
and Kim Bronson. I believe it was Kim's way of letting me know they
had gotten married. The irony was that I was happy for Charlie in that
he had someone who would care for him. I was never a threat to Kim.

The last time I saw Charlie was a few years later. He was in the back
of a golf cart at a horse show. His eyes were vacant as he stared
ahead. He was just there, not moving a muscle. Charlie, as I knew
him, was gone. He was not the man I remembered. I sent him some
love through my heart to his. He passed away not too long after that.
Unfortunately, I was barred from his funeral.

# # #

The summer of Jill's passing, my friend Julie Tolman invited me to the
Greek Theater to see the band Crosby Stills and Nash. Julie's husband
Gerry managed Stephen Stills and filled other positions with the band
as well. I jumped at the chance to go! CSN was my favorite group of
all time. When I was a college student, I would drive all over California to see them in concert. My big crush was on Stephen Stills. I
thought he was out and out, the sexiest man alive. I would literally
spend hours holding the album covers in front of me, staring at him

and wondering what it would be like to be his girlfriend. My favorite album cover was the one that had the three of them on an old couch, in front of an old house, on an old porch. Stephen was in the middle, holding a guitar with David Crosby on one side and Graham Nash on the other. I must have stared at that album cover for hours on end.

When Julie and I arrived at the Greek, I was excited to be seated where we were. Gerry got some great seats for us, right in front and dead center. The band performed all my favorites, and I was in heaven. After some really great sets, they called an intermission. Julie looked over at me and asked, "Do you want to go backstage?"

Well, who doesn't want to do that?! Of course, I wanted to go! As we walked to the back area of the stage, someone came up to me and said, "You know, you look just like that actress who just died. What was her name? Jill? Jill Ireland! You look so much like her!"

I loved hearing that, being both happy and sad at the same time. As I followed Julie, I was thinking about the irony of it all. Here I was, enjoying a rock and roll concert. I was backstage, and the one person I wanted to call and tell her all about it wasn't around anymore. I was still lost in thought when Stephen Stills came over to greet Julie. And then he noticed me standing with her. He introduced himself, and there was something in his demeanor that made me think he was interested in me. Julie picked up on that also. Twenty years had passed since I had my big crush on him, but I was still happy to finally meet him. He hung around with us for a bit before he had to go onstage again.

"I think Stephen is hitting on you," Julie said, not without some trepidation. "I need to go tell him you're married and just not interested." With that, Julie disappeared, returning a few minutes later.

At the next break, Stephen came back and began hanging out with us again. He asked about an antique cloisonne pin shaped like a guitar

Three & Me

that I was wearing and told me how much he loved it. He also said he collected guitar-themed jewelry. Well, that was a huge hint, wasn't it?! I don't really get attached to too many things, and I had no real emotional attachment to that pin. So, I took it off and gave it to him. I surmised that if it made him happy, then I was happy.

Stephen continued to flirt until Gerry pulled him aside and told him it wasn't going to happen. I don't know if Stephen saw me as a groupie, a one-night-stand kind of thing, or if he had a genuine interest in me as a person. I'm guessing he was hoping to get lucky for the night, which wasn't going to happen. I did get a kick out of the whole thing, though. True to form, I've always gotten most of what I wanted when I didn't really want it anymore. This was a classic example. I do wonder, from time to time, if he still has that pin. Maybe he'll see this and tell Julie.

# # #

Toward the middle of 1990, Theresa got some great news. Arthur Jackson would be tried on charges of making terrorist threats. When she told me, I was elated. She had been watching the calendar with dread as the days changed into months and months into years. With every fiber of her body, she knew that Jackson was getting closer and closer to release. It had been all she could talk about. It wasn't even going to be a parole situation. It was to be a full release, with no conditions attached. Never mind that he was probably going to be extradited to England to face murder charges, he still posed a huge danger to her. He had implied in his threatening letters to her that he knew where her family lived and that he had forged friendships with other prisoners. Any one of them could come after Theresa upon their respective releases.

Theresa *was* a nice person with a heart of gold. And when I say *nice*, I mean it. She wanted only to be a wonderful mother to her daughter and to be a source of comfort for victims of crime. Her foundation helped heal so many scarred women, which I witnessed first-hand. I met many of the women who benefitted from Victims for Victims over the years, and their tales were heart-wrenching. Somehow, these brave women were able to come out on top of the bad. I believe it was through the mentoring and care that Theresa and the foundation gave them. A great deal of those women were stage performers, so I was able to witness their talents first-hand. One woman named Patty, who was part of Victims for Victims, came to my living room with her husband, a scriptwriter, and director, with Theresa in tow. Patty and her husband performed their new play for me as I sat on my own couch at home! Truthfully that was one of the best plays I have seen and with those seats. WOW!

Jackson's trial date had been set and was coming up soon. Theresa asked me if I would attend the trial. Not totally understanding what that entailed, I readily agreed to her request. I had completely forgotten my fear of entering a courtroom lest someone discover that I was the sister of the gunman at the Van Nuys Courthouse. I only remembered my fear as I walked in, but by then, it was too late. During my first few steps inside, I was afraid I was going to fall into a crack within a dark abyss of fear and depression. Thankfully, I didn't.

Theresa also asked a few survivor friends from Victims for Victims to come. They would also be in the gallery. We all wore pink armbands, which, thinking back on it, surprised me that we were allowed to do that.

It was the beginning of December 1990 when I walked into the Superior Courthouse in Hollywood. I quickly found the other women who had come to support Theresa, which was comforting. The only person who was "missing" was Theresa. Witnesses are not allowed to be in the courtroom as their testimony can be tainted by the testimonies of others. I learned that while I was serving as a government witness. Movies and television always show a witness in the gallery, as in "Your Honor, I now call Mr. Johnson to the stand," and then a man stands up and walks over to be sworn in. But that's all theater. In real life, witnesses are sequestered away from any proceedings, brought in when it's their turn to testify, then escorted out again.

I took my seat without paying attention to where I was in relation to everything else in the courtroom. As I looked up, a chill came over me. I realized that I was seated directly behind Jackson and his defense attorney. I noted how poorly dressed his public defender was and how much he was sweating. I also realized I could have stretched my arm out and reached Jackson. That's how close I was. I was seated on the left side of the courtroom because I didn't realize that was the defense side. Had I known, I would have taken a seat to the right.

I remember staring at the back of Arthur Jackson's head, wondering just what the hell was going on in his brain. First of all, you've got to be a special kind of terrible to want to kill someone, to begin with. Then once you cross that line between sanity and insanity, who tries to kill someone they have never ever met? What kind of a person does that kind of thing? I know he was mentally unstable, yes, but his brain did fire some cylinders. The planning he took, and the detailed execution of his plan, was not a simple task. That took a modicum of creativity and intelligence. And now, here I was, seated right behind him.

Courtrooms are not as exciting in real life as they are on television. Lots of legal wrangling between judges and attorneys, and everything moves at a slow pace. I could not sit still for very long because of my ADHD, and I was starting to squirm. I have always had ADHD; it just wasn't diagnosed until I was an adult. My sit-down capacity, which was usually an hour, was quickly reaching its limit. I tried stretching. That didn't work. My brain wanders when things get slow, so I began focusing on the seams of the defense attorney's jacket because they appeared to be stretching in odd directions. I was completely checked out until I heard the prosecutor call Arthur Jackson to the stand. I came to attention almost immediately!

Learning To Read The Room

To my complete surprise, Arthur Jackson walked over, was sworn in, and took his seat in the witness box. Defendants, especially in cases like these, don't usually take the stand due to protections against self-incrimination. I was shocked that his attorney allowed Arthur Jackson to testify. I perked up, razor-focused. This was bound to be testimony I would never, ever forget. I still haven't 30 years later.

As prosecutors do, they lead the witness down a particular path of questioning. They build a logical path forward, slowly edging the witness closer to exposing the things the prosecution needs in order to prove their case. Prosecuting Arthur Jackson was a petite woman named Susan Gruber. I loved her spunk from the get-go. As she began to question Jackson, she reminded me of a cat playing with its prey right before the kill. I hung on her every word as she took Arthur Jackson through his paces, eventually landing on his intentions regarding Theresa Saldana. And then he said it.

"First of all," he began slowly, "I'd like to start by saying I'm sorry..."

I was momentarily surprised when he began what I thought was the beginning of an apology. I expected him to continue with, "I'm sorry I caused so much pain," "I'm sorry for all the suffering," or something equally contrite—anything to get some sympathy from a jury or a judge. But Arthur Jackson was a different kind of animal with a brain that fired its cylinders in different and mostly illogical directions. So, he continued on his path to self-destruction with no hesitation. "I'm sorry that Miss Saldana did not die!"

He really said that! I mean, he really actually did say those exact words! Upon hearing those words, I sat bolt upright in my chair, every muscle tightening against the ugliness that was coming out of that man's mouth.

Considering all the insane moments of my life—the botched kidnapping, escaping the Simi Valley rapist/murderer, just missing a terrorist bomb blast, living in a war zone, an aviation near miss, all of that—nothing prepared me for those words that flowed all too easily out of Jackson's mouth. Nothing. Watching him on the stand saying those things was almost too much for me to handle. My heart exploded.

I sat glued to the edge of my seat, watching the prosecutor. She was a lioness going in for the kill. Ms. Gruber had him now. And she knew it. With the instinctual craftiness honed by years of prosecutorial experience, she deftly handed him enough rope to hang himself. "And why is that Mr. Jackson?" she asked with a wry smile accentuated by the sharp, curt tone of her voice.

"Because," he continued as if not having a care in the world, "no one has the right to rob me of my divine mission. No one!"

"And what divine mission is that, Mr. Jackson?" Susan Gruber had a slight grin in the upper corners of her mouth. She knew now it was an open and shut case.

Arthur Jackson dutifully complied with his answer. "To murder Miss Theresa Saldana and be executed by the electric chair in the State of California so that our souls can be married in heaven forever." (Note: California never had the electric chair. It had the gas chamber in 1990.)

I sat there dumbfounded. Here it was. This was no movie. This was no John Grisham novel. This was real life, as raw and gritty as it gets. Emotionally, I was spent. I was grateful that Theresa didn't hear this testimony. I heard it and was ready for the psychiatrist's couch. I couldn't imagine what this would do to her. I wished I could share all of this with Jill. She would have been dumbfounded. Jill liked Theresa, especially since Theresa starred opposite Charlie in *The Evil That Men Do*. I could almost hear Jill telling me how it must have been absolutely "Dreadful!" to hear such testimony.

Learning To Read The Room

As Jackson was testifying, his attorney sat there, stunned. His posture said it all. He was going to lose this case. He slumped forward and put one of his hands on the back of his head as if to acknowledge defeat. I don't remember him going up to resurrect the witness, his client. If he did, I was in too much shock to notice.

Court was adjourned, and I, along with the other supporters for Theresa, left the courtroom absolutely drained. None of us could believe it. We all wanted to somehow wash Arthur Jackson's words off our bodies.

That evening Theresa phoned me. She wanted to know what happened in court. I didn't want to tell her for several reasons. One, I didn't want to freak her out, and two, ethics were involved. I kept hedging, dodging, and out-and-out ignoring her pleas. Finally, I decided I could throw her a bone and not compromise my own values. "Theresa," I said, "Jackson was Jackson. That's all I'm going to say."

Theresa laughed. "Thank goodness, right?!" The following day Theresa testified. I was so proud of her. She stood her ground and kept her composure. She relayed how his threats terrified her to the point where she had to return to psychiatric therapy to help her through it. She told the court how she had a solid belief that if he didn't kill her himself, he could easily get someone else to get the job done. She was terrified.

In the end, Jackson was found guilty of making terrorist threats against Theresa and her family and was sentenced to prison for another five years. That would be five more years away from Theresa. On the day of his release from that second sentence, British authorities were waiting to take him to England to stand trial on an old murder charge. Eventually convicted, sentenced, and imprisoned, he was shanked by another inmate in 2004. Theresa was finally free.

#

Three & Me

Around the same time as the trial, my mom's health declined rapidly. After a lifetime of eating meat and potatoes, and many years as a smoker in her teens, 20s, and 30's (she quit in 1968 at 43 years old), the damage was done. She needed a quintuple bypass. She was admitted to Century City Hospital and woke up in the CCU (Cardiac Care Unit) after the bypass. Yaniv and I waited until we could visit her. My dad was there almost the entire time, not really sleeping at home. Mom woke up, but she had a look of despair on her face. Yes, she was connected to a million machines, with tubes going into and out of her, which would make for some severe discomfort and lead to a depressive state of mind. It soon became apparent to all of us that she didn't want to really "wake up" from the anesthesia, nor did she want to do what she needed to do to get out of the CCU. Most patients are only in the unit for a day or two before being transferred out to a regular hospital room. My mom, though, languished in the CCU for five long days. Finally, she found it in herself to rally, and she began to do her prescribed breathing exercises. She constantly complained about the pain, wanted to be largely left alone, and needed to be coaxed to start the healing process. My mom had lost her will to live.

Somehow, my dad convinced her to take the breathing exercises seriously. I know he bribed her with the promise of some travel to give her a gold ring to reach for. Watching my mom struggle with recovery was terrifying. I'd never seen that side of her before. There was an emptiness in her eyes, pallor to her already pale skin, and no facial expression other than the blank despair she wallowed in. I was worried for the very first time that my mom might not make it.

As hard as it was growing up under Rita, I knew how big her heart was. I saw the generosity she shared with complete strangers as well as her friends. One of my favorite memories of her generosity was at a Passover Seder at their house. There were about 20 people present, and I was seated between Yaniv and a man I had never met. We had all gotten our Haggadahs, and, as usual, I counted the pages we had to read before we got to eat. As I was counting, the man seated to my right chuckled. He said he did the same thing and introduced himself as Brian. I shook his hand and asked him if he was a close friend of my parents.

"Oh no," he said. "I met your mother this afternoon in the checkout at Ralphs."

"Seriously?!" I exclaimed, wondering how *this* happened.

"Yeah. We were in line, and she had a whole cart of food, and I just had essentials. She asked me why I was buying so little, and I told her that I was alone for the holiday. So, she invited me over, and here I am!" Brian made a huge gesture with arms spread wide and a big grin on his face. Personally, I loved that story. But I also was grateful that she didn't extend the same invitation to a Ted Bundy or someone equally nefarious!

Over the years and over the many dinners she threw, there would always be some stragglers. Some were strangers, and some were newly single or freshly widowed friends. If my mom met a young Israeli, he or she would get an invitation, whether my mom knew him or not. Her heart was huge and open to the world, and I loved her for it.

I also knew how much my mom loved animals. If she saw a sick or injured animal, she'd get distraught and immediately want to do something to help. When I was leaving Israel to move back to the U.S., I wanted to bring my dog. Israelis have a different attitude about pets, or at least they did back then. Pets were extra. They really didn't become part of the family. So, when we were asked about what we planned to do with our dog Shemesh, I said that I was taking her with me to the U.S. When people heard this, just about everyone told us we were crazy to spend that kind of money to ship a dog overseas. They all suggested we should give our dog to someone else. "Why would you do that?" they'd all ask. But Shemesh was family. And when I told my mom I would be bringing Shemesh to Los Angeles, she was absolutely delighted.

When I finished my years at Bezalel, I wrapped things up and set my sights on returning to the United States. To get a degree from the school I attended, I had to have completed my liberal arts education, four years in my major and passed a final exhibit of my work. The degree and ceremony would only be held in the fall, even though the school year had ended in June. I didn't want to stay for the ceremony. I knew my parents would never show up. So, I left Israel a few months before Yaniv while he finished his Master's thesis in electrophysiology.

When I landed at Los Angeles International Airport, my mom and dad were there to pick me up. Shemesh had to go as baggage with a layover in New York for a night. She was shipped from Israel a day before me because, by law, an animal cannot travel more than a designated number of hours. She had to spend the night in the kennel at Kennedy Airport instead of flying straight through like I did.

I was nervous and scared for her and outwardly panicked because I had no visual confirmation of my dog on arrival in NYC. I was just told not to worry because she would be on my flight. When I sat on the plane headed to LAX, a kind flight attendant assured me that she saw my dog being loaded onto the plane.

As soon as I made it through customs, my mom and I rushed to the cargo area in another terminal. She was as nervous as I was. Once Shemesh's orange crate appeared, we both let out a yelp of happiness and immediately began soothing and cooing to my dog, who happily wagged her tail and gave us all kisses through her kennel grid. Once in the car, I let her out of the crate, and she quickly kissed everyone, especially my mom. That was the moment Shemesh officially became the granddog. My mom spoiled Shemesh up until the day she crossed the Rainbow Bridge.

▼

As these thoughts swirled in my head, I felt the sharp contrast between the woman I saw in the hospital bed—the diminutive woman with no energy or will to live—and my mother, a brilliant woman with a heart of gold whose life had no chance to fully shine. Instead of being angry with my mom for the tirades, the false accusations, and the willingness to turn me over to an institution, I had a great deal of love for her. I understood her. I had long ago forgiven her mistakes and didn't want to lose her.

I visited her every day. While her progress was very slow, she was eventually released from the hospital. She was instructed to walk daily, as well as change her diet. My dad would drive her to the shopping mall at Pico and Westwood Boulevards, and she'd mall walk. Of all the crazy things my mom would learn to love, it was walking around a mall in circles. She quickly learned the stores' names and made mental notes about which ones to shop in after completing her mileage. Mom was slowly coming back into the world of the living while my dad was simultaneously supporting the local merchants.

Three & Me

Me and Heather loved to just sit around and chat.
Especially when there was food around!

The Sound Of Friendship

## ELEVEN

The Sound Of Friendship

Around the year 1992, Heather and Bob Urich moved to Deer Valley, Utah. Deer Valley is right next door to Park City, the famous ski resort town in the Wasatch Mountains, about a 40-minute drive from Salt Lake International Airport. Before cell phones, Heather and Bob changed their landline numbers regularly. There were people whom they wished to drop all contact with, and changing phone numbers regularly ensured that. A married couple who worked for them, named John and Liz, were responsible for giving the people who were still part of the inner circle the new info. I would always feel relieved once I got a phone call with the new number.

Park City is one of those quaint small towns that you read about or see in movies or commercials. Up Main Street, the buildings are all in the style of the original mining town. A fire raced down Main Street in 1898, destroying almost all the buildings, but the strong-hearted residents decided to rebuild. What you see now is pretty much how it was back during the coal mining era, except for some improvements, signage, and many coats of fresh paint added over the last century.

Heather and Bob wanted to see a performing arts center built in the heart of the city somewhere on Main Street. It was tentatively named "The Robert Urich Performing Arts Center." Heather invested all of her energy in the project. She started a grassroots effort, created fundraisers, and hit up the wealthy for donations while using the charm of Park City as a backdrop.

Heather phoned me almost immediately and asked if I could help them in their efforts. I created a logo that was silkscreened onto t-shirts and sweatshirts. These were then offered for sale. I also helped with other graphic and advertising needs. They had planned a celebrity ski championship weekend at Deer Valley in late March 1993 to be hosted by Stein Erickson Lodge. I flew up to Utah for the event because I loved the whole project and would never give up a chance to ski in Deer Valley.

On the Friday night of that weekend, the kickoff dinner was held at the Stein Erickson Lodge in one of the main ballrooms. Because it was Park City, the dress was casual, with a bit of après ski chic. I looked around the room. There were many familiar faces from television and movies who were colleagues of both Heather and Bob. I didn't feel like working the room, so I fell back on my training from Jill. I walked over to the bar and grabbed a drink, found a spot I liked, and pretty much parked myself there. It wasn't long before a friendly silver-haired man spotted me and walked over to say "Hi." I had no idea who he was, but I figured if he was at the event, he was probably somebody. In another corner of the room, I spotted the famous skier and namesake of the lodge, Stein Erickson. He was dressed in a red ski sweater and stood out from the rest of the guests. I liken ski sweaters to ugly Christmas sweaters. People wear them, but why?! But Stein was a celebrated skier, and it was his lodge, so he could pretty much get away with wearing whatever his heart desired.

The gentleman who came over to chat asked me who I was and where I was from—the usual banter. Then after the pleasantries, he told me about a book of his that was being published. He had written a book about space. He went on and on about the book, describing things in space to such an Nth degree that I began to tire of it. (ADHD rears its ugly head yet again.) As he was droning on about space, I kept thinking about Ramona Bradbury, a girl I had gone to school with. Her father was Ray Bradbury, the famous sci-fi author who would come to school and read to our class on occasion. I had read most of Ray Bradbury's books, which in my opinion, were classics. As I looked at the gentleman speaking to me, I assumed that he was talking about having written a sci-fi novel as well. With a bit of smugness, I quietly reasoned his book would never be as good as a Ray Bradbury novel.

Finally, a little lady, much older than me but much younger than the gentleman in front of me, came over and pulled him away. She made it clear to him that she didn't appreciate him chatting up a much younger woman who obviously came stag to the party. I didn't mind her grabbing him mid-sentence because I was just happy *that* she took him.

As soon as the silver-haired guy was gone and had left the banquet room with his lady, Heather walked over to me with a big smile. "What were you doing talking to Buzz Aldrin for such a long time?" she asked.

"Who?" I said, slightly surprised. "Buzz Aldrin? Moonwalking Buzz Aldrin?! The guy who went up in the rocket with Neil Armstrong, Buzz Aldrin? That guy was Buzz Aldrin?! Holy shit!"

"Yeah, him. THAT guy! I saw his wife get pretty pissed when he spent so much time with you and literally grabbed him away." She paused for effect. Then Heather threw this out into the universe, "You know, he crashed the party, right?" At that point, we both started laughing. Then I told Heather that I thought he was just another wannabe writer with a novel. That brought on more belly laughs.

"Well... I guess he does know a lot about space, having walked on the moon! I feel pretty stupid right now!" Heather and I couldn't stop laughing at how funny that was. However, after we giggled about it for a bit, I realized that, yet again, I was conversing with history and was too stupid to recognize it.

Saturday was a ski day, and the celebrity skiers did their thing. Heather and Bob were hosting a party that evening at their Deer Valley home on Bald Mountain. Bob and Heather had a room with a pool table in it. It was my first time inside Heather's new house, and I was delighted to see the familiar green felt stretched across a table. After spending those many years shooting pool with Charlie Bronson, I was up for a game. Lots of my favorite TV stars were packed into that room. The actor who played McGyver, Richard Dean Anderson, was there, as was Jay Thomas, the actor/DJ who played Carla's husband on *Cheers*. There were many other people in the pool room as well. It quickly dawned on me that they were all guys. All famous guys, including Bob. Suddenly I realized that I didn't really belong there. One of the things I learned from Jill was how to read the room and when to make an exit, so I quietly left the room and joined the other women.

Heather, always the gracious hostess, was happily showing off her relatively newly built home. A couple of years before that, Yaniv and I joined Heather and Bob while they were on vacation in Deer Valley. I remember Heather getting a twinkle in her eye and one of her wry smiles. She grabbed my hand, pointed downhill, and said, "Come with me. I need to show you something."

We skied down to the bottom and got back up on a chair lift. At the top, she motioned for me to follow her. Heather took a slight detour off the main trail, then stopped. I caught up to her. She was beaming now. "Guess where we are?" she said excitedly.

I looked around, and honestly, all I saw were spruce, aspen trees, and lots of snow. I looked up at Heather and took a shot. "We are somewhere between the top and the bottom!" I said smugly.

Heather laughed. "Good try. But right now, we are standing in my new kitchen!" She twirled around with her arms extended outward, which showed surprising talent because she was on skis in the middle of trees! "Isn't this view just spectacular?" I had to agree. It certainly was.

As I joined the other women, I asked Heather if we could go into the kitchen. I needed to see that view again. "Suzie, it's pitch dark outside!

You're not going to see a thing!" But if I'm anything, I am stubborn. I still looked out the windows. I could see shadows of trees, slightly highlighted by the lighting from Heather's home. From what I could tell, the view would have been beautiful had there been daylight.

As the party broke up and I was about to leave, Heather asked if I wanted to stay a little longer past the weekend to hang out and ski together. I was gung-ho about staying, but I knew in the back of my mind that Passover began Sunday evening, and I had to be home for the Seder. I had a flight scheduled the next day, Sunday, in the early afternoon, which would get me back in time. (The time change was in my favor.)

Knowing full well I would get shot down, I called my mom to feel her out about me staying the extra few days, which is a lesson I have yet to learn. If I know I will get shot down and still make an attempt, am I a complete idiot? Or am I aggressively pursuing something I really want? I've come to realize I'm basically the idiot. I called my mom anyway. She answered the phone, and as I gingerly began to ask if I could miss the Seder, all hell broke loose.

"I can't believe you'd ask me that question!" she said. "Knowing how much work I put into this. And you don't know how much longer I'm even going to be alive to have Passover with you!" (Jewish guilt played well with that last sentence.) "You know what?! Do what you want to do! I don't care at this point! I just don't care anymore." She hung up abruptly, angry with me yet again.

What was the result of that stupid call? One, my mom was angry with me. Two, I would be going home anyways because the Jewish guilt thing worked. Three, if the first Jewish guilt thing hadn't worked, the "Do what you want!" thing definitely worked. I could have saved myself the guilt trip and the cold shoulder once I arrived had I just thanked Heather and told her I couldn't stay.

Three & Me

Yaniv and I were married on January 16, 1973. That turned out to be an ideal date for an anniversary because we sometimes got a three-day weekend due to the celebration of Martin Luther King. In 1994, our anniversary fell on a Sunday. MLK Day was Monday, and we looked forward to the long weekend. By then, we had moved to Northridge into a cute two-story home on a cul de sac. That morning, I woke up in a foul mood, for which there was no explanation and entirely out of character for me. I was always the one who woke up ready to hit the deck running. But not on that day.

For weeks, I felt funky vibrations coming through my house as I lay in bed. It was almost like a buzzing sound that only I felt and heard. On Sunday, the vibrations seemed to be stronger. I asked Yaniv if he felt anything, and he said he hadn't. I asked him if he'd heard anything, and again, he said he hadn't. I told him I had heard it for the past few weeks and had no idea what it was. He told me I was probably dreaming and continued with his business. My mood was still foul when I got up out of bed. I couldn't explain it, so I tried to shake it off. Because it was our anniversary, Yaniv asked me what I wanted to do.

"Nothing," I replied.

"Do you want to go on a hike?" he asked.

"Nope. I don't want to do anything. I have a bad feeling."

Yaniv was perplexed. It was such a warm and beautiful day outside. The kind of day that Easterners would kill to have in the middle of January. Blue skies and in the high 70's. "C'mon," he said. "Look how great it is outside. Let's go on a bike ride. You love to ride your bike."

That was true. I did love to ride my bike. We had gotten into mountain biking in a big way, and beating ourselves up in the hills of the

The Sound Of Friendship

Santa Monicas was our favorite activity. There were so many trails that we could never get bored. "Let's ride up to the hub," he suggested. I agreed but reluctantly, even though I loved that ride. I should have been more enthusiastic, but I wasn't. What was wrong with me?

We loaded our bikes into Yaniv's Isuzu and headed over to the top of Reseda Boulevard, where the pavement ends and trails begin. I still had that gnawing feeling that something terrible would happen. But I had no idea what it was. Soon, I focused on the steep hill that was right before me. Climbing hills is easy for me, but not with cold legs. The first hill was immediately at the edge of the parking area, and there was no getting around it. I had to concentrate on making it to the top while Yaniv just floated up. He was that athletic. After the climb, there was a great deal of downhill, a turn, then more downhill until a very steep uphill. It was rutted from some rains, and climbing it became a chore.

I'd nicknamed this hill "Hell Hill." I was already in a bad mood, and I didn't want to kill myself in the ruts, so I got off my bike to walk it up to the top. For some unknown reason, I turned to look behind me. There below, in a long straight line, was Reseda Boulevard stretching to the other end of the valley. As I looked down at the boulevard, the sinking feeling in my stomach intensified, and my sense of foreboding became even more intense. I looked up at the sheer mountain wall to my left side as I faced Reseda. I spotted a Diamondback rattlesnake climbing straight up, grabbing the juts in the wall with his scales, each undulation of his body propelling him just a bit higher. Suddenly, I felt something menacing about the sheerness of the wall, so I got on my bike and decided to brave the deep ruts and ride to the top instead of walking.

Yaniv kept trying to cheer me up as we rode, but I wasn't having it. Always self-aware, I was more and more alarmed at the way I was behaving. This was not me! We rode to the hub and made the circular trail around Eagle Rock, then headed back down to the car. I was relieved when we made it home in one piece. The awful sense that something horrible would happen hadn't left me. To make matters worse, Yaniv decided we should go out to a movie. That's the last thing I wanted to do. Again, he talked me into it, trying to get me out of my funk.

We went to a multiplex in Northridge to watch *The Shawshank Redemption* starring Timothy Robbins and Morgan Freeman. As I sat in the darkened theater, I felt panic begin to rise in my throat. I looked around me. No gunmen. No fires. Everything appeared to be safe. I forced myself to pay attention to the movie but was still on edge. Thankfully, when the movie ended, we went home, mostly in silence. Yaniv couldn't figure out my mood, and I told him I couldn't either. I kept telling him that something bad was going to happen. I knew it. And I knew it would be really bad.

I refused to go to sleep before midnight. I wanted to make sure the day was over. With no romance, except a hug and a kiss, we both fell asleep. We slept soundly until a little after 4.30 in the morning. That's when the Earth erupted with such a loud crash it woke us instantly, throwing us up off the bed. We dodged flying objects coming at us from every which way. I let out a blood-curdling scream. After that, I just kept saying, "I knew it. I knew it," to no one but myself.

The noise was so intense that my head hurt from the sounds and the vibrations. Artwork came crashing down from the walls; broken glass was everywhere. Cabinets opened up, spilling their guts in sticky and dangerous messes throughout the house. Through the windows, I could see electric transformers blowing up all around, creating huge flashes of light. Doors swung open and shut with the undulations of the house. There was no light because the earthquake had damaged the power supply, so we had to pick our way around in the dark to find our way out of the house. All our pets were accounted for, and we were able to put them in the cars that we'd parked in the driveway. Our garden walls had crumbled, as did everyone else's. Neighborhood pets were running loose, frightened by the Earth's sudden liquification. The thousands of aftershocks began to hit one after the other, and the ground was not the ground anymore but a liquified mass instead. I actually started to feel seasick.

One of the things I've learned over time is that there is no way a horrible situation can't get worse. I once again proved that theorem when I got my period during this horrendous act of nature. Bingo! Right in the middle of a monstrous earthquake! I would need more than luck finding Tampax in the piles of mess that covered my bathroom floor.

The aftershocks were coming in huge quick waves, and I had no desire to walk back into our house. It was trembling and shaking, making all kinds of moans and groans. Lastly, I didn't want to go back up the stairs and get pitched over the rail if a huge aftershock were to hit. However, I couldn't just stand there and bleed, could I? I had no choice. As I re-entered the dark and scary house, I began to think of my options. One thing I knew was that I couldn't crawl because there was broken glass everywhere. We were in our pajamas with bare feet, standing outside on the sidewalk along with everyone else on our block. Thankfully it was an unseasonably warm night for January. (Warm, unmoving air would soon become known as "earthquake weather.")

I decided to just walk as quickly and carefully as possible, trying my hardest to be as brave as I could. I gingerly picked my way up the stairs with a death grip on the railing. Thankfully, I made it into my darkened bathroom. My toiletries and cosmetics were strewn everywhere. As luck would have it, before the earthquake, I'd placed a box of Tampax on top of the toilet, where it miraculously stayed put during that horrible shake. After I took care of my hygienic needs, I grabbed a robe and put on tennis shoes. Then I found a sweatshirt and tennis shoes for Yaniv. With shoes on, I could step on the glass and make it quickly back out before another sharp jolt hit, which it did. Thankfully, I was safely outside when it hit. My legs were shaking, and my gut was cramping, but a sense of relief was also washing over me. The bad thing I was so afraid of, the thing I had no idea what it would be, finally revealed itself, and we were still alive. We survived a war 21 years earlier, and we survived a massive earthquake in 1994.

Ground Zero was at the intersection of Reseda and Roscoe Boulevards, which explained my unease when looking down at Reseda Boulevard earlier in the day. Our house was at the epicenter, within two miles of Ground Zero. That was one big jolt coming in at a 6.7 magnitude. To add to the horror, it was a shallow quake, classified as the thrust kind. That explained the big bang as we were thrown from the bed. The intensity of the shaking isn't reflected in the magnitude. Magnitude is established by energy released and the time span of the quake. If that quake had lasted longer than it did, it would have easily been a 10. People died in the earthquake, and that made me sad. An entire apartment building pancaked, killing many people living on the lower floors. Even today, if I stay in a hotel, I want to stay up high. It might not be such a good idea in a fire, but it's a great idea in a massive earthquake!

The area around the epicenter slowly began to recover, and life took on a somewhat normal rhythm. We had to live without water, gas, or electricity for what seemed a very long time. Electricity was thankfully restored in two weeks. The Gas Company was still going house to house, checking meters that were turned off before turning them back on again, so there was no gas. And we had no water. We weren't too worried about the water situation because I collected extra bottles each water delivery, storing them in the garage. I had bottles and bottles of drinking water. I had so much that I gave water away to my grateful neighbors. We still had many bottles left. We used the water to flush toilets (only flushing when solids made their appearance), water plants, and give to the dogs and cat.

During the January 17 quake, our toilet had been jostled loose enough from the base where the hose disconnected. We had no idea the toilet was broken, that is until the water was restored. Initially, water was restored without enough pressure to really become an issue. No water reached the second floor of the house at all. But one Friday afternoon, when no one was home, the Department of Water and Power gave it full throttle. Once the water made it up to the second floor, the hose began to squirt water with no one around to switch the shut-off valve at the base. It sprayed unhindered for hours. I was the first to arrive home and confront an indoor waterfall from ceiling to floor. The wood floors buckled under the saturation, the ceiling caved in, and I was again staring at a huge mess. I ran upstairs to stem the flow of water. Then went downstairs and cleaned up the flooded mess. Thankfully the dogs were in an enclosure in the backyard, and the cat was perched up on a shelf in the upstairs closet.

In the aftermath of the big temblor, we both worked hard to reassemble our home from all the mess. It took a long time to clean up all the broken glass and make sense of the mess of papers that were strewn about. We also had to contend with medicines, towels, blankets, dog food, and everything else that was kept behind cabinet doors but ejected out during the quake. The worst was the refrigerator which had toppled over, spilling its contents in a yucky mess all over the kitchen floor. We thought we had earthquake proofed our home when we moved in, bolting heavy pieces of furniture to studs in the walls with eyes and hooks. Thankfully, we had done that, but we never ever thought about cabinets and the refrigerator. Next time!

Two days after the great flood, we went shopping for food. It was a Sunday and about a month or so after the original quake. And, of course, I got my period again, complete with cramps. When we got home, I said something quite odd to Yaniv. To this day, I don't understand how these words even came out of my mouth. But they did. I said, "Yaniv, will you put the food away? I'm going upstairs to lie down. Let me know when the earthquake is over. I'm just gonna ride it out in bed." And with that, I went upstairs.

Yaniv thought, "What the Hell?" and began to put food away. We had cabinets in the laundry room where we stored all the canned dog food. He had those cabinets open as he added more cans to the already full shelves when an absolutely huge aftershock hit. It measured 5.7 on the Richter Scale. Its epicenter was directly underneath us, making it that much more intense. All the cans of dog food flew out at Yaniv, striking him in the head and leaving some pretty good-sized bruises.

When the shaking stopped, he came running upstairs, looking as if he'd seen a ghost. "How the hell did you know that was going to happen?" he said. "How did you do that?" I was lying in bed. Just before the quake hit, I was able to take some Aleve for the cramps. "I don't know," I said. "I just knew there'd be one. I'm as surprised as you are that I knew."

# # #

After that earthquake, the rest of 1994 was uneventful. We'd been trying to get pregnant over the years, but nothing happened. I was diagnosed with a horrible case of endometriosis, which explained the cramps in a big way. Endometriosis is where the lining of the uterus sloughs off during menstruation, then attaches itself to whatever it can land on nearby. It's not picky. It can land on the intestines, ovaries, and the outside of the uterus, basically wherever it finds a good spot to go. Once landed, it stays there for the rest of your life or until it's surgically removed. My insides looked like victims of sloppy housekeeping. Endometriosis continues to throw the uterine lining out every month of the cycle until menopause. Fun, right?! Here's the best part of endometriosis: Once those pieces of the uterine wall are outside the uterus and attached to wherever they may be, they act like the inside lining of the uterus during every menstrual cycle. All those endometrial cells cause menstrual cramping. I honestly thought that my cramps were normal cramps that everyone gets. The kind that all women complain about. Due to my high threshold for pain, I had no idea that my case was beyond the pale.

When told of our unsuccessful attempts at pregnancy, my gyno, Dr. Howard Mandel, suggested I undergo a laparoscopy to clean up my insides. Endometriosis gets in the way of pregnancy, so it was a step forward in the right direction.

In late spring, I entered the Short Stay at Century City Hospital to be prepped for surgery. Three little incisions would be made—one near my belly button, and the other two on each side of my hip area. I was on the table when I was brought back to consciousness by the doctors. Howie looked at me and said, "How were you not begging me for morphine each time you had your period? That was the worst case of endometriosis I have ever seen! It was all over the place! The cramps had to have been off the charts!"

I just looked at him in wonderment. "Howie, I controlled the pain with Aleve, that's it. It took the edge off."

"I still don't know how you got through it," he said. And with that, I was whisked off to post-op to ensure I could eat and drink without vomiting before I was released to go home.

After my laparoscopy, I was treated with six months of the drug Lupron to suppress my periods for those six months, thereby inhibiting my uterus from shedding more junk. That "wonderful" drug put me into a false state of menopause, and I got to experience first-hand what happens to women a bit later in life. After that time on Lupron, the night sweats, the hot flashes, and everything else related to menopause, I was convinced this was not something I was looking forward to in the future!

Even after all the therapy I'd undergone, I still couldn't conceive. To say that Yaniv was very disappointed would be a gross understatement.

Many years earlier, when he was with his Israeli girlfriend, she'd gotten pregnant. She wanted the child, but Yaniv didn't. He pressured her to have an abortion. All the guilt about forcing the abortion was now coming to a head in his psyche. I couldn't conceive a child, but he'd already successfully impregnated a woman and then had it terminated. A distance opened up between us that wasn't there before. The only problem was, I didn't see it.

# # #

Life as I knew it was about to change in a big way in 1995. My parents suggested that I should do an adult Bat Mitzvah since they didn't have the money to give me a celebration when I was 13. I figured, why not, thinking that it might be a fun thing to do. Jerry had his Bar Mitzvah at Temple Isaiah, and the reception was held at my mom's bridge club (of course). My mom enthusiastically allowed that expenditure to take place.

In 1995 we were all members of Stephen Wise Temple in Bel-Air, where I am still a member to this day. Cantor Samuel Levy was giving the adult Bat Mitzvah course. He'd pre-picked a date for the ceremony to be held in the sanctuary without having first checked what Torah portion would be read on that day. According to Jewish law, the date of the Bar/Bat Mitzvah determines which Torah portion is read during the ceremony.

The date that Cantor Levy– at that time one of the powerful leaders of the synagogue – had picked was linked to the absolute worst Torah portion for women ever! Back in Biblical times, menstruating women were considered dirty, as were women who were not virgins. This Torah portion compares those women to dead carcasses. The Torah portion begins with the Aramaic/Hebrew translation, basically saying, "I am filth. I am a dead carcass. I am impure." Being the only one in the adult Bat Mitzvah class who understood and spoke Hebrew, I was absolutely horrified as I began to read our portion, realizing that I couldn't say this stuff at all. I choked on those words.

Like an idiot, I raised my hand in front of the entire class and asked Cantor Levy to change the date in order to get a better Torah portion. I'd forgotten about his ego, which was quite large. He wasn't having it. He'd already set in process the printing and delivery of the invitations, and it was too late to change. Still, I continued my challenge, explaining why, when he erupted at me. He was absolutely furious! He pretty much told me if I didn't like it, I could always leave. I still argued, and with that, Cantor Levy stormed out of the classroom, leaving me in an awkward position. Everyone stared at me, speechless because of the conflict I had provoked. That kerfuffle happened on a Wednesday night.

I was in my office on Thursday when the phone rang just after lunch. It was my dad. "Suzie, your mother is in the hospital. She's having surgery tomorrow. You should come to visit her tonight."

"Dad, what happened?"

"I've been noticing that your mom has been having TIA's (little mini-strokes) lately. So, I called Dr. Gindi and set up carotid scans for the both of us." His voice sounded heavy with worry. "I didn't want to scare her, so I just suggested that due to our advancing ages, it might be a good idea for both of us to undergo this test."

I suddenly felt panic set in. Over the previous weekend, I had been in Arizona for a huge mountain bike race. One of my clients was Iron Horse Bicycles, and I was there with a photographer to take photos of our sponsored rider. She was one of the top female racers on the circuit at that time. I was staying in a podunk hotel room with her as my roommate. She was a great mountain bike racer, but as a roommate, not so much.

Three & Me

I had fallen asleep relatively early in the evening since she insisted on lights-out at around 9 pm. She was the athlete, so I went with her schedule. I fell into a fitful sleep. The bed was uncomfortable, the room was too warm, and the air conditioning was as noisy as it was ineffective. At some point, I began to dream. In my dream, Jerry came to visit me. I asked him why he was there. "I came for Mom," he said. Then I asked him why. "I can't tell you why, but I'm here to help Mom." When I woke up, it was as if Jerry really was there. I tried as hard as I could to shake it off; by Tuesday, I had almost forgotten about it. Except now, right now, my father was telling me that my mom was experiencing mini-strokes, at which point I developed a deep sense of foreboding. It was the Northridge Earthquake and courthouse shooting premonitions all over again.

"Is she going to die?" I asked him, getting right to the point, without telling him I thought Jerry was around us waiting for her.

"No, no... She'll be OK. They took her straight into the hospital from the doctor's office. I need to go get her a robe as soon as we hang up."

I told my dad I'd meet him at the hospital as soon as I finished work. I called Yaniv and told him he should stop in at the same time on his way home from work. Yaniv worked at the Aerospace Corporation in El Segundo as an engineer. It was right off the 405. My mom was in Century City Hospital so it would be an easy commute for him.

I got to the hospital just as the sun was beginning to set. My dad had gone to run an errand, and Yaniv hadn't yet arrived. It was just me. When I found my mother's room, she smiled. "Isn't this just idiotic?" she asked. "I've still got so much to do for Passover, and here I am stuck in bed. I feel fine!" (Passover was two weeks away, but my mom always started early.) She shook her head. "I shouldn't be here right now, but you know your father. He insisted on me taking that stupid test!"

The Sound Of Friendship

"Mom, Dad said you're 99% blocked in your carotid artery. You need to be here. You could drop dead if you're not careful."

"Nonsense!" she said. "Who knows how long I've been walking around like this, and nothing has happened."

I sighed. No sense in arguing. The fact that she was in the hospital, scheduled for surgery, and none of her whitewash efforts would stick anyway made it moot. "So, what's new with you?" she asked, changing the subject away from herself.

"Well... I just got yelled at by Cantor Levy..." I said with a bit of a wince. Inside my head, I heard my inner voice yelling at me for even bringing that up! She didn't need to know that. Why did I always stick my foot in it with my mom?

The lighthearted mood suddenly shifted to a darker tone. "What do you mean you got yelled at by Cantor Levy? WHAT DID YOU DO?" she asked.

"I speak Hebrew too well," I said. "Cantor Levy picked a week where the parashah (Torah portion) started off with me saying that I am as filthy as a dead carcass, and I just couldn't do it. He lost his load on me when I asked him to change the date."

My mom shook her head back and forth. "Oh Suzie... you never, ever learn, do you?! Why would you open your mouth over something no one else understands? Do you think anyone else knows what that means? THEY DON'T!"

"I couldn't help myself," I said in my defense.

My mom shook her head in disgust and disappointment. "Well, I hope you apologized," was all she could say.

Three & Me

At that moment, my dad walked in with Yaniv. They had met in the elevator coming up, and my mom's face lit up. Her men were here, and she was delighted. She made a big fuss over Yaniv and tried to downplay her situation. My dad, of course, tried to comfort her, telling her she had nothing to worry about. He told her he would be right there with her in post-op. He'd gotten permission from the surgeon. That made my mom happy, and she began to crack jokes about her situation, trying to lighten her own mood. It was time to leave, and after some lighthearted chit-chat, we left with goodbyes and wishes for a great outcome.

The last thing she said to me, just as I was leaving, was more of a plea. "Don't tell Beatrice." I turned and crossed my heart. She seemed pleased. Beatrice was her sister. Their relationship always baffled me. It was of the love/hate kind. They'd regularly speak on the phone, and then bam... nothing. Right at that moment, it was a whole lot of nothing, especially after the trust fund nightmare. That little innocuous promise I had just made as I left my mom's hospital room would come and bite me hard in the ass the following week.

The next day my mom went in for surgery. My dad phoned me from the hospital, relaying that the surgery went well and that he would join her in post-op, and that we should come to the hospital to greet her. I didn't go to work that day, and Yaniv didn't either. We were both home awaiting word. It was mid-afternoon on Friday when my dad made the call. We piled into the car and headed out of the Valley into Century City. It was bumper-to-bumper traffic at that time, so getting to the hospital took quite a while. My dad was waiting at the elevator for I don't know how long when we arrived. His face was as pale as I'd ever seen it. "What's wrong?" I asked. The pit that formed in my stomach from last weekend was growing ever larger.

"Your mother had her surgery. They cleaned out her carotid and thought they'd gotten it all. While I was with her in post-op, I witnessed her having a stroke. I called the nurse, who called the sur-

The Sound Of Friendship

geon, who, luckily, was still in the hospital. They wheeled her back into surgery, and she's still in there. Apparently, a bit of plaque dislodged, causing the stroke. We'll know more later."

I was so worried. In my wildest dreams, I never thought I would lose my mom. She wasn't perfect. She wasn't motherly in the general sense as other mothers, but she was still my mom. I sat in the hospital chair, waiting and worrying while my mom underwent her second surgery of the day. I wished we'd had a better relationship. I was so tortured knowing that I never made her happy. Survivor's guilt was something I suffered from after Jerry died. I couldn't help thinking that the wrong kid died in 1988 and that my mom would have been happier if Jerry were still here. She wouldn't have lost her will to live if I had gone instead of Jerry. I sat in that chair, re-running my childhood over and over in my mind. To make matters worse, I was furious with myself for telling her about Cantor Levy, knowing that my mom's last conversation with me was yet another disappointment.

We sat in that waiting room for hours, hardly speaking to each other, each of us lost in thought. My father had tears streaming down his cheeks. Yaniv was stoic. I was striving so hard to put on a brave front but losing that battle as every minute ticked by on the hospital wall clock. Nothing is worse than a hospital waiting room (except in maternity). Everyone sitting in that same room with you is praying for someone they love, not knowing what their outcome will be, yet hoping for the best.

Looking around me, I decided that even the décor was offensive. To be as nondescript as possible, hospital designers purposely design everything to be non-controversial. Beige this. Beige that. Beige in the artwork. Beige walls. Beige upholstery. Beige tile floors or beige woven carpeting. Fucking Beige Everything! I hated it.

Finally, at about 11.00 that night, my mom was wheeled into post-op. My dad was allowed in. The doctor explained the damage the dislodged piece of plaque caused and said my mother's stroke was massive. There was a huge amount of bleeding in her skull, and they hoped they could stop it. He also told my dad that the next day or two would be critical. He hoped the damage wasn't too severe. Then he left my dad alone to look down at his wife, a woman he had loved for over 46 years. Their 46th anniversary was days away on March 27. He looked sadly at my mom, still sedated, and offered up prayers to the Almighty, the God he'd trusted in and believed in his entire life. I know he called upon all his angels to help my mother heal; such was my father's spirituality and belief system.

Yaniv and I were instructed to leave. I got a brief glimpse of my mother as she was wheeled into the critical care unit, and I knew it was game over. I couldn't say anything, but in my heart, I knew. My father followed behind her gurney to hold the hand of the woman he so loved.

On Saturday morning, my dad called. He sounded upbeat. Mom was awake, but she couldn't speak. She couldn't really move, but she was alert. She could blink her eyes in response to a question. Yes, was one blink. No, was two. My dad suggested we get dressed as soon as possible and come visit. The hospital would allow us to spend time with her.

Like two jackrabbits, Yaniv and I jumped into our clothes and into the car. When there was no traffic, we could make the drive to Century City in about half an hour. We made it in even less time, so I'm pretty sure I was speeding as I drove. We went to the ICU, and the nurses buzzed us in. Immediately I saw a petite woman who looked especially small in that hospital bed. She was lying flat on her back. Her eyes were open. I walked over to her and put my hand on her face. She felt cold and clammy to my touch. There was an unforgettable look of horror in her eyes. She was like a trapped animal, trying to get out of the cage she was in. Her body had trapped her, rendering her helpless against the loss of mobility. Her eyes said it all. Her huge brown eyes were darting back and forth, trying to tell me something, just what I couldn't comprehend. Was she trying to tell me she loved me all of those years? Was she trying to tell me she tried her hardest to be a good mom? Was she trying to apologize for all the pain I'd suffered? Was she finally trying to tell me the words I'd longed to hear my whole entire life, that she loved me? Or were her eyes darting around, trying to find an escape from the hell she found herself in, not wanting to die, and panicked in the knowledge that she could die, or worse, survive in the condition she was in now, for the rest of her life? I had no way of knowing, but I felt every bit of her pain coupled with that of my own.

While we were there, an orderly came to take her to imaging to find out what was happening with the bleeding in her brain. My dad, Yaniv, and I waited in that same awful waiting room. About an hour later, she was wheeled back. We again buzzed ourselves into the ICU, and Dr. Gindi came to see us. He explained that the bleeding was severe and getting worse. My mom's situation looked dire. He pulled my dad over and asked him if he wanted to take heroic measures to save her life, whatever that life would be. My mom had a DNR (Do Not Resuscitate) directive filed with admissions at the hospital. My father walked over to my mom's bed and lovingly looked down at her, staring into her eyes that were still open in despair, then walked back to Dr. Gindi—no heroic measures. Dr. Gindi nodded and then wrote the orders that would ultimately lead to her death. Pneumonia was already settling into my mom's lungs. If you are on your back and unable to move, the bacteria begin to grow at a rapid rate. Because of the DNR, no medication was given to stop the pneumonia.

By that afternoon, pneumonia had become bilateral. We waited for hours and hours at the hospital, taking turns visiting my mom as she slowly slipped into an unconscious state, finally and laboriously taking her very last gasps of air before she stopped breathing altogether. My dad was with her throughout her passing, and he said he could feel her soul leave her body. This was the day before their anniversary.

The next day, Sunday morning, I went to my dad's house in Bel Air. This was his first day as a widower, and he wasn't good at being alone. He had been a loving husband during their entire marriage, working through my mom's mental difficulties with the same intense love he had for her from the very beginning. And now, on his anniversary, he was alone. We had an appointment at Mount Sinai Mortuary to plan her funeral and pick out her casket. I kept thinking that it was absolutely the worst thing imaginable to plan a funeral and pick out a casket for your lifetime love on the exact day of your anniversary. There was something so unfair about it.

As we drove to Mount Sinai, I finally told my dad about Jerry in my dream. It gave him comfort hearing it. He told me that he absolutely believed Jerry was visiting me to let me know he would help my mom's soul transition out of her body into her new being. He said he'd also felt Jerry's presence in the days leading up to Mom's stroke. We both sat back, feeling a bit better.

My mom's funeral was held on Monday. It was quite literally standing room only. Rabbi Zeldin and Cantor Levy were officiating. My mother had a huge circle of friends. Not only did she have all of her lifetime bridge cronies, but she had also been president of the Sisterhood at Stephen Wise Temple, then co-president a few years later. She had also been president of Beverly Hills Hadassah and then president of Na'amat, another Jewish women's organization. My parents donated to many Jewish charities, including Shelter Partnership, which built senior centers in Israel. Their reach was broad, and the community came out to bid their last respects to my mother. My mother's casket had a huge arrangement of white flowers decorating it. (Jewish people do closed caskets.) When we were finished in the chapel, the coffin was carried by six pallbearers to her gravesite. At her final resting site, I was struck by the most beautiful wreaths waiting for my mother, which also matched the flowers on the casket. I later learned that Michael Viner and Deborah Raffin sent the flowers. They heard of my mother's passing and arranged for a beautiful floral send-off.

The Sound Of Friendship

After the burial ceremony, a reception was held at my dad's house. Hundreds of people passed through, some bringing food, others just coming to pay their respects. Rabbi Zeldin cornered me in the kitchen. "I heard about what happened between you and Sam in your class," he began. "And he feels absolutely terrible that your mom passed just a few days later." Rabbi Zeldin paused for a moment, then he said, "You know Sam's a Cohen." (Cohens are the high priests in the 12 tribes of Israel, and they are not supposed to go into cemeteries.) I nodded in acknowledgment. "But he insisted on doing the service for your mother with me; that's how bad he felt. I nodded silently as Rabbi Zeldin spoke. Then he gave a little laugh, "The problem you had with Sam is that he knew you were right in your protest. He didn't think anyone knew Hebrew that well to have picked up on what you did, but his hands were tied. You were too smart for him. He was understandably upset; you understand that, right?" I didn't tell Rabbi Zeldin I planned to drop out of the Bat Mitzvah class. My mom had passed, and I didn't see any reason to go up onto the bema (altar) and say those degrading words. I was doing that ceremony for her benefit; now, she wasn't here anymore. However, the longer I spoke with Rabbi Zeldin, the more resolute I became in dedicating my adult Bat Mitzvah to the memory of my mom. Besides, I thought she'd get a kick up in heaven, hearing me announce to hundreds of people that I was basically filth. It would be an inside joke between myself and my mom's soul. Suddenly something initially so abhorrent to me became the thing I wanted to do the most. In the end, when I went up and proudly sang those words, the clueless audience expressed their approval, and Yaniv? Well, he laughed, along with my mom's soul.

About a week after the funeral, I got the call I didn't need from my Aunt Beatrice. She was fuming, spitting bullets, mad! She let me have both barrels because I didn't contact her about her sister's passage. I kept telling her that I had made a deathbed promise and had to keep it no matter what. It wasn't my decision, but Aunt Bea never saw that side. From that moment on, she would repeatedly express her hatred of my mom, her sister, until about two months before she died.

Years later, I visited her to pretty much say "goodbye," knowing that her time was coming. She was in her late 80s, a hypochondriac for the better part of her life, frequently visiting the Mayo Clinic for one imagined illness after the other until she finally really had something. Cancer. I had driven down from Minneapolis, where I stayed with her son Michael and his husband, Morrie. Once I sat down at her bedside, she began the old rant about my mother this, and my mother that, and some made-up history that I know never happened, which pushed me right over the edge. I had finally had it with that family!

"Auntie Bea! STOP! STOP TALKING!" I demanded. She abruptly stopped, in utter shock that I had dared talk to her like that. After all, she was a dying woman. My voice softened once I had her attention. "You have so little time left on this side of the dirt; why do you want to fill those moments with the hatred you've carried your entire life? Why don't you want to spend probably your last moments alive think- ing nice thoughts? Doing nice things?" Auntie Bea's face softened as I spoke. "You haven't been very nice. I know that for a fact. It's time you gave up all the bad and began doing good. You'll have more visitors in your last days or weeks. Isn't that something you would want for yourself? To be surrounded by love?"

As those words flew spontaneously out of my mouth, I realized that it had to be Jill who was placing them between my lips to spit back out. I would have never said such things to my Aunt Bea had I not had Jill's influence in my life. Had I not watched her valiant fight against disease. Had I not carried her with me in my heart, and had I not benefitted from her very being.

Auntie Bea began to cry. All the hatred left her face, exposing the once beautiful features she'd had in her youth. She agreed that she needed to let go of the bad, think better thoughts, and leave this world a better person. According to my cousin, she did just that. Her end came a few months after our visit. My cousin told me that during that time, she was absolutely delightful. When I heard this news, I quietly

The Sound Of Friendship

hoped she and my mom patched things up once they had a chance to sit on a cloud to chit-chat and share laughter as they used to in days long past.

Me and Dad.
Mom had died just two months before my birthday.
At this time, I had no idea how negatively his romantic life would impact my life.

Three & Me

I'm a MOMMY!
Out of everything I did in my life, this was the one thing I did best!

Some Of My Best Friends Are...

< **TWELVE** >

Some Of My Best Friends Are...

My dad seemed at a loss without my mom. So did I, actually. With all the disharmony and discord we'd shared over my 44 years of life, I wasn't prepared for her sudden departure to the heavens above. It felt like the floor was pulled out from under me. I'd finally learned to cope with some of her insanity, and now my emotional skill sets had no purpose. I missed her. I missed, most of all, her infectious laugh and her ridiculous jokes, most of them dirty!

After the obligatory after-funeral feast at my dad's, he asked a few people to stay while he went into my mom's closet and brought out a pile of outfits. Then he went back again and brought out more. Then more. Then more. Then he graduated to accessories. Some of my mom's friends and relatives were there, and he told them to dig in, to take whatever they wanted. The living room suddenly transformed into a ladies' dressing room, with clothing flying absolutely everywhere. The only thing missing was a cashier.

When the women left, each holding as many clothing items as they could carry, my dad began to put what was left into bags. Yaniv and I helped him clear out her closets, her toiletries, shoes, bras, underwear, and even her stockings, and put everything into giant garbage bags. By evening, my mother's footprint was pretty much erased. I couldn't understand my dad's urgency in eliminating my mom, but he said it was too painful to look into her closet and know she wouldn't be wearing her clothes anymore.

Suddenly, the loss hit me hard. I was sobbing inside but stoic on the outside. I had to be. My father would occasionally break down in tears of his own, and watching my own father cry was too much to

Three & Me

handle. I know how he faced the hardships life threw at him, and it was always head-on, without complaint. But now, he appeared to be a broken man. And when he looked towards me, I knew he saw the last member of his family still standing.

Grief is dealt with in many ways. Some spouses withdraw from the outside world, wanting to grieve in privacy. Other widowed spouses, after a period of time, step out gingerly into society. These people don't necessarily want to move on with someone else; instead, they seek the companionship of friends. Other widowed spouses go out and get animals, obsessing over their new fur babies until they feel the need for more human companionship.

My dad? Well, three days later, he went out on his first date as a widower. He already had a dog for companionship, but he craved a woman's touch and her company. Women literally came out of no-where, contacting him, trying to console him, while at the same time trying to cajole him. It worked. He had a date every night that week with different women. Mind you; this was well before online dating was a thing. My dad was 75 years old and still very handsome. He kept his Hungarian good looks by eating healthy, exercising, and be-ing the beneficiary of great genetics. He also had a personality that women his age found very appealing. He was always a gentleman and a fabulous lover. (That last part was a little TMI for me when I first heard it from one of his women.) All my male friends told me they wanted to one day "be just like my dad." I would just roll my eyes.

Within weeks my dad had his first girlfriend. He introduced Ethel to me and Yaniv one evening at dinner. She was age-appropriate, had a beautiful smile, dressed very well, and her hair was perfectly coiffed. I could see she lived a good life. I liked her immediately. I figured if my dad weren't out dating, he'd be sitting at home alone, brooding, and quite possibly dying. I'd heard too many stories of one spouse dying suddenly and then the other following suit almost immediately after.

As long as I can remember, my dad has always had heart issues. He was born with an enlarged heart, so I was afraid of losing him to a heart attack. I was thrilled my dad had someone special to spend his time with.

In mid-summer of that year, my father retired. He chose his birthday in July as his retirement day. I had a hard time imagining my father not running into his office early in the morning and staying until late at night. Nor could I imagine him not running out to make house calls when someone couldn't get themselves out of bed or off the floor. He was always available to his patients. He treated everyone like they were the most important people in his life, and to tell you the truth, they were!

I attended his retirement party at a restaurant in Beverly Hills, thrown by two of his longest and most loyal patients. He made his farewell speech boldly and confidently. He choked and teared up when he mentioned my mother and how she had begged him to retire so they could spend more time with each other. I wasn't sure how well this retirement thing would work for him. I secretly dreaded him facing lonely days and lonely nights when he wasn't with Ethel.

I needn't have worried, though. He closed down his office and sold the building where he had spent every day for the last 30+ years of his life. He brought one of his treatment tables home with him, put it in the multi-purpose room, and continued to treat his patients as if he'd never retired. But there were major differences. He had no reception-ist, but more importantly, at this point, he took no money. He treated everyone for free. He kept up his license in order to practice legally, and his life was as busy as it was before. However, just like when he had his office, he took Thursdays off.

So, it was on one Thursday in August that I decided to give my dad a treat and take him on a drive up into the mountains to go to Big Bear Lake. Once I had grown up and left the house, I had never been alone with my dad in the car unless I was taking him to an appointment, to the hospital, or to a doctor. I thought it would be nice to take a small road trip with him and hoped he'd enjoy the scenery. While we meandered up the mountain, the car engine humming with every gear change, my dad began to push me softly into considering adoption. He wanted to be a grandfather in the worst way possible. He had obviously prepared this speech because he came up with every good reason why I should and a rebuttal for every reason I found that I shouldn't. All that was good until we got to Big Bear, and my dad started to literally turn blue around his lips.

I couldn't have picked a worse place for my drive with my dad. While the ride was beautiful-- one of those fabulous bluebird days with an intense cloudless sky—my dad couldn't take the altitude. He started filling up with fluid once we got to Big Bear, which is just shy of 7,000 feet above sea level. His heart immediately began to go into congestive heart failure, and he didn't have his medication with him. His breathing became labored, his skin clammy, and his face an ashen gray. I wanted to take him to the hospital in Big Bear, but he practically demanded I take him back down to sea level ASAP. So, I drove the winding highway like a race car driver. Not to endorse a particular car, but I have to tell you BMWs hug the road, especially on curves. I was lucky I didn't pass any California Highway Patrol on my way down. We made the descent in record time. As I looked over, I could see my father was beginning to recover from my blunder. At least his cheeks were pink!

My dad phoned me at my office the very next day to see if I'd called any adoption attorneys yet. That was my dad in his purest form. Once he got something in his head, it had to be acted upon immediately. Even a five-minute delay would send him into a tailspin of anxiety about when I would actually do what he wanted me to. I sighed. Not because I hadn't yet called anyone, but because of his fragile state, I didn't want to upset him. "Dad, I promise I'll get to it later today. I don't even know who yet to call. Let me get back to you."

Some Of My Best Friends Are...

Satisfied with the answer, my dad hung up. Two hours later, he called back again. Same conversation. Same polite end to the conversation. I knew I couldn't beg off a third time, which I figured would be in under an hour from the last call. So, I picked up the phone and called Heather. At this time, Heather was still living in Utah, and I was quite happy I caught her at home. Heather's two kids, Ryan and Emily, were adopted through the Catholic Church in closed adoptions. Heather explained that wouldn't be an option for me, but she did say her very close friend, Gregory, had adopted through a well-known adoption attorney. She told me she'd call Gregory and then call me right back.

It wasn't 10 minutes when Heather phoned me back with the name and telephone number of David Radis. I called and made an appointment with his office. He was booked about six weeks out, so we scheduled an appointment with him for the end of September. Coincidentally, my dad did his own legwork, and through a patient of his, Laurie Ackerman, he got David Radis' information also. Meant to be!

David was a nice man. His low-key energy made him easy to speak with. I got the impression he loved matching unwed mothers, who were scared and lonely, with prospective, loving, and hopeful parents. Yaniv and I were like two babes lost in the woods when we sat across from him. It was a four-hour meeting. David explained the process of open adoption, advertising in Midwest newspapers for unwed mothers needing to find adoptive parents, along with a whole host of other details that we found overwhelming. Adoption wasn't going to come cheap. At least not through a private attorney, but he would ensure all the "i's" were dotted and the "t's" were crossed. We needed to cover all the expenses for the birth mother—food, clothing, rent, transportation, as well as doctor visits and the actual hospitalization for birth, not to mention his fees. After we were three and a half hours in, David Radis looked at us both and asked us this question: "Do you have any preference for color?"

Three & Me

Huh?! I couldn't believe what I'd just heard. Yaniv had the same surprised reaction. It was a question you asked about a car. Or a house. Or a pair of shoes, a purse, or anything other than a baby. At least in our minds. In Hebrew, so David wouldn't understand, I asked Yaniv, "Does this matter to us? Because I don't think in those terms. What about you?"

Yaniv answered me back in Hebrew. "Color is for things. Not for babies."

Once I heard that, I turned and looked at David Radis and uttered the words, "Happy. Healthy. We don't see color." We also told him we didn't want to do any advertising in the Midwest newspapers. That felt wrong to us. We wanted to adopt the baby who was meant to be ours, the baby who otherwise might have had a hard time finding the right parents. That's who we wanted. After David Radis made his notes in our file about what we'd said, we thanked him, went to reception, wrote out a huge check for the four hours we spent there, and left for home.

About a week or two later, I came home to a message on my answering machine. David Radis had given this young woman our number, and she was hoping we'd want her baby. I immediately phoned her back before she changed her mind. Her name was Angela Rachelle Nading. She was 22, already had a two-and-a-half-year-old girl, and she couldn't handle another child financially on her salary as a cocktail waitress. I detected a sound of desperation in her voice. This was because the baby was due in about three weeks. Something in her voice made me fall in love with her and the baby. Rachelle told me that the baby would be biracial. She said that white families only wanted a white child, and black families only wanted a black child. I immediately told her we wanted the baby. He was meant to be ours. Yaniv agreed, and we immediately set in motion what would change our lives for the better. We flew Rachelle and her toddler daughter to Los Angeles from Kansas City, Missouri, to live with us. I had just three weeks to prepare for motherhood.

Some Of My Best Friends Are...

As soon as Rachelle stepped off that plane and into our lives, I knew that not only was I adopting a baby, but I was also adopting Rachelle. It didn't seem right to me that our son wouldn't know of the heroic and wonderful thing that Rachelle was doing for him. She was giving him opportunity, stability, and a promising future. Rachelle never looked back on the decision. She was resolute and knew she was doing her best for this baby. I will always love her for her strength of character. She is still, and will always be, an essential part of my family.

I have never believed in denied access. I don't think it's healthy for anyone involved. I was not going to be one of those adoptive mothers who lived in fear of the birth parent changing their mind. Yaniv and I named our baby Jonah. I knew that by allowing free access to Jonah, Rachelle would feel good about her decision, and Jonah would grow to know two women loved him. How could that be bad? During Jonah's childhood, I would explain to him that he didn't grow in mommy's belly. Instead, he grew in an Earth Angel's belly, and when it was time, she came and brought him to us. While we use the term Birth Mother now, during introductions, she is referred to in the family as "Rachelle." However, I still quietly think of Rachelle as Jonah's Earth Angel.

Rachelle stayed with us for the rest of October. On Halloween evening, after we took Rachelle's daughter trick or treating, we drove to Cedars Sinai Hospital. Rachelle was going to be in induced labor. We waited and waited for something to happen during the night, but Jonah still hung out in the warmth of her belly. The OB/GYN who was to deliver Jonah was a patient of my dad's. His name is Dr. Stuart Fischbein, and he couldn't have been more gracious. He wanted to deliver Jonah as a gift to my father. There would be no bill from Stuart. Stuart, wherever you are, I am still grateful to you.

Stuart would come in periodically and check to see how far along Rachelle was. She was progressing toward birth, but it still seemed like we had some time. At close to 9:00 in the morning, Stuart came in to check on Rachelle again. He asked me if I had a camera to photograph my son's birth. I hadn't even thought of that, mainly because all of Rachelle's business would be in those photos. Rachelle told me she didn't mind having photos taken, so Stuart sent me down to the hospital gift shop to buy a disposable camera. (This was before camera phones.) So off I went. Buying the camera was quick and easy, but before I went back up the elevators, I decided I wanted a bagel from the cafeteria.

Sometime between the time I left the room and got into the bagel line, Jonah made the decision that he wanted out. I hadn't yet returned, so Stuart began to worry. He called the gift shop asking where I was, and when they didn't know, he really began to sweat. Then he had me paged, but I wasn't really listening for my name on the PA and never heard it. A few minutes later, the delivery room nurse went down to the gift shop in hot pursuit of me. They told her I'd already left. Luckily, she figured the only other place I would be was in the cafeteria! She sprinted over and found me in the bagel line. Quickly she grabbed my hand, and we ran to an emergency elevator. In a flash, I was in delivery, just in time to watch Jonah crown.

Jonah was the most beautiful baby I'd ever seen. He had such a peaceful aura about him. As I looked down into his newly opened eyes, I heard him tell me, "I'm really a good boy." I can still feel the warmth come over me as I remember that moment we had together. I suddenly felt like a mother. Up until then, I was incredibly worried about maternal instinct and whether or not I had it. Pregnancy gives a woman nine months to develop and nurture impending motherhood. I had three weeks. I was pretty much on the outside of it all. I never shared my fears with anyone, lest they think I didn't deserve to have the baby. Happily, in the end, my worries were for naught. As soon as I held Jonah, I became Jonah's mom, the best job I would ever have in my entire life.

Yaniv was in school at the time of Jonah's birth. He told me he felt uncomfortable being in delivery as she was not his wife, and he respected her privacy. So, I phoned him with the news that Jonah was born, and he was ecstatic!

New motherhood notwithstanding, I still craved a bagel. Jonah had been whisked away to the nursery, and Rachelle was exhausted and needed rest, so I thought it would be a great time to go back downstairs. When I got to the bagel line, it was still long and slow. I stood there for what seemed to be an eternity. There was a woman in scrubs in the line to my right. She, too, was losing patience with the wait. She looked over at me and smiled. "I hate this damn line. It's the same thing every single day! Long and slow!" she said with a look of extreme impatience.

I laughed, and without thinking about how this would sound to someone, I declared, "You're not kidding! A little while ago, I almost missed the birth of my son, standing in this line!" That statement made perfectly good sense to me.

Staring at me like I was some kind of idiot, she grabbed her hospital badge, showed me what it said, then replied, "I'm an OB/GYN! You're really going to have to explain!"

Oh yeah. Only I would think I was being logical. I laughed as I explained to her that it was the birth mother giving the actual birth. I was in the cheering section. We both had a really good laugh. I'll bet, to this very day, that the obstetrician in the bagel line remembers our conversation more than 27 years ago.

Of all my friends who were excited to meet Jonah, I think my friend Julie Tolman was the most excited. Julie is the friend who took me to the Crosby Stills & Nash concert and is one of my lifelong till-death-do-us-part friends. We may not talk all the time; in fact, long periods pass when we don't see each other or hear from each other, but we are still friends nonetheless. She took me shopping for baby stuff one day in Sherman Oaks, telling me, "You know how we have all this stuff for our horses? Well, now you need to have all kinds of stuff for your baby." Julie was absolutely instrumental in my choosing the right kinds of baby equipment, clothing, bedding, and everything Jonah could ever need.

Because Jonah was a boy, he would have his bris (circumcision) on the eighth day after birth. On top of that, Julie wanted me to have a baby shower, so she helped my dad organize it. Between the bris and the shower, I wanted for nothing. Jonah was fully supplied!

Of my other friends, the second most excited was Theresa Saldana. She was so excited she could hardly contain herself. I HAD to bring him over to meet Tianna, her daughter. I told her as soon as I could take him out, that would be my first stop after the stable.

Jonah's pediatrician was another patient of my father's. His name is Dr. Robert Landow, who we affectionally referred to as Dr. Bob. He, too, said he would take no money for anything Jonah related. Dr. Bob was true to his word. I was never billed for any of Jonah's medical care all the way through to when Jonah aged out of the practice. (Forever grateful, Dr. Bob. I hope you know that and are enjoying retirement.)

At our first out-of-hospital visit, Dr. Bob told me on the fifth day of Jonah's life to "get him out there. Expose him to everything. It's OK if he gets dirty. Don't try to protect him from germs at this stage. He needs to build up his immune system. Take him everywhere." So, on Jonah's fifth day of life, I took him out to the barn. At the time, I owned a horse by the name of Famous Amos, or Amos for short. He was an appaloosa and looked like a very big chocolate chip cookie. Amos was a very friendly horse until you went into his stall. His attitude was that if you weren't carrying hay or other treats, your side was the outside!

Respecting Amos' boundaries, I stood just outside of the stall, cradling baby Jonah in my arms, when Amos stuck his head out of his "window" to see what was going on. He'd never seen a baby before and was naturally curious. Amos lowered his big horse face down to sniff Jonah. At that exact moment, Jonah raised his little arm, made a little fist, then shoved his arm right up Amos's nose! Well, Amos had been eating hay at the time, and Jonah's fist up his nostril tickled him. All of a sudden, a very big horse sneeze came out of Amos, along with a lot of slimy green hay goo. Jonah was covered head to toe in horse slime! On that very day, Jonah was "baptized by horse" and is an animal person, just like his mom.

I cleaned Jonah's face off, but his clothes were now stained the color of hay. No matter. It was fine with me. After we bid Amos adieu, we hit the road for Theresa's condo. In the early 1990s, Theresa got a gig playing Rachel, the wife of the Michael Chiklis character on The Commish. She finally had a regular job with a regular paycheck. Being stabbed stalled her career, as producers and directors, as well as money men, were hesitant to cast someone who was such a famous crime victim. Instead, they chose other actresses with the same features and qualities as Theresa. It was infuriating. Finally, though, she had a regular job with good pay and was able to purchase a condo in the same building where she had always rented. She was thrilled. Now she was an owner in a Hollywood high rise, with a doorman and security. She could relax and stop worrying about money. I was so happy about the security the show brought her. Good friends want good things to happen to their friends. And I wanted lots of good things to happen for Theresa!

As soon as I walked in the door with Jonah, Theresa grabbed him and cradled him. She was smitten! Tianna was sitting down in an armchair, and Theresa placed little Jonah in her lap. Tianna held on to him with such loving care. She was five or six years old at the time and promised Jonah she would always be his girlfriend, no matter what. Little Tiana meant those words with every fiber of her body; she was so smitten by baby Jonah. Lucky kid! Jonah grew up knowing he already had a girlfriend.

Three & Me

Tianna grew up to be a well-known model and dancer. Her beauty, on a scale of 1-10, is a 20! Pure of spirit and soul, with her mother's talent and father's support, she blossomed into an incredible human being.

When Tianna was 11, she was in a dance recital in the San Fernando Valley on a hot summer Sunday. I took my preschool-aged son to watch her perform. He knew he was going to watch his girlfriend dance, although the concept of a girlfriend wasn't something he understood just yet. He just accepted the fact that Tianna was his girlfriend for life.

The heat outside was brutal. It was 104° F. To make matters even more uncomfortable, the recital was being held outside in the parking lot with a makeshift stage. There was no respite from the sun. The black asphalt of the parking lot was quickly heating up and softening. Tianna's number was still agonizingly some time away. I was melting, as was Jonah. When I asked him if he wanted to leave or go indoors for a bit to cool off, he shook his head. "Mummy," he said with great authority, "I have to stay and watch my girlfriend! I'm not moving until I do!"

I was so impressed with Jonah's loyalty at such a young age. It's a trait that has never left him. He is the best boyfriend any girl could ever have. We taught him well.

# # #

A little over a month after Jonah's birth, Heather and Bob flew to LA from Park City, Utah, because Bob was getting his star on the Hollywood Walk of Fame. I ran up to greet Heather the minute I saw her on Hollywood Boulevard. It had been a while. She was wearing a camel-colored pantsuit, and my first thought was that she was swimming in it. She looked frailer than I remembered, and worse, I could feel bones when we hugged.

Some Of My Best Friends Are...

"What's wrong?" I asked her. "I know something's wrong. I can see it, and I can feel it."

Heather shook her head, smiling, "There's nothing I can hide from you," she said. "Is there? I just dodged a huge bullet. The Cancer Bullet!"

"You're kidding me? What the Hell, Heather?!"

"I was feeling kind of funky, so I went to my doctor, and they found it during a pelvic exam. I had Ovarian cancer! It was huge! I think grapefruit or apple size. But it was completely encapsulated! So, they were able to easily take it out. No follow-up chemo or radiation. They got the whole sucker out!"

"Holy crap!" I declared happily!

"Yeah, I'm still recovering from surgery. And I'm really trying to re-cover from that huge scare! That was fucking huge!" (Heather and I dropped F-bombs all the time together.)

I gave her another hug. I kept thinking how very lucky it was that her cancer was encapsulated. No metastasis, no nodes, no nothing. Rare-ly do you hear the words "cancer" and "lucky" in the same sentence.

I gushed about baby Jonah, thanking her again and again. She was super excited as well, and we talked a bit about how great it was to adopt. She said she had the same initial fears as I did about maternal instinct and whether or not it would kick in. It was so good hearing that from her, as she was Super Mom.

Sometime after the Hollywood Star ceremony, after Heather and Bob had returned to Utah, she asked me how my experience with David Radis was. I told her it was wonderful. Not only was he a good law-yer, but he was also giving children a chance by helping them find loving families. Heather seemed pleased. I had no idea that she was considering another addition to her family, this time through David Radis.

A year later, Bob Urich was diagnosed with synovial cell sarcoma. Heather and Bob put their Park City home for sale and moved back to the Los Angeles area, specifically to the San Fernando Valley. After his treatment protocols, Heather and Bob went through David Radis and adopted an adorable baby girl. Jonah was two at the time. They had a house under construction in the new community of Lake Sherwood, and in the meantime, they were renting a home in Studio City.

Jonah and I would spend a bunch of time at that house, just ooo-ing and aaa-ing over little baby Allison. Jonah was smitten with Heather's baby. On warmer days, we'd sit out in the backyard near the pool. Thankfully, there was a fence around the pool, and it was locked. But Jonah kept gravitating towards it, which understandably made me a bit nervous. I made up my mind that when I could, I would have Jonah take lessons so he would learn how to not drown.

Motherhood suited me. Everyone in my circle loved Jonah. He was possessed of a sweet disposition and not prone to bad behavior. He was also absolutely beautiful, the beneficiary of all the best features from his mixed genetics. I never once looked at him as anything other than my baby, then my toddler, my boy, my teenager, and now my handsome young man. But sometimes, the world throws you curveballs when you're expecting a fastball, and you miss it completely.

That curveball is racism, which was surprising since I lived on the West Coast in a suburb of Los Angeles, and never once thought it would hit. But it did. The most shocking aspect was that most of the racism we encountered came from within the Jewish community. To be fair, we lived in the Jewish community, so I have no idea what if any, racism and prejudices we would have encountered had we lived somewhere else. Racism is still very shocking and surprising. I won't bore you with all the events, but I'll share the few that stand out the most in my mind.

Jonah was enrolled at the Bernard Milken Jewish Community Center in the heart of the San Fernando Valley for his first year of nursery school. He was three years old. I would pick him up every day at the same time, waiting outside the closed doors of his classroom until they were thrown open by the happy, smiling children who poured out into the hallways, joining the cacophony and chaos of all the other children from the other classrooms. It was the Friday afternoon before Mother's Day when I arrived at the usual time. When I walked into the hallways, I saw open doors to all the classrooms, including Jonah's. It took me but a puzzled minute to realize that there was a celebration going on inside all the classrooms and had been going on for quite a while. When I entered Jonah's classroom, he ran up to me with tear-stained cheeks and immediately grabbed my leg, wrapping his little arms around it. "Mommy, why didn't you come to see me in my play? Where were you?" I put my hand on Jonah's head, cradled his face, and told him that no one had told me about the event. He still cried his little heart out, not letting go.

I walked awkwardly toward the teacher, who grabbed Jonah by the hand and told him to sit next to her. "Can you please explain to me what is going on here?" I asked as politely as I could, the anger rising quickly in my throat.

"It's the Mother's Day Luncheon," she said. "Jonah was looking all over for you. I finally had him sit near me because you weren't there. Why didn't you come?"

"I was never informed about this!" I said, betraying my anger. "Why wasn't I informed?!"

The teacher looked embarrassed. She then pointed to two women who were about ten years younger than I was. They looked like wealthy

Three & Me

Jewish American Princesses with perfect hair, expensive clothes, and long manicured nails. "Those are the room mothers. They planned the event. You should speak with them."

I thanked the teacher, walked over to the two princesses, and inquired as to why I wasn't informed about the luncheon and the play. The two empty-headed and mean-spirited morons looked puzzled. Finally, the first one spoke, "What's the name of your child? I'll check the list." I told her that my son's name was Jonah Dotan. The one princess holding the clipboard gazed down at her list and then let out a little gasp, raising her hand to her lips. "Oh my God!" she said spontaneously. "We didn't know you were *WHITE!*"

That stopped me dead in my tracks. *THEY DIDN'T KNOW I WAS WHITE!?!* And what the hell does that have to do with anything?! Their bigotry harmed an innocent child simply because they didn't wish to share their space with a woman of color. To this day, I'm still upset about the Mother's Day experience I missed out on because they hated an innocent child whose skin color differed from theirs. And I vehemently deplore the anguish they caused my 3-year-old boy. But the main thing I deplore was the overt racism they exhibited. I cannot tolerate someone excluding anyone because of the color of their skin!

After that bout with racism smacked me hard in the face, I was a bit more prepared for the next time it reared its ugly head.

Later that summer, I fulfilled a promise to myself to make sure Jonah would learn to swim. I enrolled him in the swim program at that same Jewish Community Center. His swim instructor was a pretty girl who looked to be college-aged. She had blonde hair, a slim athletic body, and a beautiful smile. That's all it took for Jonah to develop a little-boy crush on his swim teacher. Jonah was the youngest in the class and also the smallest. That didn't bother him one little bit. He jumped in the water with much enthusiasm and caught on quite quickly. Jonah was a natural in the water.

As the kids were learning water safety and how to float, parents sat on the pool deck waiting. Most of the other parents knew each other from the public schools in the area, and they socialized freely with one another. I chose to sit by myself and either read or watch my son's progress in the water. After a few days of lessons, Jonah was able to propel himself off the wall toward the waiting arms of the cute swim instructor he so crushed on. Most of the other kids were still too afraid to leave the safety of the wall and had to be coaxed extra hard. I was so thrilled with Jonah's talent in the water that I had no time for the parents on the deck whose conversations mostly revolved around the new television series, *Survivor*.

One day, after a couple of weeks of lessons, Jonah and I arrived a few minutes early at the pool. We sat down on the deck, waiting for his instructor when I spotted her walking rapidly toward us with a very open and purposeful stride. She didn't look happy. By this time, a few other parents had arrived and had taken their usual places behind me.

I was seated, legs crossed on the deck, as she approached where I was sitting. She stood, hands on hips, looming quite large over Jonah and me. "If you don't like what I'm doing, then you are free to leave!" she said. "I don't appreciate people going around my back spreading shit about me!"

I was completely startled. "What are you talking about?" I said, not without some anger. "Jonah loves your lessons. I love your lessons!" I let this sink in for a moment. Then I said, "I don't talk to anyone here on the deck. I'm always alone. Tell me you saw me somewhere other than right here every time we come! Tell me!" I stood up and faced her, awaiting an answer. Then I saw her look towards the back at two people, both with smirks on their faces. They were the parents of the oldest kids in the group, at least three years older than Jonah. Their two kids were two of the biggest wall-huggers while Jonah was swimming circles around them. I knew immediately what I was looking at. *The Big R!*

I walked over to them and said, "YOU DID THIS! DIDN'T YOU?! YOU LIED ABOUT ME! WHY WOULD YOU DO SUCH A THING!?"

Undaunted, they looked me straight in the eye. "We will do anything and everything to protect our children!" "PROTECT THEM?! FROM WHAT?!" I was angry because I knew what the response would be. But I wanted them to say it. To say it in front of all the other parents. To say it in front of the young college-aged swim instructor.

They pointed at Jonah. "From that!" they said.

"You're trash. Hurting a little boy is something trashy people do." Their smirks turned to snarls, and before they could open their mouths, I took Jonah's hand and walked back towards the swim instructor, who stood where I left her, looking deflated and humiliated.

"You were had," I said. "And you were used. Since you basically kicked us out before you knew the truth or even tried to verify the truth, we're out of here. Thank you for the good times."

Jonah was devastated, and he cried all the way to the office, where I requested my money back. When asked why, I told them the swim instructor kicked us out, and he could ask her why. He handed me my refund, and Jonah and I headed for the women's locker room, where surprisingly, the young woman was waiting for us.

"I'm sorry," she began. "I should have come to talk to you first before I yelled at you. I'm so sorry." I noticed she appeared crushed by the events. Still, she made a choice.

I felt terrible for her. I really did. But there was no way we would go back if those hideous people were still there. If they tried to hurt a child once, what's to stop them from harming the same child again and again? So, I just shook my head back and forth, conveying that what she said was too little too late. "Maybe something good will come of this," I told her. "Maybe you learned a few valuable lessons. You're young, and you were used. Maybe next time you won't be manipulated so easily. Thank you for everything. Jonah loved your lessons."

And with that, we left. They say success is the best revenge, and Jonah certainly got his. He went on to swim club with the CCAT swim team, made Junior Olympics every year, and qualified for the top USA swimming meets, eventually ending his swimming career with California Reportable Times in freestyle and backstroke. He had AAA times and AAAA times in USA Swimming. Jonah was and still is a fast fish in the water.

The last instance of the *Big R* that I wanted to share was probably one of the worst. Jonah was enrolled in Kindergarten at a Jewish day school. He was a high-energy kid, and in retrospect, that school was not a good match for my son. But the Rabbi wanted him to go there; my dad was a huge donor to the high school program, having donated money for the Physics Lab, so my dad wanted him to go there also. Besides the high price tag for every grade level and the high-tech and beautiful campus, I was told the education was one of the best. Jonah is highly intelligent, so I thought it might work. In hindsight, he would have been better off in another setting.

He was assigned to a classroom taught by an Israeli ex-pat who had taught at that school for many years. I was informed that she was a good teacher and that Jonah was lucky to have her. Jonah had been potty trained for over a year before he started Kindergarten, so I was surprised when I picked him up one day and he literally reeked. The stench was unmistakable. He'd pooped his pants. Well, I figured

Three & Me

accidents happen. The same thing happened the next day. And the next. This went on for two weeks when I decided to take him to a psychologist to find out what was going on. The doctor told me Jonah had developed encopresis, where children regress and leak into their pants. He told me the best way to solve this would be to have Jonah hand launder his own soiled garments in the sink. I did this, and it seemed to do the trick.

A few nights later, though, I got a phone call from the teacher's aide in the classroom. It's the kind of phone call that no parent wants. I'd met her at Parents Night, and she was a lovely young woman, in her twenties, straight out of college. Now, on the phone with me, she was crying. "Suzie, you have to do something. You have to get Jonah out of Miss Zohar's class. She is abusing your son." The young aide sobbed some more before continuing. "I couldn't take it anymore. I quit today. I tried as hard as I could to protect him, and now that I'm gone, I don't know what's going to happen."

The Mother Bear in me began to rage. "How is Jonah being abused?" I asked her. I was literally sickened to my stomach.

"Miss Zohar sends him to the corner, in the cubby area, and makes him stand there for hours. If he has to go to the bathroom, she denies him. So, he has to crap his pants. He has no choice. The other kids then make fun of him. He isn't learning anything because he isn't part of the class at all. If he's tired, she still makes him stand there. He has to be perfectly still. It's torture for a little boy."

I thanked her and hung up, my head spinning and my stomach turning. I was dizzy with anger. I went downstairs and told Yaniv, who was feeding the dogs while Jonah watched *The Little Mermaid* on the VCR. Then I phoned my dad, who, within two seconds of hearing what I just said, hit the roof. "Get him out of that classroom!" he demanded of me.

Some Of My Best Friends Are...

"Dad, I know that. But I need your help. You need to call the school tomorrow and get me an appointment with the principal. You're the big donor there. I'm just a nobody."

My dad did as he was asked, and I met with the principal. I was told the school had a zero-transfer policy, and Jonah would have to stay in the classroom with Miss Zohar. It would be a bad precedent to transfer a child because the teacher and child were incompatible. What lesson would Jonah then learn? There would be no transfer.

My dad, upon hearing this, called the Rabbi, who was the final authority on all things school related. The Rabbi hit the roof and made several phone calls, and wham bam boom, Jonah got his transfer to a lovely young teacher who made all the difference in his early education.

Miss Zohar, however, was still free to do what she wanted to. I couldn't prove any racist intent at this point, although I knew in my gut that it existed. Towards the end of the school year, though, I was handed her head on a silver platter. It was during the physical education period when all the Kindergarteners were out in the yard along with the PE coach, that she finally hung herself. Miss Zohar was standing with a few teachers when she pointed Jonah out to them. "See that kid," she said as she watched Jonah. "He's fairly athletic. I just hope he doesn't turn out to be another Mike Tyson or O.J. Simpson."

I got a phone call from one of the teachers who witnessed Miss Zohar's racist comment. I wasn't surprised, as I already knew she was probably a closet racist. At the same time, I was appalled by the comment. Is every black child in danger of growing up to be an accused murderer or a wife-beater? Would she have said that she was worried a white child could grow up to be another Timothy McVeigh or Charles Manson? Doubtful.

The teacher who told me about the comment was also appalled. When I went to the high command at the school and told them of the

Three & Me

comment, they didn't believe it. I gave a list of names of the teachers who had witnessed the incident and requested that they investigate. They did. Then they called in Miss Zohar. When confronted with what she allegedly said in the yard, she didn't dispute it. She saw nothing wrong in her comment. Her contract was not renewed, and she was effectively gone.

Jonah's harsh treatment in her classroom was most likely the *Big R*. Racism can be overt, or it can be subtle, almost impossible to detect sometimes. I am still so grateful for the people who witnessed these wrongs thrust on Jonah and contacted me. Without them, Jonah would have had to endure an entire school year facing abuse, and I have no idea what that would have done to him as a person.

294

*Jonah and his birth mother,
Rachelle. She is an important part
of our family. I will be
forever grateful.*

Some Of My Best Friends Are...

THIRTEEN

The Good, They Die Young

Heather and Bob finally finished building and moved into their Lake Sherwood house. As luck would have it, their home was literally down the street from where I kept my two horses. I was excited because I could see Heather much more often.

I had stepped up into the Jumper Division, and I trained with an old coot named Tom Blakiston. Tom was past his prime as a top trainer of Grand Prix horses. He had his heyday way back when, and I knew that. I had no intention of going Grand Prix, and I would never have a Grand Prix horse. But I figured Tom forgot more than most people knew, so I became one of the few amateurs in his barn. His barn was situated deep in Hidden Valley with vistas all around. The drive over Potrero Road was picturesque and relaxing as I wound my way through, passing stables, mansions, and fields. The biggest horse farm with the most fields was a property owned by Castle & Cooke founder David Murdoch. He practically owned that entire Valley. While he was the largest landowner, the visual candy he provided the onlooker was unsurpassed.

Tom's barn was, for lack of a better word, bucolic. We were surrounded by foothills and open fields as far as the eye could see, together with the quiet sounds of wildlife and nature. From our ring, we watched the filming of some scenes in the movie *Seabiscuit*. If I had to choose a place where I would want to spend most of my time, Blakiston Ranch was that place.

After riding, I'd stop in and visit Heather. It became a regular thing with us. Somehow, I convinced her to get back in the saddle, so we both took lessons from old Tom. To my great satisfaction, Tom and

Three & Me

I graduated to the Jumper Ring on a wonderful chestnut mare named Agatha. She was born on Jill's birthday.

Sue Lika Dotan

Heather immediately hit it off. She was very tenuous on a horse, and he was able to instill the confidence she needed to enjoy herself. It was just like old times from my days at the Los Angeles Equestrian Center in the 1980s. My horse buddy was back in the ring with me.

One day in Heather's kitchen, she gave me a long Heather-type stare. I started laughing because she looked so serious. "Would you help me with something?" she asked. "Because I need you," I told her I'd help her with whatever she needed. "Good!" she said. "Because I need a logo for our Sarcoma Foundation."

I told Heather to give Bob a felt tip marker and to have him sign his name a million times, leaving space between each signature. I scanned the best of his signatures and created his logo from it, pairing it with a yellow star. (Hollywood Walk of Fame was the inspiration.) It was a logo that was appropriate for the time, but years later, after Bob had passed from complications of cancer, I needed to change the logo to something more emotional. And then I was stuck. I wanted to design something amazing and wanted it to be one of my best logos ever. With the pressure I'd placed on myself, I came up empty. Bupkis. Zilch. Nada. Nothing.

I was struggling to find just the right elements for a new Robert Urich Foundation for Cancer Research and Patient Care logo. Heather would call and ask about the progress, and I would tell her I was still working on it. Damn! I still couldn't find a visual solution that I was in love with.

I was in a deep sleep when I heard Bob's voice in my ear. "Suzie, look at my initials, especially the R; it's right there in front of you. Play with it." I woke up, keenly aware of what I'd just heard. It wasn't my imagination. I was convinced that I had heard Bob. So, I jumped out of bed, threw on a robe, walked down the hallway to my home office, jumped on the computer, and put a big R down on the page. Then I copied the R, flopped it, and placed it next to the regular reading R.

Three & Me

And there it was right in front of me. The very beginning of a butterfly! I worked for a few more hours, refining a butterfly created out of the two R's, then took the "U," stretched it out a bit, and cupped the butterfly in it, as one would cup a real-life butterfly, caring for it, admiring it, but not capturing it. I had my logo! Every once in a while, inspiration hits, and part of having talent is knowing when to listen or look for inspiration. I listened to Bob's whisper and came up with one of my favorite logos.

One day after we both rode, Heather and I went back to her house to hang out. She mentioned that she and Bob were flying to New York City the next day for some business Bob had. She was excited about the upcoming trip. I told her I'd see her in a week, gave her a hug, and left shortly after since I had a ton of errands to run that day, not the least of which was a preliminary design for a brochure I was designing for the USC Sea Grant program.

Some days later, I was asleep in bed when my dad called, waking me. Yaniv had already left for work, and I was worried that maybe he had an accident. I looked at the time. It was 5 minutes after 6 a.m. I didn't yet have caller ID, so the ringing was not only jarring, unpleasant, and loud, but it was also disconcerting. "Hello?" I said with the raspy sound one makes when woken up.

"Suzie, wake up. Turn on the news right now!" The urgency in my dad's voice scared me.

"What's wrong?" I asked nervously.

"Just turn on the damn television, and you'll know what's wrong!" My dad was never one to mince words, and he hated explaining things when he thought the answer was incredibly obvious. Never mind that half the time, I had no clue what he was talking about. Not to digress, but a typical conversation with my dad went something like this: "Get me the phone number for whatshisname," or "The whaddyacallit isn't working right, and I can't find the thingamajig to even fix it!" Clear as mud, right?!

I turned the television on as instructed and was aghast at what I was looking at. Almost all the channels were covering the same horrible thing. That was the morning of September 11th, 2001. At the time I turned the television on, only the first Tower was on fire. The newscasters said that a plane had crashed into it, which seemed inconceivable to me at the time. I had no idea that it was a terrorist event, and it was clear the newscasters weren't following that line of thinking either.

I crawled back into bed, wondering what the hell had happened. As I watched the news broadcasts, with different newscasters hypothesizing about what caused such a horrific accident, I began to get a gnawing suspicion that it just might be a terrorist attack. I lived in Israel all those years, with continuous terrorist attacks. From that experience, I learned that shock and awe are the hallmarks of terror, as well as striving for the highest body count. This would have both. I began to wonder if the plane flying through Tower One was a variation of the car bomb theme.

As I watched the Tower burn with growing unease, I flashed on the people above the damage, and I realized they had no way out. My heart stopped. Suddenly I realized that there were possibly hundreds of people who could not be saved and who would soon die. I had no idea that my calculations of hundreds dying were ridiculously low. I was having high anxiety about the people in Tower One, ruminating about their fates, when the camera crews picked up the sound of another low-flying plane. And then I saw it. The cameras followed a low approaching aircraft as it hit Tower Two with a huge impact. I began to cry for the people who, just seconds ago, had lives, families and had simply gone to work. I grieved for those who had innocently boarded planes to the West Coast and had no idea they would die in a ball of fire, incinerated.

Three & Me

After the second plane hit, I had no doubt. The United States was a victim of terror. As I sat in bed, working through the shock, I suddenly remembered that Heather and Bob were in New York City. A huge lump in my throat began to form, and I prayed they were nowhere near downtown Manhattan.

I found out later that Heather and Bob were in the middle of the chaos, but thankfully they were OK. It would take some miracles for them to get back home, though. All air traffic was halted. This was definitely not the trip to New York they had planned. But it wouldn't be the worst of their problems.

Bob's cancer, once thought to be dormant, was waking up with a quiet roar. A tumor near his heart was detected, and he was put on an experimental chemotherapy drug, usually used to fight breast cancer, which was supposed to shrink the tumor down to an operable size. Bob seemed fine with this protocol, and he was still looking forward to the future.

Not only was he back in demand as an actor, but he was also embarking on a new business venture involving an online food boutique. He needed a logo and other marketing materials. He chose me. (Happy dance!)

The name of his new venture was Eastlake Farms, named for a lake near his Canada retreat on West Lake near Picton, Ontario. He wanted a folksy image that embodied Heather's family tartan. Heather was a Scot, and her family had a tartan specific to them. He also wanted a cardinal (the bird) as part of the image. I listened to Bob intently and translated his ideas into a visual that he immediately fell in love with. I hit all his points, and he was sold on the imagery. I was also pleased with the result.

He was scheduled to meet with his investors and took the visual identity with him. Bob was proud of it. But as usual in business, people want to use their own people. His investors wanted to do just that, but Bob wasn't having it. He put his foot firmly down, surprising them when he told them unequivocally that if I wasn't going to be part of this project development, then he wouldn't be either. His investors acquiesced, and I was able to hold on to the gig. Heather used to brag to anyone who would listen that Bob was my biggest fan. Not too bad if you ask me! It's something I like to hang onto as I remember Bob and Bob and Heather together. My "biggest Fan" (besides my husband) was a pretty amazing man.

Bob and Heather had the kind of love that is a once-in-a-million event. I remember Bob looking adoringly at Heather when she wasn't noticing, and the same with Heather gazing at her husband. They fought his cancer together, never once giving up. Unfortunately, Bob did not make it to 56 years old. He passed six months after 9/11 on April 16th, 2002, from some unforeseen complications. Heather never recovered from the loss. Bob was her life, but he was also her heart light. When he left, she felt like she was half the person she was.

The day Bob passed I drove to their house with Jonah in tow. He was six years old at the time, and Heather and Bob's little daughter, Allie, was going to turn four just two days later. Heather had a million and ten things to do, so Jonah and I took Allie to the park to play in order to give Heather some breathing room. She had a lot on her plate, not the least of which was planning a funeral and a child's birthday party. While some may think it's incongruous to do both, how could she not? Little Allie needed something happy after losing her dad.

Allie seemed fairly normal when we picked her up. My guess was that she didn't comprehend what dying really meant. As the kids played, Allie began crying because she missed her daddy. Jonah came over to me to tell me that Allie was very sad and wanted to know what he should do for her. I told him to hug her. He was so in tune with her feelings, and it was heartwarming to watch him care so deeply for her. I'm convinced he was born an old soul. Jonah

Three & Me

nodded in agreement, wrapped his arms protectively around Allie, and hugged her into his chest as she cried. It was just the two of them sharing her grief. It turned out to be just the hug Allie needed. When we took her home, Jonah held her hand until they were inside. My heart melted into one big gooey mess.

Heather gave me a list of things to do to help her with the reception at their home after the Mass for Bob. Jonah and I headed out to find the items she needed. On the way back into the Valley, we noticed a great deal of police activity, including news helicopters and crews racing into Hidden Hills, a wealthy gated community. We turned on the radio, tuning into the news, and discovered that Robert Blake was being arrested on charges that he allegedly murdered his wife, Bonnie Lee Bakely. (He was later acquitted. He passed away on March 9th, 2023.) I found that to be an odd synchronicity that his arrest came the day Bob died.

Some months before Bob died, he was working on a Western movie project near Saugus. The set was way out in the sticks, not really accessible by any major road or highway. You really had to know how to follow trails to access the set; it was that far out from civilization. Bob was feeling tired after shooting, so he decided to take a nap in his trailer. He was fast asleep when he awoke to the feeling of someone staring at him. As he opened his eyes, he saw a male figure sitting in a chair across from him. Trying to focus his sleepy eyes, he slowly realized it was Robert Blake. Surprised, Bob immediately sat up, wondering how the hell Robert Blake not only made it to the set but how he found his way into Bob's trailer.

Bob told us that he was initially alarmed since he really didn't know Robert Blake that well. (Theresa was good friends with him once, usually referring to him as Bobby Blake. She absolutely adored him.) To Bob's surprise, Robert Blake began baring his soul, venting about the suspicion that surrounded him over the shooting death of his wife. He swore to Bob that he never touched her, never hurt her, or never wanted anything or anyone to hurt her.

The Good, They Die Young

Bob listened to Blake's sad tale about being tried in the court of public opinion, fearing that he would be arrested, charged, and convicted in a court of law when he was innocent. Bob lent him a sympathetic ear, and once Blake got it all out of his system, he left the trailer, probably headed home. Bob was very confused over this experience and slightly troubled. He told us he didn't really know what to make of the whole experience. Bob's story about that day in Saugus came rushing back as I watched the chaos surrounding Robert Blake's arrest on that April day in 2002.

# # #

About a month before Bob died, Theresa's life was beginning anew! The Grove at Farmer's Market opened in March 2002. For the residents of that area, it was a wonderful piece of news, but for Theresa, it gave her a lifeline to the outside world. She quickly made it her home away from home, especially upstairs at the Barnes & Noble Starbucks. It was there that she held court. For reasons still unknown to me, she went there almost every day unless she had a doctor's appointment or other such thing. She did continue to get Tianna to her dance lessons after school, but while Tianna was in school, Theresa was at The Grove.

I would take Jonah to The Grove from the San Fernando Valley, which was a bit of a schlep, to visit with Theresa and Tianna on weekends. Or sometimes, if I had some free time, I'd run over, and we'd have lunch together at one of the many places to eat.

On the days I'd bring Jonah, he and Tianna would go off on their own and meet us at a designated time. Tianna was already in her early 20s, and Jonah was already in high school, so we were completely at ease with them spending time by themselves. Theresa exuded an air of ownership over the mall. She was proud of it, almost as if it were her creation. I loved that because it brought out her positivity.

Lots of times, we'd go see movies together at The Grove. Jonah and Tianna would find seats on their own inside the theater and meet us outside afterward. Of course, Jonah was becoming more and more smitten with Tianna. She was gorgeous. She was his fantasy older woman, and her picture was prominently displayed in his bedroom. She became the fantasy older woman for all of Jonah's friends as well. As Tianna aged, Jonah followed right behind her, acting like her willing servant. It was adorable. The two of them together had nothing but love for each other. I loved that. Tianna saw a wonderful person standing before her, and Jonah saw the same. Theresa and I would oftentimes wonder what would have happened if the age difference had been the opposite. She thought Jonah would make a wonderful son-in-law and husband. I had to laugh, knowing she was right, but they were the ages they were, and Tianna would one day find a man that she would want to marry well before Jonah would even be out of school.

Paparazzi were still stalking Theresa. When one would pop out from behind an object or walk straight over to her with a camera aimed right at her, she'd give a little gasp or jump, betraying her still lingering PTSD. I always felt terrible for her, but I realized this was her path in life. A few times, I'd want to jump in front to protect her, but Theresa instinctively knew how to take evasive action, so I would just follow her away from the "action."

Theresa was also big on email. It was something she did during her time at Barnes & Noble, making full use of their Wi-Fi. Her emails were mostly light and chatty. But sometimes, she would send out long emails describing quite a lot of unpleasantry. She would hear of someone in dire straits and send every one of her friends, including me, their story. Sometimes it was financial troubles a friend was having; other times, it was a friend with a terrible disease. Theresa cared deeply about these people. She would transmit daily reports on their situation over the Internet. I was floored by the amount of compassion she had for others. She clearly took everyone's misfortune to heart. I saw her emails as a way for her to help her friends recover from whatever malady or trouble they were going through, as well as a way to help herself heal from her emotional injuries sustained during the attack. By focusing her attention on the hardships of others, she was also able to deal with her own demons and her own lifelong recovery.

One day, I got an email from Theresa. Her daughter had a bug bite on her foot, which was in itself no big thing. The very next day, they went to Venice Beach, and then that innocuous bug bite became a huge thing. Tianna went body surfing in the waves. It was within two weeks of an odd rainstorm that hit the Los Angeles area in the summer. The California Coast was filled with bacteria and viruses that the rainstorm washed through storm drains into the ocean. One of those bacteria entered through Tianna's bug bite. That bacteria was staph. She ended up in the hospital with heavy antibiotics pumped into her body via IV in an attempt to save her leg. Staph is a terrible infection. It's hard to predict and needs an arsenal of medication to fight it over an extended period of time. I remember Theresa telling me that Tianna had MRSA (medically resistant staph aureus), which is especially hard to treat. Hearing about Tianna's battle with a virus brought me back to the days when I caught meningitis from the ocean too soon after a rainstorm.

Once I saw the email, I grabbed Jonah, and we ran to the hospital to visit Tianna and Theresa. Theresa was sleeping in Tianna's room, never leaving her bedside. Jonah was particularly shaken seeing Tianna in so much pain. He wasn't exactly delighted by all the machines Tianna was hooked up to, as well as the IV pole staring him in the face. Somehow, he managed to get her to want to walk down the hallways. She buzzed the nurse, who made her ambulatory. Jonah and Tianna began walking in circles around the hospital floor. I think that was the first time she'd been out of bed since she was first admitted to the hospital. Theresa was thrilled to see her daughter up and about, albeit for a short time. Thankfully, Tianna recovered. But Theresa was a nervous wreck for a long time after that. Tianna was her passion and her reason for living.

Three & Me

After Bob passed and Heather had some time to heal, she went full bore raising money for the Robert Urich Foundation. Heather had many willing friends who absolutely adored her and wanted to help. We all became soldiers in that effort. Heather would pay out of her own pocket to host fundraisers, and they would be spectacular events. My favorites were the celebrity golf tournaments played at the Sherwood Country Club. The dinners the evening before were star-studded events, as was the golf.

My contribution towards these events would be securing auction items that could bring in high bids. I would hit up everyone I knew, especially my clients who manufactured products or sold much sought-after services. I was lucky in that I had a wide range of people to go to for auction items. Always a big seller, sports memorabilia was something I could secure through my friendship with Reggie Smith of Red Sox and Dodgers fame. Reggie was still a big name after his playing career ended. He was the batting coach for the United States Baseball Olympic Team as well as the World Baseball Classic. Besides auction items, I was very happy to do grunt stuff, like creating silent auction sheets or creating and wrapping baskets filled with goodies to be placed on tables at the silent auction. I loved helping Heather. And, as much as I loved helping Heather, I knew that my efforts would translate into funding that would hopefully be able to save people's lives or, if not that, at least prolong their lives.

One of my favorite banquets that Heather threw was held at the Sherwood Country Club on October 27th, 2002. Because it was so soon after Bob's passing, just about everybody who was anybody wanted to attend. The proceeds would benefit the Comprehensive Cancer Center located at the University of Michigan, one of about 51 such centers in the United States today. Bob had been treated at that center because they were always on the cutting edge of medicine.

The event fell on the evening of the final game of the World Series between the Anaheim Angels and the San Francisco Giants. Baseball fans such as myself were in a quandary because we were not only dying to see the game, but we also were so heavily invested in the banquet. I was able to record the game and watch it when I got home. (Angels won! Yay!)

For the event itself, I recruited my friends, Reggie Smith, and Jermaine Jackson, to play golf the next day with big donors. We were all seated for dinner, waiting for the program to begin, when Wayne Gretzky (yes, THE GREAT ONE!), who was seated at the next table, turned and noticed Reggie Smith. "Hey, Reggie," he called out, one athlete to another. "What do you think of that Bonds guy thinking he's too good to practice with his team?! I mean, what's up with that?!"

I gulped. Wayne referred to Barry Bonds, Jimmy Bonds' son, who was notorious for wanting to practice alone. I looked over at Reggie, who had a wry smile on his face. Undaunted by Reggie's lack of a response, he continued, "You know, I don't know how you guys in baseball handle guys like that, but in hockey, we handle it by sending our largest guys after the dude, and when they've got a good hold on him, we each take turns punching him."

I was laughing now. I looked over at Reggie. "Should I tell him, Reg?" Reggie nodded his head, so I turned and looked at Wayne and said, "Barry Bonds is Reggie's cousin."

"Helluva Ball Player!" Wayne replied, not missing a beat. It was hilarious. We all had a good time after Wayne's recovery from his faux pas. That was definitely one for the books! (Actually, Jimmy Bonds and Reggie Smith are first cousins. Barry would be Reggie's second cousin, but he was family nonetheless.) I couldn't have scripted a better conversation!

It was not too long after Bob died that I was at Heather's. The sun was beginning to set. Jonah and Allie were playing together somewhere in that huge house of hers when her landline rang. Heather answered it with her usual "Hello." I saw her face change from casual to absolute shock. "WHO is this?????" she asked with an air of incredulity. "Who?... You're kidding me...How did you get my number?" (Heather had an unlisted number.)

Heather silently motioned for me to come over and listen as she opened up the receiver. My mouth dropped. It was either former President Bill Clinton or an excellent actor! He'd called to express his condolences on Bob's passing, telling Heather that Bob was one of his favorite actors. As for how he got her number? Clinton explained it perfectly. "Heather, I'm the former President. I can get just about anyone's telephone number."

That was no imposter. Heather and her son Ryan were guests at the opening of the William J. Clinton Presidential Library in Little Rock, Arkansas, in November 2004.

Heather back in the saddle!!!

The Good, They Die Young

FOURTEEN

Cinderella With A Jewish Twist

M y dad's love life was something that shouldn't have been a big deal in my life, but it was. I was happy for each and every relationship he was in at the time he was in it, but for some reason, most of the women he chose, after the first few months of being sweet, turned into absolute horrors. To this day, I can't figure out why these women became so needy and exclusionary when they were in a late-life relationship. It makes no sense.

As for me, I don't have a jealousy bone. Never had it. So, it's hard for me to understand why some people, some women in particular, think every other woman is a huge threat to their security and relationship. I just wanted to be a daughter. That's it. A daughter! My role as a daughter is completely different from that of a girlfriend or wife. Those roles are miles and miles apart, but from the women my father chose as partners, it became obvious that his women blurred the lines between roles. There was only one woman in my father's widowed life I loved unconditionally, and she loved me back. In my opinion, she was the best thing that ever happened to my dad, as wild a concept as that relationship was.

The woman I loved the most for my dad was my Aunt Esther. (Yep, my aunt!) Aunt Esther was married to my mother's brother. She was the only person in the family who recognized the huge wrong thrust on my mother in that whole mean-spirited trust debacle. She made the situation whole again by making restitution after her husband, Bob (my mother's brother), passed away. Esther was a class act. She and my dad connected romantically, and I could not have been happier. My dad was absolutely thrilled to have Esther in his life. Not only was she his physical type (big boobs), but her sense of humor was sharp,

Three & Me

Esther, Jonah and Dad. I grieved over her passing. She was the best woman for my dad, for me, Jonah and for Yaniv. RIP Esther.

Cinderella With A Jewish Twist

witty, and fun! She would do standup comedy at Jewish events to raise money for charities, never once charging for her sets. One of her favorite lines, which I loved, was when she first met someone. She'd put her hand out for a shake and utter, "I'm so glad you met me!" It was hilarious to see the look on people's faces. Eventually, everyone would laugh. Esther possessed a joie de vivre. Every time we got together as a family, it was fun, loving, and filled with laughter. Jonah loved Esther. He'd bounce on a bed, and Esther would catch him. They'd spend hours together. Jonah was the closest thing to a grandson she had, and she spoiled him with all her love and gifts. She would often say, "Isn't he something!?" or "That Jonah…" and then trail off with a wistful smile on her face. When Jonah would sit on her lap and hug her, Esther was absolutely in heaven.

But it wouldn't last. Esther succumbed to cancer, and we were all heartbroken. My dad cried when she passed, as did I, Yaniv, and Jonah. She was such a special light in our lives, full of positivity. I later learned that she had needed anti-depressant medication for years. Somehow, that was never an issue. She just never showed her downside to us. Esther was, right up until the very end, a positive and upbeat person. My dad was at her bedside at the hospital when she passed. Another bright light extinguished too soon. The last words I heard her say were about my dad. "Isn't my boyfriend the most handsome man you ever saw!?!" I nodded happily when she said that. She was lying in bed with a vomit tray near her mouth because she was completely blocked in her intestine. Anything taken by mouth would immediately come back up because it had nowhere to go. Not a great end for such a wonderful spirit as Esther.

After Esther's funeral, at the reception in Esther's condo, I noticed one of her best friends flounce down next to my dad, bat her eyelashes, put her hand on his knee, and before I could say "Jack," Esther was replaced. In record time too. Just like my mom had been years before.

And so began a new era, one that would make the time I spent growing up under my mother's insanity seem like paradise. The worst was yet to come. Those were the Bertha years.

Bertha was one of Esther's lifelong friends from the time Esther and Bob moved out from Iowa to a beautiful home in Encino, California. Bertha had three adult children, two of whom were daughters and a son, whom she rarely mentioned. Bertha had been divorced for many years before landing my dad. She worked as an admin in an office in the valley and owned her own condo. For an older woman, she had a perfect figure, although her teeth were a tangled mess, so until she finally got veneers, she'd usually smile with a closed mouth. Photos of a young Bertha showed a woman full of confidence who appeared to be the life of the party. She had a tall, slim model's figure, full dark hair worn in the period's style, a twinkle in her eye, and a song and dance in her step. I don't know exactly when the twinkle faded or when the song and dance left her, but the Bertha I got to know had none of that.

Initially, Bertha seemed a good fit for my dad, who had just surrendered yet another love to the grave. In the beginning, Bertha was sweet as pie to both Jonah and me, but I could tell she had a rough edge when it came to Yaniv. Something didn't quite click. But she was yet only dating my dad, living in her own condo, while spending some nights at my dad's Bel Air house. She hadn't established herself as my father's partner and didn't wield the kind of power she was silently, patiently waiting to get. We'd have Sunday dinners out, usually at Bertha's favorite Encino haunts, which was just fine with me. It split the difference between my dad's house and mine. Those first few months were fun. I was happy my dad had Bertha in his life because he seemed happy to have her. While it still gnawed at me that Bertha pounced on my dad within minutes of Esther being buried, I tried to push those feelings aside for the sake of my dad's happiness. I was beginning to understand that as strong as my dad projected himself to be, he was still the self-conscious immigrant with no money who married into a family of the entitled. He needed continued validation of his own worth. My guess is he got that validation from the women who threw themselves at him. And Bertha threw herself at him with complete and utter abandon.

One day, my dad phoned me up. "I'm selling the house," he said, "and I'm throwing all the family photos away except two albums I made for you."

What?! I couldn't believe my ears. "Don't throw the photos out, Dad. I want them." I was a bit panicked. That was my history he was about to get rid of, much like he got rid of my mom's footprint when she passed.

"Too late, Suzie. I already threw them away. You can come pick up the albums tonight if you want. Otherwise, I'm going to throw those away too."

What the hell? I was stunned into silence. Sadly, I replied, "I'll be over as soon as I pick up Jonah from school." Satisfied, my dad hung up rather abruptly. When I went to the house, I noticed that the pottery I had made for my parents when I was in college was gone. Gone, too, were the sculptures I'd made and given him, as were the photos, the portrait of my mom, and any memento of my past. I had no idea where this was coming from, but I had no choice but to accept this new now. I learned early in life that if you can't change something, you have no real choice but to accept it or at least deal with it.

The house in Bel-Air sold in record time, primarily because he took the first offer that came in. He had 30 days to pack and move, but he'd already gotten rid of so much there really wasn't much he needed to do.

My dad phoned me two days after he signed the sales contract. I was in my car when the call came in. His voice was angry. He started off in a normal voice range, but the more he talked, the louder he got.

Three & Me

The louder he got, the more he yelled. The more he yelled, the louder his scolds became. The louder the scolds became the more rage came out. My dad went from 0-60 in under a minute. He told me that I was the worst daughter in the world, was spoiled rotten, and didn't deserve all the love he had given me over the years. I couldn't get a word in edgewise and had no idea where this rage originated. He had never spoken to me like this before, even when my mom had him riled up. This was a whole new lexicon he was using. Because I couldn't get a word in, I decided to just let him rant, thinking he would eventually tire. Then I could find out what was really going on. I pulled over into a parking lot because driving didn't seem like a good idea while I was being verbally assassinated.

My predictions were right. He was finally tired. I could talk now. "Can I ask you why you are so angry with me?" I asked him.

"You haven't come over to help me pack, GODDAMNIT!" OK. I wasn't expecting that two days after he'd signed the contract, with 28 more days before he had to pack up an already empty house that he needed help right now. But maybe he was right. Perhaps I should have offered to come over and immediately help him pack. So, I apologized and told him I'd be over every day to help him. Never mind that I was busy with work, busy with Jonah and Jonah's sports and practices, I'd figure out a way.

"Don't bother," was the reply. "I don't want your help." And then he hung up on me without another word, which was strange behavior for him at that time. Unfortunately, it was just the beginning of absurd behavior patterns from which I had no idea where it all came from.

I honestly didn't see the degradation of the relationship coming. He was much loved by his patients, his friends, and his students. By students, I meant those who came to his home to study Kabbalah with him. My dad was an expert in Kabbalah, which was quickly becoming a thing to study among Jewish people and non-Jewish people alike. Kabbalah is Jewish mysticism, and I guess the most famous of Kabbalah followers was Madonna, who studied it and lived it. Besides his Kabbalah people, he had other followers as well that would go to his home and listen to him speak about Judaism and the teachings of the Torah. He was not an ordained rabbi, but my dad pretty much had his own private congregation. My father was an amazing man whose flaws were something he only showed to me. To everyone else, he was the guiding light in their lives. In fact, I believe if my father were the nefarious kind, he could have had his own cult of followers. But he wasn't that kind. He was pure of spirit and soul. Except when it came to me.

He was also a prolific writer, extolling his love for the Almighty in his beautiful poetry. He wrote books that centered on finding one's self and finding a spiritual connection between self and God. Every so often, I pick up one of his books, and I'm blown away by his spirituality and unwavering faith in and love of God. He was true to himself in that sense until the very end of his long and storied life.

I'd always had a key to my dad's house ever since I could remember. Once he moved into his new condo, he gave me a key to that place as well. Then Bertha moved in with him on a full-time basis. She had stopped splitting her time between her Encino condo and my dad's. It was no longer Dad's place; it was now *their* place, which was fine with me. I was glad he had someone full-time with him in case something happened. (His enlarged heart was always a chronic problem.) The first time I visited my dad after Bertha moved in, he demanded that I give him the key back. I handed it to him, wondering what that was about. However, I complied without protest. I figured in any emergency Bertha would be right next to him and could handle it. In the first few months after his move, I'd already made at least two midnight runs from my house to his apartment, taking him to the ER for heart symptoms.

Three & Me

Bertha's two daughters quickly became the apple of my dad's eye, as I was simultaneously becoming public enemy number one. Right before my dad moved out of his home, he had a dinner party where he proudly showed off his two "daughters," Janice and Charleen. I sat next to a friend of his, a plastic surgeon named Gregory Kirianoff, who looked at me and said, "I thought YOU were his daughter." I just shrugged my shoulders, thinking maybe my dad meant to say that he was introducing his two NEW daughters into the fold. Whatever it was that my dad was doing that night was something I didn't understand.

One night soon after Bertha moved in, Yaniv came home on a Monday night. It was early, and I was surprised to see him. Monday nights were the nights he and my dad hung out together, discussing all things Jewish. "Your dad told me he was too tired to do Monday nights anymore," Yaniv said, betraying the sadness in his voice. THAT blew me away. Monday nights were always a thing, from when I was a baby, first with me and then with Yaniv, ever since we moved back from Israel in 1977. As surprised as I was by the cancellation of Monday nights, another surprise was about to hit us smack between the eyes. Saturdays were the days that Yaniv took Jonah to spend with my dad, Jonah's "Saba" (Hebrew for Grandpa). This was a regular custom among the three generations, and it started on the first Saturday of Jonah's life. Every Saturday, they'd sit around the dining table at my dad's house, eating, talking, and playing. Then suddenly, one day, my dad informed Yaniv that Saturdays would be no more. He couldn't bring Jonah over on Saturdays because he was now "way too busy." I suspected Bertha was behind my dad cutting off the contacts to steer him away from his family towards hers. But I kept those fears to myself.

Bertha was still being sweet towards me and Jonah, so even though I had my suspicions, I couldn't confirm them. I also wasn't fully aware of the crumbling relationship Yaniv and I had as a married couple. Yaniv was always a loner, preferring to study his bible or material he was working on for yet another college degree, so I hadn't realized he was becoming lost without the direction of my father. Yaniv was moving further and further away from both Jonah and me. Yes, he was a soccer coach. Yes, he still drove Jonah to school in the mornings, adjusting his work hours to accommodate the trip to school. Yes, to a lot of things, but suddenly No's were popping up out of the blue. No more watching swim meets. No more watching baseball games. Until one day, we looked at each other and realized we were on different paths. He was moving into a religious-based future, while I still wanted to be secular. Without my dad to guide him, Yaniv was living a lost existence. Any intimacy was gone between us. He was too lost to feel love. And while this was going on, I gave Yaniv his space to hopefully figure things out. I never dreamed that he couldn't. I just didn't see the end of the marriage the way he did.

The only place I could go, and feel whole, was to ride my horse and visit Heather or Theresa. We'd talk about what was happening in my life, trying to figure out what was going on. It was Heather who pointed out to me that Bertha was behind the sudden changes. While I had my suspicions, I didn't want to believe them. Bertha hadn't yet overtly played her hand, so I took Heather over to visit with my dad and Bertha. Bertha was courteous but cold, contrasting with my dad, who was warm and fuzzy toward Heather.

Earlier my dad gave Heather some critical help in the aftermath of Bob's passing. He was still in the Bel Air house back then. Heather had a pain in her arm that wouldn't go away. I took her to my dad's so he could help alleviate her pain. My dad was able to adjust her arm, but he also got inside her head. He explained that a great deal of her pain was caused by the trauma of Bob leaving. He told Heather she had to try and let go of the sorrow and replace it with the love she had for Bob during their entire marriage. Somehow, he found the magic words to heal her soul, as well as the magic touch to heal her arm. Heather had no more pain after that one visit, something she reminded me of many times.

Three & Me

When Heather and I walked into their apartment, my dad literally gushed over seeing Heather again. The chill from Bertha was unmistakable. For the first time, I noticed something dark in her eyes. It was jealousy and, dare I say it—hatred.

A week later, at our Sunday night dinner out, Bertha brought up Heather and told me she didn't like her at all! I was stunned. She didn't know Heather, and Heather was absolutely delightful during the short visit with my dad. It was then I knew. Heather was right. Bertha was behind the new and negative changes in my dad.

An almost identical experience happened with Theresa. She wanted to visit my dad. He had helped her out of severe pain in the past. When I took Theresa to see him, Bertha responded with the same cold chill she had aimed at Heather. "Suzie, that lady has a very bad vibe to her," Theresa told me. "Watch your back."

At that time, Bertha and my dad had been together a few years, during which time my dad lavished her with some beautiful pieces of jewelry as well as a Middle East cruise and trips to D.C. to visit her sister. Again, I was happy my dad was having fun with a partner he loved and cared about. Bertha appeared to be healthy as a horse and was in no danger of dropping dead any time soon, which was a good thing. She would be around for him. He also paid cash for a new car for her. Bertha was his woman, and my dad always treated his woman right.

But then, my dad's health began to deteriorate rapidly. He began to have horrible back pain that he described as excruciating and could find no relief. He was given steroids to alleviate the pain. Then his kidneys failed, and he was taken to the hospital in a near unconscious state, put on dialysis, and told he'd have to dialyze for the rest of his days. The circulation in his legs became a huge problem at about the same time, causing more excruciating pain and preventing him from walking until surgery correcting it. He got shingles on his face, which went into his eyes and across his head. He pretty much got hit with

Cinderella With A Jewish Twist

everything at almost the same time. He was placed on a cocktail of some powerful medications.

Bertha became his Florence Nightingale and took amazingly good care of him. And that's when she finally laid the cards down on the table with an unbeatable royal flush. She had total control over my father, and all bets were off. She was going to take me out! Operation Nuke Suzie was put into play!

It started off when my dad was going to go in for vascular surgery to correct the painful constriction of the veins in his legs. I had called one evening to talk to my father, which I did every day. Bertha was now the only one who answered the phone in their house if she wasn't out shopping or out with friends. My dad had a cell phone but refused to use it. He was a landline-only kind of guy. When I asked Bertha if I could speak with my dad, she told me he was asleep and was not to be disturbed. I found that odd since I'd called him right after dinner at 7.00 pm. But I had no reason to think that wasn't true, so I just told her to let him know I called.

The next day I was at the Long Beach Aquatics Center with Jonah. He was in a very prestigious swim meet. Jonah didn't make finals that day, so we were done after the morning session. We were having lunch with a friend from high school when my cell phone rang. It was my father. He was at Cedars Sinai Hospital, having just woken up from surgery, and wanted to know, "WHY THE HELL I WASN'T THERE!" He was furious, screaming and yelling, calling me all kinds of names, telling me that I was the worst daughter on the planet, and using a bunch of expletives at the same time.

I sat there stunned. The only thing I could say was, "Dad, I had no idea you were in the hospital. I didn't know you were having surgery today. NO ONE TOLD ME! You have to believe me!"

"LIAR!" he screamed back at me. "Bertha told me she told you, but you decided you had other things more important to do! DON'T BOTHER COMING HERE! I DON'T WANT TO SEE YOU!" And with that, he hung up. I let out a huge sigh and told Jonah we had to get to the hospital to see Saba. I had to beg off from lunch with my friend, who said he'd take care of the bill. And once again I was called a liar when telling the truth.

Off we went from Long Beach all the way to Cedars Sinai Hospital. I had tears stuck in my throat the entire way. I didn't want Jonah to see me cry, so I kept them inside me, painful as it was. My head was racing in a million directions, not the least of which was why Bertha would put me in such a bad light with my dad. SHE LIED! It wasn't me! I was a spinning ball of emotions as I made that horrible drive.

Of course, I ran into airport traffic, then all kinds of street roadblocks because of the Los Angeles Marathon, which was being held that same day. After what seemed like hours on freeways and streets, we found our way into one of the few parking lots at Cedars Sinai Hospital. I went to registration and found my dad's room. Jonah and I ran in and found Bertha and her two daughters by his bedside. My dad angrily looked over at me. "I told you not to come, didn't I?" I thought he was going to erupt, but he realized Jonah was in the room, so he tempered his comments. "You can sit in that chair by the door. Jonah can come to see me." He looked towards Jonah and said, "C'mon, Honey. Come give Saba a kiss." The entire time I was in the room, he said nothing to me, never once looking in my direction. However, he brought Bertha's two daughters over and kissed them, telling them they were his real daughters. I knew that was for my benefit. I sat there and took it. Who was I to confront a hospitalized man?!

My dad still needed me for his IT issues, though. Once he left the hospital, he told me I needed to fix something on his computer because he couldn't log in for some reason. I immediately drove there to help, knowing how important it was for him to use his computer. He spent

Cinderella With A Jewish Twist

his days writing books and poems on the computer. The computer was his lifeline. He and Bertha stood in the room when I asked him for his password. Apparently, he'd changed it for some odd reason. I guessed the change was inspired by Bertha.

My dad spelled his password out to me, but he was right. It didn't work. Then I tried the same password with a lowercase letter, and I got in. I told him his password was case-sensitive and to remember that the next time he tried to log in. He was pleased, then went to answer his phone, which was ringing in the other room. I was left in the room with Bertha. She was silent the entire time I was there, so I concentrated on my dad's computer. I didn't pay much attention to her silence. When I stood up, I looked over at her and smiled. She gave me a mean grimace in return, whispering just loud enough for me to hear, "You little *CUNT!*"

I took a step backward. Bertha was an old lady! Old ladies don't use the word "cunt" do they? I must have misheard because there was no way she would use a word like that. "What?" I said, completely baffled. "You heard me, you little *CUNT!* I called you a *CUNT!*" As she said the last "cunt" my dad walked into the room. Seeing him, Bertha stormed out of the room, went into her bedroom, and slammed the door.

"What did you do?" my dad demanded. (Why was it always me who did something?!)

"Nothing Dad. But Bertha decided to call me a cunt for some reason."

"Stop lying! She'd never say that!"

I shook my head in disbelief. "I'm gonna go now. I fixed your computer." And with that, I left, thinking the craziness I got from my mom was nothing compared to the evil I saw in Bertha.

Three & Me

After that day, the phone conversations I had with my father became more contentious. He would start off calm, then escalate into a full-fledged rage. He still had shingles pains, and he was still on a million different medications, so I figured I would just let him rant. I would sometimes put the phone down and go into another room, and when I returned, he was still yelling. This was my new normal. I missed the days when my mom called me "rotten." Rotten was a word I could handle. But this new set of circumstances was getting out of control and clearly beyond my pay scale.

Eventually, I got another call from my dad needing computer help. I had no desire to go there, but again, I knew how much he depended on his computer to write his poems and stories. His computer was going wonky on him, and he couldn't figure out why. So, I drove over there to take a look-see. I left Jonah with Yaniv. After that last visit, when Bertha called me a cunt, I figured she was too X-rated for Jonah. It's a good thing I left him at home. My dad didn't tell Bertha I was coming, which was a huge mistake.

I rang the doorbell, unaware of the rage that would soon welcome me. Bertha answered the door, and her facial expression said it all. She was beet red! As I crossed the threshold to go in, she slammed the door with a huge force missing my face by mere millimeters. The slam caused the doors and windows to shake with such intensity that it felt like the Northridge Earthquake all over again. I have to admit, that scared the whack out of me. Had that door hit me, it would have rearranged my face and probably broken my nose and most of my front teeth. I was shaking from the sheer ferocity of her action. I had never witnessed such unbridled hatred in my entire life. Not even from my grandmother! And that's saying something!

Bertha had declared war on me for reasons I didn't understand, and it was beginning to scare the living daylights out of me. I ran from her into the relative safety of my dad's office space, unplugged the external that he had plugged in, rebooted the computer, and it worked

Cinderella With A Jewish Twist

just fine. As I was leaving, Bertha was on the phone with the police. "If you are not out of here in one minute, you're going to be arrested for trespassing," she said. "The police are on their way!" I thought she was bluffing until I heard the sirens. I left, but not before calling her a bitch, which surprised me. Unfortunately, I never wanted to stoop to her level, but for one brief second in time, I did. My dad, sadly, heard it too. When Bertha informed him that she called the police on me, he seemed very pleased and complimented her decision.

As I walked out that door, I was resolute to never return to that horrible place again. My dad was completely useless, so pussy whipped; he was willing to throw me under the bus and let it back over me again and again. That was when I realized that my dad's sexual needs outplayed his loyalty to his own daughter. It all flooded back in a torrent of tears as I recalled my father's role in my life. He let my mom get within a second of signing me over to become a ward of the state. He never stood up to her when she physically or verbally abused me. Now he was letting Bertha force Jonah and me from his life. The realization was brutal.

After that, the phone calls with my dad got worse. He'd call me up, screaming at the top of his lungs. It was a period of total insanity. There were no calm starts to the conversations. It was out-and-out rage right out of the gate. "I DEMAND TO SEE MY GRANDSON!" he'd shout. "BRING HIM BY. YOU WAIT OUTSIDE IN THE CAR. I'LL SEND HIM OUT WHEN WE'RE DONE!" It was crazy, but that's what I did; worried sick about Jonah's safety the entire time he was inside.

After doing that a couple, three times, I decided I'd had enough. I was wiping my hands of them both. I called my dad's lawyer, Marty Singer, and asked him to take me out of the will if I was even still in the will. Marty told me that I was being ridiculous and he wouldn't do that. Besides, the only one who could change my dad's will was my dad. I refused to call my dad at that point, so it would have to wait.

Three & Me

I didn't call my dad that day or the day after. I needed to heal. I spent the time riding my horse, trying to let the serenity of the outdoors calm the storm of emotions swirling within me. Heather had moved to Toluca Lake, a longer commute from my home and barn, so it was harder to visit her all the time, but we could talk on the phone, which we did a lot. She always knew to call me when I was at my lowest point. There was such a strong connection between us. She called, and I told her I was giving up on my dad. He was beyond help at this point. She calmed me down. "Suzie, I love your dad. He's going to come around. Just give him time."

When Heather said this, my sadness was too heavy to accept her insight. I was too close to the situation to see that there was quite possibly a light at the end of the tunnel.

After the third day of my not calling, my dad called me. The conversation went like this.

"Hello, Suzie"

"Hello."

"How are you?"

"Fine."

"What are you doing?"

"Nothing."

Long pause on my dad's end. Long pause on my end.

So, I ended the conversation by saying, "Thank you for calling. I need to go."

Cinderella With A Jewish Twist

He called the next day, and it was the same conversation. And the next day, and the day after that. Then he skipped a day, hoping maybe I'd call. When I didn't, he called, and the same conversation took place, word for word. This went on for two weeks. Then my dad did something I never thought he'd do. He called me, but he changed it up a bit.

"Hello, Suzie. Will you please talk to me?" I detected some sorrow in his voice, but I was done. I wanted nothing more to do with him.

"No," I said calmly.

"I don't understand. Why not?" he said, genuinely surprised.

I wasn't about to get sucked into a conversation. There was no good to come from any of our discussions. I didn't believe that this conversation would end up on a good note, either. "I need to go," I said softly. "I'm going to hang up now."

"PLEASE! DON'T!" he begged. "I want to talk to you. I've been very sick. I've been on so many medications that I became crazy. I don't know what I did to push you away. Please talk to me. You're my only daughter. My only child. The only one left of our family." And then he started to cry. At that point, I just broke down and sobbed quietly also. I had no idea why people hurt the ones they love the most. It's not something I would ever do, to Jonah, or anyone, for that matter. I just didn't have that in me. Feeling my dad's pain for the first time and not wanting to hurt him, I agreed to come over, but Bertha had to be gone. I was done with her. He said he'd call me when Bertha left to play cards with her group. He called me the next day. Bertha was gone.

When I walked in, he looked like a broken man. His shoulders were hunched over, and his eyes sagged in defeat. My strong and stoic dad was gone. Instead, I was facing the shell of the man I had loved my

Three & Me

entire life, the man I admired for his genius, his spirituality, his ability to help people out of pain, his compassion for animals, his wisdom, and his love for his family—all of that and more. Tears fell from his cheeks. "Will you please tell me what I did to hurt you so badly?"

He might as well have fired a canon at me; that's how far I fell backward. How could he not know?! "You honestly don't remember?" I asked incredulously. My dad shook his head from side to side. He said he didn't. "You don't remember screaming at me like some maniac on the phone?" Again, he shook his head. "And you don't remember calling the police on me when *YOU* asked me to come over to fix your computer?!" Same response. "You don't remember shutting me out at the hospital when you had your vascular surgery and calling Charleen and Janice your real daughters right in front of me, right in front of my son, your grandson?!" Nope. He didn't remember that either. My dad was either so medicated that he didn't know his name, or he was lying.

Because I hated not being believed when I was telling the truth, I had to give it to him. I had to try and believe him. He explained that he had discontinued most of those medications a few days before, and he had begun to see and think with more clarity. He also said the pain from shingles had thankfully become nothing more than a nuisance, and his legs had healed, causing him no more pain. He expressed his dismay over the fact that I appeared to be so cold to him. He just didn't understand that.

I sat and stared at him, not knowing what to do, so I decided to forgive him. Even if he did remember all that stuff, he was now putting himself out to me to mend the relationship. I had no choice but to try and let it go.

As I was getting up to leave, Bertha walked in the front door. Seeing me, she instantly flew into a rage, confident that my dad would support her unequivocally. My heart stopped. There were knives in that kitchen. I'd seen her blind rage, and I was now in a very vulnerable spot. Bertha stood between me and the door. But then my dad did something so wholly unexpected. He stood up and faced Bertha. "SHUT UP, BERTHA. SHUT UP AND SIT DOWN RIGHT NOW!" Bertha stopped in her tracks. She began to scream about calling the cops, and then my father looked at her and said, "ONE MORE WORD OUT OF YOU, AND YOU CAN GO BACK TO YOUR CONDO IN ENCINO!"

Bertha didn't say another word. She sat down on a chair, glaring at me as if she was saying, "You haven't seen the last of me, Missy! Just you wait. I've got more... much, much more." My dad wasn't finished. He looked at Bertha. "From now on, you will treat my daughter with respect. Do you understand?" Bertha held steadfast. She was probably wondering if my dad was really going to throw her out. He'd given her a lovely lifestyle. Would she risk losing it? "Well... Are you going to treat my daughter with respect or not?" Bertha began to protest, and my dad cut her off. "This is a yes or a no question. What is your answer?!" Bertha realized she had lost this battle. She softly muttered that she would treat me with respect. At this point, she got up and went into the bedroom, slamming the door behind her. Bertha had lost the battle, but she was resolved to win the war.

After that baring of souls with my father, he returned to the dad I knew in the pre-Bertha days. I would stop and visit him often when Bertha was not around. Our relationship was back in a good place. Bertha had one more ace up her sleeve, though. My dad's 90th birthday was coming up, and she intended to throw me one last curveball.

# # #

Janice, Bertha's daughter, was a pleasant and personable woman, and we shared a love of horses. Her husband, David, absolutely worships the ground she walks on. They have a beautiful home in the hills near the San Fernando Valley, and it's the perfect setting for a party with its open-concept design and a lush garden out in the back. It was Janice she'd turn to when she needed something, and it was to Janice she turned to put on the party for my dad's birthday.

I had no idea this party was in the making. I called my dad earlier in the summer, asking what he wanted to do for his 90th. All he could say was that he thought Bertha was planning something for him and that he'd get back to me. Ever since I was a little girl, with the exception of the time I lived in Israel, I'd helped my dad celebrate his July 4th birthday.

On Sunday, the 4th, I hadn't heard about anything going on. I was alone as Jonah was in Omaha, Nebraska, at a baseball tournament with Yaniv. My cell phone rang, and it was one of my dad's friends who wanted to know why I wasn't at the party yet. He said my dad kept looking at his watch, wondering why I was so late. Because my dad had a cell phone that he kept with him, turned off at all times (I'll never figure that one out, but OK), I couldn't call him. I quickly got my purse and jumped in the car. It would take me 15 minutes or so without traffic, which is what I was counting on, to get to Janice's house.

I parked down the street, afraid someone would recognize my distinctive red Mini Cooper and lock me out or just not answer the door. My heart was pounding as I nearly sprinted up the street to the front door. I rang the bell. Janice answered with a look of complete surprise. "What are YOU doing here?" she asked as she started to close the door on me. I put my foot inside, stopped the door, and quickly brushed past her.

"He's *MY DAD!*" I said in response, rushing towards the backyard where I saw him sitting. I don't know if Janice followed me in, but as soon as my dad saw me, it was game over for them. They couldn't eject me in front of my dad and all of his friends, most of whom have known me for many, many years. I was in. Bertha shot visual bullets towards me, her anger as obvious as the nose on her face, but she had to put her poker face back on in front of the partygoers lest she be outed for the evil, vindictive person she was. Many of my dad's friends were among Los Angeles movers and shakers, and Bertha delighted in being part of that world, who, without my dad, would have ignored her completely.

I avoided Bertha the entire time, instead visiting with many of my dad's longtime friends. I didn't stay that long, just long enough to mix it up a bit with the guests and my dad. Jonah and Yaniv were flying into Burbank airport a bit later, and I had to pick them up.

When I finally made it to my car, I let out a little "Whoop," with the knowledge and satisfaction that I had spoiled Bertha's plan. It was pretty apparent what she wanted to do, which was to throw the party, not invite me, then tell my dad that I didn't think he was important enough in my life to attend his 90th celebration. It was the hospital/surgical playbook all over again, only this time, with a little luck, it didn't work. Hatred is a terrible thing, and I believe it makes one a terrible person. Bertha was certainly a shining example of that.

329

The following May, Bertha went in for the same surgery my mother had on her carotid. She had quite a bit of blockage and was headed for a massive stroke if she didn't take care of it. She was admitted to Kaiser Permanente, right near my Woodland Hills home. On the day of the surgery, my dad phoned me up. "Suzie, I think it would be nice if you met me at Kaiser while Bertha was having her surgery." I sat bolt upright.

My thoughts ran the gamut. *Are you kidding me?! Why in the name of Sam Hell would I do that?! And don't you want Bertha to recover? If she saw me there, she'd actually have the stroke!* Of course, I said none of that, even though those thoughts were banging around in my head like Taiko Drums! "Dad, I don't think that's such a good idea," is what I did say. "I wish her well, but I don't want to be there with her daughters. She's their mom. She's in surgery. No one needs me there. You go without me."

Three & Me

Somehow my dad cajoled me into going. He said something to the effect of, "It's time to forget all the bad and move on. Develop a little amnesia over the past. She needed support. Seeing me would make her feel well." I just shook my head. As much as my dad knew about almost any other subject, he really didn't understand women. My presence could set Bertha back years. The other big thing on my mind was that as much as I hated being near her, I didn't hate Bertha. I only hated what she did and truly didn't want anything bad to befall her.

In the end, I reluctantly went and waited with my dad and Bertha's two daughters. Finally, Bertha came out of surgery with a much better outcome than my mom. She was wheeled into a semi-private room, where I gave her well wishes and then left, wondering why the hell I was even there. I did feel bad for her, though. I don't like seeing people when they are down, even the woman who hated me as much as she did.

Bertha healed enough to be discharged in a timely fashion, but she went home with stomach pains. Everyone thought it had to be residual pain from having had anesthesia or the medications she was taking. No one thought that there could be other underlying reasons for the abdominal pain, not even my dad. After a week or so, still suffering from the pain, which seemed to grow progressively worse, my dad called me to ask if I could drive over and take Bertha to the doctor. I agreed and arrived about 45 minutes later. Bertha refused to go with me, which is what I knew she would do. But I was willing to take her, no matter the past.

Bertha finally got a hold of Janice, who came and took her to the doctor. He immediately ordered Janice to take her to the Emergency Room at Kaiser's main hospital in Hollywood. Once admitted, they immediately began administering a bunch of diagnostic tests to get to the root cause of all the agonizing pain. Her results came back, and it wasn't good news. Bertha had stage 4 pancreatic cancer. My dad called me up and asked me to come down to the ER in Hollywood

Cinderella With A Jewish Twist

with Jonah. We drove down there as quickly as we could. She was lying in an ER room because there were, as yet, no beds available upstairs. They were in the middle of discussing the pros and cons of treatment, as well as the kinds of treatments, versus letting nature take its course. Jonah and I wished her well, then left, not wanting to impose on her more than we already did.

The next day Bertha was still in the ER, and my dad asked me to come down again, which I did. They were going to announce Bertha's plans. As I entered the room, both of them had a look of dread on their faces, and I knew immediately what the plan would be. No chemo. No medical intervention. She would be set up with hospice in their living room, where she would die. As I stood there, listening to them speak, an orderly came for Bertha's gurney. A bed had finally opened up in the main hospital, and the orderly was taking her upstairs, where they would begin palliative care. Basically, that translated to morphine in high doses. As the orderly navigated the tight corners of the small ER room and the corners of the hallway, I ran over to the side of her bed. As I looked down at her pale face, it softened for the first time since I'd known her. Her eyes flashed no more anger, only sorrow. Looking into those same eyes that just a few weeks ago held only hatred for me, I told her I forgave her for everything and that I had a great deal of love and gratitude for how she took care of my dad. As I was speaking, I saw a tear fall from her eye and roll down her cheek. I couldn't let her die without her knowing I only had forgiveness in my heart. She squeezed my hand in hers, closed her eyes, and was wheeled away to begin her journey.

I felt Jill Ireland beside me as I spoke to Bertha. It was the exact kind of thing Jill would have done. I also have the feeling it was Jill who gave me the nudge to run to the bed as Bertha was being wheeled out. Out of all the wreckage and landmines that Bertha put in my life, I emerged intact, and I felt that I had done the exact right thing in forgiving her. Bertha passed a little over a week later. My dad lost yet another love to the grave, and believe it or not, I grieved for his loss.

Three & Me

Dad at 90!
I finally got my dad back after several tumultuous years.

Cinderella With A Jewish Twist

FIFTEEN

Lessons Learned

My dad didn't find a Bertha replacement at her funeral, nor did any one woman flounce down next to him afterward. We all attended the funeral, preferring to hang in the back row with Jonah. Bertha's immediate family, along with my father and Jonah, sat together in the reserved chairs up front. No one thought to include me, and it was just as well. Jonah was called upon to be a pallbearer, which he did so stoically. Several of Bertha's friends whispered when they noticed me sitting in the back row. It was like the game Post Office. I'd see someone turn and look at me, then whisper to the person next to her. And then, that person would turn and look at me and continue whispering to the next person until that entire row saw me sitting in the back. Everyone wanted a good look at Public Enemy Number One. So much so, in fact, one woman turned and actually asked, "Are you Suzie, Sandy's daughter?" I nodded my head, but the whispering and staring continued.

In the days following Bertha's passing, her daughters went to the condo to collect their mother's belongings. I tried to stay away during that time. My dad phoned me up, sounding a bit heartbroken. "They took the car, Suzie. They took the car that I bought for Bertha."

"Was it in her name?" I asked.

"Yes, it was. I thought I would go before she did, so I didn't see any reason to put it in my name."

"Well, Dad, then it's theirs. I know you paid for it, but they have every right to take it." I sighed when I said it, sad for my dad. He now had no car. He wasn't driving anymore, having aged to the point where

*Me and Heather at lunch in
Beverly Hills.
We never lacked for passion on any
subject we talked about.*

Lessons Learned

his depth of field was impaired. However, in Bertha's absence, he was hiring caretakers and now would have to ride around in whatever car they had, comfortable, safe, or not.

"I think they should have asked me if I needed it. They knew I paid cash for it. I think they could have given me that courtesy." For the first time, my dad was annoyed with Bertha's daughters. In the past, he had held them up as the standard of perfection, comparing my deficiencies to their accomplishments and skills. Hearing the sadness in his voice, I felt so bad for him, but nothing could be done. Once he put the car in Bertha's name, it belonged to the girls. Lesson learned.

# # #

About a month after Bertha's passing, Theresa called me in a panic. Her daughter was now, and for quite a while, the breadwinner in the family. Theresa was the Momager (Manager Mom) over Tianna's modeling and dance careers, which were going very well. Tianna was gracing the pages of many magazines and setting herself up for acting roles as well. Unfortunately, Tianna was ill and presently not working. But the big problem was money. Theresa had long ago gone through the money she'd stashed away from the television series, and she had no paying gigs on the horizon. She was behind on her HOA fees. According to the rules and bylaws, the HOA could seize her condo and sell it to recoup the fees owed. She had gotten a few notices, which she didn't take seriously until she got a scary legal notice from a law firm that her condo would be put up for sale within 30 days of that notice. Could I help her pay off her HOA fees?

"How much do you owe?" I asked her. She gave me the amount, but I didn't have that much in cash, so I asked her, "Would they be willing to take it in three payment installments?"

Theresa said she'd ask. They came back to her initially saying they wouldn't, but after she told them she'd be on solid ground again when her daughter began working, they relented. So, I sent a check for one-third of the monies owed to her HOA. My dad always told me that once you loan money to someone, you'll never see it again. So, before you loan the money make sure you know it's going to be a gift in the end. I had no delusions I would ever see the money again. But she was my friend. Someone whose lot in life had many challenges placed in its path. How do I say no? Again, I felt Jill beside me, knowing it was what she would have done, only differently. She would have just written a check for the full amount right then and there, as well as giving Theresa a bit extra to tide her over. At that time, I didn't have that luxury.

Money was tight for me too. Yaniv and I had sadly separated and were waiting for the final divorce to go through. We hired a mediator, who was also friends with my dad, for the legal proceedings. Yaniv and I didn't want to hurt each other during the process, and we certainly didn't want to hurt Jonah. We had agreed on how to split assets, as well as custodial issues. There was no acrimony, and a settlement was reached. But now, instead of two incomes supporting my household, I had just one, plus a little bit of child support. There was nearly no alimony due to my own income, which, when it was a second income was wonderful. Now that it was primary, I had to give up some of what I was used to enjoying.

But Theresa needed my help. I couldn't let her lose her home to auction. I did what any good friend would do and helped her out. I made it work. Tianna recovered, began working again, and all was right with the world.

Life began to get hard financially. I never fully appreciated the financial freedom a two-income family had, with all the benefits such as health insurance, life insurance, and a 401K. Health insurance became my biggest expense, second only to my mortgage. Because Yaniv worked for a corporation, all those things were taken care of. Now that I was newly single, they became monkeys on my back.

Lessons Learned

My second most significant awakening had to do with men. I never realized what it would be like to date in my 50s. If someone had told me that I would find myself in that position, I would have clawed, tooth and nail, back to the safety of my marriage. The problem was we'd grown apart, wanted different things, and while we still had a loving dialogue and a wonderful son, I didn't want to keep Yaniv from what he wanted the most, which was to become a rabbi and to have a child with someone who could conceive. Yaniv loved Jonah with all his heart, but he wanted to give Jonah a sibling. I wasn't the person who could do that, and we both knew it. Hiring a surrogate never entered our minds since it was still such a new pathway to parenthood. But that wouldn't have solved the Rabbi part anyway, so we parted.

I jumped into the dating pool feet first. I was lucky in that I found a guy, rather quickly, who was attractive and funny. His name was Dave. He hailed from a Boston family that had built a manufactured stainless steel restaurant supply business.

Dave graduated from Wharton Business School and owned his own business in Culver City. He was a pilot and owned a Beechcraft Bonanza plane, which he kept at Santa Monica Airport. The big red flag was that he'd never been married. But I dismissed that out of hand because he'd lived with a woman for 17 years, and I figured that counted. Dave and I had a ton of fun until we didn't. I loved him but couldn't fall in love with him. He was my political opposite, and as hard as I tried to ignore it, I couldn't. I'd argue with him, which was no fun for the both of us. He loved animals as I did, a commonality I found more important than whom he voted for. Dave was also a good lover, so that was a big plus in his favor.

Having been married for so many years, I liked the idea of having a man by my side, and even though I wasn't in love with Dave, I enjoyed being with him. He still had a lot of life in him, even though he was six years older than me. He would fly his plane to Sedona, where he had built a second (and sometimes primary) home with his bare hands. He tinkered all the time. He bought a junker of a boat and tried to restore it. He eventually gave up on that boat and bought a beautiful like-new yacht, which he keeps in Marina Del Rey. Dave is now tinkering with his new boat, even today as I write this. Dave would also tinker with cars. In fact, he was a race team pit crew member. I think he's the spark plug guy. Dave would fly to the different races across the western part of the United States in his own plane. He liked and specialized in Funny Cars, having raced them in the past himself. The drag race kind, with the nitroglycerine fuel shooting fire out the rear as they race in a straight line for the Finish.

Because we lived at opposite ends of the vast Los Angeles region, seeing Dave became harder and harder. We were GUD (Geographically Undesirable) to each other. Additionally, he was always gone, either in Sedona or at a race. I was more alone than I wanted to be. I think I was a bit of a nag on that subject as I look back on those times. Ultimately, Dave decided he wanted to live in Sedona permanently and found a new lady who eventually became his woman. Upon reflection, I resolved after Dave never to get involved with anyone who had not been married before. Lesson Learned.

The guys I got fairly serious with, like Dave, I would introduce to Theresa and Heather to get their opinions. Women do that, and I suspect that men do that too. Theresa really liked Dave. He was always the perfect gentleman. One evening, he took us all—Theresa, Tianna, Jonah, and me—out to the Ivy in West Hollywood, which is a very chic restaurant. When I informed Theresa that we were no more, she was sorry to see him go. I think she liked being spoiled by him, and who can blame her? Dave knows how to charm his way into the heart.

After Dave, I dated a slew of guys, each one with his own specific quirks. I realized that once you are past 30, trying to combine your set ways with someone else's set ways is quite difficult. Not to mention, there is the problem of attraction. I've always been slim and fairly athletic. I quickly learned that men over a certain age lose their looks, waistline, hair, and desire to do anything that takes effort. Not all, but a vast majority of them fit into that category. It's a dirty trick that young men have the energy, the hair, the bodies, and the willingness to partner with someone and grow together in an everlasting relationship. And then Kapow! Nature takes it all away! I think women take better care of themselves, and slow the aging process down, much more so than men.

My next relationship was with a guy named Jeff. He was a blast! He had the same energy level as I did, loved to do most of the same things I did, was into exercising and staying fit, had hair, was trim, as well as highly intelligent. He loved books and movies, and we were on the same page politically. He had a heart of gold, and I absolutely adored him. He had my back 24/7. When I struggled, he was right there with me, offering me his support. Especially during the Bertha period.

We traveled quite a lot in the time we were together. My favorite trip was to Russia. Jeff was perfect. Except I couldn't figure out how to fall in love with him. I loved him a lot. But I wasn't IN LOVE, and that kept gnawing at me.

Additionally, Jeff was in the middle of a bitter divorce, and it was all he could talk about. He was constantly angry over lawyers and the inability to reach a settlement. It got old after a while.

But Jeff, as much as I loved him as a person and a partner, was a dead-end relationship. Yes, it was fun, but I knew he wanted to move back to the Bay Area, which he eventually did. Throughout the few years we were together, I realized more and more that there was no future for us. And we both knew he would never want to live with someone after his divorce, which he has yet to do. Another lesson learned.

Three & Me

Heather and I would have discussions about men and dating at this age. Since Bob died, she may have gone out a few times, but no one was as good as Bob. I felt, in my heart also, that using Yaniv as the baseline standard was probably unfair to the men I was meeting and seeing. It's hard when you've known young passionate love, the kind that picks you up off of the ground, to feel that way again. I had no idea how to find that in midlife. I kept looking. Heather stopped. No one was going to be able to fill Bob's big shoes. But I was still hoping someone would fill my heart. I couldn't let go of the dream.

# # #

One day while I was in my design studio working away on a fitness catalog, Heather called me. "Suzie, I'm moving back to Park City! Allie is struggling at Campbell Hall. I just met with her teachers, and the school is just not a good fit for her. So, I'm moving back to Park City to enroll her in the public schools there!"

I was speechless. I'd gotten used to being able to drop in on Heather. She was in a newer, smaller house in Toluca Lake which suited her perfectly. On the other hand, I knew Heather hated being in the same place for too long a time. Her inner alarm clock went off, signaling that it was time again to move on. It was part of her pattern. I was saddened to hear that she'd be even further away than the distance from Toluca Lake to Woodland Hills (a 30-minute drive). "Are you sure this is the right decision?" I asked. "I mean, Campbell Hall isn't the only school, you know. There are a zillion of them, like Buckley, or..."

Heather quickly interrupted me. "Suzie, I've already listed my house. I'm going. I don't want to put her in yet another private school and have her flunk out. I think Park City will be good for Allie!" I sighed. There would be no convincing her. Oh well, we'd just have to do email and phone calls. At least there was that.

Lessons Learned

I remembered back to the time when mobile phones were really only in cars. That was when I got Heather into riding road bikes with me. I convinced her to buy a really expensive, super light Tommaso. Tommaso was one of the elite Italian imports. At the time, I was riding a Vitus, a French-made road bike. We were very Euro together. If you've ever seen the movie *Breaking Away,* you'd understand how I felt. Between Heather and I, we could have been speaking Italian or French!

One day, when we were on a ride, Heather wanted to stop for a break. She needed to do something. We pulled off to the side of the road. She stretched her hand back around her waist, over to her cycling jersey's back pocket, and pulled out a thing that resembled a grey brick. She flipped it open and began dialing a number. She was calling Bob. I just stood there, mouth agape. Here we were in the middle of basically nowhere, and she was making a telephone call! No wires, no antenna, no nothing! When Bob answered the phone on his end, and Heather actually began having a conversation with him that was perfectly clear, as if she'd been speaking into a landline telephone, well... my head nearly exploded with wonder! Heather had one of the first-ever cell phones. I had to have one! It was just too cool!

I was grateful for technology when Heather told me she was moving. We could stay in touch no matter where we were. Cell phone technology had advanced. They were smaller and easier to carry around in a purse. So, we'd be able to reach each other at any time. Besides, she'd be back. There were more fundraisers to put on!

Three & Me

My father and his caregiver, Maura, waiting to speak to the head of cardiology at Cedars Sinai about a new heart valve.

Pain? What Pain?

## SIXTEEN

Pain? What Pain?

After Bertha died, my dad settled into a new normal without a woman by his side for the first time since he was 29. He often told me about meeting my mother and proposing marriage three days later. He said he just knew that she was the woman for him. That one sentence pretty much summed up my dad. He made a decision and then acted on it, rarely studying the pros and cons of that decision, relying on his gut instinct instead. Some people might call it reckless. Other people call it self-confidence. I was somewhere in between, sometimes scratching my head, other times in awe at how he moved things forward, never looking back.

My dad hired two sisters to help him who would trade off days. They worked for him full-time, taking him to appointments, shopping for food, and helping prepare his meals and any other needs he had. They were a lovely pair, and I saw and appreciated the loving kindness with which they treated my father. Any adult child would be grateful for the kind of love and care these two provided.

His health was about to go completely haywire. He got pneumonia right after Bertha passed. He was hospitalized for his pneumonia at UCLA Medical Center. As I walked into his room, he exclaimed, "Well, you just missed me spewing vomit across the room. Damn, medications made me sick!" I was kind of glad I missed that. Projectile vomit was never my thing. He looked fine otherwise.

For the first time in my life, my dad was my dad without the interference of women who were jealous of his relationship with me. From my mother to his other girlfriends and finally, to Bertha, the women in his life just couldn't handle a father's love for his daughter or a

343

daughter's love for her father. We were spending time together, trying to get to know each other again. I had the opportunity to see my father not only through my own eyes but through the eyes of others. He was such a well-respected individual, and for the first time since I was a little girl, I got to experience him as others saw him. The rage was gone. There was only love in his eyes.

I used to talk to Jill, Heather, and Theresa about my relationship with my dad. I couldn't understand how he was the most amazing father to me as a little girl, spending time teaching me things no one else could about the world and humanity, then changing course during my adolescent years and onward. I definitely had whiplash from all those changes. He sporadically reverted from good dad to raging dad and then back to good dad again. I used to think it was me that was the problem. I tried doing everything I could to be the daughter he'd be proud of, but there was always a woman whispering negative things about me in his ear. During the period after Bertha, I finally realized it wasn't me. It was my dad's own weakness. His desire was to be with a woman, no matter the cost. To put it bluntly, his big head was controlled by his little one, and he inadvertently hurt his own flesh and blood in the process.

Jill used to tell me that my dad would soon realize what a great person he raised and that he would be proud of my accomplishments. She said he'd probably wake up one day and see me for the first time. As for Theresa, she loved my dad unconditionally. He would take care of her aches and pains for free. She, too, would tell me my dad would come back around. Heather was of the same mindset as Theresa, so convinced my father was a miracle worker and that he would realize what a great daughter he raised. It was during that last year that all three of my friends were right.

My dad was 91 when we were reconnecting. His mind was still sharp, but his body began throwing punches. His heart needed a

Pain? What Pain?

valve replacement. That entailed open heart surgery. Very few doctors wanted to perform that kind of surgery on a man his age.

Additionally, Medicare wouldn't pay for it. His prognosis without the surgery was pretty much certain death. My dad, being my dad, wanted the surgery at all costs. He'd pay for it if he had to. He just needed to find a doctor willing to operate on a 91-year-old man.

My dad found his way to the head of cardiac surgery at Cedars Sinai Medical Center. He was a world-renowned surgeon, and after examining my father, he decided he'd do the surgery. He suggested a synthetic valve replacement because of my father's advanced age. Somehow my dad managed to get Medicare to pay for it. Right before his 92nd birthday, he had open heart surgery at Cedars. He was placed, post-surgery, in the Saperstein Cardiac Care Unit, surprising all the nurses and doctors with his ability to recover. He was up and walking the very next day. Apparently, I inherited my high pain threshold from my father.

345

I was very excited to go visit him. When I arrived, I went to sit in a chair by his bed. My father grew suddenly very agitated. "DON'T SIT THERE!" he barked. "DON'T YOU SEE THAT MAN SITTING IN THE CHAIR?! YOU ALMOST SAT ON HIM!" I literally jumped forward. I looked back at that chair. It was empty. So, I stood. No use in getting him riled up the day after open heart surgery. He had a smile on his face now. He pointed to the wall across from his bed and remarked, "Look at all those amazing books. I can't believe I'm in a room with the most fantastic library."

I kissed my dad and told him I'd be right back. Then I went to the nurse's station and told them of my dad's hallucinations. "He's probably got Sundowners," the nurse said. "We see it all the time. It's also called 'ICU psychosis.'" Apparently, when an older person has anesthesia, the drugs do funny things. If they've had anesthesia a few times within a short time frame, the drugs are even more potent. Also,

Three & Me

in an ICU, patients don't know what time of day it is. There are no windows, and the lights are on 24/7. So, their circadian rhythm gets turned around, and the mind plays tricks on them.

I was concerned that my dad, whose mind was always sharp, was now fading into dementia. "Will he be all right?" I asked, not without a great deal of trepidation.

"Oh, he'll be fine once he's transferred to another room. His circadian rhythm will adjust to day and night quite rapidly. It'll take a couple of days, though." With that knowledge, I returned to my dad's room and happily played along with the odd things he was seeing and saying. I dealt with the spitting people who were stuck on the ceiling, the lost and afraid dogs hiding under his bed, the Hasidic gravestone salesman who wanted to sell me my own gravestone, the gentleman who never left that chair, and an assortment of other strange statements.

I felt like I was in the middle of some strange dream of my father's. One of the best comments he made was to his doctor. Dad was seated at a table eating dinner in his room when the doctor walked in to see him. Dr. Maasatchi wore his white medical coat with dark pants and a white shirt underneath. My father looked up at him as Dr. Maasatchi asked him how he was doing. "Sir!" my father said with an indignant tone. "This is chicken, and I ordered the fish! I refuse to pay for this. What kind of resort are you running here!"

I could tell Dr. Maasatchi was stunned, so I motioned for him to meet me outside the room. I told him my dad was saying weird stuff like that all day. When my dad saw the white medical coat, I surmised that he mistook his doctor for the maître d' of the restaurant he believed himself to be in. We both had a good laugh, but I secretly worried that my dad had lost his marbles just when I had gotten him back from the dark side.

Pain? What Pain?

Just as the nurse predicted, my dad was eventually transferred to a regular hospital room, and the hallucinations stopped. His recovery at his age was nothing short of remarkable. The surgeon said that there were men in their 50s who went through the same procedure and didn't recover as well as my dad at 91. He was on his way.

Eventually, my dad was discharged, and he began his recuperation. Jonah and I would spend a great deal of time at my dad's place, or we'd go out to dinner at his favorite deli, Junior's, on Westwood Boulevard. He was a completely different man than the man he was around, Bertha. Whether it was age or being single that made him so, I cherished all the time I got to spend with him—the post-Bertha days started to look like the pre-Bertha days once more. People that Bertha had cut out of his life began to return, and he had many friends to socialize with. People she had either chased out or quietly dropped gathered with my father again. The broken relationship that Bertha had engineered between my father and Yaniv was now healing. Yaniv began his Monday night lessons all over again, almost as if they hadn't stopped. While already divorced from Yaniv, I was thrilled Monday nights were back being a thing. Life became conflict-free for me with my dad and I would be lying if I didn't say that I hoped my dad would live forever.

My dad was still undergoing dialysis. Medicare paid for transport to his dialysis and back via private ambulance. They would pick him up at 4.00 am three days a week. My dad was the kind of guy who never let his gas tank get below half empty, never let a bill sit unpaid for more than an hour, and was never late for anything. I remember him leaving for the airport to pick up my mother from a trip to Minnesota to visit her sister (when they were still speaking). He actually left for LAX before my mother's plane even took off! He literally sat at the airport for hours by the gate, waiting for her. (Before TSA security lines, you could do that.) God-forbid he ran into traffic on the 405 and was late picking her up!

It was right around Labor Day that my father woke up for his dialysis, dressed in his typical sport shirt, slacks, Members Only jacket, and beret, and sat down by his front door in a wheeled dining room chair on a cold hard tiled floor, to wait for the ambulance. When they arrived, my dad's caregiver, Maura, tried to buzz them in. But the buzzer wasn't working, and the door didn't open. They tried buzzing again and again to no avail. Finally, my dad told her to go downstairs and open the door herself. Maura left the door to the unit open as she left without her key and went downstairs to let them in. In that span of a few minutes, my dad managed to nearly kill himself. He had gotten up instead of waiting for the wheelchair that he usually took. The wheels of the chair he was sitting in slipped out from under him, and he fell hard on the tile floor, hitting his head on the open door, which then slammed it shut. Maura and the ambulance crew were immediately locked out.

I got the phone call from the ambulance crew and literally jumped from a deep sleep into my car. I drove over 100 mph on an empty freeway with the key in hand in order to save my dad, who was lying helpless on his entryway floor. I got there in record time. My dad was placed on a gurney and was transported to UCLA Medical Center Emergency. They had to dialyze him there and care for his gaping head wound, concussion, and newly detected broken hip. I didn't realize it then, but that was the beginning of the end.

Something else was wrong with my dad physically, and it would prove to be a medically unsolved mystery. His body had so many things going on, between pneumonia, open heart surgery, dialysis, and now his fractured hip. And lately, he seemed to catch the stomach flu quite often, either that or food poisoning, as he would tell me. He spent a great deal of time vomiting, which was something he had really rarely done his entire life. After the first few times, which started in UCLA during his pneumonia stay, I kept a diary to track the days he told me he vomited. After about the third vomiting episode (not including the one from when he was at UCLA), I doubted it was

Pain? What Pain?

a stomach bug. What started out as vomiting episodes six months apart grew into episodes three months apart, then six weeks apart, then three weeks, then ten days, then weekly, then daily, eventually turning into multiple times a day.

Not only could he not walk anymore due to his broken hip—relegated to a bed full time—he was vomiting profusely. He was in and out of hospitals trying to find the root cause of his nausea and vomiting, but not one definitive diagnosis was made. It was thought that dialysis and toxins were making him ill. It was also thought it was something else. No one could definitively ascertain what was happening to his body. The doctors didn't seem overly concerned, though. His weight was good, and besides the vomiting, he seemed fine for a man his age with a broken hip. At his age and level of mobility, I was told that he didn't need that much nourishment to keep him going. That was of little comfort to me as I watched my dad suffer those horrible bouts of nausea.

He was in the hospital in December 2012 when he looked at me and said, "They want to put a feeding tube into me now. I'm not able to walk anymore. I've got dialysis three times a week, and I'm becoming a potted plant. This isn't the life I want to live anymore." I started crying because I knew his end was coming. I just wanted him to stay around a while longer. I wanted him to watch Jonah, the apple of his eye, graduate high school. I wanted him to be around so I could continue building our relationship. I loved him with all my heart. I had just gotten him back 18 months prior. It wasn't enough time. It didn't seem fair.

I witnessed first-hand how hard he worked to stay alive, how he would always have miraculous recoveries from surgeries, rarely having a sick day his entire life. He survived being Jewish in pre-War Europe. He survived as an American spy against Nazi Germany in World War II. He survived my grandparents' hatred, my brother's death, the loss of his wife, the loss of Esther, and so many other calamities. My heart broke, but I understood. I know I wouldn't want that life either. Hard as it was, it was time to let go.

My dad phoned his doctor and told him he wished to have hospice set up at home. Once discharged, he wanted to go one last time to dialysis and say goodbye to the many friends he made there. He brought a cake with him that last time. It was a goodbye party of sorts. He then called his friends, told them of his plans, and gave them the opportunity to come to say goodbye.

For the first three days after his last dialysis, he was alert because his body didn't yet know he was missing the treatment. He enjoyed seeing his many friends who came by to bid him a peaceful passing and to say the things that he could hold in his heart through this last journey. My friends also took the time to come and spend time with my dad, including Theresa. Bertha's daughters, who referred to him as "Dad or Papa," also came. Heather phoned him from Utah and said her good-byes. His book editor, Tracy Creech, flew halfway across the country to say goodbye to my dad one last time. It was non-stop people from all walks of life coming to bid their farewells to this extraordinary man. My dad enjoyed the company and appreciated the outpouring of love for him. He had so many well-wishers to send him off with so much love to carry him into the next world. I considered it a parade of love.

My dad used to tell me that the day you die is your first real birthday because your soul is freed from its earthly body to begin its journey in the heavens. He wasn't at all afraid to face death. He was welcoming it. By the fourth day, his body was suffering from the toxins that kidney failure causes. No dialysis meant the toxic buildup would cause his organs to slowly shut down. He started to slip into a renal coma, but the vomiting prevented that. He'd wake up to vomit, then lose himself back into the process of dying.

On the seventh day, my dad was pretty much out of it, only waking to vomit, then falling back to sleep. But a strange thing happened

Pain? What Pain?

in the early part of the afternoon. He woke up and was completely lucid. He demanded to see a dog, so I ran to his neighbor and asked if she could bring her Yorkie over. The sweet little girl was placed on my dad's bed and began licking his face, wagging her tail, and kissing him all over. My dad loved it. Always an animal lover, this was just what he wanted and needed to send him on his way.

Suddenly, out of the blue, my cell phone rang. It was Rabbi Zeldin, my father's old friend, calling from his retirement home in the desert. He'd heard about my dad's decline and wanted to know how things were going. I passed the phone to my dad, who had a wonderful conversation with the Rabbi. You would have thought my dad was just hanging around the house, casually conversing with an old friend; it was so normal. At the end of the call, I heard my dad say, "It's been a pleasure knowing you too." I couldn't help but think that this conversation could have been over something as normal as friends moving away, or a business associate leaving for another job, or any number of nondescript subjects, rather than a final goodbye for the grave. After they hung up, and while he was still lucid and awake, I told him that I'd found his discharge papers and arranged for him to have a full military funeral. I also told him I didn't want him carried in a limo but instead in a horse-drawn carriage, hailing back to his early years in a European village. He cried when I told him and softly said, "Thank you, Suzie. I love you more than you know." He put his hand on my cheek, lay down, and fell back into his coma.

My dad left on the eighth day, just like in the days of the Maccabees when Jewish tradition tells us that the oil in the Temple lasted eight nights instead of one. On the eighth day, the light it provided went out, just like my dad's light. His storied journey was over. Right up to the end, he was stoic and strong. He faced death like he faced imprisonment in Hungary. He knew he was going to be with his angels and with God. His faith was so strong throughout his life, and it was even more vital during his death.

Three & Me

The most remarkable thing about my dad's last year was that he never complained about the pain of his broken hip, the pain of open-heart surgery, or the pain of dying. It was as if the pain didn't exist. He skated through it all with an unmatched determination. Stoic until the end. I hope to be as brave as he was when it is my time.

The next day Heather called me. I was crying on the phone. She was crying on the phone. We were sharing our broken hearts over my dad's passing. "Suzie, your dad was such a wonderful man. I'll never forget how he healed my pain. I'll never forget him telling me in that Hungarian accent of his to 'let go of the pain from losing Bob.' He was right, Suzie. I haven't had any pain since. He was so wonderful to me and to Ryan." Because of that one phone call, Heather was a healing light in my life. She helped soothe my pain. She managed to get a smile out of me as I fondly recalled that day when she emerged from seeing my dad, grinning from ear to ear.

As soon as Heather and I hung up, Theresa called. She was devastated. My dad meant so much to her. "Who am I going to go to now when I'm in pain?" she asked. "No one was like your dad. He took such good care of Phil and me. He would talk to me, and I immediately felt his inner peace. Suzie, I am so sorry he's gone. It's such a huge, huge loss. Please come over when you can."

Life and death are interconnected. You can't have life without death. It's something we are taught as children, learning that in time all things die. But it's just a concept at that stage of life. Maybe a child experiences death through the passing of a dear pet, grandmother, or grandfather, but it's still not "real." As we age into our twenties and thirties, death is still just a concept, except for the few who actually experience it through accidents, illness, or suicide. As we age, though, it becomes something real to fear and try to prevent. In the age of Covid, death became more than real. For people my age, death can come at any time. Or life can continue for years to come.

Pain? What Pain?

About a week after my dad's funeral, I got a call from someone who knew both Bertha and my dad. This person was close to Bertha for many, many years, so I was more than a little surprised to get the call. "Suzie, I just wanted to let you know just how sad I am to hear of your dad's passing. He was a fine man." There was a pause that was almost too long when I heard, "And I wanted to let you know that you did nothing wrong. Bertha was out to get you from the start. She would tell me and others just how much she hated you. She wasn't one to put up with any kind of competition, and she could be quite ruthless, as I'm sure you found out."

I was in a state of disbelief but extremely relieved to hear this. "Thank you. Thank you so much for telling me this. At times I thought I was the crazy one."

"No. You weren't crazy. I'm even afraid of her, or at least I was. I know how hard she made your life. She bragged about it incessantly. You got lucky in the end, though." I knew this person was referring to her passing so suddenly. I shudder to think what would have happened had she outlived my dad.

"Thank you again," I said softly. "You've made me feel so much better. Those were pretty rough years. I'm glad they're over." After a bit more chit-chat, the call ended. Validation was important. My feelings were right. Bertha put a target on my back, and it could have gotten much worse had she lived to continue her reign of terror. I had no way out with her. She would have done who-knows-what to eliminate me from my dad's life. But I put all that in the past. I had forgiven Bertha and all her crazy antics toward me. She was with God and her angels now. Forgiveness means forever in my heart.

Yaniv, Jonah, and I took my dad's death pretty hard, but it seemed that Jonah took it especially hard. After a playoff baseball game in Arizona, he quite literally had a breakdown in the car, sobbing uncontrollably. I thought I was going to have to take him to a hospital for some medication, but he managed to calm down enough to talk it out. His performance on the mound wasn't typical, Jonah. He was a pitcher on his club team, and he had a very bad outing in a critical game. He couldn't find the zone, and when he did, he got lit up. Granted, the team he was up against outmatched his size and power. Once in the car, he broke down into an inconsolable mess of tears, sobs, and wracking wails. His pain was real, and it was intense.

Jonah struggled after my dad passed, and it wasn't isolated to that baseball game. He was now a senior in high school, and schools were after him for his pitching arm. His grades were middle-of-the-road, but his SAT scores were off the charts. He was able to satisfy the student-athlete criteria for university acceptance with ease.

Jonah had a childhood friend one year ahead of him in school but at least five years ahead of him in "maturity." Unfortunately, his friend introduced Jonah to alcohol. They both lied to me on the evening before Jonah was supposed to fly to a school in Nebraska for a campus visit. That school was recruiting him for their baseball team. The boys told me they were just going to a movie. His friend assured me on the phone that they would be home early. It was the evening of March 8th. Our flight was early on March 9th.

When Jonah wasn't home at the designated time, I called him. He said he was close to home. I called him again about 45 minutes later because he hadn't yet come home. He said he got confused and went the wrong way on the freeway, and he'd be home. Again, no Jonah. This went on for two hours, and I knew something was very wrong. After midnight, the morning of March 9th, the anniversary of my brother's death, a call came in from a phone number I didn't recognize. It was from a physician. He had stopped to help my son, who had crashed into the wall of a freeway offramp after hitting the center median and caroming across all freeway lanes. My son was drunk. His friend had taken him to a college party where there was booze in the punch. His friend then let him get in his car, as inebriated as he was, all because

354

the friend wanted to stay and party. I still can't get over that. (Whatever happened to "Friends don't let friends drive drunk?")

I threw my coat on over my pajamas and drove to the accident scene. There were only two California Highway Patrolman there when I arrived. They told me Jonah was taken under arrest for DUI to the Ventura County Hospital to treat his concussion. I was completely crazy with fear for my son's well-being and safety, let alone confused as to how my son got that drunk.

I somehow found that hospital. It was not a nice place at all. Still in my pajamas and coat, my hair a complete wreck, I found someone who would help me. Jonah had turned 18 a few months before, so in the eyes of the law, he was an adult. Police or hospitals don't talk to the parents of adults. Because he was under arrest, I was not allowed to see him in the ER. I was going crazy. And then, it hit me—the nausea. I've always thought that when I saw someone in the movies vomiting when they saw something terrible or heard something terrible, it was theater. Nope. It happens. I ran to the bathroom, where I was sick, sick again, and fairly dizzy. I couldn't believe what was happening. The only thing I was grateful for was that Jonah was alive. I'm sure my dad did everything he could from Heaven to protect him.

A policeman did come out to talk to me, and it turned out he was a very nice guy. He explained that Jonah would be transferred to the county jail once the doctors deemed him healthy enough for processing. He also informed me that because this was Jonah's first offense, he would probably be released to my custody without bail, but he suggested I call a lawyer because Ventura County had zero tolerance for drunk driving and was fairly harsh with punishment at trial. I thanked him for speaking with me. He was very gracious and anxious to return to his job guarding my son.

Marty Singer set me up with a good DUI attorney who helped us navigate the Ventura County legal process. Eventually, Jonah was sen-

355

tenced to 48 hours in the county jail. Those were the longest 48 hours of Jonah's life. Being in jail scared him straight. He definitely learned the hard way about responsible drinking and driving. For that, I am grateful.

Jonah paid dearly for his mistake in many ways. Not the least of which was the teasing he had to endure for his last two months of school. But he made it. He graduated and went on to college. One of the things he did, though, was turn this experience around into a positive. He returned to his high school the following year to talk to graduating seniors about the dangers of drinking and driving. When those kids heard his horrific story, I'm pretty sure they made better decisions for themselves. Of that, I'm proud.

# # #

In October of 2012, before my father died, my wonderful horse, Aggie, died. She died two months before Dad. I think she timed it in order to give him a ride up to Heaven. That was a comfort to me during and after both their passings. I was now without a horse for the first time in a long time. Jonah had already packed up and left for college in Santa Barbara, leaving me an empty nester. I decided I'd get back in the saddle and take lessons with a trainer. Eventually, I found a horse to lease and then purchase, and I was horse happy yet again.

Heather and I talked on the phone regularly. She loved being in Park City but realized she needed to move yet again. Allie was having a difficult time in her middle school. Heather was beside herself. She decided to move Allie to the lakeside home in Canada. Heather's older daughter, Emily, had emigrated to Canada, married, and had her own kids. It was a natural choice for Heather to move up north. Heather was convinced the Canadian schools would be a better fit for Allie both socially and academically. In true Heather form, she packed up Park City and moved into the Canada house without so much as a second thought. Heather was a great deal like my dad in that way. Once her mind was made up, the plan was executed with lightning speed.

After a couple of hard winters in the Canada house, complete with exorbitant heating bills, Heather told me that she'd be moving again. This time to New York City. Allie would stay with her older sister, Emily, during the school year. Heather would return to Canada to spend summers, escaping the New York heat and humidity. She would have the best of both worlds. Heather told me she was done with owning houses, except for Canada. She now wanted to rent. She was tired of being tied down and was looking forward to a tenant's life. "Let someone else worry about maintenance," was her new mantra. Like a fancy cut of steak, she was done.

My friend was moving even further away. Theresa was busy being Momager to Tianna's career. Jonah was away at school, and my mommy duties were pretty much over. I had the horse and my dogs and cat. It just wasn't enough. One day after riding, I stopped off at a restaurant close to the barn for a burger. Two women were sitting at a table, both wearing volunteer t-shirts for the Wildlife Waystation. I knew that place, having taken an injured raven there years before, and more recently, I tried to take a Mallard duckling there that I found wandering on the freeway shoulder of an onramp to the 405. (They re-directed me to a Mallard duck rescue in Agoura Hills.) I asked the women about becoming a volunteer also, and they told me to go to the website. They also told me that there had been a purge of volunteers fairly recently and were in the process of rebuilding their volunteer base.

So that's what I did. I went onto the website, did the training, and became a volunteer at the Wildlife Waystation. Suddenly, my world opened up to a magical place filled with every kind of animal imaginable. Lions, tigers, bears, hyenas, foxes, chimpanzees, exotic birds, giant tortoises, African crested porcupines, wolves, coyotes, bobcats, leopards, mountain lions, raccoons, a camel, pot-bellied pigs, llamas,

Three & Me

alpacas, a zebra, monkeys, lemurs, ligers, reptiles, and more. I felt like I'd ascended to Heaven, only I wasn't dead. I was still very much alive in this magical universe! It's hard to explain that magic, the feeling I got in the presence of so many beautiful souls. I felt a strong sense of belonging to a wonderful community of volunteers with the same love for animals. The Waystation eventually closed due to a lack of funding, but I am happy to say that currently, I volunteer my time at a zoo in Salt Lake City and two other animal sanctuaries in California. My heart is filled with fur.

Dad getting his last "Lubbies" from a sweet little Yorkie. It was a the most appropriate send-off for his journey.

Pain? What Pain?

SEVENTEEN

Did He Kill Her?

On March 17th, 2016, I went out to the barn to ride my horse. I was briefly aware of a small stitch on my right side that was almost imperceptible. I rode for about an hour, then ran to meet a friend named Jeannie Cooke Maceachern for lunch in Valencia. Her daughter used to ride in the same barn as I did. I was looking forward to lunch with Jeannie because I hadn't seen her in a while and wanted to know how things were going with her and Skye and their new trainer.

I hopped off my horse Dan, cleaned myself up, and drove out to meet Jeannie for lunch. We had a fabulous time at this cute little restaurant that Jeannie found. We chatted about a million things, all related to trainers, past and present. After lunch, I needed to go to the lady's room, and once my pants were down, I noticed just a bit of bloat. I paid no attention, figuring it was gas, plus I had just eaten lunch. No Big Thing.

After lunch, I ran some errands, and by the time I got home, I found myself shaking with chills. It was a warm day outside, and for the life of me, I couldn't understand why I was so cold. I felt fine, so I didn't think I had a fever, but better to err on the side of caution. I pulled out the thermometer and was shocked to find out I had a 102.5° temperature. Wait! 102.5°! That's nuts. I felt perfectly fine. I figured maybe the thermometer was wrong, so I waited for it to reset, then took my temperature again. Same result.

Wasn't it Einstein who said, "Insanity is doing the same thing over and over and expecting different results"? Well, like the idiot that Einstein knew I was, I waited for the thermometer to reset itself, took

I had just woken up from an appendectomy at UCLA.
I had to lie to get seen, they were so crowded. Good thing I did!!!

Did He Kill Her?

my temperature yet a third time, and was amazed that I got the same result yet again!

I wondered what this fever was about. I thought maybe I might have dehydrated myself, or maybe I might be coming down with some virus. Except I felt perfectly fine. So, I called my friend Bob Jaffee, a former Emergency Room doctor who worked at Urgent Cares. I figured he'd know. So, I called him.

"Hey Bob, I've got kind of a high temperature, and I have no clue why I have it," I said to him. Bob laughed on the other end. He wanted to know how high it was. "102.5°." That got his attention. He told me to come over to his place right away.

Bob lived in a condo near my home in Woodland Hills. There were a great many stairs to navigate before I got to his second-floor door. He heard me climbing the stairs and opened the door to watch me pretty much sprint up all of them. "You certainly don't present as someone with a high fever, do you?" He was laughing. "Let's take your temperature the old-fashioned way." He stuck a thermometer in my mouth and waited for the beep signal, letting him know I was thoroughly cooked. It read 102.5°. "Hmmmmm, go lie down on the bed."

I walked into his bedroom. He pulled up my shirt and began to palpate. He pushed on my lower right side. Nothing. Then he pushed harder. Still nothing. Bob had a serious expression on his face, and then with all his might, he really gave me a shove on my lower right quadrant. "Did you feel that?" he said, not without a look of exasperation.

"I felt a little something, but nothing terrible. But you rammed me pretty hard there, Bob."

"You need to go to the hospital right away. I think you have appendicitis. You don't present as anyone with appendicitis, but I'm pretty sure you have it. You need to go now, to at least rule it out as a possibility."

Three & Me

I was a few weeks away from being able to apply for Medicare. The timing was horrible for me, but Bob was insistent. So, I drove myself to UCLA Medical Center and walked into the ER. The lady at the front desk took my temperature, and I handed her a note from Bob, saying that he had examined me and that he diagnosed acute appendicitis. Since Bob wasn't on staff at UCLA, she threw the note down on her desk. I did have a fever though, which didn't seem to bear any weight. She then asked me what my pain level was on a scale of 1-10. "I don't really have any pain," I answered truthfully.

"I need an answer," she said impatiently.

"Ok. It's a 2," I said pulling the number out of my head.

"Go sit over there. We'll call you when we're ready for you."

So, I sat. And I sat. And I sat. Six hours had gone by and it was going on 3:00 am. I walked over to the lady at the desk and asked her how much longer. "It's St. Paddy's Day, and we are inundated with drunken drivers crashing their cars," she replied. "And then there's Obamacare, where now everybody is using the ER as a trip to a doctor they can't afford. So, you have quite a few people ahead of you yet."

I told her I wasn't going to sit much longer, that I had a fever and a note from a doctor, and I should be given some kind of exam. "Do what you please. You're not going to be seen anytime soon."

So, I drove home, crawled into bed, and slept like a baby. I still had a high fever but otherwise felt fine. I showered, had a small breakfast, and went to see a new client about a brochure I was designing for his gym on Ventura Boulevard. At about 1 pm, Bob called me on my cell. "WHERE THE HELL ARE YOU?" he demanded of me. "I just phoned UCLA and they have no record of you. WHAT ARE YOU DOING?!" I told him about the futile wait in the ER, and that I had just finished

Did He Kill Her?

my meeting with a client in Tarzana and was on my way to another meeting. "GET YOUR ASS BACK TO THE HOSPITAL. YOU HAVE ACUTE APPENDICITIS AND YOUR APPENDIX IS PROBABLY CLOSE TO BURSTING!" Bob was in a frenzy. I told him I'd go back, and that made him happy. "Wait," he said. "What did you tell them about your level of pain?" I told him the truth. That's when he emphatically said. "SUZIE, YOU HAVE A HIGH THRESHOLD! GO IN AND LIE!"

I took his advice and that's exactly what I did. I drove into the valet parking lot outside of the ER, walked in through the front door, and gave an Academy Award-winning performance, grabbing my side, limping, and moaning loudly. With my high fever and perfect performance, I got into triage right away, where I continued the act. Bam, I was in a room, blood drawn and waiting to see what was going on. A nurse came in after I'd been there for an hour and told me I was being sent up to imaging because my white blood cell count was off the charts on the high side.

When I came back from imaging, I was going through email on my phone, when a bunch of residents walked in with one holding a syringe, another holding a chart, and another one writing something down on a clipboard. "What's the shot for?" I asked.

"It's medicine for your pain."

I laughed. "Oh, I don't need that," I said. "I only faked pain to get in here!" Ooooops, I let that cat out of the bag.

"Well, it's a good thing you did, said the one with the syringe. You have acute appendicitis, and you're going in for emergency surgery within the next half hour. Are you sure you don't want anything for pain?"

I told her I was feeling great and didn't need anything. They all laughed and shook their heads. "When was the last time you ate?"

Three & Me

asked the one with the clipboard," I told him I hadn't had anything since breakfast, which was about 17 hours prior. They nodded, happy with that answer. One told me that I certainly didn't act like I had acute appendicitis, and then they all left the room. I called my son at school in Santa Barbara and told him I was going to have emergency surgery but not to worry because I felt fine. Within a few minutes, an orderly came and told me that I was being prepped for surgery. With that, I was whisked away.

I woke up at 6:00 in the morning in post-op, feeling great! I jumped out of bed and walked over to the nurses' station dragging the I.V. pole I was hooked up to. I wanted to know where my purse and my clothes were. I wanted my phone. The nurse told me my stuff was probably still back in the ER, so I turned to follow the signs in that direction. "Wait! You can't go there. You just had surgery!" I told her I felt fine, wasn't dizzy, needed to pee, and I really wanted my phone. So, she assigned an orderly to follow me around, just in case I did a face plant. I went into the lady's room, did my business, then followed the signs to the ER to get my stuff. Satisfied with my purse and my bag of clothing in hand, I headed back to my bed in post-op with the orderly still behind me. As I entered my curtained cubicle in the post-op ward, I saw two doctors waiting for me. They both had smiles on their faces as I entered. "I wish all my patients were like you," one of them said. "We were wondering where you were. You're only a few hours out from surgery."

I asked them when I could go home. "If you can eat breakfast, without vomiting, you can go home. Do you need anything for pain?"

"Nope! I feel great. I just want to go home." I asked the nurse if I could get oatmeal, and they brought it right away. I chugged it down, and it stayed down. I was hoping I could get sprung soon. I didn't feel like being in bed, so I walked laps around the ward. It made the nurses crazy. One of them finally came up to me and said that I had to go back to bed for hospital liability purposes. As soon as I got into

Did He Kill Her?

bed, reluctantly mind you, my son and his friends descended on me. They had driven down from Santa Barbara to see me before class. Had I been meandering around post-op they might have missed me. It was so nice seeing them, but the visit was a quick one. With the same speed with which they arrived, they left back to Santa Barbara to continue their lives as college students.

True to the doctor's words, I was allowed to go home. They warned me about my high pain threshold, telling me that I would probably want to do everything I did before surgery, but that I couldn't, because it would risk tearing my inner stitches. I had six weeks when I had to refrain from riding horses or any other strenuous activity. I could walk and that was about it.

Theresa phoned me later that morning in a complete funk. I didn't tell her I had just gotten out of the hospital because I didn't want her worrying about me. She was depressed because everything in her condo was old and ragged. Phil wasn't working, she wasn't working, the only one who was working was Tianna, and that just wasn't enough income to purchase all new furniture or rugs. I could feel her pain coming through the phone receiver.

I immediately made a Facebook post without specifically naming Theresa, asking if friends had stuff in good condition that they didn't want anymore because I had a friend who really needed some nice things in her life. A horse friend of mine, named Kathy Hittleman, told me that her mom was getting rid of a ton of stuff, and if there was anything that I thought my friend wanted, then it would be hers. I was absolutely elated. I could hardly wait to tell Theresa. Kathy is a truly generous person. She threw herself behind helping my friend. But alas, it wasn't to be. Life sometimes takes over when you're making other plans.

I was still healing from my appendectomy when a few days after our phone conversation, I got an email from Theresa. Theresa's emails required a mental process to decipher them. It was like she'd invented her own shorthand, leaving out vowels, consonants, words, punctuation, etc. Each and every email was a brain exercise, some more so than others. When I sat down at the computer a few days after my own medical emergency, I saw an email from her that really required I put my thinking cap on. I managed to pick out "Cdr Sni" and realized she was talking about Cedars Sinai Hospital. With more scrutiny, I realized that she'd been admitted and wanted me to visit her.

Staphylococcus bacteria thrive in hospital settings. No matter how hard hospitals try to control it, it's such a nasty little organism that it has developed ways to escape all cleaning agents. I was petrified of getting a staph infection. There was no way I was going to go to the hospital. Add to that the traffic and distance from my Woodland Hills house, and my fear grew. I was resolute in calling her every day instead of a face-to-face visit. I called Theresa and told her I wouldn't be coming because I still had stitches, which meant little openings for staph to find and settle into.

"I need you to come," she said. "I'm not getting out of here alive." Her voice was airy and fun, so her almost off-the-cuff remark about not getting out alive, seemed completely incongruous. She sounded fabulous, just like the Theresa I knew. If you want to talk about ironies, well, her voice sounded happy and fun, and yet she was telling me she was going to die. That just didn't compute in my brain at all.

"You're joking, right?" I asked her. "What were you admitted for?"

"I have the flu." She replied.

"The flu?" I asked her. "How bad is it? What are they giving you?"

"I'm on a fucking Z-pak!" she said, her voice suddenly flashing anger. "I told them that I needed more powerful drugs than a Z-pak, but my doctor is on vacation and the attending wouldn't listen to me! You need to come. This place is going to kill me!"

Initially I thought Theresa was being overly dramatic. She didn't sound like someone who was facing her end of days, but who was I to judge? I took a deep breath, hoping she was just exaggerating her situation, and then told her I would leave in an hour after I cleaned up. I was confused for sure. The flu is horrible, a disease that really knocks a punch, and it makes one feel like shit. I thought only people who were immunocompromised, too old or too young, died from influenza. Not someone as robust as Theresa.

I thought back to when I last had the flu in my 40's. I decided then and there that it would be the last time I would ever have it. I've gotten vaccinated every year since. I had a breakthrough case once in all those years, and it was a very mild and manageable case lasting a couple of days. I am a believer in vaccines. Unfortunately, Theresa was not. When I asked her if she got the flu shot, she said she didn't because she didn't believe in them. I shook my head, but there is almost no way to convince someone who doesn't want a vaccine to take it. And it was at this point a fait accompli anyway. At the moment I wasn't too worried about her. She was in the hospital with influenza, and they would monitor her, cure her and eventually discharge her.

"I have a surprise for you," I told her when I arrived at the hospital. Theresa smiled, happy to see me and very pleased that I had made the drive to visit. I told her about the new furniture and rugs that Kathy and her mom were going to give her when she got out, and I also told her I would try and give her an allowance every month, to hold her over until she got back on her feet. She mentioned that she felt safe in the hospital and loved having cooked meals served to her in bed. I began to worry less about her dying.

I thought of my own father who took care of so many of his friends and family. He supported his parents, he supported his sister, and he sent monthly payments to some of his friends. He'd always helped me when I needed it. He also sent my foster brother money over the years. My dad helped so many people during his lifetime, both financially and spiritually, that I felt compelled to follow in his footsteps. Offering to help my good friend Theresa was an easy decision for me.

I settled in for an hours-long stay. Theresa was dressed in some cute pajamas. She had little regard for the open-backed hospital gowns worn by most patients, and she looked absolutely adorable. She was animated and full of life, bouncing around on the bed, but not too much, lest she dislodge the IV in the top of her hand. Had she not told me that she was sick, I never would have known. She pointed to the medicine bag on the pole. "Look!" she said as she pointed. "That bag is a fucking Z-Pak in IV form!"

I got up out of my chair and read "Azithromycin" on the label. Yep. She was right, a Z-Pak, although I'm pretty sure the dosage was higher than the run of the mill pills you pick up at the pharmacy. Theresa gave just a hint of a deepening cough. I'm no doctor, but it hit me that my son, when he'd had the flu and subsequent bronchitis, sounded much, much worse. Still...

"My fucking doctor, who knows my fucking history, who has helped me out of this situation in the past, is out of the fucking country right now," she said, letting her anger flash once more. "Can you fucking believe this?" Theresa did like throwing around F-bombs, especially when she got mad. "And he won't fucking return any calls, because I think he's in fucking Turkey."

I tried assuring Theresa that she'd be alright. I had complete confidence she'd recover fully. She's had the flu before, and she's had pneumonia before, and she'd always come out OK in the end. "Not this time," she told me. "Not this time!"

Did He Kill Her?

I needed to change the subject. So, I switched to my love life. That was one subject we always enjoyed talking about, and we'd end up giggling like two teenagers when I'd get to the juicy stuff. Sometimes she liked to live vicariously through me. At least, that's what she said.

As Theresa sat on the bed, I described a relationship that was changing shape. I had been going out with an Italian guy, same age as me, named Jimmy. Jimmy was born in Brooklyn. Theresa already liked the guy, especially because I told her that he had a really thick Brooklyn accent. We'd gone out for about a year, from last April to this April. I told Theresa that I had an expiration date for the relationship already on the calendar-- the one-year anniversary of our beginning to date. That is unless we both saw reasons to move forward from just dating. In the end we didn't, but instead morphed our relationship into an incredible friendship.

I told Theresa that in the very beginning, I would hear Jimmy speak about this deal and that deal, and this guy owes him, and that guy owes him, peppered with some tough guy talk about the losers that owed him money, and so on. "Did you ever see the movie, Get Shorty? I asked her. She nodded her head that she had. "Well, I had nothing to do one night and the movie was on. I'd watched it in the theaters, years ago when it first came out and I loved it, especially the line from John Travolta's character about his new minivan being the "Rolls Royce of minivans." Theresa laughed at that line. She remembered it also. "Anyway, as I'm watching it, I'm listening to the dialogue and thinking, 'Huh! Where have I heard that before?' and 'Huh! that character sounds like one of Jimmy's debtors,' and you know, Theresa, all of a sudden, I had one of those 'AHA!' moments."

"What do you mean?" she asked me, with a huge smile on her face.

"It dawned on me that Jimmy was either a loan shark or a shylock! Or both!!!"

Three & Me

"You're kidding me!" she said, eyes wide open and mouth agape. "You're serious?"

Laughing, I continued my story. "And the next day at lunch, I mentioned it to him, 'You know, I watched the movie Get Shorty, last night.' As I mentioned this, Jimmy looked up at me from his sandwich. 'Soooo....?' I asked him. He responded in just one word. 'Yeah.' That was his answer. Just 'Yeah.' And then he continued to eat."

"That's crazy!" Theresa exclaimed.

"YES! And get this! One Saturday night we go out to a restaurant that's owned by a friend of his. That friend of his happened to be some big kingpin in the Mafia! He was there that night and gave us a great table. Jimmy was giving him the respect a big gun in the Mafia gets, while I was incredibly shy and reserved. I had no idea how to meet big Mafia people, so I figured 'less is more.' I remember having the chicken parmesan for dinner, and afterwards, Jimmy's friend came over with a very sugary dessert and placed it right in front of me."

"You don't eat sugar," Theresa said laughing. "What did you do?"

"Well, I started to say 'Thank you, but...' except when Jimmy gave me a look like I needed to zip it quickly. I ended up saying just the 'Thank you' and a huge smile. So, his friend smiles back, and walks away telling me to enjoy the desert, and to please let him know how I liked it."

Theresa was laughing loudly at this story. Her nice little Jewish friend, hanging around big Mafia kingpins, faced with a sugary dessert, or else. "So, what'd you do?" she asked between giggles.

"He was MAFIA! What do you think I did?! I ate some of it! Then I told him it was absolutely delicious, gushing about it so profusely that I thought I had a sugar high! And of course, Jimmy couldn't stop

Did He Kill Her?

laughing." As I was telling this crazy story to Theresa, I was happy because I saw that she was able to take her mind off of her situation and relax, thanks in large part to our girl talk.

Eventually, Theresa's daughter arrived. She was spending nights at the hospital with her mom but had to do her own business during the day. She had just returned from her day's activities. After greeting each other, I looked at my watch. I'd been there almost two hours, so I decided to head home into the Valley before traffic got too bad. "You're coming back tomorrow, right?" Theresa asked, reverting suddenly to the sick patient. I told her I would. "See you tomorrow!" and with that, she blew me a kiss, then got back under the messy covers of the hospital bed as Tianna settled in for the long night ahead.

I got another email from Theresa later that night. It was hard to decipher, her usual code was all over the map. I was able to ascertain that she was beginning to feel worse and was worried. I shot back an email telling her not to worry and that I'd see her the next day.

When I went back the next afternoon, I couldn't believe how much worse she had gotten in 24 hours. The medical staff were still following the same protocols, even though she wasn't showing any improvement, and in fact was declining. I didn't want to alarm Theresa, so I kept up a poker face.

"I liked your stories about Jimmy," she said. "Tell me a few more."

"Ok, this one involves a stalker, though. Are you OK with that?" I asked, genuinely concerned about how that might hit her given her own history.

"Yeah, I'm fine. I know it ends OK because you're sitting right in front of me, so tell me the story."

Three & Me

"OK," I began, "There was a crazy post by a neighbor who lives around the corner from me, on that website *Nextdoor*. I sort of knew the person who posted it, just by sight, and I knew which house she lived in. She claimed that her burglar alarm went off, and she got notice on her phone, so she stopped what she was doing and drove home. On her way home, she noticed an African American male in his early 20's wearing basketball shorts and a tank top walking down the street. She was convinced he was the burglar. When she got home, nothing was taken, no windows or doors were broken, and she claimed that the burglar alarm must have scared him off. She hypothesized that he probably jumped the wall of her backyard and was therefore able to make it to Winnetka Avenue undetected."

"Are you kidding me?!" Theresa asked. "What a racist! She had no proof. What a terrible thing to say!"

"Exactly!" I exclaimed a little too loudly. "So, I posted a comment on her thread that she had no proof that kid was a burglar, nothing was taken, and if a burglar is going to come and steal, wouldn't he have a car waiting for a quick getaway, and to be able to haul the stuff in? He didn't even have a backpack! IF HE WAS the burglar, what was he going to do? Stick a television in his basketball shorts pocket?!"

Theresa laughed. "How stupid, absolutely ridiculous for her to make that allegation."

"Well, that isn't the half of it. All of a sudden, all these neighbors from different areas around Woodland Hills are talking about shooting the guy if they saw him, or beating him up, or having the cops arrest him. They threatened bodily harm if they saw that kid in their neighborhood, or our neighborhood again. This completely freaked me out because even though Jonah is at school in Santa Barbara, Donte Jackson is living in my downstairs bedroom and he always wears tank tops and basketball shorts in the warmer weather, and he takes walks up and down the street."

Did He Kill Her?

"OH MY GOD!" Theresa gasped. "What the hell did you do? I know what I would have done. I would have gone postal on that lady!"

"I posted exactly what I told you. That she was endangering my son, and she was endangering my 'other kid,' Donte. I asked her to take her post down, but she refused. And then, the texts started coming in from a nut job in my neighborhood demanding that I apologize to the *crime victim.*"

"Are you kidding me?" Theresa was aghast. She was one of my friends who was completely color blind and I loved her for that. She could see the racism emerging in the mob rule mentality of *Nextdoor* and was as upset as I was. "So, what did you say to this guy?"

"I told him that there was no evidence of a crime. She was not a victim. Her alarm went off, nothing more. No signs of forced entry. Nothing was taken and I believed this entire story was a complete jumble of conjecture on her part. And I would not apologize for asking her to take down her incredibly inflammatory post. That's when he told me that he would harass me until I apologized to her publicly on *Nextdoor.*"

"I would have called the police," she said. Then Theresa began to cough a deep wet cough, one that I hadn't heard from her before. I looked up at her and her skin was gray, nothing like the pink cheeks she had the day before. My concern was rising, but I didn't want to focus on that, so I continued my story when the coughing stopped. I had to wait because Theresa buzzed the nurse and asked for a breathing treatment. Within a few minutes, a technician came in with the equipment. Theresa inhaled some steamy vapors, first in more shallow breaths, ending in some deeper ones. The vapors were clearly soothing her lungs, which appeared to be battling whatever was multiplying inside of them. Once the tech and the equipment left the room, Theresa sat in bed, trying to breath as normally as possible. I waited patiently beside her bed, putting my hand on her back

Three & Me

to offer support. She finally looked up at me and said she felt better. She wanted me to continue.

"Anyways, that guy, named Alex, was true to his word. His texts were coming in fast and furious. All the time. It was like he was obsessed. I couldn't figure out how to block him, so my phone kept pinging with absolutely nasty texts to me. Each one got worse, his anger spilling out into the digital world he was living in. So, I did what I knew how to do best. I researched his profile and found his business phone number. Turns out he had an office in my neighborhood. So, I called Jimmy and told him the whole story. I forwarded him the texts this guy was sending me."

"Really? You called Jimmy about this?" she asked smiling broadly now.

"Oh yeah. Absolutely! Jimmy told me to demand Alex stop immediately, that I wasn't going to put up with his bullshit anymore. And if, after that, he still harassed me, well, to let him know and send a copy of the text over."

"And he didn't stop, right?" Theresa knew. Stalkers never stopped.

"Right. So, I sent Jimmy the text and gave him the guy's office number. Jimmy, he's got this gravelly voice and a really thick Brooklyn accent, right? So, he calls the guy up and the conversation kind of went like this..."

"Hello, is this Alex?"

"Yes, this is Alex."

"Hi Alex. I'm calling you because I have a problem. You see, you've been harassing a friend of mine lately, and she's very unhappy about it." Alex was suddenly silent. "And you see, Alex, when my friend is unhappy, then I'm unhappy. If you continue to make my friend unhappy then the problem is going to be between you and me and you don't want a problem with me." Then Alex said he understood. "Good! Because I'm asking you nicely, man to man, to just stop with the texts. Forget her."

"According to Jimmy, Alex's voice became extremely quiet, as he agreed to leave me alone. And that was the end of it. Theresa, you should hear Jimmy talk. He sounds like a bona fide mobster, and I'm half convinced he is! Alex must have shit his pants when Jimmy started talking!" Theresa was smiling and laughing now. I was happy I could make my friend's day a little bit more entertaining.

The morning of April 12th, I woke up to an email from Theresa. *"I Got Worse."* Just those 3 words caused my heart to sink. I am the quintessential optimist, always have been. But sometimes I get hit right between the eyes when I'm just not ready. I wasn't ready to face yet another person in my life leaving for the great beyond. It was starting to feel as if every time I turned around, I was mourning a loss.

Later in the morning, I got this email from Theresa:
> *"My doc is back. Catscan & Chest xray had terrible results. I'm worsening rapidly. I'm drowning in liquid or junk in lungs including infected scar tissue from stabbing. Tests showed possible rare fungal infection. Only 30 people yearly. In order for Dr P to be approved by insurance to treat for fungal infection meds, insurance insists that I have a sedated procedure (bronchoscopy) along with a biopsy to rule out the Big C."*

I immediately emailed her back that I would be there later in the afternoon after her procedure. Theresa had massive scar tissue from her stabbing. Scar tissue has no vascular. If any organisms were hiding in her scar tissue, no medication could reach them, and they could have full rein to create havoc in her body. A strong feeling of panic began to well up in my throat. If Theresa died because of the bacteria or

Three & Me

fungal particles hiding in her scar tissue, does that mean that Arthur Jackson actually killed her? If it did, would his soul be able to marry her soul in Heaven, just like his "divine mission" stated would happen? My imagination was running away with me, and I was clearly freaked out.

Heather must have been reading my mind because she phoned me inquiring about Theresa. I told her that Theresa was getting sicker by the minute from when she first was admitted to Cedars. I brought up my fears about Arthur Jackson. If she died, did he actually kill her some 34 years later? I know police can charge someone with murder if they injure someone and that person doesn't die immediately, instead dying years later from those same injuries. Jackson was dead, so he couldn't be charged if she died. But would he have been? My mind was racing, because I wanted her soul to have a peaceful transition, and to spend eternity in a state of bliss. I didn't want her soul tormented by that of Arthur Jackson. Who knew what his soul was planning up there? I sounded like a babbling idiot when Heather finally said, "Stop! You're torturing yourself over nothing! His soul can't reach hers if she dies. He's in hell." I sat upright with that thought. As a Jew, I don't believe in Hell.

Jews believe that everyone is forgiven of their sins once they die. I'd never even considered the possibility of Hell. As soon as Heather uttered those words, it was funny how quickly I began to believe in Hell. Thank goodness for clear-thinking Heather, otherwise, I would have been a complete basket case. Or at least more of a basket case than I already was.

Anyone who lives in Los Angeles knows there's a time to get on a freeway, but there are more times to NOT get on a freeway. I was dreading the drive to Cedars Sinai because I would be sitting in rush-hour traffic for hours. It was either that or sitting in a hospital waiting room for hours, so I opted for traffic. At least I could listen to the radio. It took me about two and a half hours to get to Cedars on a crowded 101 Freeway coupled with bumper-to-bumper traffic on all the side streets. I arrived in a panic that I might be late for who-knows-what. I needn't have worried so much though because when I got to Theresa's room, she was still in imaging. I ended up waiting anyway.

Finally, Theresa was wheeled into her room, and I wasn't prepared for just how bad she would look. She looked absolutely horrible. And she was angrier than I've ever seen her in my life. She had been told that her bronchoscopy would be performed under sedation. But someone in imaging didn't get those orders, and she had to have the procedure done without. She was in pain, crying, and humiliated. To make the whole situation that much more awful, her lungs felt worse and she had trouble breathing. She could hardly speak. I was completely shocked. "How could they do this to you?" I asked her, completely bewildered.

"I don't know. I kept asking to be sedated, and they refused. They went ahead anyway, holding me down. So many people had to wrestle with me. It was awful." And with that, she began to cry even harder. My stomach was in knots. I have a hard time watching anyone suffer, let alone anyone I love. I was powerless to do anything, even consoling her seemed as if my words would just sink unheard into the darkness of her mood.

I kept thinking back to her words, that she wasn't going to leave the hospital alive. I didn't want that to be true. In fact, I never believed those words to be true. That is, until that afternoon. I had been fighting those words with every fiber of my mind. I was beginning to lose that battle, just as I watched my friend of three decades, lose hers.

Theresa was inconsolable, and a dark pall fell over all of us. Phil and Tianna were there also and were deeply disturbed by what had happened to their wife and mother. Phil kept muttering that when Theresa was finally well, they should consult with an attorney, he was that angry. Theresa was in agreement, although I could see that it was a weak response because of her weakened state. I was hoping that come the next day, she'd bounce back and be full of piss and vinegar. She always did. She managed to escape death before, I was hoping she'd rally and be able to do it again!

After a while, I saw that Theresa was tired to the point that my even being there was not only of no use, but I felt it would be a detriment to her getting much-needed rest. As I left, I told her how much I loved her and wanted her to heal. Those would be the last words I would ever get to speak to her while she was in a state of consciousness. Later that night she crashed. She was transferred to the Saperstein ICU building the same one my dad was in when he had his valve replacement. During the night she was placed on a ventilator and put in a drug-induced coma, dialyzed, and monitored 24/7. Tianna also moved over to the ICU, where she slept every night on a recliner, keeping vigil over her much-loved mom. I was so admiring their strong mother-daughter bond. Looking back, I wished I could have shared that same bond with my mom.

Hours passed and became days and then weeks. During that time, Theresa needed a tracheotomy after seven days on the vent. The ventilator was then attached to her throat. She was still unconscious and undergoing dialysis. Tianna was still spending every night in the ICU with her mom. If sheer will from all of us could save Theresa, it would have, such was the love and devotion her husband, daughter, and friends had for her.

On one of the days when I was at the ICU with Tianna and Phil, the doctors wanted to try and wake Theresa up. They had discontinued the medically induced coma and were waiting for her to come to. She wasn't responding and was still in a deep coma-like sleep. One of the doctors walked over to the head of her bed and began to shout her name and clap his hands. "Theresa! Theresa! WAKE UP! Theresa!" We all stared at her from the foot of the bed hoping that she would open her eyes. The doctor kept calling her name for what seemed like an eternity. We were standing there with bated breath when Theresa slowly began to open her eyes. And then I saw it; the look of horror on her face. She couldn't talk because of the tracheotomy and the ventilator, but the contorted and angry expression she was making said it all. And then I remembered that certain something she had said to me years and years before after Jill died. *"I need to tell you it is the most wonderful feeling you'll ever experience. Dying is incredible!"*

Those words hit me hard. I sensed that her expression of anger was probably because we interrupted that process, just like the surgeon did when he revived her those many years before. Instead of being happy that we woke her up, I felt a sense of shame and I looked around me. Tianna and Phil were so happy to see her open her eyes, and initially, I was too. But that look on her face said it all. We all took turns talking to her, but her expression never changed. Eventually, she closed her eyes and went back to sleep. However, everyone, including the doctor was optimistic that she had awakened from her coma. I don't know if I was the only one in that room who was worried, but the sense of dread was growing in me.

Tianna kept up her vigil. Phil spent endless hours in the ICU, trying to get his wife to rally. This went on for days. Finally, at the beginning of June, Phil and Tianna told me that they were going to take Theresa off life support on the coming Monday. Theresa, at this point, was being kept alive only by the ventilator and dialysis. It was clear she was not going to regain consciousness. I asked them what they thought of me finding Jeff Fenn, the man who rescued her during the attack. They agreed that it would be a nice thing and gave me the green light to try and find him. But I didn't have a lot of time. It was Saturday, June 4th which left only Sunday, the very next day, for a possible visit, if I could even find the guy.

I didn't know what I was thinking, except I had an urgency to find Jeff Fenn, a needle in a haystack. Something in me felt that if I could find him, the man who saved her life those many years ago, it would prevent Jackson's soul from being able to get near her. I didn't tell anybody, but I kept thinking that Jeff Fenn needed to be there to protect my friend once more.

I contacted a friend that I met literally through Facebook. He was a retired Los Angeles Police Officer named Marty Fentress. Marty was one of those guys with a gregarious personality, a gentle giant. He was tall, like many LAPD officers, had a full head of greying hair, and a smile that would light up a room. He had an interest in antiques and fine antique China and wasn't ashamed to discuss those subjects. I really liked Marty, so I jumped onto my computer and texted him about finding Jeff Fenn and why. I figured that he would know how to do that, especially since I knew that police officers have a great brotherhood that lasts a lifetime. Jeff Fenn was not LAPD, rather he was a retired Sheriff's deputy, but I had faith in the connections and friendships that peace officers have amongst themselves.

Marty pulled off what most people would call the impossible. He immediately put the word out to LAPD, and he got a hit. Someone was actually friends with Jeff Fenn and called him to tell him why I was looking for him. Jeff was at a baseball game in Anaheim with his son when he got the call. He called me immediately, and I felt a rush of calmness come over me, penetrating deep into my soul. I was never so happy to talk to someone I had never met. Of course, he said, he'd meet me at the hospital the next day. I quickly told Phil who was as happy as I was.

On Sunday, the day before Theresa would be taken off the ventilator, I drove to Sapperstein ICU for one last time. When I arrived, Jeff was already there, speaking with Phil and Tianna. It was as if they were old friends, the camaraderie and mutual respect were obvious. Jeff walked over to Theresa's bedside and began to talk to her. As he did so, something in me knew that she heard him. I also felt the danger of Arthur Jackson's soul leaving with each word that Jeff spoke. It was as if a magical spell was being cast over Theresa, protecting her from any more evil. I felt lighter than I had in the last six weeks and calmer.

Did He Kill Her?

No one knew how grateful I was to Marty Fentress and Jeff Fenn. Jeff Fenn's presence gave me peace, knowing my friend was protected for all eternity; that her passage would end her suffering and would send her into that same light she saw many years ago; free of baggage, free of evil, with only love to carry her.

I too said my goodbyes to Theresa, someone who was there for me in thick and thin. It was hard for me, to leave her, but Phil and Tianna needed their time alone for those last agonizing hours. On Monday, they took her off life support and she peacefully slipped away into the light.

Heather called me once the news hit. "I can't believe she died so young," Heather said. "How are you?"

"I'm OK. It's really starting to get old losing people, though." Besides Jill, Theresa, my brother, my mom and dad, my friend Deborah Raffin, had also died from leukemia. She fought breast cancer some years prior, and sometimes chemo can bring on leukemia a few years down the road, especially breast cancer chemo. (I knew Deborah Raffin from the Jill and Charlie days. If you remember, she had been married to Jill's manager, Michael Viner but had an acrimonious divorce about 10 years before she passed.) As my heart recalled all the losses, I began to panic about Heather. "You better stay healthy!" I demanded of Heather. "I can't lose you too!"

Heather laughed. "I have no intention of getting sick," she said. "I'm not going anywhere! Besides, I'm having too much fun in New York City. When are you coming to visit?"

Relieved when I heard her resolve toward life, I exhaled. "I'll try and come in a few months when it gets cooler." She would be leaving for Canada any day, anyway. I wasn't too worried about Heather. She was fit as a fiddle, still young and so full of life. And, she still had her mission to raise as much money as she could for cancer research through Bob's foundation.

Three & Me

Me, Karla DeVito and Heather
at the 25th Anniversary Celebration
for the animated movie,
Beauty and the Beast.

EIGHTEEN

Love And Other Goodbyes

In August, Heather called me, sounding very excited. "Sooz! Robby just invited me and a plus one to the 25th celebration of Beauty and the Beast here in Lincoln Center! You're my plus one!" Well, that's not an offer I could refuse! Our mutual friend, Robby Benson, voiced the Beast in the Disney movie, and I was excited to go to the big celebration. And I was even more excited to be going with Heather!

"I'm booking my ticket as soon as I hang up with you," I said. "Thank you so much for making me your plus one! I love you!" I was super excited. I met Robby in the mid-1970s, within a year of my return to the United States from Israel. His brother-in-law, Moshe Elimelech, was married to Robby's sister, Shelli Segal, who had established her own brand in the fashion industry. Moshe was a designer and an incredibly talented artist. He was also Israeli. I met Moshe through another designer friend who was my colleague at the Art Center of Design in Pasadena, where we both were instructors. Moshe and Shelli became good friends with Yaniv and me. Robby's parents, Ann and Jerry Segal, lived close by in Woodland Hills, and we all spent many summer days hanging out by the pool. We were in our 20s back in those days, with so much of life to look forward to.

Robby and his dad wrote the movie *One on One* about a basketball player who was unfairly treated by his coach. You can imagine how funny it was when one day, we played a basketball game with me on Robby's team, while Moshe and Yaniv played against us on the other. Our team won, of course, because Robby was an entire team by himself. He could nail a shot from just about anywhere. I had fun running around pretending to be of help. I remember those days fondly because all of us were young and happy, with few cares in the world. Robby is a talented actor, author, singer, playwright, composer, musician, basketball player, and runner. There seemed to be nothing he couldn't do. Shelli also had more talent in her pinky than most people have in their entire bodies. She still kept her old apartment in New York City (rent control kept it ridiculously cheap), and when Robby was cast as Frederic in the Broadway production of *The Pirates of Penzance*, I flew out to stay with her and attend the show. It was wonderful, to say the least. Robby's leading lady was Karla DeVito (female vocalist for the artist Meatloaf), who played Mable. Robby and Karla fell in love while doing that show, and I'm happy to say they are still together, a wonderfully creative couple with a strong sense of social consciousness. They have always stood up for the oppressed and defenseless, making me proud to know them. (I love them both with all my heart.)

Heather and Bob met Robby and Karla through their mutual friend Burt Reynolds. It's incredible to me how there really are only a few degrees of separation between people because here were me and Heather, mutual friends with Robby and Karla, through entirely different paths.

Robby's parents eventually sold the Woodland Hills home and purchased a beautiful penthouse condo in Studio City. Robby and Karla lived near them. They recently sold their home and were preparing to move out of state. One day when I was hanging out with Heather together with Jonah, she said she wanted to cruise by Robby and Karla's house to say goodbye. Jonah was about seven or eight at the time, and Heather's daughter, Allie, was about five or six. *The Beauty and the Beast* video was quite literally played to death on our kitchen television VCR. All the Disney movies were. Once Jonah saw a movie, he wanted to see it again and again. He could recite the entire dialogue of each Disney movie and knew all the songs. When I told him we were going to go visit Robby, who voiced the Beast in the movie, Jonah looked at me like I had taken leave of my senses. Allie didn't believe it either when Heather told her.

When we arrived, the first thing Heather said to Robby was that the kids didn't believe he was the Beast. Robby is a handsome man with piercing blue eyes that sparkle with love. He didn't look like a Beast. In fact, he didn't even sound like a Beast with that sweet, whispery soft-spoken voice of his.

Robby is also a good-natured guy. He smiled his Robby Benson wry smile and walked over to Allie and Jonah, who were both standing quietly in his backyard, trying to find the Beast. He leaned in very close to Allie's ear and whispered in that distinctive voice of the Beast just loud enough so that they could both hear, "Hello, Belle."

Both Jonah's and Allie's eyes widened. There was no mistaking it. Robby *was* the Beast. They both stood there staring at Robby with new eyes. After that day, every time we watched the movie when the Beast would make his appearance, Jonah would scream out, "Look, Mommy! Here comes Robby!" He never once referred to the Beast as a Beast again, instead calling the animated character "Robby." I could tell that Jonah had found a new hero because he told all of his friends that he knew the Beast personally!

I flew to New York in mid-September of 2016. Heather and I had a ball trying to figure out what we were each going to wear. We both had our tried-and-true black pair of pants at the ready, which I paired with a black top. Heather opted instead for a red dress and beige crocheted sweater, leaving the trusty black pants for another occasion.

When the time came, we entered Lincoln Center and almost immediately spotted Karla. She ran up and gave us both hugs. It was a wonderful reunion because we were all living in different parts of the country. While Heather and I communicated over the phone and in person, Karla and Robby were always somewhere else doing something else, so our connection was mainly through Facebook.

Three & Me

Say what you may about Facebook and Mark Zuckerberg; he gave us a great platform to stay connected. I'm pretty sure he wasn't thinking of an older demographic when he created the social media giant. Still, as it turns out, that demographic uses it more often than the younger generations, who have opted into Instagram, Snap Chat and Tik Tok, and whatever new thing will come along.

The celebration was fantastic; the highlight was Angela Lansbury, singing the title song accompanied by the song's writer, Alan Menken on piano. Heather and I went nuts. Angela Lansbury got a standing ovation that lasted a long time. It seemed like magic was happening right before our eyes. It was over far too soon. Heather and I went backstage to visit, having been invited by Karla, who came out to get us. I loved becoming part of the background. I saw Angela Lansbury up close (Charlie Bronson was a huge fan of hers and would have loved being there), as well as Paige O'Hara, who voiced Belle. Robby was there, but he wasn't feeling that well. He came out to greet us quickly but had to get back to the business of being interviewed. Karla told me later that Robby was suffering from food poisoning. I had to hand it to him. He was stalwart with the old adage that "The show must go on." Kudos to Robby, ever the professional.

Heather and I left Lincoln Center and headed back to her place facing the Hudson. She had a beautiful view of the river as well as New Jersey on the other side. Heather had found a wonderful place that was quite large by New York standards. It boasted two bedrooms (one was an en-suite), and two full baths, with a smaller room that could be used as a guest room or an office. The apartment included a formal dining room as well as a large great room.

Heather had a "roommate" who hailed from her California days. He was previously married but was going through a divorce from his husband. Danny was suddenly without a permanent source of income. Heather let him move in, in what she told me was a temporary situation until he could get back on his feet. He eventually became a permanent fixture. I had the feeling that while Heather complained that he didn't share in the expenses as much as he should have, at that time, she enjoyed the company. They used to joke around, telling everyone that they were a *Will and Grace* couple. In the beginning, it definitely appeared that was the case.

I slept on the pull-out couch in the living room and had to share the hallway bathroom with Danny, whom I'm guessing wasn't too pleased with that arrangement. Oh well. There was literally nowhere else to pee, so Danny was stuck with me. I remember buying more soft soap because I didn't realize I was using Danny's personal bottle of the stuff while I showered and cleaned up. Once I found out, I was embarrassed and bought a bottle quickly before I left for California. Sharing that bathroom was definitely a bit awkward.

Every morning, I woke up around 10 am New York time, which is about 7:00 am Los Angeles time. Heather would sleep until about noon. I'd watch television until she got up. We'd then walk uphill towards the Manhattan Diner, a kind of retro eatery in a true diner style. Heather always ordered off the breakfast menu while I ordered lunch. The food wasn't great, but the wait staff was personable, and I loved the genuine retro décor.

After eating, we'd hop on the subway and go somewhere, usually shopping. Heather and I liked the same camp-shirt style blouses, so we went to Macy's and stocked up on a few. We also had the same taste in sweater coats, each of us purchasing an identical sweater. We laughed at each other and promised we'd never, ever wear that sweater coat at the same time. I wasn't too worried. I was taking mine back to the West Coast, and hers was staying in New York City.

While I was in the City, Heather wanted me to visit with Bob's former driver, a guy named Tony Hillery, the same guy who drove them around NYC on September 11th, 2001. She couldn't stop talking about what a great person he was and how he had started a non-profit aptly named

"Harlem Grown." Heather was speaking in fragmented sentences because she was so excited about Tony's project, constantly interrupting herself to begin saying something else about it, then interrupting herself again. My takeaway was that Tony liked to grow things in Harlem and was an amazing person, but I still had no idea what Harlem Grown was all about.

We took the subway to Harlem so I could see first-hand what Tony's non-profit was all about. Of course, Heather got lost. We got off at the wrong stop in an industrial area. I finally looked around at where we were. I only knew what Harlem looked like from seeing movies and photos, and nothing I was looking at even remotely resembled what the movies had portrayed Harlem to be like. I was convinced we were hopelessly lost and in the wrong neighborhood. "Heather, I think this isn't the place," I said with about as much tact as I could muster. Heather had never been good with directions. In fact, she would get lost many times when we drove to places together. So, I was well-versed in getting us out of situations like this.

A couple of years back, we visited Albuquerque, New Mexico, to visit her son Ryan, who had just had a baby boy with his wife, Nancy. From the hotel we were staying in, it was pretty much a straight shot up one street, a turn, then a straight shot up another, and then another two turns, and we'd arrive at Ryan's house. But Heather couldn't do it without panicking, so she'd always ask me to drive, especially at night. Getting lost was her thing.

So, there we were, roaming around an odd part of uptown New York City when I suggested she go on her phone and pull up Tony's address in the Uber app. That way, the Uber driver would get us to our meeting with Tony in time for our appointment. In concept, that was a great idea, except Tony forgot to tell her that the address she had was for a school and not for his office. The Uber driver dropped us off in front of an elementary school and left. Heather and I roamed around again, trying to figure out where we were. We walked into the

Love And Other Goodbyes

school, thinking that maybe Tony had an office there. When we asked about him, we were told that Tony didn't, in fact, have an office there, but he frequented the school quite often, working with the kids who attended that school. We left the building, and I asked Heather to call Tony, who answered immediately and told us to wait for him. He was expecting us in an office a few blocks away, but he'd meet us in front of the school. Heather and I waited, and it wasn't too long before Tony showed up on foot, elated to see Heather again.

"Tony, this is my good friend Suzie from California," she said proudly, "and I wanted her to see your operation. I tried to explain to her, what you did exactly, but I wasn't too clear because she had a puzzled look on her face the entire time I was talking."

I laughed. "That's because you never finished one sentence before beginning another!"

Heather's excitement about Tony Hillery and his non-profit was more than justified. As soon as Tony walked us across the street into one of the group's vegetable gardens, he explained that children are the ones who grow the food and then pass the knowledge down to the younger children who are just beginning in the program. I was hooked. Tony Hillery is an exceptional human being. He identified a problem for kids in Harlem and actually did something about it.

As he explained it a great deal of the kids live in small and sometimes crowded apartments with only a single parent, usually the mother, who has to work to support them both. Tony explained that these kids are typically latchkey kids and are raised on fast food because it's cheaper than buying groceries which can carry inflated prices in their neighborhood. He said their diets are horrible. Before he came around, most of the kids had no idea what a vegetable even was. So, he found a plot of land and decided to teach kids how to grow their own vegetables, how to raise egg-laying chickens, how to prepare food, and how to eat healthily. Each kid gets to keep what they grow.

Three & Me

Tony wasn't done with just the one garden. He built a greenhouse next to the outdoor garden and taught the kids how to keep the garden multiplying by planting sprouts. He's found multiple locations for gardens, each now producing food, creating employment opportunities, educational opportunities, and keeping kids out of gangs. One of his gardens is self-sustaining, utilizing solar power and humidifiers to create moisture to water only the roots.

The kids can also sell their vegetables at fresh-air markets in Harlem. They get to keep the proceeds. Tony took us to one such market to see his kids in action. These kids were high schoolers, and you could see the love and admiration they had for Tony as soon as he walked up to greet them. Their faces literally lit up in appreciation, and they began to excitedly tell him about the events of that day.

More, Tony decided that taking care of their stomachs was not enough. He needed to take care of their minds. So, he opened up his office to the kids, letting them have access to computers and the internet so that they could do homework and learn. Many of Tony's kids graduate high school and go on to higher education because of his mentoring and his generosity. He's a believer in the old adage, "If you give a man a fish, you feed him for a day. If you teach the man to fish, you feed him for a lifetime." That's exactly what Tony was doing for these kids.

Tony has big plans for his program. He bought a food truck that he outfitted with a television and a cooking station. He takes the truck into new areas of Harlem and teaches kids how to cook what they grow. He is all about education. Tony has dedicated his life, and his own money and is fund-raising to keep the program growing (hint hint).

I was so impressed with Tony and Harlem Grown that I nominated him to be a CNN Hero for 2016, but I was too late. The nominations were already closed. I had just missed the cut-off. Not one to be deterred, I nominated him again in 2017. I must have done something right when a CNN Hero producer interviewed me because Tony was

Love And Other Goodbyes

selected to be a *CNN Hero* in 2017! I remember my excitement after I hung up with the producer. I was jumping up and down. She said that my enthusiasm would go far in Tony Hillery's selection, which happened pretty soon after my call. CNN did a wonderful story on him, which was shown on national television many times. Unfortunately, he didn't make it all the way to *CNN Hero of the Year,* but being one of the Heroes is still a huge accomplishment, and people can still access his story online. Not only that, but I am hopeful it helped to bring bigger donations to his noble cause.

# # #

Once I returned home after my wonderful New York visit, I felt I needed more out of my life from a relationship standpoint. I had been going out with a former newscaster, and while I liked him a lot, I knew I couldn't ever fall in love with him either. I was seriously beginning to think I was broken. He said that he was crazy about me, and I knew he would be the kind of man who would want to give me the best of everything, but still... I just couldn't get that loving feeling. So, I became obnoxious. I hate hurting people, so I figured if I were a brat, he'd find his own exit door. But he didn't, so I kept on seeing him. I did have a lot of fun with him, though. He was zany, quirky, completely nuts, and endearing. (Unfortunately, I heard he recently passed away, and I am extremely saddened by that news.)

I was still on the Jewish dating site JDate, which was how I met the newscaster, whom I was still seeing. I was less than enchanted with the site because of what I considered to be a thin selection. The men in my age group were mostly either physically unattractive, waiting around to die, looking for a nurse or a purse, or had other unattractive qualities. I was done. Convinced I was doomed to spend the rest of my life alone simply because I couldn't find a man whom I could fall head over heels in love with, I wasn't sure if I had unrealistic expectations, or if Mother Nature intentionally ignored women who had left child-bearing age behind. I was still full of energy with an unbridled zest for life and new adventure, and I worked hard to stay physically active. I couldn't understand why I couldn't find a partner that would want to share all that youthful energy with me.

The thin choices I had for men in my age group, notwithstanding, weren't the only reason I was unhappy with the JDate experience. I woke up one morning to find my mailbox had exploded with emails from a wide range of men, all giving me their personal emails, along with notes telling me, in one form or another, that "YES!" they wanted to see those naked pictures of me.

WTF! First of all, at the time, I was 64 years old. In my wildest dreams, I couldn't figure out *what kind of lunatic wanted to see naked pictures of a 64-year-old Jewish woman!* After shaking my head at the lunacy of the whole thing, I opened up my JDate outgoing mail and saw that a message went out from "me" to just about every guy on that site. It said something to the effect of, "If you'd like me to send you naked pictures of myself, please send me your private email." Yep. I was hacked.

Once I peeled myself off of the ceiling, I phoned the parent company for the dating site. I explained what had happened, and they told me that I was the third person calling about the same problem. The person on the other end of the phone said that I should feel complimented because it had only happened to the more attractive members. HUH?! No. I didn't feel complimented. I felt violated, especially since I knew men from other social situations in my life who were on the site as well, and they probably wondered when I had taken leave of my senses!

I wanted the company to shut down my account, my subscription was ending anyway, but they insisted on migrating me to another portal with a new handle and extending my subscription. They told me I didn't have to use it if I didn't want to, but they wanted to make things right. Ugh. Before I hung up, I asked them to make sure it wouldn't auto-renew, and they assured me that when the newly-subscribed-to period was over, my account would drop off.

After that, I forgot about JDate and didn't answer any emails from men on the site. I went on with my life. Then on Yom Kippur, the holiest day of the Jewish calendar, I was notified through my banking app that money was deducted from my account because JDate auto-renewed. It was YOM KIPPUR, and there was nothing I could do about it because the corporate offices were closed. Annoyed as I was, I went to services at my synagogue and tried to forget about it.

I usually don't take my phone with me to Yom Kippur services, and I didn't that night either. It wasn't until I got home that I noticed I had an email from a JDate guy. To be clear, under normal circumstances, I would have ignored that email. However, not this time. It caught my attention in a huge way. I wondered, "What idiot hits on a Jewish woman on Yom Kippur through a Jewish dating site?!" I absolutely had to find out who that idiot was.

393

So, I went into his profile. He was nearly nine years older than me, which was not, particularly a good thing but not a bad thing either. Under closer inspection, the one thing that really stood out to me was that he basically had a firm grip on life, maximizing every moment, not to mention the most gorgeous blue eyes, second only to Yaniv's. If he was telling the truth in his profile, we appeared to enjoy a great deal of the same activities. Judging by his profession, he would be good for intelligent conversation, which I absolutely had to have in a man. So, I responded to his email, giving him my phone number. Except I made a typo and gave him a number that was one digit off. It was my mistake.

Well, as you can imagine, he didn't reach me. I was curious as to why he wanted my number if he wasn't going to call, but I shrugged it off to dating site hell and didn't give it a second thought. The next day I got an email from him, letting me know that I had given him

Three & Me

the wrong number. He wrote HIS number down for me to call him. I went back into the email I sent him and saw that indeed I had given him the wrong number. I laughed at how funny that was because it seemed like God above was trying very hard to get us together, but I kept making a fumble. I had a mental picture of my father, up in heaven, slapping himself in the head, uttering the same phrase he'd use when I'd mess up: "OY! You are *such* an Idiot!"

I called the number, and it turned out that the "idiot" was a pretty cool guy named Ron. As it happened, Ron lived just a few blocks from me. Once we were actually on the phone together, he described his near-futile attempts to reach me through the number I had given him. He left a few voice messages, but none were returned, and he was getting ready to move on when a woman called him back, telling him that no Suzie lived at the number. We both had a good laugh over my huge faux pas. And, as expected, our phone conversation confirmed we had a great deal in common. It also appeared that our sense of humor was on the same track, which I liked.

Over the telephone, Ron confessed that he really liked a photo of me, where I was wearing a cute hat and scarf. That photo was taken at a Super Bowl party at Mrs. Jackson's home in Calabasas. I told him I would wear both when we met so he'd recognize me immediately. He also said he was leaving for Italy in two days for a three-week trip, taking his assistant and her husband with him as a thank-you gift. Ron's wife passed away unexpectedly nearly eleven months prior to our speaking, and his assistant, Bev, was critical in helping him maneuver through the days, weeks, and months following her passing. Bev had become an incredibly important part of his life, and the trip was to show his appreciation for everything she did for him. Even though he was leaving in two days, he wanted to meet me before he took off for Europe. So, we arranged to meet at a California Pizza Kitchen in Tarzana the following evening.

Love And Other Goodbyes

When I met Ron on that October 5th evening, my heart jumped for the very first time since I'd met Yaniv some 46 years prior. That surprised me. I wasn't expecting it. He pretty much had me at *"Hello."* It wasn't a luxury date at an expensive eatery but a step up from the Starbucks dates I'd go on as my usual first meet and greet. Both light eaters, we ended up splitting a Caesar salad. As we sat and talked, I noticed him fidgeting with a straw the same way I fidget with a straw in my drink, putting a finger at the top of the straw, trapping the liquid, pulling the straw out, and drinking what's in the straw from the bottom of the straw! WHO ELSE DOES THAT AT OUR AGE? I was blown away and excited at the same time. One more quirky box checked off.

When dinner was over, I felt as though I'd known Ron for a long time. A certain unexplainable familiarity was taking hold. When he kissed me goodnight, his hand descended lower and lower on my back. Strangely, it felt right. It just did.

If the lack of complication of that night could have carried over into the rest of our lives, we would have had a smooth transition into our relationship. Unfortunately, it didn't happen that way. While I went home walking on air, feeling like I had finally found the guy I was supposed to be with forever, landmines were waiting for me. They were soon to blow up as I journeyed into my new relationship with Dr. Blue Eyes.

Early on in the relationship—exactly three weeks in—on our first long-distance outing to a friend's vow renewal ceremony in Las Vegas, Ron let me know that with absolute certainty, his friend and assistant, Bev, was the number one woman in his life and that the woman who occupied the number two spot was his business partner of many years, a physician named Gail.

As I said before, I don't have the jealousy gene. Hearing from Ron about this female hierarchy didn't really phase me one way or another.

It wasn't my place to question him. I just accepted what he had to say and didn't think too much more about it. But I probably should have.

I'm not going to lie. I was smitten with Ron, and I was very attracted to him on so many different levels. I wanted nothing more than for us to have the perfect last chapter in our lives. I wanted that fairy tale with all of my heart and soul. We were still in the "honeymoon" phase of our relationship, and usually, during that phase, both parties are on their very best behavior. Men typically show their true colors after about six months. Because I had nothing to hide, my true colors were out already. I was a WYSIWYG (What You See Is What You Get). What I didn't realize at the time was that Ron was a WYSIWYG also!

I remember one particular night we went out together. We were standing in my driveway, having a nice kiss goodnight. It felt heavenly. And then Ron, who had no idea about behaving well for the first six months, pretty much laid his cards out right there. "You know what the best thing about our relationship is?" he asked me. I was waiting to hear something nice, like, 'I really think we get along great,' or 'I could see myself falling for you,' or something equally mushy. I liked mushy. Instead of mush, though, I got cold hard truth. "The best thing is that at our age if something happens to either one of us, the other can just walk away." And with that, he got in his car and drove away. I stood on my porch watching his tail lights disappear down the hill, wondering just who I was getting involved with.

In Ron's world, though, nothing had happened. He had just let fly with a thought that was in his head without thinking about how it might land. We weren't yet boyfriend and girlfriend, although I believe that was the goal for both of us. He just said what was on his mind and practically forgot about it by the time he'd reached the stop sign two houses down.

Love And Other Goodbyes

I called Heather the next morning. "Hey, so if a guy told you that if you ever got sick or hurt or something, he'd just walk away, how would you take it?"

"I'd kick him to the curb," Heather said. "You're what? A couple of months into dating?! You need to have a man who worships you, who would go to the ends of the Earth for you. I mean, he just did you a huge favor. He let you know where you stood, right?"

"You know I'm number three in his female hierarchy, right?" I told Heather. "He has two women in his life ahead of me."

"Suzie, I'm just going to tell you this one thing. Bob chased after me. He let me know from the very beginning how much he loved me. He held me on a pedestal. There was no way he would let me go, no matter what life threw at us. You need a Bob in your life!"

I nodded my head in acknowledgment. Perhaps in spite of the bone-headed thing he just said, Ron could be my Bob or at least a close second. I still had my fingers crossed.

To my surprise, Ron called me later that evening. He had previously spoken about us traveling together, but I thought it was mostly talk. JDate men did a lot of talking and hardly ever carried through on what they talked about. But Ron wanted to go to Cuba for a short trip and wanted me to come along. My head spun. I really thought he'd kissed me off the night before, and now he was inviting me to Cuba.

During the same conversation, he also invited me to meet him for dinner at a funky little restaurant on Ventura Boulevard. He liked a Greek place down the street from his house called Pozi. He invited me to drive over to his place, and we'd leave from there. When I arrived, Bev answered the door. I'd met her before at a somewhat awkward lunch that Ron had orchestrated. At that lunch in an Israeli restaurant, they both sat together on one side of the table, and I was alone on the other side. It felt more like a job interview than a casual lunch. Which, in hindsight, I suppose it was.

Bev worked for Ron in his home office. He sold his radiology business earlier in the year and had wisely kept Bev on. When Bev let me in, she smiled and said, "I heard Ron is taking you to Cuba in February." I said that was true and let her know I was excited about the trip. "You know that's the trip I turned down," she said. "He asked me first, but I just said, 'NO WAY!'" And then she laughed.

Well, OK then. My excitement for the trip just went down a couple of notches, but then I remembered my place. I'm number three. Get over it! Of course, Ron asked her first. She was number one! And I was lucky enough that he was taking me to a place I would find absolutely fascinating. So, I just sucked it up and tried not to let it bother me too much. But it did.

I again called Heather. "So, Ron invited me to Cuba. How crazy is that?"

Heather laughed. "Well, that's a step in the right direction, isn't it?! Are you going to go?"

"Of course, I'm going to go! But his number one lady, Bev, let me know that Ron had asked her first, and she turned him down."

Heather laughed. "Just go and have a good time. Ignore what she said. In the end, it's you who is going." As always, Heather's advice was good advice. I let the entire thing slide and ended up having a wonderful time in Cuba.

One night at dinner, Ron surprised me with his relationship Wish List. These were things that were very important to him, which he hoped I could deliver on.

    1. I had to learn to drink wine. He and his wife loved to

crack open a bottle and share it, on occasion, over dinner. I wasn't a wine drinker at all. Yaniv and I never touched the stuff.

2. I had to learn to eat more exotic foods. Ron was a foodie. I was the kind of person that ate to live. Ron was the kind of person who lived to eat.

3. I had to learn to sleep in a room with a higher temperature than I was used to. I liked to sleep when it was 67° and Ron likes it at 70° or warmer.

4. His friends had to like me. (They ended up hating me.)

5. I had to consider living full-time in Utah. Ron was moving there, and he wanted his person to be there with him. (Well, I had just bought a new home, but Park City, Utah, was a spectacular place, so that was one I could consider!)

I was stunned. I'd never had a man give me a list before, but here it was, all laid out and delivered. (I later learned that most men have wish lists, but they don't really verbalize them that quickly.) After my initial surprise, I told Ron that I would try to check off the items on that list but that it couldn't possibly happen overnight. These were huge lifestyle changes, and I needed time to adapt. While I had no demands of Ron in return, and I realized this list was a one-way thing, I was still quite willing to go along with it. I figured I might gain some new insights into wine and food, subjects most people held in high regard.

In March of that year, I flew with Ron to a cheese festival where we would be meeting up with his office people, people who had worked with him for many years and knew him as well as his wife very well. I was excited to meet his friends and start developing memories that we could share with each other down the road. To say they hated me on sight would be a complete understatement. His former COO spent hours on the phone with Ron trying to get him to leave me in the dust and move on to a better woman. Of course, I was hurt upon hearing this from Ron.

Three & Me

But hindsight is 20/20. It never dawned on me that they all loved Ron's deceased wife, Phyllis, and absolutely hated seeing Ron with someone new. To them, I was an intruder, a complete outsider, and could never fill Phyllis' shoes. Additionally, I represented the cold hard reality that Phyllis was gone. It took me about five years to come to this realization when I found myself on the other side in a similar situation. Then it hit me like a ton of bricks. Suddenly, the light bulb went off, and I got it, albeit five years too late.

That three-day weekend felt like an eternity. Ron really didn't help much. He walked away, happy to be with his buddies, leaving me to fend for myself. It was obvious that Ron was really enjoying his reunion with his office group. I was just the tag-along.

While my mind was sorting things out, my damn heart was still beating hard for Ron. I felt something when I was with him, alone, with no outside interference. I felt love for him from such a deep place in my soul that the idea of leaving him, or him leaving me, was horribly painful. I knew I was in love with him, but I didn't think my love was enough for Ron. Life plays crazy tricks, doesn't it? I couldn't fall in love with men who ranked me number one, but I fell in love with a guy who ranked me down at number three. Go figure. I think a shrink would have had a heyday with that one!

Meanwhile, his friends were harping on him to find another woman and to move on from me. I know he was listening intently and waffling because while he didn't want to cut bait, he began to see me through their eyes. And once someone begins to see you through the eyes of another, things can get dicey.

For some unexplained reason that I didn't understand at all, and completely out of the blue, Ron invited me to spend a few days with him in Mexico City in late spring. I became hopeful yet again and looked forward to the trip. It was obvious to us both that we traveled well together. It was also obvious that the more we saw each other, the more history we created between us. A history that would help bind us as a couple.

Once we got back from Mexico City, the realities of life set in. Yaniv informed me that he planned to lower the amount of money he contributed to Jonah's college education. We didn't need lawyers to work out finances. If he couldn't pay, he couldn't. There was no need for me to get angry or upset. Yaniv was the good guy who had continued helping beyond the terms of the divorce agreement. I was grateful for whatever help he could give me toward Jonah's college expenses. I paid his college tuition, and most of his living expenses, but Yaniv helped with Jonah's Santa Barbara rent.

Losing that income, or gaining more expense, depending upon how you looked at it, was going to be a hit financially, but I would have to make do. At that time, I was living in the San Fernando Valley, with the hottest temperatures in the summer, sometimes reaching highs of 122° Fahrenheit, and the lowest in the winters, often in the 30s and 40s. As a result of the extreme weather, my cost of water and electricity kept escalating and was outrageously high. My property abutted Corbin Canyon—always a fire threat—so I needed greenery between my house and the canyon. That meant water. I was seeing bills of over $6,000 for two months in the summer and not much less in the winter since rain was becoming close to nonexistent. Simply put, Los Angeles was in a perpetual state of drought. I had to face the reality that the house I loved was something I could no longer afford.

With no real choice, I made the decision to sell. Right before I left for Mexico City, a For Sale sign went up in my front yard. Within an hour, an offer, close to asking, came in. The buyer wanted to buy the house "as is" with no inspection. This meant no fixing things, no renegotiating the price and no headaches. I gladly accepted it, and we went into escrow. Once I returned from the trip, I was faced with packing up a huge five-bedroom house and two storage sheds, pretty much all by myself.

Three & Me

I quickly found a house in Moorpark that offered small-town living with large-city conveniences not too far away. The weather is much milder in the summer and in the winter. The home had solar panels, so I could kiss my huge electricity bills goodbye. My lot size shrunk from nearly half an acre down to just under one-third of an acre, so my water bill would shrink as well. It was a newer home, so I wouldn't have to struggle with a leaky roof or other expensive repairs for quite a while, hopefully. My Woodland Hills house had been a money pit. An expensive surprise was always waiting for me when I least expected it, and usually at the worst possible time.

None of this was good news to Ron. I didn't have much time for him now. He had a house in Park City, Utah that he was transitioning to and wanted someone there with him full time. We were still fairly new to each other, with the bad history of his friends' disapproval of me to boot. With the timing of my move, he became frustrated. Ron was already in Park City, hoping I would be spending a great deal of time there with him. The fact that I had to spend almost two months of summer packing up my life was a green light he took to find another woman who would fit his needs. We drifted. Ron dated. I packed.

My old boyfriend Dave called me in July. He had broken up with his girlfriend of many years and moved back from Sedona to his Santa Monica house. He wanted to get together. Ron had informed me earlier in the month that we were not exclusive, so I told Dave my move would be in two weeks, and after that, I'd love to see him.

By the end of the first week in August, I had moved into the Moorpark house. I called Dave shortly after, and he came over the very next day. Dave was his usual pleasant self, greeting me with all the compliments I needed at the time. I was worn out, not only from the move but from the emotional roller coaster I was on with Ron. The first thing Dave did when he saw me was give me a huge kiss and a bigger hug. It felt like old times. I loved him but still wasn't in love.

Love And Other Goodbyes

Ron was busy in Utah, meeting local women through Match.com, trying to find one that would fit his lifestyle and needs. Ron still called me, but not every day. And when he did, the conversations were rather beige in nature. Dave and I went out. I enjoyed his pampering, the endless compliments, and the fun times. But I missed Ron terribly. Dave would make the drive from Santa Monica to Moorpark, up Pacific Coast Highway, over the canyon, and then back again. It was a long haul. Dave hated the drive—I thought that was funny because he was an ex-race car driver. He hated it so much that he once flew his plane to Camarillo Airport from Santa Monica Airport just to see me. I adored Dave. But the timing was all wrong for us. I wanted Ron, maybe because I realized I couldn't have him. Who knows? But it was all I could think about.

During that same time frame, I was planning a trip to Picton, Ontario, Canada to visit Heather at the end of the month. Heather wanted me to help with her first-ever fundraiser on her beautiful lakefront property. She had given me about a year's notice that she wanted me to come at the end of August, and I already had my ticket in hand, ready to go. Ron let me know he was coming to LA from his Utah home that weekend. He was going to a fundraiser with his son, Scott, who was flying in from Portland, Oregon. He'd invited me to go, but I told him I would be in Canada. I'm pretty sure he wasn't too pleased. But I'd made the promise to Heather 11 months before when the idea of the fundraiser was percolating in her brain (before I even knew there was a Ron in the world). I had to keep my word. Ron found a date with a woman he enjoyed spending time with, so it all worked out.

# # #

Once we moved into our new house, Jonah wanted me to buy the biggest television ever made for the family room off the kitchen. UCSB was on the quarter system, and Jonah took summer quarters off. Student housing in Santa Barbara began in mid-September and ended in mid-June. It was nice having Jonah home during the months of the move-out and move-in period. I promised him we'd get that big television. So, on a warm August Sunday, we drove over to the Best Buy in Thousand Oaks to look at and purchase the biggest television made.

I had just pulled into the parking space, the engine still running, when Heather called. I clicked "accept" on my Bluetooth to take the call. Heather and I usually started our phone conversations with one of us saying, "Hey!" so that's what I did when I clicked "accept." Except, I didn't get the "Hey" back. Instead, I heard sniffles, and immediately I knew this wouldn't be a good call.

"What's wrong?" I said, "You sound like you're crying."

"I am. I've been crying all morning. Ryan called me. He walked out on Nancy. He said he couldn't take it anymore. He's found someone that he is in love with, and he rented his own apartment and everything. And now it's all a big mess!"

As Heather told me about Ryan, Nancy, and the details of Ryan's new love interest, my mind harkened back to a few years before. On Ryan's last residency weekend when he needed to finish the required hospital hours for him to complete his M.D., Nancy became critically ill and was in the hospital. Heather wanted to know if I could go watch the kids because she was snowed in, and her driveway was impassable. Not only that, but it would take hours to get from the Lakeside home to Toronto Airport. Time was of the essence. She didn't have to ask twice. Within the hour, I was on the road for the 6+ hour drive to Scottsdale.

I arrived in good time, sometime before midnight. Ryan was relieved to see me, as he could now finish his hospital requirements for his Residency. The weekend went quickly, with just a little bit of a hiccup in the form of the stomach flu for the youngest daughter. Later that night, I called Heather to tell her everything seemed to be under control.

Love And Other Goodbyes

Now, here I was a few years later, sitting in the Best Buy parking lot on that August day, trying to console my friend, realizing that I was doing a pretty miserable job of it at that. I kept telling Heather that it was for the best. If Ryan had no more love for Nancy, then the best thing for both of them would be for him to leave.

I told Heather that I felt Ryan *had* tried working things out with Nancy. I told her that lots of people divorce and it's not the end of the world. I was divorced! Life doesn't end with divorce. I told her that it's like an unscheduled right turn, which gets you a bit lost but you see new things you wouldn't have otherwise. All that fell on deaf ears. Heather's baseline for life was her absolutely perfect marriage to Bob. Heather couldn't wrap her mind around anything that was less than perfect. Messy wasn't part of her life.

After some time, I managed to talk Heather down. We talked some more about Ryan and Nancy, and I finally got Heather to realize that she wouldn't want Ryan to stay in a non-functioning marriage.

405

A few weeks later, I finally flew into Toronto to help Heather as planned, and what an experience that was. It was no surprise to me that the customs guy was a total jerk. He kept asking question upon question. I noticed other travelers being waived through after they presented their passports and immigration card. But not me.

The customs officer wanted to know precisely why I was in Canada. Why was I visiting my friend? How did I meet Heather Urich, to begin with? How long did I know Heather? Why was I staying at her house? How long did I intend to stay? (I showed him my return ticket, and he still asked me.) How much cash did I have on me? He got mad when I asked him if credit cards counted. All these intrusive questions while the clock was ticking. The plane was delayed, and we'd arrived late. I was becoming nervous that I'd miss my ride to Heather's. I told the customs officer that I'd prepaid a coach to take me into Picton, Ontario, a six-hour drive and it was leaving soon. It would be the last coach of the day so I couldn't miss it. That only got him angrier, and he began to ask me more questions just to irritate me, or at least that's what I thought.

# # #

During my whole life, customs agents the world over have picked me apart. In England, when I was just 19, agents pulled me at the gate just as I got off the plane. No one else had been pulled, and I was curious as to why I was singled out. I was escorted into a little room away from the rest of the terminal. Isolated. The room appeared to be some kind of police interrogation room, which was unsettling to a 19-year-old. I wasn't there for ten minutes when they came in with my luggage. I was on my way to Israel to see Yaniv. To my surprise, they opened my bags, pulling everything out piece by piece.

They took my toothpaste and opened the back end, squirting it into a container. They shredded my Tampax, patted me down in my crotch area, and examined the soles of my shoes. Every time I tried asking them why I was going through such a crazy search, they told me to be quiet or else. I chose quiet. "Or else" didn't sound like a good place to end up. I was with them in that room for more than an hour. Finally, they told me I could go. My belongings were absolutely everywhere, strewn about on the table, the chairs, and on the floor. I had a two-hour layover but still had to get to another terminal far away. I didn't have time to neatly repack, so I threw everything in my luggage, praying it would close, ran to recheck it, then sprinted to my gate, arriving just in time to board. I literally just made it. Oh, and the reason why I was detained and searched? I found out at the end that I fit the physical profile of a wanted terrorist. Interpol alerted the English authorities to the plane I was on, thinking I was that terrorist traveling under a fake name. Fun, huh?!

That wasn't the only time. Every time I'd land at LAX from abroad, before I could even get luggage, right at passport control, I'd feel a hand

Love And Other Goodbyes

on my shoulder. It was always a customs agent, and he'd accompany me to get my bag for a search.

Once, when I was coming back from China, where I'd been doing quality color control on bikes I'd designed, I was pulled out of the crowd. By then, I was used to this drill. This time, the customs agent really put the screws to me. He went through my luggage, finding nothing. I had a coat with me because it was winter, and it actually gets cold in China. The customs agent sliced open the lining of my coat with a knife. "What are you doing? That's an expensive coat," I blurted out without thinking.

"One more word out of you, and it's a strip search," was the response that came back. Not one more peep came out of my lips, that's for darn sure. The next day, I called my friend, a federal agent named Kent. I had been his witness in the big fraud case he had investigated and subsequently won at trial. "Hey Kent, can you do me a favor? Can you find out why I am always targeted in customs. It's getting pretty old. Yesterday they literally ripped out the lining of my coat!"

Kent laughed. "Of course, I'll find out for you. Give me a day or two."

Kent called me back the next day. "So, Suzie. I called my buddy in D.C. He's up at the very top in Customs. When I asked him why you were always targeted, he asked me to describe what you looked like. You know, I told him you were a cute, petite woman with long hair, and my buddy stopped me right there. 'No need to explain further,' my buddy said. 'Your friend fits the physical profile of a drug smuggler. A mule. That's why she's always stopped.'" Kent laughed when he told me this. "But my buddy said not to worry because one day you'll age out of that profile."

Well, I'm not so sure that's good news, but at least I had an answer. So, while I was getting the third degree from the Canadian customs agent, I thought, "I'm 66 years old, I haven't aged out yet, and I still fit that damn profile of a drug mule!!"

Three & Me

I arrived at Heather's more than seven hours after I landed. It took me longer to get to Heather's from the airport than it did for me to get to Canada from LAX. And the coach ride was right up there in price. Note to self: "Rent a damn car!"

Before I packed, I asked Heather about the type of clothing I should bring with me. "T-shirts, shorts, tennis shoes, bathing suit!" she said. August temperatures in Southern California vacillated between warm, to hot, to extremely hot, and I took Heather at her word. As soon as I stepped off the coach in Heather's driveway, I knew I was in trouble. It was freezing cold! Heather was up when I arrived after midnight. But then again, she was always up at that hour on East Coast time. She'd never really shifted from West Coast time, apparently. Or at least that was my theory.

We chatted for a while before I realized I was tired at around 3 a.m. Heather told me that another friend of hers was staying in the guest house on the property, a woman by the name of Sarah Boone. Heather said Sarah was rehearsing for a show in NYC in November and that Sarah's voice was to die for. She told me that Sarah would be doing her vocal exercises in the mornings and that we could hear her from the main house where I was staying.

My room was Ryan's old bedroom from when he was a kid. It was right across from Heather's. Heather showed me where the towels were, along with pillows and blankets. I quickly gathered the bedding, undressed, and was lights out within minutes, falling into a very deep sleep.

I wake up with daylight. It's one of the reasons I never get jetlag. When the light hit my window, I woke up. Heather was still asleep, so I pulled out my phone, opened my Kindle app, and began reading. It wasn't long before I could hear Sarah doing her voice exercises. Heather was right. That woman had an amazing voice.

I needed to go to the bathroom, so I threw the covers off, immediately feeling the chill of the cooler temperatures. Brrrrr! I made it down to the landing where the bathroom was, acutely aware that I needed warmer clothes. After I did my business, I ran back up to the room, grabbed a towel, all my toiletries, and ran back into the bathroom in the hopes that a nice hot shower would warm me up.

I know that a shower is a shower, but in today's world, a shower is an exercise in engineering. You practically have to have a degree to figure out most showers nowadays. What turns what on, how to aim, where is the spray regulator, and so on. I was standing in the shower stall trying to figure things out when I managed to hit the wrong thing and make a huge watery mess. Ugh. I finally got the shower to work right, but I couldn't figure out how to get the shower head to give me more of a stream. Heather was sleeping, so I made do with what I had.

After I was sufficiently clean, I pitter-pattered up the steps to where my suitcase was opened and looked at all the summery clothes I brought. Thankfully, I brought one pair of long jeans, but I needed warmer tops. I knew we'd have to go shopping to get supplies for the upcoming fundraiser picnic that Heather had planned for Sunday, so it would be an opportunity to find something warmer to wear.

Heather finally woke up, probably because she heard me in the hall-way. Once she showered and dressed, we went across the lawn to the guest house and got Sarah. Sarah was younger than us by at least a decade. I liked her on sight. First and foremost, she had an amazingly upbeat personality that shone through her big smile. She was outgoing and friendly, and I could tell she liked to laugh. She was on board to help with the fundraiser, also. Heather's daughter, Emily, and her husband, Steven, were also on board. We had a team! I was excited for Heather. It looked like another successful fundraiser in the making.

Before we went anywhere, we walked around Heather's property. To say it was absolutely gorgeous would be a great understatement.

Situated on the banks of West Lake in Ontario, Canada, the property had a private dock, a small boat, a main house, a guest house, and a guest apartment over the garage. There was a big fire pit between the main and guest house for nighttime bonfires. Besides dramatic views of the lake, one of the main features of the property was the park-like front lawn that went from the house all the way to the main road. It was absolutely huge. That's where Heather planned to put up a tent and hold a silent auction, have a dance floor, tables and chairs, and a stage for the band. Heather absolutely knew how to put on a party!

The three of us got into Heather's SUV and headed for the small town of Picton for lunch. Girls gotta eat! We went to a cute little restaurant, ordered a nice meal, and when the time came to pay, the owner told us he'd comped us because he held Heather and Bob in such high regard. We all appreciated the generosity and thanked him profusely.

I noticed a quick moment of sadness on Heather's face, the kind of sadness one gets when missing a loved one. I hadn't really thought about how hard this weekend might be for her but realized right then that it had to be tough. Not only was this weekend about Bob and cancer, but the Canada property was also Bob's refuge from the grueling days of series television. He would take breaks and come up to Canada to relax, fish, sit out by the pit, and enjoy doing nothing, usually surrounded by the sweet company of his family. If he was anything, Bob was a family man first and foremost!

Once I became aware of Heather's sadness, I couldn't let it go. I was picking up on little tells, the kind of things that would have gone unnoticed had I not been made acutely aware. She kept talking about Bob in Heaven and how she was beginning to feel lost without him. Life had little to no meaning suddenly. She said she dreamt of him often lately, and missing him was becoming more intense over time instead of less. I'll admit, I was getting concerned.

Love And Other Goodbyes

The mood picked up once we went shopping for clothes to keep yours truly warm. Heather took us all to a shopping mall and walked me into Eddie Bauer. Heather was wearing a zip-up sweatshirt with white piping. She'd gotten it at that store, so she walked me over to the area where they were displayed. I found one in a rust color and bought it. I just added another item to the wardrobe choices that we shared between us. I looked like a mini version of Heather, at least wardrobe-wise.

Parking for the event would be at the church across the street from Heather's property. Bob was buried in the small cemetery there. Before we'd gone to lunch, Heather walked us over to visit. He had a huge cross as a headstone, and I noticed that some of the letters were a bit weather-beaten. I silently hoped that no more erosion would take place and that the carvings would be visible for many, many years to come. I picked up a rock and placed it on his gravesite. Jewish people place stones instead of flowers on someone's headstone. It's to protect their souls from evil spirits. Flowers, although pretty, die off. I lowered my head and silently said a prayer for Bob before we left.

411

One of the items Heather needed to buy for the event was a sign with an arrow. She had an arrangement with the church that allowed for free parking. She wanted to have an arrow pointing in that direction so the attendees would know where to park their cars. Attendees would be mostly locals who would be driving their own vehicles. We went into Staples, looking for the perfect sign with an arrow. I quickly found a pretty good one with a space where we could add the word "PARKING" in big bold letters. I handed the arrow to Heather to get her opinion. "I like it, Suzie, but it's facing the wrong way," she said as she looked at it.

Sarah and I instantly burst out laughing. "Heather," I said between laughs, "Turn it upside down. You're holding it the wrong way!"

The three of us were laughing pretty hard by then. "You're holding it the wrong way" became our go-to phrase the entire weekend and beyond.

Three & Me

On top of the wrong-way arrow, we bought supplies to design and print out silent auction forms, donation forms, auction item tags, and other fundraiser communications. I was busy at work the rest of that afternoon, working my magic on the computer I brought with me. Heather was busy in the kitchen making what smelled like a spectacular dinner. We ate it outdoors on the patio, and it could not have been better! After dinner, we bathed ourselves in mosquito repellant and sat by the fire pit. It was such a welcome change from the hectic last two months of my life. I embraced the change of pace that this little slice of heaven in Canada was offering.

When the fire extinguished itself, Heather and I headed indoors into the main house, and Sarah went back to her guest house. She was working on her show, which was coming up in just a couple of months, and wanted time to rehearse.

Heather and I sat in the living room, watching television and talking. We were never at a lack for words; the conversation flowed quickly and easily between us. She was still obsessed with the separation and impending divorce of her son and his estranged wife, flashing anger with her soon-to-be ex-daughter-in-law from time to time. We talked mainly about the upcoming fundraiser and how happy she was to be doing it up in Canada instead of at some fancy restaurant with a rubber chicken for dinner. And, of course, we talked about Bob and how these next few days would be hard on her emotionally. I remember her telling me how much she missed being with Bob, even though he'd already been gone 15 years.

We found an oldies TV station and happily watched the Smothers Brothers. I'd forgotten how funny those two brothers were together. Tommy Smothers uttered my favorite line, "Mama always liked you best!" throwing me into a fit of laughter. When the program was over, and Heather and I had done a run-through of our favorite Smothers Brothers lines, I looked up at the clock. It was past midnight, so I decided I'd cash it in and go upstairs to bed. The way the house was laid

Love And Other Goodbyes

out, there were a few steps, then a landing with the bathroom. Then a left turn, up some more steps to the entrance to my bedroom just ahead on the right. It literally took a minute or two to reach my bedroom. I sat down on the bed to take my shoes off when I heard what sounded like someone vomiting. What?! Two minutes ago, I had left Heather on the couch, and she was fine. Good color, no complaints, and good cheer. Not a hint of nausea or feeling ill in any way. So, I figured my mind was playing tricks on me. Heather probably had swallowed wrong and was coughing from the small aspiration. Happens to me all the time.

I'd gotten both shoes off when Heather knocked at the open door and entered. "Want to hear something funny?" she asked me.

"Sure," I said, waiting for something funny.

"I just vomited a whole bunch!" she said rather lightly.

Well, that's not exactly funny, but I wasn't totally surprised because I heard her retching.

"So, how do you feel?" I asked her. She said she felt perfectly fine. I looked at her to see if she was pallid, sweaty, or had any other tell-tale signs of illness. I could find nary a one. "We all ate the same thing, so it can't be food poisoning," I said. Heather agreed. "So, what made you vomit so violently?"

"I have no idea," Heather said. "But it was projectile! I just opened my mouth, and out it flew!"

"But I left you sitting on the couch just minutes ago." I was perplexed.

"I know. I was totally fine. Then I got up to go to bed and walked by the toilet and threw up!" she said as if she had not a care in the world.

Three & Me

We both shrugged. "Well, as long as you feel good now, that's what's important. But if you start to feel sick, I'm right here. You can wake me up at any time. OK?"

I fell asleep, wondering what made Heather so sick. In the morning, I got up, pulled myself together, then went downstairs to continue my work on the event graphics. Heather woke up a bit later, and we walked over to collect Sarah. Heather was fine. There were no hints of her having been sick the night before.

Of course, we went to Picton to eat lunch! After walking through a few shops in Picton, Sarah found a second-hand store with (gasp!) a sweatshirt for just a couple of bucks. I quickly snapped it up, adding it to my "Let's keep Suzie warm" collection. While we were still at lunch, Sarah went to run an errand. While she was gone, Heather confided in me that she wanted to be with Bob sooner than later. "You're not thinking of doing anything stupid are you?" I asked, seriously concerned.

Heather vehemently shook her head. "Oh, gawd no!" she said. "Bob used to say that people who committed suicide pissed him off because they were wasting what he wanted more than anything but knew he could never have. I could never do that."

"Thank goodness!" I exhaled a huge sigh of relief!

After lunch, we went back to the house to label auction items and assign the silent auction sheets that I'd created to the corresponding items. Emily and her husband Steve, along with their daughters, came to help as well. We were a regular factory inside that lakeside cabin. Heather had done a wonderful job getting the auction items together, publicizing the event on local radio, in articles and ads in the local papers, as well as on posters in local businesses. I was impressed with how she pulled it all together these last few months. The stuff we were doing in the living room was basically tying all of Heather's efforts together in one big bow!

Love And Other Goodbyes

We worked feverishly all afternoon. Dinner was served at the indoor dining table. Little Allie, now a grown woman, showed up with her then-boyfriend (now husband). We had a very full table and a huge mess in the kitchen. After dinner, the bug spray came out. We all sprayed it on ourselves and went to sit by the fire for another night of camp-side fun. I was really enjoying sitting outside, watching the day turn into night, lit up by a bonfire. The lake was placid and beautiful and reflected the changing colors of the sunset. Paradise.

Again, when everyone went home, Heather and I sat on the couch talking. This time she asked me about Ron. I told her I had no idea what was happening with Ron. I couldn't read him. I was in love with him and had no idea at the time if he loved me. It turns out, though, that he did. I just kept missing the tells.

Heather could sense that I was conflicted when it came to Ron. After thinking about it for a minute, she told me not to overthink things. It would either work or it wouldn't. Solid advice. After chatting some more, Heather got up to go into the kitchen. She wanted to pour herself a glass of wine. Heather very much enjoyed a glass after dinner. It helped her relax. She was gone for a little while longer than I expected. As soon as I thought to get up and investigate what was taking so long, she walked in smiling and holding her glass of white wine.

She sat down on a chair next to the couch as if nothing had happened, completely unaware of the bloody footprints she had left behind. I looked at the top of her bare foot and saw quite a bit of blood oozing out. "Heather! What did you do?" I asked as I got up to find a bandage and clean up her bloody footprints.

Heather looked down in surprise. "I have no idea," she said. I jumped up and sprung into immediate action, cleaning up the blood she had left behind. Then went to sleep, worried and wondering just what was going on with Heather.

The following day was a copy of the day before. We worked feverishly preparing the auction items and tying up loose ends. The big tent was put up on the front lawn, rented tables and chairs were set up, and the mood at the house was festive. Even though we were working hard, we were all laughing and enjoying our time together. Sarah and I wouldn't let Heather forget the bit about the wrong-way arrow, pretty much beating it to death.

Emily and Steven came by to help out also. They owned a party rental business, and Steve was bringing a whole slew of fun things for kids and adults to do at the picnic. He went outside to scout where he would put his big inflatables and oversized games.

I was in the kitchen when he walked back in. He looked happy, and he gave me a hug. "I'm so glad you guys are here to be with Heather," he said. "I mean, I hate thinking of her up here all by herself for the entire summer. She's so frail lately."

That got my attention fast! "Huh? Heather? Frail?" I wasn't sure if Steve actually knew something or was just assuming that because she was 68 years old and he was so much younger, age and frailty went hand-in-hand.

"Well, yeah. She's been falling down, getting hurt, and I worry about her up here all alone. I hope you guys can make this a regular thing every summer. I was going to tell Heather that maybe she shouldn't spend all summer here by herself. You know, she should arrange friends' visits in a more condensed timeframe."

My brain was having a hard time wrapping itself around what Steve, Heather's loving son-in-law, was describing. Heather was a dynamo! I mean, all one had to do was look out the window to see what she was accomplishing! Frail? Oh my God, that would be the last word I would use to describe my buddy.

Love And Other Goodbyes

She was a dancer, for crying out loud. He mentioned falling; well, that could be explained. The cabin was a bit crowded, and it would be easy to trip, not to mention being outside at night in the dark. There were steps all over the place as well. Other than vomiting for no obvious reason and the cut on the top of her foot, she was pretty much the Heather I knew and loved.

Two days later, people came pouring in from all over the area to participate in the fun. There was a food vendor, band, music, dancing, silent auction, and plenty of fun things to do thanks to Emily and Steve's donation of activities from their party rental business. The weather didn't disappoint either. It looked like it was going to be a gorgeous day. The silent auction items attracted a lot of interest, and soon, there were bids on everything. I had my eye on *The Sound of Music Scrapbook,* a book containing memorabilia from each Sound of Music kid while filming the movie. The book was autographed by all of the "kids" in the movie. Even Charmian Carr, who had passed away 11 months prior, had autographed the inside cover. I wanted that book with a passion. I put a bid down, and when I checked I saw that someone else upped it. So, I upped that person's bid. And then that person upped my bid. This went on the entire time until at the very last minute, I put in the final bid and won the book. I was absolutely thrilled that I won. It's one of my most prized possessions. I had no idea at the time how precious it would become to me.

When Heather was still living in the Lake Sherwood house, she showed me the plans for the scrapbook. We sat at the table in the family room, and she pulled out all kinds of memorabilia from her days acting in the *Sound of Music.* She told me that all the other "kids" were putting together similar items from their time in the movie. As the book progressed, Heather showed me proofs and then, finally the finished product after publication. In a way, I felt like that book "grew up" right in front of me since I saw the very genesis of it in Heather's family room.

Three & Me

The next morning, the coach would be coming to pick me up for my flight to Minnesota. I had decided to make a detour in order to visit family. I really enjoyed the trip to Canada and felt I'd made a new friend in Sarah. Her performance was scheduled for November 6th, and I promised her I would fly to New York to see it. Heather was happy about that because it meant I'd stay with her during my visit. I was really sad to leave Heather and the peacefulness of the Lakehouse. Before I left, I had one more thing I needed to do. I called Emily. I just wanted to go on record about the vomiting and the bleeding foot and to let her know to keep her eyes open. She promised she would.

We all said our goodbyes, gave each other big hugs, patted ourselves on the back for a job well done, and wiped away tears. Heather told me that all the proceeds from the day before were going to the Robert Urich Foundation. She'd bankrolled the entire event, and not one dime would be used to pay for any of the fundraiser's expenses. Heather had a huge heart and a wonderful soul. Her mission was to raise as much money for cancer research and patient care as she could. No matter the financial burden she bore in order to do so, she wanted to fulfill her mission. Soon the coach arrived, and I was facing at least a five-hour ride to the Toronto airport. Sarah was smart and took the train. It took far less time and cost a whole lot less. Note to self: Next time, rent a damn car!

▼

I flew to Minnesota from Toronto through Newark. What a pain in the ass that was. It took forever! At last, I arrived, and my cousin, Mikey, and his husband, Morrie, picked me up at the airport. I would rent a car the next day to drive down to Rochester to see my mom's sister, my Aunt Bea. In the meantime, though, I enjoyed visiting with my cousins. Mikey and Morrie bought a beautiful home in the plush neighborhood of Edina, just outside the Twin Cities. Their backyard abutted a gorgeous natural river and was lush with the sounds of nature. The sounds of the rushing water from the river below did make me think of running to the bathroom, though.

Love And Other Goodbyes

My Minnesota visit was pretty brief. I crammed in as much as possible before I flew home. That was the visit where I told Aunt Bea to stop with the family hatred. It had been a success. I had garnered a more positive outlook from my mom's sibling; my work there was done. Aunt Bea passed not too long after that last visit, and I was grateful I took the time to drive down to Rochester.

Back at home, I had to rush around, trying to unpack more boxes, before leaving to visit Ron, at his invitation, in Park City. I wasn't looking forward to the visit, though. I had so much more work to do at home. At that time, I was doing some remodeling while also trying to unpack.

When Ron and I traveled together, we slept in the same bed. When I was in Park City, I was relegated to the furthest bedroom away from Ron at the opposite end of the house. The best guest bedroom was labeled "Bev's Room," and I didn't dare go in there. I ended up in the bedroom facing the driveway with basically no view. I'd get lonely in that room, and I missed my animals and my friends terribly. Ron had a philosophy that visits weren't much use if they were under ten days. So, I was looking at ten days in relative isolation.

A lovely woman named Shirley, whom he was also dating, had been there visiting right before me. Ron told me how absolutely every-one who met her loved her. His number two lady, Gail, sat next to Shirley on the plane to Burbank Airport at the end of Shirley's visit. Gail and her husband also have a home in the neighborhood where Ron lives. According to Ron, Gail loved Shirley, also. Naturally, the first thing I thought was, "Why the Hell am I here?" I already knew how much Ron's posse hated me, and now I knew how much they loved Shirley. Sigh.

Ron and I did have fun, though, once we were out of the house. He took me up to Mirror Lake, and we did a beautiful hike around that picture-perfect slice of nature. Mirror Lake is up in the Uintas,

Three & Me

a spectacular mountain range only accessible in the summer months. Ron was in his Drone Period. He loved playing with his drone, so we took it with us. He was able to get some nice shots from the drone near a waterfall, which was on the way up to Mirror Lake, but once we got to the lake, he found out quickly that no drones were allowed. That kind of put a pall on the rest of the afternoon. Ron is not one to accept denial easily. But we managed, or at least I managed, to have fun despite the no-drones-allowed policy.

We also went out to eat at nice places, hung out with his Utah friends (some of whom actually *did* like me), and basically tried to get to know each other. Ron wasn't big on me leaving any personal items in that room, so I'd have to pack up things like shampoos and other necessities that were a pain to travel with. I threw my stuff into a plain duffel bag, which I kept in the hall closet for my next visit. I had skis and ski boots in the garage, and I had a few pairs of long johns and a pair of ski pants that I kept in that duffel bag as well. I considered buying a mountain bike since there were so many beautiful trails near his house. Initially, Ron had been for it, but as time wore on, he tried to talk me out of it. Every time I brought it up, he would tell me to not waste my money. I saw that as another relationship red flag. He was afraid of me putting down roots in Park City at that time.

Once I returned from Utah and was back home, I made a big push to get all the construction work done as quickly as possible. I still had a mountain of boxes to go through, hardwood flooring to lay down, and travertine to replace the hardwood in the kitchen area. My closet needed work, as well as some modifications to new walls and built-in shelving.

Heather came into town from New York for the annual *Sound of Music Sing-Along* at the Hollywood Bowl. She called and said she wanted to come by to see my new house. She was staying in Studio City with one of her closest friends, Sue Mullen, and she wanted to bring Sue and another friend named Jodie over as well. I was also friends with the two ladies and was thrilled they'd be coming over. Heather suggested we all have lunch. She knew of my culinary skills, or lack thereof, in the kitchen, so suggested they bring lunch with them. I thought that was funny but practical! While my mom was a great cook, she never once thought of teaching me how to create meals. I had to learn on my own from friends, and it wasn't easy! And not effective. Remember, I'm the kind of person who eats to live and not the other way around.

A couple of hours after the call, they walked in with a beautiful Chinese Chicken salad and some side dishes. We all sat around my kitchen table, enjoying each other's company. As we were wrapping up lunch, Heather announced she had a housewarming gift for me. With an exaggerated, almost ceremonial gesture, she took it out of a bag and handed it to me. I could not stop laughing once I saw it. It was a wooden arrow painted blue with the words "Wrong Way" in dark pink script. A more perfect gift could not have been found. I immediately hung it up in my kitchen, where it remains today.

That day Heather looked great! She sounded great! And she was on top of her game! She was Heather, the way I always knew her. Heather had this positive energy about her that exploded into a room the minute she walked in. That September day in my kitchen, it was the same kind of energy. There was nothing frail about her. I surmised that she must have been fighting off a bug while in Canada, which seemed the most likely explanation for my concern.

Somewhere in the middle of lunch, Ron called me. He had just returned from a trip to Australia with his brother, Howie. Not one to sit around and gather any moss, Ron was planning a trip in a few weeks to Italy, as well as Paris, France, and ending in London, England. He wanted to know if I was interested in joining him. That invitation caught me by surprise, and the girls noticed I had a funny look on my face. "Yeah," I said to Ron. "It sounds fun." I then told him I had friends visiting and would have to call him back.

"Well, it looks like I'm going to Europe," I announced to the girls. Heather shot me a piercing glance. She knew how much of a roller coaster ride I'd been on in the last 11 months since I met Ron, but the other girls didn't. When she had a moment when no one was looking, she mouthed the words, "You need to call me!"

Heather had a busy schedule while in California. We didn't get to chat until she was back in the City. "So, it looks like things are progressing," she half asked, half stated.

"I think so," I said, mostly unsure. "Ron's kind of a tough cookie. One minute I think things are great; the next, I think they're not so great. I haven't figured him out yet, and I'm super afraid of getting hurt."

Heather listened as I went on and on about not really understanding Ron's sense of humor, my frustration with his wish list, and my inability to consume anything more than a little bit of wine, as well as being number three or four or five or wherever the hell I stood at the time. Heather laughed at that last comment. "Don't be surprised if you end up number one! When I spoke with him on the phone last week in the supermarket, he sounded really nice. Besides, he does keep coming back to calling you and inviting you to different countries, doesn't he?!"

She had me there. Ron didn't totally disappear, but he did appear to be waffling in interest. As to why he kept coming back, I wasn't really sure. He was pretty upset that his best friends didn't like me. And he was upset that I couldn't drink more wine. Not to mention, some of the things he put on his plate, like tongue and snails, grossed me out. (He even ate brains.) How was I ever going to hit the items on his list? I liked chicken everything, an occasional burger, and Italian, which was as exotic as I got.

A few weeks later, we landed in Paris and arrived at Ron's favorite hotel, the Park Hyatt, at the Vendome. I loved it the minute we walked in. I'm not sure if I loved it because it was such a great place, a fabulous location, or if I loved it because the possibility of a bed was looming just within reach. I'm pretty sure it was a little of both, and thankfully Ron was exhausted from the flight as well. We both fell into a deep sleep the minute we lay down. Heaven. There isn't one reason why people love Paris. I'd have to say there are many reasons. Even if one walks away thinking the people can be a bit *"froid"* (French for cold), the sights, sounds, and smells are definitely worth experiencing. When I lived in Israel, it didn't cost much to fly to Europe, which made traveling through Europe easily accessible. I would be in Paris many times in my 20s, and every time I came, I would rough it, staying in funky hotels or youth hostels on the Left Bank. I mainly subsisted on baguettes and cheese, capped off by a cup of tea. Admittedly, I didn't weigh very much after each trip, but it was worth it!

Being in Paris with Ron was a dream come true. I realized that I was an adult in Paris, far removed from the young lady in tattered jeans and a backpack. We were at a luxury hotel in a picturesque location, within walking distance to the Champs-Élysées as well as all the chic shops and eateries. Nothing better. Traveling with Ron is quite an experience. We both like to walk around each place we visit, independent of any tour guide. Time is ours, and we cherish the unscheduled freedom that time allows us. Some people like pre-planned tours, but we both like being immersed in the culture of each new place by doing things on our own. If all we do is go to a supermarket or a laundromat in some far-off country, well, that works for us. Walking the streets gives us insight into the way people live, shop and eat. It's quite wonderful, really.

From Paris, we flew to Milan, where we rented a car and drove the two or so hours to Alba, Italy. Alba is one of the white truffle capitals in the world. Before I visited Alba, I thought truffles were little chocolate goodies. Boy, was I wrong! Once in Alba, Ron exposed me to the delicate flavor of these little fungi, which are considered a true delicacy. I loved the scent and the way truffles interact with certain foods and wine (yes, wine!). And I love the fact that these little "rocks" from the ground are sniffed out either by dogs or pigs, two of my favorite critters.

Ron was friends with the innkeeper/owner where we stayed. It was a hotel of sorts but unconventional. The suites differed one from the other, and the inn was quite small and intimate. Our room was something to remember but for all the wrong reasons. A big tour came through and booked all the fabulous rooms. Ron and I got the leftover room; you could sit on the toilet and shower at the same time. The bed had to have been no more than six inches off the floor, with a mattress made of thin foam rubber. At least we had a view of the garden. We could watch old guys sitting on lawn chairs, speaking a variety of different languages.

At dinner with friends of Ron's who came from Germany on their annual truffle trip, the innkeeper brought out a white truffle to eat with our dinner. He announced that the small rock he was holding was worth $500. That got my attention! Truffles are not cheap, but they are delicious.

From Alba, Ron and I drove to Firenze (Florence). I'd been there many years before with my parents. Ron booked us a beautifully upgraded suite at the St. Regis Hotel, right on the scenic Arno River. From the balcony, we could see the famous Ponte Vecchio bridge. My mother had pronounced it incorrectly as the "pont-day-VEK-eeyo" I could clearly hear her as I stared out onto the bridge from my spot on the balcony.

From Italy, we flew to London to spend a few days there before returning to the United States. We stayed near the Marble Arch and St. James Park. It was cold in England at that time of year. The leaves had all fallen from the trees in the park, and the ground was barely visible. I wanted to visit Kensington Palace, where Princess Diana had lived post-Charles.

When we were in Paris, our hotel was very close to the Ritz Carleton, where Diana spent the last few hours of her life before that fateful drive into the tunnel. Ron and I decided to visit the hotel lobby and public areas downstairs and were wowed by the opulence of the décor. On one of our walks, we ended up at the tunnel where the princess lost her life. I will admit I was very sad when I was at that site. I sent up a little prayer for her soul as I watched cars enter and leave that very tunnel. Since we'd witnessed where Diana's life ended, I thought it would be more positive to see where she had lived.

London is a lot like New York City in so many ways, just with different weather and different English terms. There is an active theater district, just like Broadway, and you are never at a loss for a place to eat or to shop. A lot of the architecture reminds me of NYC also, along with the hustle and bustle of the City. There is a certain high energy emanating from London on the same level as New York.

We had dinner reservations at the oldest and most prestigious restaurant in London. I was excited and looked forward to going. When we arrived, I couldn't help but notice how stuffy the place was in the furnishings and attitude. It was completely overdone, in my opinion. But it was considered one of the best places, so I held my tongue and relaxed in the atmosphere of London. We ordered dinner, and Ron ordered the wine. This was where I told myself I would finish a glass of wine, come hell or high water.

About halfway through the wine, I started to feel dizzy, but I didn't want to say anything about it to Ron because I wanted to hit at least *that* on his wish list. So, I kept sipping, each sip adding to my discomfort and escalating instability, until finally, I had to stop. Ron was talking to me, but the room was spinning around, slowly at first, then gaining momentum. I closed my eyes to shut out the quickly blurring surroundings, but instead of seeing the room spin, I then felt it, the G-force holding me erect in my chair. Ron was still talking to me, and I had all I could do to nod and offer up some one-word

425

responses. I heard him ask the waiter for the check. I didn't know at that point whether or not I should be relieved or panicked, but I was too sick to even care. The last thing I wanted to do was vomit in a restaurant, so I did everything in my power not to.

Getting up out of the chair would prove to be one of the more difficult things I had to do on the trip. Somehow, I managed. When I took a few steps, I knew I would stumble, so I grabbed Ron's arm. "I'm so sick," I said to him. "I'm dizzy. ... I need to sit outside in the fresh air."

Thankfully, Ron guided me out of the restaurant, and I found a spot on the sidewalk and sat down, letting the cold fresh air heal me. I don't remember how long I sat there with my back against the building and Ron standing sentry nearby, but I could eventually stand up without feeling too terrible. We ordered an Uber back to the hotel. I remember that ride being sketchy, with nausea hitting at different points during the ride. When we got back to the hotel, I walked silently, in shame, into our room, angry with myself for not being able to finish a glass of wine and letting us both down in the process.

When our plane touched down at Los Angeles International Airport, Ron's driver, a nice guy named Mike, picked us up and drove us back to his house, where my car was parked in his garage. I placed my carry-on luggage in the trunk, kissed Ron goodbye, and drove home to Moorpark. There wasn't much to say at that point. Although we'd had a great time together, I was still stuck, not knowing where the relationship was headed.

Somewhere in the back of my mind, I started to think that he would make a nice friend, and so my behavior began to shift in that direction. My intuition was right on target. Ron had started a telephone relationship with the former college roommate of one of his friends who was also a neighbor. Amanda lived in New York City, was a few years younger than I was, and was very pretty with an upbeat, infectious personality. At that time, I didn't even know she existed.

Love And Other Goodbyes

The funny thing, though, is that Ron kept calling me, albeit much less frequently than before. We still had a connection, but I noticed him picking at things about me more and more. In hindsight, I hypothesized that this was because he couldn't quite put an end to us as a couple, so he used the little annoyances as fodder to help him get there. I recognized the methodology because it's one I employed when I didn't want to continue in a relationship, and I was too chicken to just say so, hoping my behavior would scare the person off.

# # #

In the meantime, I was looking forward to my trip to visit Heather in New York City and to hear Sarah sing! I was super excited about the upcoming trip and spoke with Heather regularly. This time I knew not to ask Heather about my wardrobe and was constantly checking the weather app on my phone to figure out what kind of clothes to bring. I figured it was safer that way. November should be a cold month in New York. For some reason, my weather app kept showing milder weather, so I brought a wardrobe that I could layer if it got colder and peel off if it got warmer.

Heather told me that we were also going to hear Linda sing. Linda Purl, a close friend of both Heather and Sarah and now mine as well, was going to be giving her own concert with Don Most of *Happy Days* fame. She told me to get a ticket quickly, which I did. Now I was going to two concerts by amazing women. I was stoked.

I arrived, finally, at Heather's apartment around 9:00 pm, on the night before Sarah's concert. Her roommate had gone to Los Angeles to attend a wedding and left his little dog, Patches, in Heather's care. She was pretty upset about that and felt imposed upon. She was also pretty much over Danny's residency in her apartment because, as she said, he just didn't pay but somehow found the money to fly to Los Angeles. That didn't sit well with her. She was also angry because little Patches was using the hallway as his personal bathroom, and she once slipped on his urine, which ended in a nasty fall. Heather told me she was very close to asking Danny to leave.

Patches needed to pee, and Heather was about to take him when I said, "I'm coming with you!" Being a dog mommy, walking a dog to do his business was not a big deal to me. I had mentally decided that while Danny was gone, I'd take over responsibility for little Patches, who, through no fault of his own, had become a nuisance to Heather. I grabbed his lead, and we all headed out the door.

Heather's building faced the Hudson River, and right across the street from her place was a greenbelt that stretched along the riverbanks. It was quite pretty, with mature trees, bushes, and a nice pedestrian path. Most of the dog owners on that street used that park to walk their fur babies, so there was a plethora of scents for Patches to experience on his walk.

Heather and I headed down the elevator. Once we reached the park across the street, we walked casually along the path. It was well-lit by street lamps, and I think there may have been a good moon that night because everything was visible, even at that late hour. As we walked and talked, Heather stumbled over an exposed root, and down she went. As I watched her go down, I noticed she didn't put her hands out to stop her fall. She fell flat on her face in a faceplant. I literally could not believe my eyes as my brain directed me to try and stop her fall. I jumped over her to the side she was facing to figure out if I should call 911 or not when she began to slowly sit up. Heather started laughing while I wondered if an ambulance should be called. Then she stood up. Blood came oozing out from a cut she sustained when her glasses cut the lower area of her eye. I picked her glasses up out of the dirt and noticed they were smashed. The frames looked OK, but the lenses were useless.

"Heather, you're bleeding from a cut under your eye. And it looks like you'll have a huge shiner in the morning. Let's go back upstairs and clean you up."

Love And Other Goodbyes

Heather agreed with one little protest. "What about Patches?"

"I'll come back down with him after we patch you up. C'mon, let's go."

We went back upstairs to her unit, and she told me where the items I would need to clean her wound could be found. Danny had put together a kit for when Heather fell down. Wait! WHAT?! *"Heather, what do you mean, Danny put together a kit?"*

"I've been falling down a lot," she stated very matter-of-factly. "There's been a lot of that."

"What do you mean you've been falling down a lot?!" My mind was racing to a place where I didn't want it to go. I was starting to think she was either an alcoholic or there was a neurological problem. Neither thought was a good one, and I immediately pushed those thoughts out, at least for the moment. The only thing I'd ever seen Heather drink was a glass or two of wine.

429

I cleaned and disinfected her wound while she sat on top of the toilet in Danny's bathroom. Then I got some ice, sticking it in a plastic bag. After I wrapped the bag in a towel, I went back into the bathroom and told Heather to hold it up against her eye so she wouldn't swell up. "I'm taking Patches back out," I told her. "Don't move until I get back." Heather nodded in compliance.

I went back down with Patches and walked over to the offending root. I decided I'd try to trip over it, closing my eyes as I walked. I did trip. But I didn't fall. So, I tried again, dragging my feet closer to the ground. I tripped again, propelling myself further, but I was able to catch my balance. I did this about five times, each with the same result. I didn't fall. Yes, I stumbled. But I didn't fall. What gnawed at me was the knowledge that Heather was a lifelong dancer. Her balance had to be perfect, yet she did a faceplant over that root. My "spider senses" were definitely tingling. I vowed to keep my eyes open.

After Patches had done his business and sniffed enough doggie scents, I returned upstairs and walked Heather to her room. "I think you should go lie down, watch some TV. Don't eat or drink anything in case you gave yourself a small concussion. If you need anything, scream. I'll hear you."

Heather agreed with a "Yes, Doctor!" which was kind of funny. Her son, Ryan, is now an Internist and an Infectious Disease Specialist, and her daughter Emily is a nurse. And here I was, dispensing medical advice.

Patches spent the night cuddled next to me in bed. Heather had turned her office into a spare bedroom, so that's where I stayed. The problem was a hot pipe running the length of the building from the bottom floor to the top floor, right through the little room I was in, making the heat unbearable for sleeping. Not only was it hot, but it kept making strange sounds as the heat wended its way through the old pipe. Needless to say, that first night offered me little in the way of sleep. Patches, however, slept just fine. I got out of bed several times to take him downstairs to the park to do his doggie business and to just cool off in the night air.

Heather was still asleep in her bedroom when I awoke and began to putter around the flat, showering, making the bed, and tending to Patches' dietary needs. I went into the living room and turned the television on, making sure to keep the volume low so as not to wake my friend. Heather woke up around 12.30 New York time and found me sitting on the couch with Patches at my feet. "Hey, I have a great idea," Heather said. "Let's go up to the Manhattan Diner for breakfast, and then let's go to the Metropolitan Museum of Art! We can cut through the park. And later, if there's time, let's take the Staten Island Ferry over to Staten Island!"

"That sounds great, but at some point, today, I want to buy a fan! That room is pretty hot at night!"

Love And Other Goodbyes

Heather laughed. "No problem. We'll go over to Best Buy."

After Heather was dressed, we began our walk up the hill toward the Manhattan Diner. I used to struggle to keep up with her on that hike up the hill, but this trip was different. Heather was slower. Either that or I was faster. I'd been working out quite a bit, doing a lot of hiking and biking, so I thought it might be me being more fit.

We had a wonderful meal at the Manhattan Grill, not so much because of the food, because it was more or less diner food, but I loved the conversation we had. When we sat down in our usual booth, she was back to being the ebullient, energetic person she's always been.

We cut through the park on our way to the museum, and I caught her making some funny poses near statues we passed along the way. Whenever we got together, the two of us behaved years younger than what our driver's licenses said. We were like two kids, goofing off, enjoying our lives, without a care in the world.

Once we made it to the museum, we walked through the Old Masters area, slowly taking in the beauty of the paintings. We'd found our way over to some Van Goghs when Heather turned to me suddenly. "We need to leave," she said with a great deal of urgency.

"Are you OK?" I asked. I had some concerns, but looking at her, I couldn't see anything wrong.

"I'm fine. Just tired. Museums do this to me. They make me tired."

I was confused. We'd only been there about 45 minutes, and I didn't quite understand what she meant when she said, "Museums make me tired."

Coming from Heather, that was an unexpected and seemingly off-the-wall comment. I surmised that maybe it had to do with the fall from

Three & Me

the night before. In any event, if she wasn't comfortable, then I didn't want to prolong our stay, so we left.

As we walked out of the museum and back towards the park, I tripped on a rock and flew forward, catching my balance so I didn't fall. I kept thinking about Heather's fall the night before. I still had no idea why she fell the way she did, which worried me. As predicted, she had a huge shiner. The glasses she broke were the only glasses she really liked to wear. We'd planned to get to an optometrist for new lenses and to get the frame repaired, but for now, she just wanted to go home to go back to sleep.

We made the long walk back to Heather's, but it seemed she felt much better once she was outside in the fresh air. We laughed and chatted the entire way back. We were both trying to figure out what to wear for Sarah's show, "Hollywood Blondes," later that evening. Mostly, though, Heather talked about the conflicts among some of the *Sound of Music* "kids." Politically, there was a divide among a few of the "kids," as well as discontent with Danny's handling of some of the business affairs. Danny had been hired to manage the group as well as to help with the writing and publishing of the *Scrapbook*. There were definite personality clashes between some of the "kids" and Danny. Heather was caught in the middle of it all, and she wasn't happy about it.

Additionally, she wanted Danny to move out. It was time. We talked again about the fact that Danny dumped Patches on Heather while he went off for a weekend in California. Heather contended, correctly, that he should have just hired a dog walker. In New York, there were professional dog walkers on almost every street corner. The fact that I was visiting, and taking over for her, was wonderful, but she was still angry with him.

We made it home without incident, and Heather retired to her room for her nap. I decided to take Patches out for a long walk

Love And Other Goodbyes

while Heather slept. Heather woke up about two hours later, and we walked back up the hill towards the subway on our way to Best Buy. Heather wanted to buy a small television for the wall in the guest room/office, and I wanted a fan! The walk up the hill was a non-event, but once we got to the subway station and began to descend the stairs to the trains, Heather suddenly froze behind me. "Suzie," she said with a panicky voice. "I can't get down the stairs. I can't feel my feet!"

I looked up at Heather. Now I was concerned, but I didn't want to worry her. "OK, let's do this together. Grab the rail and face the wall. OK. Good. Put one foot down, sideways, toe pointing towards the wall. Keep holding the handrail. That way, if you fall, you fall towards the wall and not down the stairs."

Heather did as she was told, slowly, painstakingly, taking each step one at a time. "I'm right here for you, right below. I can break any fall … There you go. You're doing it. We're almost down." Heather took the last step and let out a huge sigh of relief. The panic was gone. She was back to herself once again.

We arrived at Best Buy without further incident, and Heather was back in her usual cheery mood. She got her TV. I got my fan. But before we left, I suggested we take an Uber instead of the subway for the ride home. Heather quickly agreed. As soon as we closed the front door and were inside her apartment, I thought it was time to pepper her with questions. "Heather," I began, "When was the last time you saw a doctor?"

Heather thought about it for a few moments, then told me it was probably about a year ago. There was something in the way she said it that made me think it was much longer than that. So, I pushed back a little. "I want you to make an appointment to see your doctor! Like, call him tomorrow if you can't do it right this minute."

"Suzie, I'm fine. I'm really OK." I wasn't buying it.

Three & Me

I had a sinking feeling in my stomach and wanted her to get a physical. She was pushing back, telling me she'd do it after the first of the year. That wasn't good enough for me. I made her sit on the couch in the living room, and I called Ron. Ron is a retired physician, and I figured he could talk to Heather about the importance of getting to a doctor sooner rather than later.

I called Ron and told him about some of the things I witnessed in New York. I also brought up the vomiting in Canada as well as the foot injury. While I had a bad feeling about everything, up until that point, it was just that. A bad feeling. It could easily have been my imagination running away with me. That is until Ron actually verbalized my worst fears. "Suzie, tell Heather that she needs to go see a doctor right away to at least rule out the possibility of a brain tumor."

With that one sentence, things got real. I turned and looked at my friend, who was sitting next to me on the couch, and my heart sank. I had a sick feeling in my gut that the brain tumor wouldn't be ruled out, but hope springs eternal, doesn't it? I was hoping upon hope that maybe she drank too much wine, and that would be the source of her problems—an easier thing to fix. But first, I had to get her to a doctor for a physical, and the rest would take care of itself. Or so I hoped.

"Ron, will you talk to Heather? She's sitting right here." Before he could respond, I passed the phone to Heather. I don't know what Ron said to her, but she actually did call her doctor and set up an appointment for the Monday after Thanksgiving weekend, some three weeks away. I was happy but disappointed at the same time. There were no appointments available before that, and I worried that she might try and back out of it since it was far enough away to ignore.

After yet another nap for Heather, we went to see Sarah's show that evening. Sarah knocked it out of the park. She was spectacular. THAT VOICE! The show itself was so well orchestrated—her choice of songs, the scripted conversation between songs, the music, the lighting, and even her gown were all fabulous. She absolutely looked like a "Hollywood Blonde" from the old movie studio days. When the show was over, we all went out to celebrate. Heather seemed fine; she seemed to be enjoying herself the way everyone else was, without any hint of sickness or weakness. I was beginning to convince myself that the odd things going on with Heather had to do with a bit too much wine or something equally innocuous. I wanted to believe it so badly!

When we returned to her place, I immediately took Patches out to do his business for the night. I refused to let Heather outside, telling her that I could handle it on my own. Danny was due back the next day, and the responsibility for Patches would be his.

The following day, Heather declared that she wanted to do a Zumba class at the Alvin Ailey dance studio. I instantly grew wide-eyed. In my entire life, I'd never Zumba'd, was never once a studio dancer, and I knew Heather had been doing dance her entire life. Ugh. I forgot for a moment that just a couple of days before, she couldn't get down the steps to the subway without my help. I was in a slight panic about Zumba. "Heather, I'm going to totally suck at this!" I told her. "If we go, I'm going to stand way, way, way in the back so no one sees your dumb friend. I don't want to embarrass you!"

Heather laughed and told me I'd be just fine. So off we went, dressed for Zumba. I was nervous when I walked through the doors of the expansive dance building. It was modern, and it was absolutely huge. I signed up for the class, paid the nominal fee, and walked into a room that was clearly a dance studio with wall-to-wall mirrors and beautifully polished blond wood floors. I took my spot towards the back, as I said I would. Heather was in my sight line, so I was able to watch her do her stretching exercises. I tried to emulate what she was doing, but I couldn't really keep up with her movements, so I improvised my own stretches. The young and very fit Zumba lady walked in, started the music, got in front of the group of women, and began to call

Three & Me

out the Zumba moves. Somehow, miraculously, I caught on quickly, my brain and muscles remembering the 1980's aerobics classes I had taken regularly. I was starting to have a lot of fun when I looked over at Heather, expecting to see her throwing everything she had into the movements.

Instead, I saw my friend flailing around, falling behind in the movements, pausing intermittently, with a look of confusion on her face. Then she'd try to rejoin the rest of the group.

She was not doing what I expected her to do. I expected her to excel in the class with all of her dance experience behind her. Heather was unable to do any of the moves that required balance or effort. My heart sank. At the break, I walked up to her and told her how terrible I was doing and what a klutz I was, but I told her I was happy she made me come. She smiled warmly, without any betrayal of her own difficulties with coordination during the session. I didn't want her to feel bad about herself, so I told her I would be returning to the back so as not to embarrass her too much. My real goal, however, was to keep an eye on her.

When the second half of the class picked back up, I watched Heather, all the while praying she would be OK. I hoped she would make it through without falling, which she thankfully did. But the second half was a copy of the first. Heather couldn't do more than 50% of the moves, and the movements she made were out of sync with the rest of the group. I saw the Zumba lady look over at Heather with some concern as well, and I had a feeling that she purposely slowed the beat down to allow Heather to catch up. Heather never did catch up, though. She'd stop and just stand still for a bit, catch her breath, then try once more to sync her movements with the group.

Finally, and mercifully, the class was over. When I walked over to Heather, she grabbed my arm, walked me over to the Zumba lady, and introduced me as her close friend from L.A. The Zumba lady was very warm and welcoming, then turned to Heather and asked how

Love And Other Goodbyes

she was feeling. "I'm a bit tired," was all Heather said. "I didn't sleep well last night."

The Zumba lady nodded, appearing satisfied with Heather's response. However, I had a massive tornado churning in my brain, worried sick about my friend. I kept wondering if I should call Ryan or Emily about my concerns. I remembered calling Tony Bronson about Charlie's huge memory lapse and being brushed off. I did have a penchant for defaulting to the worst possible scenario. Remembering that, I didn't want to scare them. I reasoned she had a doctor's appointment coming up soon, and then we would all know what was what.

After Zumba, Heather wanted to eat. She was ravenous. We found a cute little hole-in-the-wall pizza place near the studio and split a pie. She was back to being Heather again, full of bubbly energy, with a spring in her step, and a take-no-prisoners attitude.

When we got back to the flat, Danny was already there. Heather was nice to him, but I noticed a change in her attitude, which I don't think he picked up on. Again, I was privy to her disenchantment with him, and I could read the slight chill she was giving off.

We all went to our separate spaces within the apartment. I plopped down on the bed, turned the fan on against the heat of that pipe, and read a book on my iPad. About an hour later, it was time to get ready for Linda's show. I showered in the hallway bathroom, probably to Danny's chagrin.

Linda Purl gave a beautiful concert with Donny Most. Her voice is very comforting. I felt like I was floating on a cloud while listening to her. Donny was charismatic, and the banter between the two of them was absolutely fabulous. They have great chemistry on stage. I'd never met Linda before, having only heard about her from Heather and Sarah, but I thought she was the bomb! I absolutely loved being there, listening to her sing her heart out.

Three & Me

After the concert, it was time to celebrate. As a group, we all went out to a Chinese restaurant somewhere near the Triad Theater. It was a great last night for me to be in the City. I really liked all of Heather's friends, except for Danny, whom I didn't like from the time back in LA when we worked together on Heather's fundraisers. The chemistry just wasn't there, but the unspoken competition between us was.

After our night out, Heather and I arrived back at her place with an unexpected greeting. Danny was standing in the hallway outside the small kitchen with a young guy. "Great news, Heather! Tommy's here!" he exclaimed quite happily.

We both looked at Tommy. He looked barely 18. Danny looked old enough to be his father! Heather and I looked at each other, said a polite hello to Tommy, and quickly walked into the living room.

"Who the Hell is Tommy?" Heather asked rhetorically. "What the fuck!"

"He looks so young!" I exclaimed. "Seriously, what the fuck, is right!"

I could see Heather simmering. She was pissed. This was *HER* place. *SHE* paid six grand a month for the apartment. According to Heather, Danny paid zero most of the time. He never asked her permission if he could have a sleepover, especially while she had a friend visiting from out of town. It would make for very cramped quarters having him here. She was raging mad. "I'm kicking him out! I've had it with him. I'm so sick of this shit!" she exclaimed, maybe a little too loudly. But Danny never heard a word, or at least he didn't behave like he had heard her.

The next day, we tried to make the trip to Staten Island but got waylaid. Sarah was leaving in the late morning. We both wanted to spend time with her before she returned to Florida, so we changed plans. We invited Sarah to join us at the Manhattan Grill for a bite.

After lunch, we said our goodbyes, but not before we took selfies! I would be leaving a few hours later, which made me sad. Heather and I went for another walk, where the conversation centered on Danny and Tommy. She was still venting about Danny bringing Tommy home with him. Thankfully, both Tommy and Danny left early in the morning. Heather would not have to deal with yet another body crowding the space in her home.

When it was time for me to catch my Uber to the airport, Heather and I stood by the front door, where I hung up "my" set of keys to the apartment. We gave each other hugs when Heather's eyes welled up in tears. "Suzie, I want you to move here. We can share the apartment. Will you think about it?"

I wasn't expecting that, as moving to New York had never occurred to me. "Wow!" I said in response, "I never thought about that."

"I love my life here, Suzie. You met my friends. Look at how much fun I'm having. I absolutely LOVE MY LIFE! Move here! Even if it's part-time. We can work something out."

"Let me think on it. I like the idea of part-time. I'm sure I can figure it out!" Heather was thrilled. And I had a new idea in my head. I did love the lifestyle New York had to offer, and I could see myself living part-time in that apartment. I just needed to figure out where my life was headed because, from where I was standing, I had absolutely no clue where it was going. This was a new possible direction that I'd not thought of before.

I knew the way Heather's mind worked. I surmised that if she could tell Danny that I would be moving in and actually paying her rent, he'd have to give up his room. This could go two ways. Either he'd have to leave, or he'd have to move to the small room with the hot and noisy pipe. I wondered if this was a passive-aggressive way on Heather's part to deal with the problem. Was this her way of getting the best result out of the lousy situation she was in with a roommate that she claimed had overstayed his welcome? Having a good friend move in, in his stead, made perfectly good sense. I could see the twinkle in her eye as we discussed my moving to NYC.

"Good!" she exclaimed happily. "I also want you to come back for Thanksgiving, OK?! There's one place left at the table, and it's for you!" Heather was absolutely adamant that I come to visit over the holiday. I really wanted to, especially since I could go with her to her doctor's appointment or, more importantly, make sure that she actually went!

"Yeah. I'll come. I'll book my reservation as soon as I get home." She seemed pleased that I said I'd be there. I was actually pleased about that myself. With that, we gave each other one last hug, and I was out the door to begin my journey home.

# # #

Jonah's birth mother, Rachelle, and her then six-year-old son, Carmelo, Jonah's half-brother, left Missouri in the fall because of a domestic situation with Carmelo's birth father. She, and the little one, were staying in my guest bedroom. I adore Rachelle and admire the way she faces adversity, something she has faced her entire life. She's a survivor of many bad people, as well as horrible circumstances, but she still holds her head high. I respect her enormously. The thing I admire most about her is her humanity. She's got a great heart. There is no one sweeter than Rachelle. (And I wish she knew that.)

She was trying to rebuild her life in California, which is pretty hard to do. Housing was expensive, jobs in her field were scarce, and one needed a car to survive. When she left Missouri, she didn't have much money and spent most of it on a car that broke down during the road trip to California. After buying another car, she arrived at my place with barely any money in hand. I was worried about her,

Love And Other Goodbyes

but she managed to find jobs quickly. They weren't in her field of quality control, but they were jobs. In my mind, I compared her to Danny. Rachelle wasn't snooty about working. She took the jobs that would put food on the table and clothes on Carmelo's back. Danny, it seemed, was happy to do nothing below his station. But in all honestly, I could only go on information Heather fed me. He could have been working at a lower-level job making money and I would have never known.

Ron was in Park City when I got back to Los Angeles but was planning on being in his Tarzana house closer to the Thanksgiving holiday. He still called me and told me about plans to visit New York in December. He was going to go for two weeks. The first week, he'd be with Bev, his friend, and assistant, who would also be staying with him. They had meetings set up that she needed to attend because she was an integral part of his finances. The second week, he'd have a friend come in to stay with him as well. At that time, Ron always got an upgrade at the Sheraton at Times Square. He'd have a conventional room, which opened up to a living room with a Murphy bed, so it could also be used as a second bedroom. When he said he had a friend, I thought he meant his childhood friend, Harriet. I never questioned him about it, though. It was none of my business.

I went online and tried to get flight reservations to New York for the Thanksgiving holiday. It was two and a half weeks out from that weekend, and there were no flights available for under a small fortune each way. That was a shocker. I suppose I could have gotten cheaper flights by crisscrossing the country with long layovers, but that seemed like a big IF. I even thought of using my United miles to get to New York City, but I didn't have enough to cover the trip because a bunch had expired. (I hate when that happens.) I finally had to realize that the fares were too rich for my blood.

With great disappointment, I called Heather to tell her I couldn't come. She sounded distant, almost as if she was having a hard time comprehending what I was saying. I figured she'd had too much wine and let it go. She didn't sound disappointed either, which puzzled me, because she was so adamant that I come just the day before. When I was in New York, we were sitting around her dining room table looking at some mementos from her *Sound of Music* days as well as a painting that her father had made of her when she was a little girl. She sounded so very proud as she displayed these items. Then we got to talking about her being honored in Park City, Utah, at the Eccles Center. The Eccles Center is the result of the Robert Urich Celebrity Ski Weekend. Funds raised were used to erect a performing arts center. Heather had been approached by the Eccles Foundation, asking her if the project needed a million dollars. Heather was thrilled.

This offer was made 27 years prior, and that million dollars would be worth closer to about ten million or more in today's dollars. In exchange for the donation, the Eccles Foundation wanted to have the cultural center named The George S. and Dolores Doré Eccles Center for the Performing Arts rather than The Robert Urich Performing Arts Center. It was not a problem because Heather and Bob got the small town of Park City their performing arts center! It was the 25th anniversary of the Center, and Heather was being honored on January 9th, 2018, at the theater she helped create. A video was made, and she would be addressing the audience afterward. She was looking forward to it and wanted to ensure I'd be there. She was going to arrange for my tickets to the event so that I could sit up close to the stage.

During that same phone conversation with Heather about Thanksgiving, I asked about how I would get my tickets to the event, but she was in a state of confusion, and it took several times repeating myself before I was able to get her to even remember the celebration at the Eccles Theater. Again, she sounded far off and distant.

The next morning, I called Heather around 10:00 am LA time, which would be 1:00 pm New York time. Heather was a bit more lucid but still showed signs of confusion. She did remember Eccles, and she did show some disappointment that I couldn't come for Thanksgiving. I

Love And Other Goodbyes

told her Ron had invited me to stay with him in January for the event, and she sounded pretty pleased about that.

Because Rachelle and Carmelo were staying with me, Jonah was coming home from UC Santa Barbara for Thanksgiving. I knew Ron would be in town, so I invited him to come over for dinner as well. He accepted. Rachelle and I worked on the turkey, but it was Rachelle's culinary skills that really helped pull the meal off. I have yet to make a good bird, but because of Rachelle, it came out beautifully. Jonah, Yaniv, Ron, Rachelle, Carmelo, and I found our places around the table. The table was set beautifully, and we all had a wonderful time. Carmelo was, of course, the center of attention. How could he not be? He was incredibly cute and precocious, with a sharp wit and an adorable smile. He reminded me so much of Jonah when Jonah was that age. Ron appeared to be enjoying himself at dinner, and when he left to go home, he said as much. I noticed, though, that he was cooler, but I wasn't sure if it was because Yaniv, Jonah, and Rachelle were around or if it was something else.

443

Late at night on the Saturday after the holiday, I got a call from Sarah. Sarah is one of those people whom I could sit in a room with and spontaneously burst out laughing over absolutely nothing. And it would be a really good belly laugh, to boot. She is always upbeat and cheery. When I answered the phone, she sounded anything but that, which was worrisome. "Suzie, Heather is in the hospital," she began. "You know I'm staying with her, right?"

My heart started pounding, and my head began to go cloudy. "How is she?" I asked.

"Well, they are doing tests." My heart jumped. "Suzie, it was terrible. Yesterday, we all went to a show and a restaurant, and Heather was stumbling so badly they wouldn't let her in. I knew something was wrong at Thanksgiving dinner because she was already having difficulty walking and needed to lean on my arm a lot!

"Then today, I had to go out and visit friends, and when I got back, Heather had already called Ryan and the paramedics. I just got back to the apartment from the hospital."

I listened intently, my mind racing; all I could think was FUCK, FUCK, FUCK! I glanced over at my clock. I was in bed watching TV when Sarah called. I was surprised as well as panicked by the late-night phone call. It was 11:00 pm my time, so it had to be 2:00 am New York time. Late-night phone calls are never ever good. I thought of the phone call the night Jonah crashed his car on the freeway when he was drunk, and the dread came rushing back. Also, I felt horrible for Sarah. Talk about a trip to the City going awry. This was the epitome of that!

I later learned from Ryan that Heather had called him at some point during the day. She was experiencing a bad case of vertigo, too dizzy to get out of bed, and described to him how fast the room was spinning. Ryan told her to call 911 and get to a hospital immediately. Heather didn't pay much mind to that directive, though. When Ryan called her cell phone a couple of hours later to find out what hospital she was in, she told him that she was still in bed. Ryan then went postal on his mom. "Either you call 911 right now, or I'm calling 911! Either way, you're going to the hospital!" Heather called.

I prayed that the doctors wouldn't find something seriously wrong. Sadly, sometimes prayers don't work.

On Sunday, I woke up worried about Heather. I'd had a fitful sleep the entire night. Too many thoughts were swirling around in my head. I'd seen too many strange things since August. The only thing I could do was get her to book a doctor's appointment for the Monday after Thanksgiving, which was one day away. She didn't even make it to her appointment. Could I have done more? I wondered about that for hours. I was in a definite funk.

Love And Other Goodbyes

Just before noon, I decided to go to El Pollo Loco to grab something to eat. There was one in Moorpark close to my house. I badly needed some comfort food, and a cheese burrito sounded like just the medication I needed. After quickly downing the burrito, I found myself in the parking lot, about to get into my car when my phone rang. I looked at the caller ID, and it was Emily, Heather's daughter. I closed my eyes and took a deep breath, expecting the worst and hoping for the best. But I knew there'd be no best because if there was, Emily wouldn't be calling me.

"Hi, Em!" I said as I answered the phone, the dread welling up inside of me, betraying my emotion. "What's going on?"

"Suzie, my mom was just diagnosed with glioblastoma." I froze instantly where I stood. I couldn't think. I couldn't speak. I almost couldn't stand. Somehow, I found my tongue. I had secretly been praying the symptoms were from too much wine. I remembered how dizzy and horrible I felt in England when I had just sipped half a glass. No such luck.

"So, what's going to happen now?" I asked, clearly distraught.

"They are going to biopsy to make sure." I listened to the strength in Emily's voice and had so much respect for her. This was her mom we were talking about. And yet she had the presence of mind to phone Heather's friends in the face of this terrible situation.

After a few more short comments, we hung up so she could continue making calls and arrange travel from Canada to New York City. I stood in place, still frozen by the news. I'd lost too many best friends in my lifetime, and now I faced the reality that Heather, the friend and confidante I had for the last 31 years, my buddy, my sidekick, was gravely ill. The tears flew out of my eyes. I couldn't get in my car and drive. I've had these tears before. I recognized the wracking sobs from when Jerry died, the tears blurring my vision to such a degree that I felt submerged under water. I walked around the parking lot, avoiding people and cars, all the while sobbing my heart out.

When my emotions finally settled down enough, I called Ron and told him about Heather. He was at home in Tarzana and immediately told me he would meet me at my house. There was something in his voice that comforted me, something I hadn't recognized since that wonderful first night we met. Did I sense love? His voice blanketed me with comfort, and it was as if he were already wrapping his arms around me. I had pulled back so far from him afraid I'd get hurt. Was it possible I had missed his love for me?

I tried to pull myself together enough to drive home without getting killed. I still cried softly in the car, because no matter how hard I tried, my eyes just would not cooperate and dry up. When I got home, I called Heather. I figured she'd answer the phone if she felt up to it or let it go to voicemail if she didn't. Surprisingly, she answered. "Heather, what kind of a mess did you get yourself into?" I asked, trying to be as lighthearted as I could.

"This one's a beauty, isn't it?!" she answered, trying to emulate my upbeat tone.

"How are you?" I asked.

"I'm not doing too good. I've been given medication for the dizziness, though, and I'm going in for a biopsy."

"Hey, I'll come visit when it's OK for you to have visitors. Just let me know."

Heather sounded happy. "I'll let you know. I like that."

Danny must have been standing near Heather when I called. He was very controlling with her, inflating his importance in her life. If he only knew he was about two seconds away from being evicted, maybe he wouldn't have been so obtrusive. But he didn't. And he was.

Danny immediately called one of Heather's lifelong best friends. She was going to fly out the next day to visit. She then phoned me and told me that Danny told her to tell me that Heather didn't want me coming out. "WTF!" I thought. I just hung up with her. I had no reason to disbelieve the woman calling me, but I definitely had reason to suspect Danny. I would take a wait-and-see approach. I knew that Emily, Ryan, and possibly Allie, were all flying out to see Heather. I figured I'd go the week after when the first wave had left. I could happily be in the second wave. I booked a room in a hotel for that second week, then bought my plane tickets. I was set. My attitude was basically, "Fuck Danny!"

Ron finally arrived on my doorstep, and I literally jumped into his arms for a long and much-needed hug. Usually, when I'm deeply upset, I'd find a way to go ride my horse, to be outside, to feel the wind on my face. I have always sought ways to feel a pulsation of life, to fully appreciate being alive. Instead, I had called Ron because intuitively, I knew he could help to put salve on my inner pain. I still craved the wind on my face and the outdoors, so I asked him if we could take one of my dogs, a little cattle dog mix named Rosie, for a hike in the Santa Monica Mountains.

Standing in the restaurant parking lot after hearing the devastating news about Heather, I looked up at the blue sky above. Why, on the most beautiful days, would I get the most horrible news? Just like the day my brother was killed the sky above was so obnoxiously unaware of the sadness in my heart. It thumbed its bright blue nose in my face. By the time Ron and I arrived at the trailhead to Sycamore Canyon, it was late afternoon, and the sky had turned gray. I looked up at the darkening clouds and felt that this was a much more appropriate response by Mother Nature.

Three & Me

Ron, Rosie, and I had a nice walk on steep hills and down steeper hills. Ron had to pick up Rosie for some of the uphill climbs because her little legs got tired. We kept the conversation light, and I appreciated him being with me. The hike, while shrouded in sadness, was doing its thing for my emotional state. Having Ron by my side, for some inexplicable reason, gave me a sense of grounding and security. But as usual, our signals misfired. Here he was, my Knight in Shining Armor, my rock and my protector, but his mind and focus were already on the new lady he'd found in his life. I just didn't know it then.

When it got too dark to hike, Ron took me to a restaurant in Thousand Oaks that allowed us to bring Rosie into their patio. While at dinner, I spoke with Ryan. He was flying out to see his mom the next day. He explained glioblastoma to me in a way I'll never forget, sending chills up and down my spine. "Suzie, a glioblastoma is the honey badger of all brain cancers. It's vicious." After I hung up with Ryan, I just stared at my gourmet mac 'n cheese dish for what seemed a long time but was really only minutes. I couldn't get those words out of my head. I told Ron what Ryan said, and he concurred. Great. Now two physicians were implying that my friend probably had a zero chance to survive, and one of those two physicians was her son.

Sometimes my mind refuses to believe the obvious. This was one of those times. I had to acknowledge that Heather was gravely ill with an insidious brain cancer. Except I didn't. I figured there were therapeutics and chemotherapies which could prolong her life. Hopefully, she'd outlive her cancer. I was hoping she'd have, at the very least a few years left. Stubbornly, I was already planning to take her up on her offer to move to New York and spend at least two weeks a month with her. I knew her other friends would also want to take shifts. I thought that with our team effort, we could make Heather's time on this side of the soil good time.

Despite Ryan's description, I really didn't understand just how bad glioblastoma really was. I was completely naïve in making mental plans to help my friend survive. After all, I'd done that with Jill, traveling with her to her doctors and hospitals. I was seasoned, broken in by the experience of helping Jill during both her bouts with cancer, and I could put those experiences to work helping Heather. I kept making plans on how to help my friend escape glioblastoma.

Unfortunately, Ryan was right. Glioblastoma is the honey badger of cancers. At the time, I didn't know that Heather's tumor was dead smack in the center of her brain and was inoperable. I also didn't realize how quickly glioblastomas grew. Beau Biden, President Joe Biden's son, died from glioblastoma. John McCain died from a glioblastoma as well. As did Senator Ted Kennedy.

I began researching this horrible nemesis that was trying to kill my friend. Usually found in older men, but not limited to that demographic, glioblastomas grow exponentially. Which means that every single day they double in size. That's a lot of growth in a short period of time. If I were to count the days from when Heather began showing symptoms in Canada, there were about 80 or so days between my time in Canada and Thanksgiving. That alone is enough to give this horrible monster plenty of time to become a big problem. Who knew when her disease actually began? Steve, her son-in-law, knew something was wrong when I was in Canada. He was right when he told me she was frail and shouldn't be left alone, only I just didn't see that frailty at the time. I wish I had. From all the research I did on glioblastoma, I learned that the maximum survival time was 18 months with surgery and chemotherapy. Without surgery and chemo, the expected survival time was 10 days to just a few weeks tops. Shit.

Heather was a shining light within a lovely circle of friends. Each one was a special kind of someone. Over the years, I'd met the people special to her, and except for Danny, there wasn't one person I could find fault with for any reason. Every one of Heather's true friends loved her for her and not for what she could do for them. And she loved each of her friends equally and wholeheartedly. Once she got sick, the circle tightened around her, like wagon trains did in the old West, creating a circle to protect against outside enemies. We all became part of a circle of light around Heather. Soon an email chain was created. Her friends who lived in New York, like Judy Rice, herself just emerging from a cancer battle, and Linda Purl, became our lifeline to Heather's situation. We didn't need to bother Heather because these lovely ladies would send daily reports to keep us informed., each of us sitting on pins and needles until we got that much-awaited email.

I was lucky that Ryan was constantly communicating with me, giving me more insight into what was happening with Heather. I made sure to share this information with the others in the email chain. Ryan, because he is a physician, was able to talk doctor-to-doctor about Heather's care, prognosis, and planned therapies. It was very helpful during those dark times. He got the skinny that we couldn't get as laypeople.

From the conversations I had with Ron, I knew he would be in the City at the same time I was and I didn't want him to think that I was following him, or in any way trying to worm my way into his trip. I booked a hotel room near Penn Station. It wasn't luxury, but it wasn't bad either. Having a kid who was an athlete that swam club and played travel ball, Jonah and I were used to clean but basic hotel accommodations. The hotel was no big thing to me. It was a clean bed in a clean room. Done.

But Ron wasn't having it. Once he found out when I'd be in New York, and why I was in New York, he insisted I stay with him. Bev had already gone home, and this was his week with his new girlfriend, but he'd asked her to leave a few days earlier so I could come. I didn't know any of this at the time, but had I known, I wouldn't have taken him up on his offer.

When I arrived in New York and went to the room, Ron had me stay in the Murphy bed in the second room. I sensed a coolness, but I was so turned upside down from the flight, the last few weeks, as well as my desire to finish a digital photo frame for Heather for her hospital stay that it could have been my imagination.

Ron went to his side of the suite while I opened up my computer and began to create the slide show to load into a digital photo frame. I collected photos from her family and all of her closest friends. I'd already had a ton of pictures of her and Bob together from my affiliation with the Urich Foundation and subsequent marketing materials. I wanted to give it to her when I saw her in the hospital the next day. Because of the three-hour time difference, I stayed up until the wee hours working on my project. When I woke up the next morning, I quickly jumped on the project to wrap it up. Once I begin something, I'm like a dog chasing a bone. I need to see completion, no matter what. Deadlines were my life during my entire career. While this was a self-imposed deadline, it was a deadline nonetheless.

Ron had something he needed to do, so he left the hotel in the late morning. I used the time to make some calls, clean myself up, review the little production I made, and catch a deep breath. I also sent up a little prayer for Heather's well-being. I knew not to go to a hospital in the morning when doctors do rounds. I targeted the early afternoon for my visit. I packaged up the completed photo frame and headed toward the hospital. Judy Rice had texted me directions from the hotel to the hospital to Heather's room. She was so exacting in her directions that I don't think Google Maps could have done any better. Judy produces fashion shows, which I imagine have a bazillion working parts to them. I could tell from those directions that Judy's shows probably ran like clockwork with not so much as a single glitch.

I got to the hospital without any problems and found my way through the maze of one building to the labyrinth of a second building with my frame in hand. I was excited to see my friend and even more excited that I could bring her the digital picture frame with all her favorite people, including some wonderful photos of Bob.

Three & Me

Heather was thrilled to see me and even more thrilled with the digital photo frame. Every time a photo of Bob would pop up, she'd exclaim, "Isn't he the most handsome man you've ever seen?" I had to agree. Bob was definitely eye candy. I included photos of their wedding, the two of them as kids in love, and of them together during Bob's fight with cancer. Each photo elicited the same excited response from Heather. If I did anything right in my life, that digital photo frame was it.

After Heather looked at all the photos in the frame, I saw her mood darken. "You know, Suzie, I've had some time to think. And the more I think, the more I think I want to just let this thing in my head do what it's going to do and not fight it. I want to be with Bob. I want this over!"

My heart sank when I heard those words, but I honestly could see her side. Knowing what I had learned about glioblastoma, I couldn't fault her for her sentiments. But I didn't want her to die either. I was completely torn.

Heather was like a sister to me. She was family. My nuclear family was gone, and while I had cousins, they lived far away. Some were basically cousins in name only, communication was sporadic, and there wasn't a close relationship that I could ever fall back on. My friends were my family. And while I had my wonderful and beautiful son, I would never want to burden him with the things that trouble me or challenge me. He needed to find his own footing and carve his life's path without my being an encumbrance to him. Even when I was married to Yaniv, I rarely would burden him with things that bothered me. Either I just sucked it up or talked things out with my friends. I suspect most women do the same.

Losing Heather would be like losing an arm, or a leg, or any other vital organ. Then I mentally slapped myself in the face. Now was not the time to be selfish. Heather's needs far outweighed mine. "Heather, you need to do what's right for you," I said sadly. "This is your life to live or to end."

Love And Other Goodbyes

"THANK YOU!" she said loudly enough to take me by surprise. "I'm already getting pushback about this. No one gets it. They are NOT in this bed. I AM!" Heather's anger flashed red hot, and I understood it. She must have gone through the five stages of dying–denial, anger, bargaining, depression, and finally acceptance–fairly quickly to have reached this point.

She picked up her cell phone and called Danny, who was a notary, and asked him to come to the hospital to take her directives. Within half an hour, Danny walked into the hospital room and ordered me to leave. Heather was speechless.

"Danny, she can stay. I don't care what she hears. Suzie can stay in the room!"

"Oh no, she can't!" Then he turned to me. "You need to leave right now!"

I looked over at Heather, who was beginning to be very upset. But I didn't want to be the cause of any conflict or distress to her, so I looked over at Danny and told him that I would be waiting in the hallway. "Suit yourself," he said.

I walked out of the room and waited in the hallway. And waited. And waited. Then I called Ryan, who was already back at work at the hospital in Albuquerque. "Can you believe that fucking asshole Danny! I flew all the way to see Heather, and that motherfucker kicked me out of the room because Heather wanted to give him directives!"

"What an asshole!" Ryan was pissed at Danny. In fact, all of Heather's friends were pissed at Danny. He did nothing to help her once her symptoms became obvious, had sponged off of her good nature for years, and now, Heather's illness threatened his very livelihood. He faced eviction if she died or moved to a care facility. He was riding a train to nowhere.

Three & Me

After I vented to Ryan on a call that was way too long (he was such a good sport about it), we both knew there was nothing I could do at the moment. Causing a scene was completely out of the question. We finally hung up, and I felt better having spoken with Ryan. I walked back towards Heather's room, and the door was still closed.

I decided I'd get something to eat across from the hospital. A nice thing about New York City is that you can always find a warm place to sit down and have a bite to eat. I was seated there when Emily phoned. She was clearly upset with what was happening, and we had a long talk that did us both good. I told her about Danny's hissy fit in Heather's room, and she sighed in disapproval as well. Danny was not making good moves, and he wasn't done yet, as we'd find out later.

I looked at the time. I was on the clock because Heather's lifelong friend Kym Karath, the youngest of the *Sound of Music* "kids," was coming in to see Heather as well. She had the evening time slot with Heather. I didn't want to step on her time, depriving them of one-on-one time with each other. Danny was essentially killing an entire day that I would never ever be able to get back.

I went back upstairs to see if Danny had left. Mercifully he had. As I walked into her room, the physical therapist came in and told Heather she needed to do physical therapy. I had never seen Heather yell at anyone in my life, but she unloaded on this poor girl. "I am NOT getting out of this bed!" Heather yelled. "I'm tired. I'm in pain. Physical therapy isn't going to help me! I'm done! You go back and tell them no more. I AM DONE!" The young therapist quickly left the room. "Good!" Heather said, nodding her head in satisfaction. "I'm sick of this shit. Physical therapy for WHAT?"

The week before, Heather had undergone a biopsy on her tumor, and it confirmed she had glioblastoma, which we began to refer to as "glio." The swelling was starting to occur due to the surgery, and

Love And Other Goodbyes

it was affecting her motor skills. She was quickly losing the ability to walk, as well as losing the feeling in the leg opposite the site of the biopsy. (If the brain has a left-side problem then the right side of the body is affected. If the brain has a right-side problem, then the left side of the body is affected.)

I don't know if it was Danny possibly pleading with her, or if her daughter Emily also plead a case for life, or if it was a change of heart, but somewhere in between the time that Danny kicked me out of the room and my return, she had decided that she'd go the next day by ambulance to see someone about putting together a program to extend her life. She would be gone for most of the day, so I would come by in the evening when she returned.

After we chatted a bit longer, mostly about politics—a lot was going on at the time—I looked at my watch and knew I had to allow her to rest up before Kym arrived. So, I left and went back to the hotel, feeling deflated, frustrated, emotionally exhausted, and incredibly angry with Danny—because I would never get that time with Heather back! He stole something more valuable to me than I can even imagine. I can never forgive him for that, and I pretty much forgive most things.

The next day, I woke up thinking about Heather. I was in a high-rise hotel with a view of Times Square. I walked over to the window and looked down at the bustling street. New York never slept, and I could feel the energy from the street below. Cabs honked their horns, sirens blared their alarms, and throngs of people walked up and down Seventh Avenue. I surmised that each person down there had a story to tell, had pain or love in their hearts, had challenges they needed to overcome, or had just given up. My thoughts went back to that day when Heather told me, "Suzie, you need to move here; I just love my life!" just a few short weeks ago. How was I going to be able to reconcile those words with the woman in the hospital bed, the same woman whom the day before told me she wanted to let the thing in her head "do what it's going to do?"

I'd already seen my two other best friends perish through disease. I knew death was a huge part of life. But this time was the hardest for me. Heather was supposed to be my "lifer." Heather was sunshine. She was a warm summer day on a horse. She was responsible for me being a mommy. She was a belly laugh. She was a lighthouse in my stormy seas. And she was a rock. Her trips around the sun weren't supposed to end like this. She was supposed to die an old lady surrounded by grandchildren and great-grandchildren. I dropped my eyes in sadness, and they quickly landed on an old woman walking on the street. I silently wished that woman well on her day's journey.

I had plans to spend the day with Ron, walking around the city. He wanted me to meet his friends, Joel and Deborah, who owned an upscale cleaning business on Amsterdam. I also wanted to have a quick lunch with my cousin, who worked at ABC as a graphic designer. Being a designer runs in my extended family. I was one. My cousin, Ruth Hiller, was one. And Mira Scharf was another. I would be visiting Mira at the commissary for her half-hour lunch break. Ron was supposed to meet me at the commissary at ABC, where we'd begin our walk to visit his friends' business. When Mira and I were seated, we chatted amicably for a few minutes before she got right down to brass tacks! "Is he the *One?*" she asked, catching me totally off guard.

I was stuck for an answer, and words just flew out of my mouth without thinking. "I truthfully don't know. Right now, though, I don't think so. We're just dating." As soon as those words were placed into the universe, they felt wrong, and I knew it wasn't true. Before I could correct myself, though, Ron walked in and sat down next to me. I panicked inside, not knowing if he heard me tell Mira he wasn't the One. I quickly realized he hadn't heard, so I relaxed a bit and finished lunch without any other major faux pas.

Ron and I walked through the city, but it was more Ron walking and me following. I learned something critical about Ron. If Ron were a horse, he would be more like a Jumper than a Hunter. I know you're

Love And Other Goodbyes

shaking your head over this comparison, but let me qualify that last statement. A Hunter is a horse that goes around a course of fences at an even pace, hitting the perfect distance (take-off point) to each fence where the fence is underneath the arc of the jump. The horse is judged for the manner and style of his round, as well as the accuracy in front of the fences. A Jumper is a horse that goes through a course of fences and is judged by clean and time. In other words, the fastest time with no faults (dropped poles, refusals, crashes). Ron walked everywhere "for time." Once that bell rang in his head, he was off like a shot, and if you weren't facing forward, you were quite literally "off the horse."

I basically chased Ron everywhere, and in fact, I still do. He gets something in his head, and he's basically gone. If I blink, I have no idea if he went straight or turned off somewhere, or worse, turned in somewhere. And that's how it was that day in New York City. I was chasing after Ron, who walked like a man possessed. Once, at Columbus Circle, I became distracted by a street vendor for just a minute, and when I looked up, I had no idea where Ron went. Hedging my bets that he would be straight ahead on Broadway, I sprinted until I spotted him a few blocks up. He left right where the road forked and turned into Amsterdam, so I had a 50/50 chance. Phew!

It turned out we didn't meet his friends that day. I wanted to find out if Heather was back at the hospital, and wanted to get over there, so we headed back toward the hotel. Heather was indeed back, and so I took my leave of Ron and caught the subway that would take me near the hospital.

Judy Rice was there when I arrived, and I was very happy to see her. I knew she had been battling breast cancer, had come out on top, and looked fabulous. She brought with her, much-needed cheerful energy into the hospital room, and all three of us had a wonderful visit. Heather had opted not to wait around to die, instead making a stab at a recovery of sorts. She wanted more time, and I was happy about her decision. The doctors, she said, had to find the proper protocols that would do the job, and that was the purpose of the day's meetings. She was exhausted but had a different outlook than the day before.

Kym wasn't there because she had another engagement to tend to. I was disappointed not to be able to meet her again. We'd met years before at Michael Jackson's Encino house, where my friend Alejandra Jackson was having a trunk sale of her line of knit clothing. I remember being in awe at how absolutely gorgeous and well-groomed Kym was. Simply put, Kym was flawless.

In the hospital room, we had the news on following an election where none of us liked the guy who was supposed to run away with the vote. We kept talking about the state of the world, the country, and the direction things were headed, and not one more word was said about Heather's situation. It was a godsend. It was as normal a night with friends as could possibly be under those harsh circumstances.

Heather was quickly losing more and more mobility as her brain continued swelling from the biopsy. She couldn't move her left leg, but it hurt. I lifted her leg ever so gently and began to massage her foot and leg, trying to bring some relief to her pain. I stood in the position, with her foot in my hand, for a very long time. Heather was happy I was helping her, and even though she couldn't move her leg on her own, the massage did offer some relief from the pain.

We stayed with Heather for a couple of hours when she said she wanted to sleep. Judy and I bade our fond farewells, went down the street to a cute place that she had found, and sat down for something warm to drink. It was the first time I'd had a chance to have a one-on-one with Judy. We talked about her own battle with cancer and how well she was now doing. She was a brave lady. I discovered the beautiful woman she was inside, her depth of caring for her friends was bottomless. I enjoyed that time we spent together, maybe due to the intense circumstances we shared, but probably, more realistically, because of the genuine love she exuded towards life.

I was becoming very impressed with Judy very quickly. Not only did she do fashion shows, but she was involved in a charity that benefited Broadway actors, not all of whom are well-paid or work regularly. She was a volunteer for Broadway Cares and threw her heart into it, helping so many creative people.

I love and have nothing but respect for people who give of themselves for the greater good. One of my pet peeves is selfish people who see and care only about themselves. People who live in a bubble, who constantly take, take, take, with no regard for anyone else. These are the people I have little respect for. But the Judys of the world, the Heathers of the world, the Theresas of the world, people like my dad, who would help people who couldn't pay him, people like Jill, who would spontaneously help anyone who needed it—those are the people I have high regard for.

459

On my last visit to Heather, before I was to head back to California, Heather spoke a great deal about how unhappy she was with the impending divorce. The continual discord was ripping into her heart. "Suzie, do me a favor! If anything happens to me, be there for Ryan. I know you will. You guys have always been close." I promised Heather I would do everything in my power to always be there for Ryan. No matter what. I am still there for him today and always will be. (He calls me his "Jewish Mother.")

My visit to Heather was coming to an end, and I gave her a huge hug goodbye. "I'll be back in a few weeks," I told her as we parted, fully convinced she would still be here. I assumed she'd be sick from chemo but still full of her usual "piss and vinegar." We hugged goodbye one last time, and I left the hospital feeling like everything would be OK.

Three & Me

However, not too long after I left New York, Heather began to slide. She quickly lost more and more of her motor skills, as her brain either kept swelling as the tumor kept growing, or both. My friend was spiraling downward. Through the daily email chain updates from Judy and Linda, I found out that Heather and Emily had decided that the best course of action would be for Emily and Steve to pick her up within a few days and drive her back up to Canada. Emily was a well-respected nurse and would ensure that Heather's care and medication would be top-notch. They were still waiting for the chemotherapy and possible radiation protocols to be implemented. The orders would be transferred to medical facilities in Picton, Canada, where Heather would be treated.

Once up in Canada, Heather deteriorated rapidly. Ryan phoned me quite upset. Heather was close to dying. With her children around her, and her grandchildren all present, Heather lay in her bed as she took her last breaths. Heather used to tell me that Christmas was Bob's favorite holiday. Ryan was even born on Christmas. As a family, Christmas was always celebrated in Canada, where Heather now lay. So, I believe firmly that on that particular Christmas Eve, Bob reached out his hand to Heather, and she took it.

Heather and her "Wrong Way" arrows.
Left side is the Canadian Arrow. Right side is my Kitchen Arrow.

## NINETEEN

Life, Love, Laughter, Tears

I was stunned into silence as the text came over my phone from Emily. It was dated December 24th, 2017, and came to me at 5.43 pm Pacific time. It stated simply, *"She has gone home to Dad."* The swiftness with which Glioblastoma took Heather's life was brutal to process. My mind was going to a million different places, mostly to Heather's big presence on this planet. The good things she accomplished in her all-too-short life were too many to count. The footprint she left was huge. Her smile, her laughter, and her wry sense of humor would be never more. I was heartbroken yet again. How many people who suffered from cancer lived on because they benefitted from the money donated through Heather's efforts?

How many people had years added to their lives because of those same efforts? I imagine the numbers are staggering. So many cancer patients have a second chance at life because of Heather and what she stood and worked for. I am so proud of my friend.

Heather's passing was not without some bad moments. While Heather was still alive, albeit in the hospital, Danny allegedly decided that he would eject her things from her bedroom with the en-suite bathroom and take that room for himself. (No one saw him move her belongings.) When the decision was made for Heather's move to Canada, Heather's New York friends got together to pack her things up. They found Heather's belongings thrown into the bathtub of the hallway bathroom—Danny's former bathroom, the one I used when I was visiting. THAT bathroom. The discovery did not go over well in our circle.

A couple of days after Heather passed, I got an email from Kymmie. We were together on that wonderful email chain that circulated

461

462

At Heather's memorial in Canada. It was held on my birthday, so I got to say goodbye to my friend as an unintended birthday present.

Life, Love, Laughter, Tears

during Heather's final journey. She asked if we could talk, something I was totally in favor of. She sent me her phone numbers, and I called her immediately. We both cried on the phone over everything that happened, and we both swore like sailors over what we perceived were horrible travesties happening behind the scenes with her room-mate. We decided to have lunch and share our opinions over our newly discovered common enemy.

We met for lunch that Saturday and asked for a booth far away from the earshot of other customers because we knew we would be dropping lots and lots of F-bombs. Oh boy, did we drop some! We F-bombed the snot out of everything and anything that had to do with all the events leading up to Heather's passing. From the biopsy that made her brain swell to the clothing in the bathtub, we F-bombed it all! Through all the swearing, and unloading of all our frustrations and anger, we found that one moment where we realized that we were destined to become good friends. Our mutual sharing of love for Heather and our ability to communicate with one another set that path in motion. Through the haze of F-bomb smoke, we suddenly re-alized that Heather wanted us to be friends to hold her memory alive and treasure her. How can I thank Heather for the ongoing gifts she gave me? With tears? With laughter? With F-bombs? Almost no words can come from my lips, but I know they come from my heart.

It's said that life is for the living, and I do believe that. But life with loss is one of the most challenging hurdles humans have to navigate. In my 70+ years, I am slightly better at it, but the hurt still hurts, and the absence is never filled. My love never dies, which I happily dis-covered from the saddest moments of my life. Even these many years later, I still love those who have left before me. Their memories are seared into my heart forever as they have become threads in my final resting tapestry.

In the aftermath of Heather's passing, almost like a Christmas miracle, she gave some of us the greatest gift of all: Eastside Judy, Westside

Judy, Gregory, Kymmie, Billy, Linda, Sarah, Sue, Jodie, and me, each of us, the beautiful gift of friendship with each other. Heather's circle of friends, all of us, closed tightly around her memory. Instead of us dispersing into a diaspora of sorts, a strong connection, the connection of Heather, kept us together and still keeps us together. It was almost like she orchestrated this before she died.

I know now that she had to know something was seriously wrong. I believe she was too afraid to vocalize it lest hearing it come from her own lips would make it true. As I mentioned before, her son is a doctor, and her daughter is a nurse, yet she didn't reach out. I am saddened knowing that her last months were probably spent in fear of the unknown.

However, through all of her fears, she was able to put us all together in the last year or so of her life. She made sure we all knew one another. It was as if she knew something, something as big as the Universe itself — friendship and love and the power of it all. I know this must be because magic happens every time we get together, either in person, through Zoom, or even Facebook. For those moments, Heather is with us, laughing when we laugh, crying when we cry, teasing us in our dreams, or in a softly blown curtain caressing us as we lunch together. Heather is definitely there. She blessed us all in life, and she blesses us all in death.

My life has always been about the people in it and less about what I have, want, or need. I learned early in life that you never cry over anything money can replace, even if you don't have the money to replace it. That one little message rang true during all the losses in my lifetime. You don't enter your eighth decade of life without having loss become a thread or more in your tapestry. Unless you are a hermit living in a cave in the mountains, you will experience the heartbreak of loss.

After Heather passed, I was determined to live my life, with each moment counting towards something good. I began to distance myself

Life, Love, Laughter, Tears

from people I thought were a drag on my soul or had values so different from mine that it was hard to tolerate. I decided instead to fill my life with people who offered unconditional love and lived a life full of goodness.

# # #

Ron paid for a flight for me to stay with him during the Eccles 25th celebration. The celebration was initially intended to showcase Heather as one of the founders of the effort to bring a performing arts center to Park City. Because of Heather's passing, they asked Ryan to come in her stead. The video she made before the event, the one she was so proud of, became a memorial video, extolling all her wonderful energies and efforts in helping to create the center.

When I arrived in Utah, I noticed a difference in Ron's attitude toward me. Just the week before, his new girlfriend was there for the New Year's celebration at his friend's ranch. I didn't know she existed, but when I went to the hall closet to fetch my duffel bag, I noticed another one that clearly looked like it belonged to a woman. (The pink bow gave it away.)

A day later, Ryan arrived at the house and stayed in Bev's room while I was still in the bedroom with the driveway view. During the ceremony, I noticed Ron was texting someone. Unbeknownst to me, Ron had told his lady that I was coming, and I'm pretty sure she wasn't too happy about it. But I put all suspicions aside regarding the texting because the ceremony honoring Heather was taking place, and I couldn't be bothered with drama. My focus was on Ryan. I was worried about his emotional state of mind.

It was a hard night for me and a harder night for Ryan. My heart broke for him. I watched him as his voice cracked with emotion while he stood on the podium facing hundreds of people, all of whom were well-wishers. I was relieved when, after a while, after he had a chance to compose himself, he sat down next to me.

Three & Me

When it was over, Ryan went to spend time with some former class-mates of his from when he lived in Park City. Ron and I went to an after-party. At the party, Ron was still getting texts and trying to dis-creetly answer back. At this point, I was doing the math. I figured it had to be a woman texting him because guys don't text back and forth with other guys to the extent Ron was texting (unless they are in a relationship). There was also that tell-tale duffel bag in the closet.

When the night ended, I went to sleep alone, with tremendous sad-ness in my heart. While my flight home was still nine days away, I considered finding a flight home the next day. But I had Ryan there, so I resolved to find a flight out on the day Ryan left. The following day, Ron and I went skiing at Deer Valley, and Ryan went snowboard-ing at Park City.

The day was pleasant, and Ron was attentive, giving away nothing regarding a new girlfriend, although he was pretty terrible at hiding it. To my surprise, he handed me a Deer Valley season pass that he had bought for me but had his girlfriend use. I still hadn't changed my flight, so I went along with everything waiting to see how it all played out.

It was at dinner, though, that things began to change. We went out to Grub Steakhouse in the heart of Park City. While there, I tried again to drink some wine with dinner and failed miserably. That's when Ron uttered the magic words. "Don't worry about the wine. It's not that important." That's when all my walls came down, and we finally had a huge discussion about "us."

I've never been the type of girl that wanted to talk about the relation-ship I'm in with the man I'm in it with. Some women like to have those discussions. I prefer to just let things move on and see what happens. Usually, when a woman says to a guy, "We need to talk," it's because she wants to talk about the relationship. I've never uttered those words. But this time, I was happy we were talking about us.

Life, Love, Laughter, Tears

As it turned out, Ron *had* met someone. He was crazy about her. She was in New York with him at the hotel right before I arrived. He had maintained a phone relationship with her for the months leading to their initial meeting and had become very fond of her. He told me she was a dead ringer for me in size, hair, and facial features, and he found her very attractive. He said she had an outgoing and friendly personality, and the best thing about her was that she was a New Yorker, just like he was. She was three years younger than me, which meant there was a 12-year difference between them. She moved much quicker into his life and heart than I did, which I believe made Ron very happy. She had the relationship all figured out and assured him that it would continue on the right track. She planned on living with him in Park City once she retired in three more years. As I listened to Ron tell me the story of him and his new lady, I wondered why he was telling me this. (Had I known about her before I flew out, I never would have stayed with him in Park City for the event at Eccles. I would have left him to his new lady.) I stared at him, wondering what my next move should be, mentally packing my bags and finding flights out ASAP. And then he said something that completely upended everything and gave jet fuel to the rocket that would take me into the Universe. *"Suzie, you're the person I've wanted since the day we met."*

I sat there totally confused. It took a moment for me to regroup, and to find the right words to say because he had just described Amanda in such loving terms, but was now telling me that I was the one. (Life is never simple.)

"It's the same with me, Ron. But we misfired on so many occasions; I figured it was not meant to be. And that damned list you gave me."

Ron laughed. "That list was not a hard line, Suzie. It was only there so you'd know about the things that make me happy. It wasn't supposed to be a deal breaker." And right there, over some poorly tasting steaks, we both fell in love with each other for the second time. When we got back to Ron's house, I slept in the master bedroom. It's my room now. Ron and I have been together since then. We will be celebrating 7 years together this fall, with plans for this relationship to last forever. He's been my rock and my best friend. He's also been, my protector.

Each of us brought different pieces of "baggage" into the relationship. We had both been married for a long time to the partners we'd met when we were young. Trying to merge two lives at this late stage wasn't easy. We have finally learned how to read each other's signals. We slowly came into sync with each other and now share our lives together completely. I'm so lucky I found Ron. Luckier still that he saw in me someone with whom he wanted to share his life. I keep thinking back to how much Bob loved Heather. I never thought I could find that kind of love, but I have. I often reflect on the way Charlie loved Jill, doing everything in his power to make her disease disappear. And I reflect on the love Phil had for Theresa, trying his hardest to protect her from the evils this world threw at her.

Ron and I traveled to China in the spring following Heather's passing. There is a place in China called the Yellow Mountains. There are no roads there. At the base of the mountain, you take a cable car up, and then the real work of the Yellow Mountains begins. Every trail is a series of steps, much like the Great Wall of China. You go down a million steps, and then you climb up a million steps. A guide is a must because without one, getting lost and dying is something that happens often enough. Packing lightly is also a must because you carry your belongings with you. Even something as innocuous as a camera is weight, and through the arduous steps up and down, can become quite cumbersome.

As you trek the Yellow Mountains to your destination, you see men with a wooden pole across their shoulders in the tradition of China, each side weighted down with supplies for the hotels en route. Up and down these men go, weighted like beasts of burden. You can see the toll these weights have taken on their bodies. As I struggled with just the dumb weight of my own backpack, I stood in awe of their determination and strength. I was told they make a lot of money while they are working, so I am guessing that is the motivation behind such back-breaking work.

The trip to the Yellow Mountains was cathartic for me. I saw the amazing natural beauty of this world from a place that was hard to reach, hard to traverse, and harder still to navigate. I felt the intensity of life surging through my body and soul from those precarious steps, steep drops, and dangerous trails. I thought of Heather in her brief battle, of Theresa in hers, and of Jill's long slow march toward her final end. With every step I climbed, I imagined their cumulative struggles. Every successful climb to a peak, I imagined their temporary respites. Climbing the Yellow Mountains for me was so much more than a tourist seeking a destination. It was, for me, a symbol of the sanctity of life and was a profound experience.

Almost immediately after returning from China, Ron and I flew to Canada to meet Heather's family and friends for a memorial at the lakeside home. It was a happy event, celebrating the beautiful life she had lived. The day was lovely, and everyone was happy and grateful to be present.

When Heather passed away, she passed away in the dead of winter. The ground freezes in winter, making burials very difficult. Heather was cremated, and it was decided her cremains would be buried in June at the little church across the street, right next to Bob. Heather's memorial and burial were held on my 67th birthday, and I couldn't think of a better birthday present than to celebrate her all-too-short life with the people who loved her most. I got to witness my friend "physically" reunite with her husband, a wish of hers that grew stronger over the years. What could be a better gift than that!?

# # #

Three & Me

Six months to the day after Heather died, I suffered a catastrophic horse accident. That morning, Ron and I were fighting about the NYC girlfriend again. I was in my Moorpark house, and he was in his Park City house, and we were fighting over the phone. Still angry, I went to the barn to ride my horse. My trainer, Mary Williams, who always rode my horse for me before I got on, had an emergency at the last minute and couldn't make it. My horse, Smylie, was an OTTB (Off -The-Track-Thoroughbred) and came with a few quirks. He was girthy (did not like the girth tightened too tight all at once), which is dangerous enough because girthy horses will shoot backward, trying to evade the girth. (The girth is the belt-like attachment that goes under the horse's chest and attaches to each side of the saddle, securing it in place.) My dad always told me that the nerves to a horse's lungs lie precisely where the girth hits, and when you jack up the straps too suddenly, some horses panic, thinking they can't breathe.

Smylie's other quirk was in the mounting. He had to be mounted jockey style. In other words, he had to be able to walk forward after you put your foot in the stirrup, swing your other leg over as he walked, and then slowly ease into the saddle.

On the day I went out, a groom newer to the barn was in charge of getting him ready for me. He'd taken Smylie to the big arena in the back area and lunged him with the saddle on. When a horse is on a lunge line, it looks like a very long dog leash is hooked to his bridle. The horse then circles around you at the walk, the trot, and the canter. Then you take the leash (lunge line) off the one side and put it on the other side, and do it all over again, this time going in the other direction. This way, a fresh horse can get his bucks out, making it safer for the rider. Smylie had his saddle on to ensure he'd be breathing freely and calmly.

I was waiting for the groom to return Smylie from his lunge when I saw them approaching. Suddenly the groom stopped, unhooked Smylie's girth, moved the saddle up on his back, and then I saw him tighten the girth to the tightest holes. I panicked as soon as I saw this. "He's girthy!" I said, "You just tightened his girth right before I get on him."

The groom sounded annoyed at this admonition. He shot back, "Don't worry about it. He's already loose from the lunge I gave him. Look how he's walking. He's walking with a full stride and not with baby steps." But I WAS worried.

The mounting block can be used on two sides. On one side, I would have been able to put my foot in the stirrup, let him walk ahead, and do the jockey mount. On the other side of the mounting block, he would be trapped between the block and the barn, with an obstacle not too far in front of him. For all intents and purposes, it was almost as if he was being led to the start gate at the track before a race. Horses don't always like going in there. If they don't, they tend to shoot backward until the jockey can get them in, and the ground handlers can close the door behind them, closing them in until the bell rings. ("And they're off!") For some unexplained reason, the groom chose that side for me to mount.

471

"I want to mount on the other side, please. Can we walk him around to the other side?" The groom was clearly in a bad mood, unhappy with my questioning him about the saddle and even unhappier still with me wanting him to take an extra minute to walk the horse around to the other side.

"Look, I've got a lot of other horses to do today. Just get on." He was frustrated with me. Do you know that little voice in your head that screams at you NOT to do something? Well, that little voice was screaming loudly in my head with a megaphone to NOT get on the horse. I hesitated.

"Please, just get on!" the groom said in utter frustration.

I didn't want to. And I have no idea why I complied since he technically worked for me. I paid a substantial amount of money every month for grooming services, as did the other customers in the barn, from which he received his salary. Every fiber of my body was telling me not to get on. But I did. I looked at my horse. Smylie was standing calmly at the block. But when I put my foot into the stirrup, he lifted his head in surprise, probably, because the groom moved over to stand right in front of him, blocking his walk forward. While the perfect storm was building, there was one more element to complete the fury of it all. In a gut reaction to Smylie lifting his head up, the groom pulled down on the reins, which got him in the bars of the mouth (a very sensitive area for Smylie). And just like that, while I was still vulnerable, Smylie shot backward in a panic. The perfect storm for disaster. Girth, Block, Mouth.

In the blink of an eye, disaster struck. "I knew it!" I thought as the horse charged backward. Behind him stood the groom stalls. (Because they are prey animals, horses' eyes are on the sides of their heads, so they can see predators and what's behind them. This is common in all hoof stock. Carnivores, however, have their eyes in front to hunt.) Smylie saw the groom stalls and quickly spun around backward to avoid colliding with them, the centrifugal force of which threw me off the back side of him onto the cement-hard ground. I immediately heard the loud cracking noise of bones breaking. The pain was instant and harsh. As I lay on the ground, I knew I was in trouble. I didn't know it yet, but I had shattered my wrist and elbow and broken my arm in a compound fracture.

The head trainer, Rainie, ran over to me, hearing my screams. I shouted, "Call 911! Call 911!" because I knew I had to be taken away in a meat wagon. She asked if she could do anything. "Call Ron," I said. After their conversation, Ron hung up, found the first flight he could take, and was on the plane without so much as a second thought.

At about 6:00 pm that evening, I underwent the first of two surgeries. The surgeon told me up front that I would probably never be the same again and would probably have limited usage of my right hand

and arm. I remember thinking, "Like Hell! You don't know me." He then made me sign a waiver to that effect, allowing him to operate. I signed gladly. The aftermath I would deal with. I just wanted to start the process.

After surgery at around 9:30 pm, I was wheeled into my room. It was dark, with some soft backlight. I could make out the figure of a man standing in my room. As the gurney I was in was pushed completely into my room, I realized I was looking at Ron. He had a look of worry on his face but broke into a smile the minute he saw me. When the orderlies got my bed and the IV poles in place, he came over and kissed me. Then he went into physician mode and probably drove the nurses crazy. I was so grateful.

The next day, the phone rang. I had posted on Facebook that I was in the hospital. I wanted to share my journey back from injury. I answered the phone, and it was music to my ears when I heard, "What the fuck!" That's what Heather would have said. She would have picked up the phone and called me with those exact words. Of course, it wasn't Heather; instead, it was her good friend, Gregory. He knew exactly what to say, and it made my day.

Two days later, I had to have a second surgery, this time on my elbow. They didn't have the part that would fit me when I had the surgery on my wrist and arm. Ron stayed with me almost the entire time but flew back to Utah to catch a Kenny Loggins concert in Deer Valley a day later.

I was finally released from the hospital after a six-day stay. The day after, I attended the Joe Jackson Memorial Service held by the Jacksons in Pasadena. Joe had died while I was in the hospital. I walked in with my arm in a sling and a huge bandage wrapped tightly from both surgeries. But I was glad I went. It was vital for me to go because Donte was still living in my home, and Joe was his grandfather. I wanted to be there for Donte and his brothers and sister, who were all near and dear to me.

My life had changed drastically from that two-second disaster. I could no longer hold anything in my right hand, let alone use it for anything. It was my dominant hand. I began to use my left hand for all my needs. I was almost ambidextrous before the accident, so it was an easy transition to make.

The main point that I want to share with everyone is that I never once had a pity party for myself. I had an accident. I didn't end up paralyzed or worse (which could have happened). I wasn't given a terminal diagnosis of cancer or any other insidious disease. I didn't lose my limb. My situation, in the general scheme of things, was terrible but wasn't fatal or paralyzing. The work to get well began and ended with me.

I ended up with six surgeries on my wrist and elbow. I transferred treatment to the Park City orthopedics office of Rosenberg, Cooley, and Metcalf. Dr. Olson became my surgeon of choice. When he looked at my arm and the X-rays he took and compared them with the X-rays I had before any surgeries, he told me that I would probably have to accept a new normal. My arm was frozen at a 90° angle. I had no range of motion at all. I couldn't move my wrist in any direction, had no motion in any fingers, and as far as my elbow was concerned, well, it was not budging a millimeter. I can understand why he'd said that to me.

"Dr. Olson, I'm getting back to my old normal," I told him. "Just watch!"

Dr. Olson smiled that beautiful smile of his and said, "I hope you do."

Jill Ireland taught me how to suffer through the pain of recovery with dignity and the single goal of getting normal life back. Theresa Saldana showed me that you could come back from the dead, having been stabbed so many times that she literally crashed on the operating table. And from watching Heather journey through the last leg of her Glioblastoma, I learned acceptance of the situation. I would have no woe-is-me days. Instead, I would march forward.

These three women were part of the confidence I had in myself to heal. I was shown the way by these brave ladies. I couldn't let them down. I couldn't cry about my plight because they went through so much worse in their lifetime.

I attacked my road to recovery with a determination to finish a winner. I spent grueling hours in physical therapy with two of the most wonderful therapists in the world, Michele and Meghan. *The Mighty M's!* They cranked on my wrist and my arm, pulling, yanking, pushing. When they asked me if it hurt and if they should stop, my response was always, "Bring it!" I didn't care about the pain. I wanted my arm back. No one thought when they first saw me that this was a realistic goal. But the harder I worked at the therapy center and at home, the more they realized that I might just do it!

It took me nearly a year to get close to an almost complete range of motion. When Dr. Olson saw what I had accomplished, he looked at me and said, "I wish all my patients were like you. Especially the older ones. They tend to just give up and live with what they have." It took me another year of just me, working on myself to get a complete 100% range of motion. I can completely straighten out my arm now, which is almost unheard of after a shattered elbow. If the scars weren't there, no one would even know I had the accident.

Today I'm playing golf, having taken it up at the age of 69. I have a pretty good swing too! I'm skiing, back on a horse, and other than some ugly scars, doing well. Were it not for the friends I've had in my lifetime, I couldn't have found the inner strength to heal myself. I still have years left to live. For how long, I don't know. But I do know that with the lessons I've been so privileged to learn, whatever life throws at me, I can take it. Even when it's my turn to face the end. I have the knowledge and the strength to face that head-on, also.

Three & Me

476

Ron and I attending the wedding of a close friend.
We were still trying (not too successfully) to figure each other out then.

Life, Love, Laughter, Tears

EPILOGUE

I'm grateful I got to enter my septuagenarian room, and I'm hopeful I can reach my octogenarian, nonagenarian and centenarian rooms without too many foibles. Life is, without a doubt, a wonderful journey to take, even with all the bumps in the road.

I carry with me a lot of my dad's lessons as well as those I've learned along the way from my three best friends. I appreciate all life in all its strange and intricate forms. I'm almost a science geek. I love learning about the different species on this planet, including plants, bugs, avians, ichthyology, and whatever else the Universe provided us with. I'm happy to fall in love with an octopus one day or a tiger the next. I see the wonder in the world, and I love it all.

Some people reading my story may think I've had it hard. I hear many times over from caring friends that I've had more than my fair share of losses and disappointments. However, if there is a takeaway from my life's story, it's that despite the loss, in spite of some hardships, in spite of anything negative, I know I've lived a life full of blessings. I would hope that somehow my story and the stories of my three amazing friends will inspire you, the reader, to look for the blessings you accumulate on your own life's journey. *Nothing is as bad as we make it in our own minds.* Things can turn around. It's always up to us to make sure it does.

As Heather used to say, *"Onward!"*

Mom's Graduation from University of Wisconsin, Madison.
L-R: Skeeze, Beatrice, Mom, Lottie, Mom's Grandma Barkin.

478

Mom and me in an awkward pose. Notice her
leaning her head away from mine.

Sue Lika Dotan

Me and Jerry outside our Los Feliz house. Dad was making money in insurance before he gave it up to become a Chiropractor.

*Jill's self-portrait painted in the 60s.
It looks like me today!*

Three & Me

The Dotan family before the amicable divorce. Me, Yaniv, Jonah.
Dogs are L-R: Dudley, Sophie and Choppie.

My shattered arm and wrist. I was
stuck at 90°.

Riding an Icelandic Horse in
Iceland in October, 2022.

Sue Lika Dotan

Made in United States
Troutdale, OR
08/02/2023

11735990R00276